CELE ATING THE REFOR MATION

ITS LEGACY AND CONTINUING RELEVANCE

CELEBR ATING THE REFOR MATION

ITS LEGACY AND CONTINUING RELEVANCE

Edited by Mark D. Thompson,
Colin Bale and Edward Loane

APOLLOS (an imprint of Inter-Varsity Press)
36 Causton Street, London SW1P 4ST, England
Website: www.ivpbooks.com
Email: ivp@ivpbooks.com

First published 2017

British Library Cataloguing-in-Publication Data
A catalogue record for this book is available from the British Library.

ISBN: 978-1-78359-509-9
eBook ISBN: 978-1-78359-510-5
Set in Monotype Garamond 11/13pt

Typeset in Great Britain by CRB Associates, Potterhanworth, Lincolnshire
Printed and bound in Great Britain by Ashford Colour Press Ltd, Gosport, Hampshire

Inter-Varsity Press publishes Christian books that are true to the Bible and that communicate the gospel, develop discipleship and strengthen the church for its mission in the world.

IVP originated within the Inter-Varsity Fellowship, now the Universities and Colleges Christian Fellowship, a student movement connecting Christian Unions in universities and colleges throughout Great Britain, and a member movement of the International Fellowship of Evangelical Students. Website: www. uccf.org.uk. That historic association is maintained, and all senior IVP staff and committee members subscribe to the UCCF Basis of Faith.

For
Mike Ovey,
heir of the Reformation and faithful disciple of Jesus Christ

CONTENTS

CONTRIBUTORS

Andrew Bain is Vice Principal of Queensland Theological College where he teaches Church History and Christian Ethics. He is also Head of the Department of Christian Thought and History within the Australian College of Theology consortium of which QTC is a member. Andrew writes and researches primarily on the theory and practice of theological education and on the history of applied theology.

Colin Bale is Vice Principal, Academic Dean and Head of Church History at Moore Theological College, Sydney. His special area of interest is Australian church history. He is the author of *A Crowd of Witnesses: Epitaphs on First World War Australian War Graves* (Longueville Media, 2015).

Rhys S. Bezzant is Dean of Missional Leadership and Lecturer in Church History at Ridley College, Melbourne. He is the Director of the Jonathan Edwards Center Australia and is Visiting Fellow at the Yale Divinity School. He has published *Jonathan Edwards and the Church* (OUP, 2014) and *Standing on Their Shoulders* (Acorn, 2015), and is presently writing a book on the mentoring ministry of Edwards. He also serves as Canon of St Paul's Cathedral, Melbourne.

Gerald Bray is Research Professor of Divinity at Beeson Divinity School and Director of Research for the Latimer Trust. His recent books include *God Is Love, God Has Spoken* and *The Church*. He is currently writing a theological commentary on the pastoral epistles.

Martin Foord lecturers in Systematic Theology at Trinity Theological College, Perth. His research interests include the historical theology of the late medieval and Reformation era, Puritanism, the doctrine of the gospel and the canon of Scripture.

David A. Höhne lectures in Philosophy and Theology at Moore College. He is currently undertaking research in the areas of trinitarian theology and eschatology. His publications include *The Last Things* (IVP, forthcoming) as well as chapters in *True Feelings* (Apollos, 2012) and *Jürgen Moltmann and Evangelical Theology* (Wipf and Stock, 2012).

Chase R. Kuhn lectures in Christian Thought and Ministry at Moore Theological College, Sydney. His current research interests are in ecclesiology, eschatology, ethics and preaching. He is the author of *The Ecclesiology of Donald Robinson and D. Broughton Knox* (Wipf and Stock, 2017), as well as several academic essays.

Andrew Leslie lectures in Christian Doctrine at Moore Theological College. He has a special interest in the early development of confessional Reformed thought in sixteenth- and seventeenth-century Europe, as well as its retrieval and expression in the contemporary Christian context. He has written a book on John Owen's doctrine of Scripture: *The Light of Grace: John Owen on the Authority of Scripture and Christian Faith* (Vandenhoeck & Ruprecht, 2015).

Edward Loane is a lecturer in Doctrine and Church History at Moore Theological College. He has published *William Temple and Church Unity: The Politics and Practice of Ecumenical Theology* and *From Cambridge to Colony: Charles Simeon's Enduring Influence on Christianity in Australia* (ed.). His research interests include Anglican and evangelical history as well as ecclesiology and eschatology.

John McClean is Vice Principal and Lecturer in Systematic Theology at Christ College, the theological college of the Presbyterian Church of Australia in Sydney. He has published *From the Future: Getting to Grips with Pannenberg's Thought* and *The Real God for the Real World*, an introduction to Christian doctrine. He is currently writing a book on the doctrine of revelation.

Joe Mock is a Presbyterian minister in Sydney, Australia. He has an interest in the Swiss Reformation and has published several articles on Heinrich Bullinger, such as 'Biblical and Theological Themes in Heinrich Bullinger's "De Testamento" (1534)' (*Zwingliana*, vol. 40 [2013], pp. 1–35) and 'Was Bullinger's Gospel Synergistic or Universalistic? An Examination of Sermon IV.1 of *The Decades*' (*Scottish Bulletin of Evangelical Theology*, vol. 34, no. 2 [2016], pp. 141–157).

Michael J. Ovey was the Principal of Oak Hill College until his sudden and unexpected death in January 2017. He was the leading theological voice among evangelical Anglicans in Britain. His theological work brought exegesis and historical theology together for the service of the churches. His most recent work was *Your Will Be Done: Exploring Eternal Subordination, Divine Monarchy and Divine Humility* (Latimer, 2016) and a book on Hilary of Poitiers is in production. A particular passion of Mike's was the doctrine of justification and the salvation that is ours through Christ alone. Mike is survived by his wife, Heather, and their three adult children.

Tim Patrick is Principal of the Bible College of South Australia, an affiliated college of the Australian College of Theology. His research interests are in gospel theology and the doctrinal history of the Anglican Church. Tim's recent work includes 'The Purging of Purgatory and the Exclusion of the Apocrypha during England's Reformation' (paper, in preparation) and 'The Pastoral Offices in the Pastoral Epistles and the Church of England's First Ordinal', in Brian S. Rosner, Andrew S. Malone and Trevor J. Burke (eds.), *Paul as Pastor* (London: Bloomsbury T&T Clark, forthcoming 2017).

Mark D. Thompson is the Principal of Moore College. His research interests include the doctrines of Scripture, Christ and justification as well as the theology of Martin Luther. He has lectured in doctrine at Moore College since 1991 and is the author of several books and numerous articles, including *A Clear and Present Word: The Clarity of Scripture* (IVP, 2006). Mark is married to Kathryn and they have four daughters.

Stephen Tong is completing PhD research on the English Reformation at Corpus Christi College, Cambridge. His particular interest is in the relationship between evangelical ecclesiology and liturgical reform during the reign of Edward VI (1547–53). He has spoken at a number of international conferences on various topics, including the doctrine of the sabbath in the English Reformation, sacramental theology and the Irish Reformation, and has been awarded three Dr Lightfoot Scholarships for essays on ecclesiastical history.

Jane Tooher serves on the faculty of Moore College where she lectures in Ministry and Mission, New Testament and Church History. She is also the Director of Moore's Priscilla and Aquila Centre which stimulates research and discussion about women serving in ministry in partnership with men. Her publications include 'Eight Ways That Humility Can Become Our Greatest Friend', in *Let the Word Do the Work: Essays in Honour of Phillip D. Jensen*, and 'Hearing the Old Testament Women in Matthew's Genealogy: Tamar, Rahab,

Ruth, and the Wife of Uriah the Hittite', in *Listen to Him: Reading and Preaching Emmanuel in Matthew*.

Dean Zweck, recently retired, was Lecturer in Church History at Australian Lutheran College in Adelaide, 2001–16. Prior to that he was in parish ministry after returning from many years in Papua New Guinea, where he also taught in seminaries. His current research interest is the early Luther ('The Communion of Saints in Luther's 1519 Sermon . . .', *Lutheran Theological Journal* 49, no. 3).

PREFACE

This collection of essays began life as contributions to the 2017 School of Theology at Moore College in Sydney, Australia. The School itself was part of a wider year of celebration as we remembered with great thanksgiving to God the theological heritage we have received from the Reformation. In the sixteenth century life changed dramatically as people came to understand afresh the gospel of grace and the authority of the Scriptures as the written Word of God. While there was plenty of turmoil in those years, and serious mistakes were made, especially in the way people on both sides treated those with whom they disagreed, it is impossible to remember the contributions of men like Luther, Zwingli, Calvin, Cranmer and the rest and not rejoice at the gift of the Reformation to the Christian churches.

At this School members of the Moore College faculty were joined by scholars from around Australia and indeed from around the world. This collaboration has been a particular joy and we are grateful for the way their insights enriched our gathering. Sadly, one dearly loved friend was not able to be with us. Mike Ovey, Principal of Oak Hill Theological College in London and one of the leading voices in evangelical Anglicanism worldwide, died suddenly on 7 January 2017. His loss is deeply personal for many of us and is a severe blow to the evangelical cause at a crucial moment in its history. Nevertheless, we were granted permission to edit and publish a lecture on justification, a subject Mike was fascinated by and about which he had intended to write a great deal this year, for this volume. We have not tried to eliminate all traces of the oral presentation, though the depth of the scholarship behind his presentation is obvious.

Our deep respect for Mike has led us to dedicate this volume to his memory. We are indebted to his widow, Heather, for her permission to do so. May the Lord raise up for us more leaders and thinkers like Mike Ovey.

We have a great many people to thank as this book is published. Thank you first of all to each of the contributors. Amidst very hectic schedules they each presented their work in time for us to get this volume published to coincide with the 2017 School of Theology. Thank you, too, to Philip Duce of Inter-Varsity Press, whose encouragement, enthusiasm and patient guidance were, as ever, greatly appreciated. Thank you to the team of people behind the scenes at IVP/SPCK who worked on this volume. Thank you to the librarians of our various institutions, who bore with incessant demands for obscure books, not least the librarians at the Donald Robinson Library, Moore College, as they did this in the midst of a major move of premises.

Our greatest debt, though, is to the faithful men and women about whom we write in these pages. Without the Protestant Reformation we would have been left in darkness. In an era which tends to like to bring heroes down to earth, it is right that we take a moment to thank God for the heroes he has given us, human, fallible people just like us, but who had the courage to say on the authority of Scripture alone, not Scripture and tradition: we are saved by Christ alone, not by Christ and the church; because of grace alone, not because of grace and merit; through faith alone, not through faith and works; to the glory of God alone, for he is the only one who deserves all honour and glory. Those are truths worth rejoicing in five hundred years after the Reformation and until Jesus returns.

Mark D. Thompson
Colin Bale
Edward Loane

ABBREVIATIONS

CR	*Corpus Reformatorum*, ed. W. Baum et al., 101 vols. (Berlin/ Leipzig/Zurich, Theologischer Verlag, 1834–)
CTJ	*Calvin Theological Journal*
ESV	English Standard Version (2001)
ET	English translation
JETS	*Journal of the Evangelical Theological Society*
KJV	King James (Authorized) Version
LW	*Luther's Works*, ed. Jaroslav Pelikan and Helmut T. Lehmann, 55 vols. (St Louis/Philadelphia: Concordia/Fortress Press, 1955–86)
NIV	New International Version (2011)
NRSV	New Revised Standard Version (1989)
NT	New Testament
OT	Old Testament
WA	*D. Martin Luthers Werke, Kritische Gesamtausgabe: Schriften*, ed. J. K. F. Knaake, G. Kawerau et al., 66 vols. (Weimar: Hermann Böhlaus Nachfolger, 1883–)
WABr	*D. Martin Luthers Werke, Kritische Gesamtausgabe: Briefwechsel*, ed. J. K. F. Knaake, G. Kawerau et al., 18 vols. (Weimar: Hermann Böhlaus Nachfolger, 1930–85)
WADB	*D. Martin Luthers Werke, Kritische Gesamtausgabe: Die Deutsche Bibel*, ed. J. K. F. Knaake, G. Kawerau et al., 12 vols. (Weimar: Hermann Böhlaus Nachfolger, 1906–61)

WATr   *D. Martin Luthers Werke, Kritische Gesamtausgabe: Tischreden,*
              ed. J. K. F. Knaake, G. Kawerau et al., 6 vols. (Weimar:
              Hermann Böhlaus Nachfolger, 1912–21)
WTJ   *Westminster Theological Journal*
Z   *Huldreich Zwinglis sämtliche Werke* (Berlin: Schwetschke;
              Leipzig: Hensius; Zurich: Berichthaus/Theologischer
              Verlag, 1905–1991)

INTRODUCTION: WHY THE REFORMATION STILL MATTERS

Gerald Bray

What has been remembered: the legacy of history

In 2017 we are celebrating the 500th anniversary of the dawning of what would become the Protestant Reformation. When Martin Luther posted his Ninety-Five Theses on the church door at Wittenberg, he could not have known what effect they would have on Western Christendom, and for the rest of his life the ultimate fate of the movement they initiated would remain in the balance. Not until the Peace of Westphalia in 1648 would Protestantism settle down into a pattern that we still recognize today. The effects of the Reformation can still be seen in the long-term consequences of the Westphalian settlement, and for that reason, if for no other, we must conclude that Luther's revolt still matters. The Reformational divisions within the Christian world are still with us, and despite the growing secularism and inter-denominational ecumenism of recent times, they show no sign of disappearing anytime soon. Despite the calls we hear from prominent church leaders in favour of Christian 'unity', and the friendly relations that are now the norm among the different denominations, little real progress has been made to overcome the legacy of the sixteenth century. Even among Protestants, the merging of different denominations has proved difficult and is relatively rare, while the Roman Catholic Church remains as distinct as ever. The 500th anniversary of the Reformation is an opportunity to remind ourselves that the events of the past cannot be undone, and that whatever the future holds, their mark will remain.

To understand where we are today and how the Reformation has had an impact on us, we have to consider two dimensions of its influence. The first of these may be loosely termed 'political', which is to say, the historical and social context which the events of the Reformation helped to shape and that continue to linger in our collective consciousness, even if many people would be hard put to identify them. The second may be called 'theological', embracing not only the doctrines that the Reformers taught but the worldview that dominated their thinking. Broadly speaking, the doctrines are still embedded in most Protestant confessions of faith, but the influence of the worldview that underlies them is harder to measure. For some people it remains as vital today as it ever was, but for others it belongs irretrievably to the past. The former see no need for any change or adaptation of the tradition they have inherited and are suspicious of moves in that direction as a dilution of the original message. The latter, on the other hand, tend to reject it altogether, regarding Protestantism not as the preservation of a now-ancient inheritance but as an intellectual impulse that drives us to ever-new reformulations of the faith once delivered to the saints. Whether this can be done without throwing the baby out with the bathwater of accumulated tradition is uncertain and is contested, especially by those who disagree about what the baby is. Are we talking about the doctrines that remain so dear to the traditionalists, or about something else – the spirit of innovation, perhaps, or freedom of conscience? How we answer these questions will determine what sort of legacy we think the Reformation left us and will help us to determine how much, and in what way, it still matters today.

The Protestant Reformation is often portrayed nowadays as the moment when the conscience of the individual stood up to the great powers of the time and prevailed against the odds. There may be some truth in this if we are speaking about the conscience of Martin Luther, but we have to remember that he, and a small number of other Renaissance intellectuals like him, enjoyed a freedom in this respect that was denied to the vast majority of the population. To focus on men like Luther, William Tyndale or Sir Thomas More is misleading because it distorts the bigger picture and imposes a modern value, *viz.* freedom of conscience, on a world to which that idea was largely alien. The truth of the matter is that the success or failure of the early Reformers was not measured by the truth or falsehood of their beliefs, but by their success in attracting political support to back them up. It was not as a result of the Reformation that individuals obtained the freedom to choose their own faith or lack of it. Instead, whole countries found themselves cast into either the Protestant or the Catholic camp, almost always because their secular ruler had so decided, and particular people were expected to conform to that or get out if they wanted to save their lives. The Reformation could be a costly business for those who found themselves on the wrong side of it, and in those circumstances, freedom of conscience was more likely to lead to martyrdom than to anything else. Admittedly, these martyrs have become part of the inherited tradition and they continue to be honoured by both sides as heroes who held firm while those around them were surrendering to compromise of one kind or another, and to that extent their example continues to play an important role in establishing group identity among Protestants and Catholics alike. But they do this precisely because they were exceptional and not typical. Like it or not, the Reformation survived not so much because of them as because significant numbers of ordinary people were persuaded, often without any appeal to their conscience or their will, to accept a particular form of the new teaching and apply it to their lives.

Thus it was that most of northern Germany, Scandinavia, a number of Swiss cantons and about half the Netherlands passed from the old to the new religion, and southern Europe remained in the Catholic fold. France was divided, mainly because it was not yet a highly centralized state and its aristocrats fought among themselves for supremacy in the so-called wars of religion. These ended when, by dynastic accident, a Protestant inherited the throne but found that he could not unite the country behind him unless he converted to Catholicism. He eventually did so but promised toleration to his erstwhile co-religionists, an arrangement that barely survived for two generations before it was suppressed and the remaining Protestants were forced to choose between Catholicism or exile. Those who chose the latter became a new ethnic group – the Huguenots, who left their mark on the countries to which they fled and whose influence is still perceptible three and a half centuries later.

England, as we all know, was a case apart. King Henry VIII broke with Rome for personal and dynastic reasons, thereby creating a Protestant state with no Protestants in it. What Henry's theology was remains a matter of controversy, but everybody agrees that the king believed in himself, and that he expected others to believe in him. Acceptance of the Reformation, such as it was, was an act of loyalty to the crown, and so it remained. When his Catholic daughter Mary ascended the throne, the country returned to the Roman obedience, but left it again when she was succeeded by her half-sister Elizabeth. It was not until more than a century later that it was finally made clear, in the so-called Glorious Revolution of 1688, that Protestantism had come to stay.

The effects of this state of affairs can still be seen. The United Kingdom is what it is because a common Protestantism brought England and Scotland together. Ireland, which had long been more closely tied to England than Scotland was, now gradually drifted away and eventually its Catholic portion seceded because it could not live happily in a Protestant state. That division is still apparent today but it is by no means unique. In Germany, Protestant Prussia united the country, but at the price of excluding Catholic Austria, which became and remains an independent state. In the Netherlands, the Protestant north revolted against Catholic Spain and gained its freedom, whereas Catholic Flanders still prefers to remain uncomfortably united with French-speaking Wallonia in a somewhat artificial federation known as Belgium, because it is too different from its Protestant neighbour to the north, even though it speaks the same language.

In the Americas, of course, the difference between north and south is very apparent. Not many people realize it now, but the Spanish and Portuguese colonies there regarded the revolt of the British colonies to their north as an inspiration. When they broke away from their mother countries, they renamed themselves the United States of Mexico, the United States of Argentina and eventually the United States of Brazil, names that they bear to this day. Yet nobody, and least of all the people we call Americans, thinks there is much in common between them and the model that inspired them. Why not? Because the northern federation was Protestant and the others were Catholic – a difference of belief and outlook that has created a different culture, despite the periodic desire of the elites on both sides to bring them together.

Nor should anyone think that this religious difference no longer matters. North Americans do not want to get any closer to their southern neighbours than they already are, and there has even been talk of building a wall to keep them out. In the European Union, everybody knows that there is a north–south divide that threatens to tear it apart. The UK has sadly voted to leave it altogether, but it might have less trouble uniting with the Netherlands or with Scandinavia – it is the Catholic and Orthodox PIGS (Portugal, Italy, Greece and Spain) that the British want to stay away from. This is common knowledge and most people understand why it is so, even if secularism and diplomacy conspire to conceal the real reason. Protestant societies have different values and march to a different tune from Catholic or Orthodox ones, and never the twain shall meet. Even in the realm of private morality, this is obvious. No British politicians, however immoral they may be, could get away with the sort of philandering that is regarded as normal among their peers in France or Italy, and the systemic corruption common in Spain and Greece would be unthinkable further north. Somewhere or other there is a collective conscience at work, and in spite of all the secularism of the modern age, that conscience has Protestant roots.

If we go back to 1517 and look at the map of Europe as it then was, we see a more wide-ranging change in the centuries since. At that time Holland was a bog with a small permanent population and little culture or industry of any sort.

The Low Countries owed their wealth and their fame to the great cities of Flanders – Antwerp, Bruges, Ghent and Brussels. A century later, all that had changed. War and the virtual expulsion of Protestants from Flanders had led to the settlement of Amsterdam, Rotterdam and the other great Dutch cities, which were rapidly becoming the richest, cleanest and most progressive places in Europe. In 1517 Scotland was a poor, divided kingdom with little going for it, but by the seventeenth century it was turning out scholars of the first rank who were recognized as the teachers of the entire continent. How had this happened?

On the whole, the growth of Protestantism was not a spontaneous movement of people who had been convicted by the preaching and teaching of the great Reformers. Much more often, it was the result of persistent education, conducted by clergy who had been trained in the universities, where they had come into contact with the new theology. It was these men who prepared the textbooks for popular consumption and who opened the schools where their ideas would be taught. The Reformers believed that the Bible was the supreme authority, not just for the government of the church but for the spiritual life of the believer as well. That made translation into the common tongue and widespread printing and circulation of the sacred text imperative. But for the Bible to have any effect, people had to be taught how to read and be encouraged to put book-learning at the centre of their lives, especially in childhood. The Reformers turned the church into a classroom, where people were taught the faith and then told to take the Bible home and read it for themselves in the bosom of the family. Parents were expected to have devotional times at meals and to teach their children how to pray. Children were systematically catechized – the concept of catechesis, if not exactly a Protestant invention, was revived by the Reformers and put into practice in a new way.

People were taught that they could pray to God without needing the intermediary of a priest. They could confess their sins to him directly, and hear his word of forgiveness in the Scriptures. They were told that they were united to Christ in baptism and that he had adopted them as children of God. As members of the divine family they were privileged, but also responsible for their behaviour. Their sins would not cut them off from God, but they would have to repent of them, recommit themselves to him and seek a deeper presence of his grace and spiritual power in their lives. They would also learn that they could do nothing to increase this power, which was not an objective thing but a relationship with God that had been sealed by the blood of Christ and applied by the Holy Spirit in the hearts of those who trusted in him.

Above all, Protestants were taught that they had been chosen by God for a purpose and given a calling in life that was meant to glorify him. The word 'vocation' was liberated from its monastic context and applied to every form of human endeavour. Even today, it is possible to see on the notice board of a Catholic church a plea that church members should pray for more vocations, by which they mean men and women who will feel led to enter the priesthood or the convent. In the Protestant world, this meaning of the word has fallen into disuse, so much so that we now have to explain it to the uninitiated. A Protestant could be called by God to do anything – the vocation to be a door-keeper in the house of the Lord was just as important in God's eyes as being a bishop or a king.

It was this sense of the spiritual worth of the individual, who had been chosen by God to serve him, that created the conditions for the subsequent establishment of free speech and the rights of the individual conscience. How could a church or the state persecute someone who had been called by God? As this way of thinking took root in Protestant societies, they were transformed. Businessmen, scientists, carpenters and teachers were all exercising their vocations before God and glorifying him in their chosen professions. Gradually, social barriers were broken down. It could be disconcerting for people to realize that God was capable of raising up servants of his from the dregs of society, but when men and women were being moved and changed by the preaching of an ignorant tinker's son like John Bunyan, how could they deny what was happening? The humble were being lifted up, and the mighty, like the Catholic kings of Spain and France, were being laid low. Slowly but surely, the modern world, in which merit counts for more than birth and the worth of the individual is respected even above the demands of the state, began to take shape.

All of this took time, of course, and it would be foolish to pretend that it was all smooth sailing. In many respects, real social reform had to wait until the eighteenth and nineteenth centuries, but it was largely under Protestant auspices that it occurred, and usually without major social upheavals in the process. No Protestant country experienced anything comparable to the French or Russian revolutions, where the church was seen to be a bulwark of the old order and was made to suffer because of it. In Protestant countries, reform and religious belief went hand in hand so that even today, though there is widespread unbelief and indifference to religious concerns, there is little or no anti-clericalism in northern Europe. The church is not seen as an alien body of religious professionals who are trying to dictate to those outside their ranks, but rather as a gathered community in which pastors and people form a single body. That body can be marginalized and ignored, but it is hard to control or persecute it outright because the leadership is not so clearly distinct from the members. The priesthood of all believers, taught in the New Testament and proclaimed during the Reformation, has changed the church, both in the way that it functions internally and in the way that it is perceived by those who reject what it stands for.

We may therefore conclude that although much has changed over the centuries and in recent times there has been considerable secularization in the traditionally Protestant lands, the legacy of the Reformation is still apparent and influences people who may be quite unconscious of its message or else reject it outright. At the same time, Protestant societies generally allow freedom of speech and of religious belief to everyone, making it possible for those who adhere to the teaching of the Reformation to express themselves without undue interference. It is true that this freedom has come under attack in recent years and the future is uncertain, but as long as the memory of Protestantism persists, the chances are that the freedom of its adherents to proclaim the gospel will also survive.

What has been forgotten: the unchanging reality of human nature

I have spent what some people may think is an inordinate amount of time on the historical legacy of the Reformation, especially as it has been felt in the social and political sphere. I have done this deliberately, partly because it is more important than many people today realize, and partly because it can help us to understand both how the Reformation still matters today and how it does not. In historical terms, it matters because it has been a major influence in shaping the modern world, whose ideals of freedom and democracy cannot be understood or truly put into practice without taking it into account. But in modern terms, the kind of Reformation that occurred five centuries ago is no longer possible. For a start, there is no longer a monolithic church that claims to control the spiritual lives of its members. There is no social structure in place that allows the person at the top to dictate what those under him or her will believe, especially about spiritual matters that lie beyond that person's reach. Thanks to modern technology, information and thought control are no longer possible and there will never again be a caste of experts, cut off from the rest of society, that will be able to dictate its wishes to every citizen. Places like North Korea may be trying their best to turn the clock back, but they are swimming against the tide and it is only a matter of time before they collapse.

But the Reformation was more than merely a social and political phenomenon, important as those aspects of it were. It was also a spiritual revolution, and it is at that level that its importance for us today is both controversial and compelling. Individualism was a rare commodity in the sixteenth century, and reading our modern preoccupation with ourselves back into it is anachronistic.

But the Reformation helped to create a world in which the individual mattered, and in that sense it has come into its own in the modern age. Today almost everyone is free to decide what his or her personal belief system will be, and the Reformed faith is only one item on a rather large table of offerings. In fact, most people, at least in the Western world, pass the table by altogether. They are not interested in a personal faith commitment or even in a secular ideology. Many ignore the whole issue completely, while others pick and mix in what is loosely called the 'new age' style of spirituality. Either way it does not matter – those who take an interest in religion do so because it is a kind of hobby or distraction. They pick it up when it suits them and put it down again when it does not. Only a tiny minority ever gets hooked, and the road to Kathmandu is more likely to lead to a shop in the local shopping centre than to some mystical Shangri-La in the Himalayas, or even to the New Jerusalem.

This is a very different world from the one in which the Reformation took place. Five hundred years ago, virtually everybody in Europe believed that there was a God in heaven, a devil in hell and spiritual powers representing one or the other at work on earth. No doubt there was a lot of superstition in this belief system, which the Reformers did their best to uproot, but if people sometimes got the details wrong, their basic perception was much the same as that of the Bible and of many parts of the Global South today. To them, good and evil were spiritual realities that impinged on their lives – for better or for worse. It would probably be true to say that most people did not think of themselves as being intrinsically one or the other, but rather that they were subject to the influences of spiritual forces that were. If a man was wicked it was because the devil had got hold of him, and children needed to have the devil beaten out of them if they were to grow up properly. Demon possession was a reality in the popular mind, and exorcism was a regular practice. When Luther cried out that he was doing battle with Satan, people understood what he was saying. They may not have had the experience themselves, but they believed that it was possible, and even to be expected from a monk or holy man whose calling in life was to fight against the world, the flesh and the devil.

How far the average person understood the official teaching of the church, which was that all human beings had fallen into sin and that none could save themselves apart from the grace of God, is impossible to say. We know that at least some educated people understood it, and many of them were critical of the church for not making it more explicit. To those like Erasmus, the ceremonies surrounding the consecration of the sacramental elements had too often become an invitation to superstition, and they wanted ordinary church members to rise above that. The bread and wine of holy communion were not there to be gazed on or adored in themselves, but to be used as a means of grace.

Frequent communion, which was a relative rarity before the Reformation, was encouraged by them as a way of combating sin and growing closer to God.

The assumption, of course, was that getting closer to God was possible. Baptism had cleansed the soul from original sin and set it free to grow in grace. The problem was that too many people stopped there. From time to time a conscience would be stirred and an individual would be spiritually awakened. A man might then dedicate his life to the service of God and perhaps go into a monastery, where he would have the time and the encouragement to grow closer to God. That is precisely what the young Martin Luther did after he fell from his horse and was miraculously unharmed. It was as he was trying to serve the Lord in this way that he discovered how sinful he really was. The more he tried to expel his inner demons, the more they returned to haunt him. The remedies offered by the church only made things worse because they held out the promise of salvation without being able to deliver it. The corruption within him went too deep for that. It was only when he realized that sin was not a disease or a weakness that could be cured by regular exercise and spiritual medicine, but a broken relationship with God that only a restoration of that relationship could put right, that Luther's eyes were opened. People could not become righteous by their own efforts, but were made righteous by the gift of God in Christ. The worse off we are in the flesh, the greater that gift is, so that to deny oneself is to glorify Christ even more. It is, in the language of the Bible, to be born again into a new and eternal life in the Spirit.

All of this is now familiar to Protestant Christians and we resonate with Luther's experience of the transforming power of God's grace, working through regeneration and faith. The point I am trying to make, though, is that this is a foreign language to most modern people. The average person today has only a vague idea of what evil and sin might be. Almost all people will admit that there is room for improvement in their lives, but this is seen as achievable by a form of natural development which does not require a radical spiritual transformation, even if the language of 'spirituality' is used to describe it. Becoming a better person is considered to be a worthwhile and achievable goal. It may well involve sacrifice, and nowadays something like raising money for charity will probably be regarded as better than saying the rosary umpteen times, giving an added air of social usefulness to the sacrifice in question. Affluent people can quite easily be made to feel guilty for not doing more to help others, and if the church is an agency that allows them to work off that guilt and become 'better' people, then why not? The outward forms of piety may have changed over time, but their inward spirit is remarkably similar to what it has always been.

The spiritual dilemma of our time, therefore, is not that people think they are perfect. They do not. The problem is that they do not think that they are nearly as bad as they really are. They do not believe in Satan or in hell, even if they say they do, and tend to think that the world can be improved with good-will, plenty of cash and hard graft. It used to be thought that education and material prosperity would cure crime and other social evils, and the welfare states that came into being in the nineteenth and twentieth centuries were built on that premise. Many good things were achieved – there can be no doubt about that. Today we are for the most part better fed, better housed and better educated than our grandparents or great-grandparents were. We tend to live longer and are generally healthier. The exceptions are either unlucky – they have the wrong genes or were caught in an accident – or stupid. In a free-market economy, harmful substances are still sold, but they are clearly labelled, and if you cannot count your calories or understand health warnings, it is your own fault. Those with a working brain can save themselves; the others get what they deserve. Either way, it is all a matter of personal choice, and if there is a God in heaven he will reward those who make the right choices.

This is why the message of the Reformation is so desperately needed in modern society. Without in any way wishing to deny the beneficial results of healthy living and prudent decision-making, we who are Christians have to say that not only are those things not enough, but in the end they achieve nothing at all. The medieval church may have been wrong, but at least it was trying to point people to heaven, where most of them were trying to go. Today, heaven has become a vague, semi-fictional place of departed souls, useful mainly as a comfort to the bereaved, and even the church seldom points anyone to a life beyond this one. Our message tends to be 'Come and join us if you are lonely, frustrated or unhappy. Be part of our community and you will be happy and fulfilled in your life.' There is nothing wrong with that as far as it goes, but where does it go? Nowhere, if you stop and think about it. If all we can do is relieve boredom, entertain people and give them a sense of belonging, we are doing no more than might be expected from a good social club. If that is the case, the church is badly suited to its newly appointed role and it is hardly surprising that few people take much interest in it.

The sad truth is that the good news of salvation, while it may be preached from any number of pulpits every Sunday, is harder to understand now than it was five hundred years ago. Most people have no idea what we are talking about or why it is important, and few of us want to risk putting them off Christianity still further by telling them the truth about their spiritual condition. Yet Christian faith is nothing without the truth, as Jesus himself told his disciples. We do not have to convey this message in a heartless and forbidding way, of course, but convey it we must. If we spare people the hard facts for fear of offending them we are doing them no favours at all – that is certainly not love. The truth will hurt, but pain is often a God-given warning that something is wrong and that there is a problem that needs to be dealt with. If a toothache takes me to the dentist, how much more should a wound to my pride drive me to the Saviour of my soul? The trouble today is that people believe in the skill of the dentist, but are doubtful whether there is such a thing as the soul and unlikely to think that it needs saving or that there is anyone who can do that if it does.

The message of the Reformation still matters because it forces us to get to the bottom of what is wrong with us. Even more, it tells us that once we have plumbed the depths of our inner being and understood how weak and corrupt our minds are from what the Bible calls 'sin', there is indeed a deliverance available to us. Moreover, it is a deliverance that cannot be lost, overruled or diluted by any power in heaven or on earth because it comes from God. It is what the Bible calls 'eternal salvation'. Jesus Christ came down from heaven in order to take our burden of sin and guilt on himself. He died on a cross in order to pay a price for us that we are unable to pay for ourselves. What we cannot do in our own strength, he has done for us. Moreover, we can know this by the presence of his Holy Spirit in our hearts. The Holy Spirit is not a substance poured into us like a medicine, but a presence in our lives that can and will be given to us if we have faith in the Christ who has died to save us. How do we know that this is so? As the saying goes: 'The proof of the pudding is in the eating.' Or as the Bible puts it: 'Taste and see that the LORD is good.'[1]

The wonder and the glory of being a Christian is that, as God works in our hearts, we come to understand him and his way with us more clearly. Those who are mature in their faith are always learning just how sinful they really are, and are discovering new depths to their own depravity every day. They find themselves dealing with spiritual struggles and temptations that would have overwhelmed them in their youth. They come to appreciate just how tangled the web of humanity is and how impossible it is for us to straighten it out. Yet at the same time, if the Spirit of God is really at work in them, they do not despair. They know, because they have seen him at work in their own lives, that God is greater than we are, that he can bring life out of death, and that he can transform evil into good. We do not change for the better in any material sense – let us be honest and admit that growing old is a form of decay as far as this life is concerned. But we do not improve in a spiritual sense either, at least not independently of his presence inside us. Instead of following a programme of self-help, we are constantly being humbled and made more

1. Ps. 34:8, KJV.

consciously dependent on the one who has rescued us from the power of sin and death.

Today we live in a world in which the spiritual foundation of our humanity is denied, but the truth will not go away. In spite of all the improvements that technology and science can bring, we are unable to answer the great questions of life. Why are we here? Where are we going? Most people brush these questions aside and prefer to think about something less taxing, but the result is a spiritual disorder that reveals itself in our mental and even in our physical state. There is no doubt that levels of stress and anxiety have increased dramatically in the past hundred years, nor that trying to deal with such things has become a major industry. Therapy and counselling have replaced confession as the staple diet of the affluent, and they bear witness to the underlying truth that we are spiritual beings who do not live by bread alone.[2] Centuries ago, St Augustine said to God: 'O Lord, you have made us for yourself, and our hearts are restless until they find their rest in you.'[3] We see the truth of that observation being borne out in our own generation. Without him, our life is meaningless, and some people, at least, cannot live with that emptiness at the heart of their lives. There has to be a meaning somewhere, and if they cannot find it, they will drive themselves to destruction. Suicide is a terrible thing, but dying for oneself is the secular alternative to dying with Christ, and we should not be surprised to see it happening all around us. The difference is that those who reject God have no Christ to give them new life after death, whereas those who die in him are raised from the dead to enjoy the new life of his resurrection.

Here we have reached the heart of the Reformation message and the promise that it still holds out for us today. There is a God who understands us and who has reached out to put right what has gone wrong in our lives. Putting that right demands death – the death of Christ on the cross, which is echoed in the spiritual death of self to the world. 'I am crucified with Christ,' said the apostle Paul, 'nevertheless I live; yet not I, but Christ liveth in me.'[4] Theologians like to talk about the theology of the cross, which is what Paul is explaining here, and they connect it to the teaching of Martin Luther. They also like to contrast it with a so-called 'theology of glory' which puts all the emphasis on the wonders of heaven and downplays the need to deal first with the sin in our lives. In fact, of course, this contrast is imaginary. The theology of the cross is the theology of glory, as the hymn-writer John Bowring (1792–1872)

---

2. Deut. 8:3; Matt. 4:4.

3. Augustine of Hippo, *Confessions*, 1.1.

4. Gal. 2:20, KJV.

understood when he wrote his famous hymn 'In the cross of Christ I glory, / Towering o'er the wrecks of time . . .' The same was true for Fanny Crosby (1820–1915), who sang: 'In the cross, in the cross, / Be my glory ever; / Till my raptured soul shall find / Rest beyond the river.' The cross is our glory, because only in and through the sacrifice of Christ for which it stands is our sinfulness taken away, our broken relationship with God restored and new life given to us in the Holy Spirit.

We live in a time in history when the future seems less certain than ever. The planet's natural resources are running out. The ice caps are melting, with consequences that no-one can fully predict. Worse still, nuclear weapons are spreading, so that it is probably only a matter of time before somebody pushes the button and we all go up in fire and smoke. Until recently most people, at least in the Western world, believed that they were working to provide a better future for their children. Now, that seems increasingly unlikely for many. The society we were brought up to believe in is collapsing around us, but still the band plays on, assuring us that everything is for the best in the best of all possible worlds, and that it is getting better all the time. To this world of ours, the voices of the Protestant Reformers come like an unwelcome message from an alien planet. Yet what they had to say to their contemporaries matters now more than ever. If I put my trust in the powers that be in this life, I shall be deceived and ultimately destroyed. There is no hope and no salvation in human achievements, however great and wonderful they may be. The only answer is the one that comes from above, from that world of God that our contemporaries do so much to ignore and exclude from their lives. Talking about it is no more popular now than it was five hundred years ago, and certainly no more popular than it was when it was first proclaimed by Jesus, 1,500 years before that. We shall not be thanked for insisting that he alone is the way, the truth and the life, that we must pass through spiritual death and resurrection in order to get what we want, and that our assurance of salvation depends entirely on what he has done for us. Less of self and more of Christ – that is the motto of the Christian, which is diametrically opposed to the self-help culture of our time which leads us nowhere.

As we remember the stirring events of half a millennium ago, let us not forget that beyond all the superficial changes that make the world of the Protestant Reformers seem so foreign to us there lies a deeper spiritual reality that does not and cannot change. Our task is to bring that reality to bear on a culture that has turned its back on it and does everything it can to suppress it. The Reformation succeeded because God had mercy on his people and delivered them from the hand of those who would obscure and deny the truth. Do we have the faith to believe that he can and will do the same again, so that the glorious message of salvation by grace through faith in Christ alone may once again be the hallmark of our culture and a beacon of light to the perishing world around us? That is the challenge that the Reformers hold out to us, and the reason why their Reformation still matters to us today.

PART 1

THE CHIEF PLAYERS

1. MARTIN LUTHER

Mark D. Thompson

Martin Luther is the enduring face of the European Reformation. Though in time significant differences would separate him from other Reformers in Switzerland and England, he was recognized by all as the pioneer or fountainhead of the entire movement. After all, it had been Luther who had first challenged the Church of Rome on the basis of Scripture's plain teaching. He was the one who had seen, more clearly than those before him, that the abuses so many deplored arose from a distorted and unbiblical theology. Even before the *Disputation on the Power of Indulgences* (the Ninety-Five Theses, October 1517), Luther had publicly and stridently attacked the scholastic theology which supported this practice, in his *Disputation against Scholastic Theology* (September 1517). He did not hold back from challenging the abuses. He would do that all his life. Yet in the end these were mere symptoms of something far more serious and Luther knew it. An avalanche of writing from his pen, together with sermons and lectures, letters and even his table conversation, called men and women all over Europe back to the teaching of Scripture and the gospel of an entirely sufficient redemption in Christ. In many ways, to celebrate the Reformation is to celebrate what God did through this spectacularly gifted German monk, who translated the entire New Testament into German in just eleven weeks, bested the most accomplished debater of his age (Eck in 1519) as well as its greatest scholar (Erasmus in 1525), and stood with seemingly iron resolve against the combined might of the papacy and the Holy Roman

Empire. He bore the cost of such notoriety. When he died in 1546 it was as one excommunicated by the Roman church and outlawed by an edict of the emperor.

It is the stature of Luther, a giant in the history of the church, that makes the study of Luther such a complex activity. How can we be sure we are dealing with the 'real' Luther? Which portrait of him is true to this flesh-and-blood figure of human history? Luther has been made and remade over the centuries in the image of individuals and groups who want to claim him and his imprimatur for their own purposes. His own self-understanding oscillated between a 'poor stinking bag of maggots' and the second Noah, seeking to rescue as many as possible before the imminent deluge of divine judgment was visited on the earth.[1] His contemporaries, though, preferred to draw a comparison with Elijah, the prophet who stood against apostasy and idolatry.[2] Melanchthon is reported to have greeted the news of Luther's death by exclaiming in front of his class, 'the charioteer of Israel has fallen', an allusion to 2 Kings 2:12.[3] Others later minted a coin with the inscription 'Martin Luther: the Elijah of the Last Age'.[4] In sub-sequent centuries Luther has been claimed as the prototype German intellectual,[5]

---

1. The comment about himself as a 'poor stinking bag of maggots' is part of a plea against partisanship which is found in his 'A Sincere Admonition by Martin Luther to all Christians to Guard against Insurrection and Rebellion' (1522) *LW* 45:70–71 = *WA* 8:685.4–15. His identification of his mission with that of Noah is found later, in his lectures on the Noah narrative, e.g. *Genesis Lectures* (1535–45) *LW* 2:53 = *WA* 42:299.32–33 (on Gen. 6:6); *LW* 2:87 = *WA* 42.324.11–13 (on Gen. 7:1). See also M. Parsons, 'The Apocalyptic Luther: His Noahic Self-Understanding', *JETS* 44, no. 4 (2001), pp. 627–645.

2. E. W. Gritsch, 'The Cultural Context of Luther's Interpretation', *Interpretation* 37 (1983), p. 276.

3. H. A. Oberman, *Luther: Man Between God and the Devil*, trans. E. Walliser-Schwarzbart (New Haven: Yale University Press, 1989), p. 8.

4. '*Mart. Luther: Elias ultimi saeculi*', C. Schubart, *Die Berichte über Luthers Tod und Begräbnis* (Weimar: Böhlau, 1917); G. Rupp, *The Righteousness of God: Luther Studies* (London: Hodder & Stoughton, 1953), p. 14.

5. 'In more ways than one, Luther is the prototype of the German intellectual. He is so in particular as a writer, in his basic contribution to the development of the German language, but also as the *representative* of the German people in relation to the Catholic Church and hence on the world scene, as witnessed by his popularity, which means that to a great extent the Germans recognized themselves in him.' L. Dumont, *German Ideology: From France to Germany and Back* (Chicago: University of Chicago Press, 1994), p. 45.

the prototype German nationalist;[6] the cause of National Socialism,[7] the cure to National Socialism;[8] a revolutionary,[9] a voice of the people against the tyranny of their rulers,[10] the man who simply replaced one bondage with another;[11] a mystic,[12] a rational individualist;[13] the true progenitor of biblical criticism and liberal theology,[14] an evangelical inerrantist.[15] It is too easy to see your own commitments in Luther and by so doing justify them. However, there have also been those who have seen in Luther 'a catastrophe in the history of Western civilization'.[16] Not everyone looks to Luther for inspiration.

Yet was Luther really any of these things? He was, undoubtedly, a sixteenth-century northern German male, an academic of extraordinary capacity and yet

---

6. H. von Treitschke, 'Luther und die deutsche Nation', *Preußische Jahrbücher* 52 (1883), pp. 469–486; for a useful study of this phenomenon, see J. H. Brinks, 'Luther and the German State', *Heythrop Journal* 39 (1998), pp. 1–17.

7. P. F. Wiener, *Martin Luther: Hitler's Spiritual Ancestor* (London: Hutchinson, 1945).

8. G. Rupp, *Martin Luther: Hitler's Cause or Cure?* (London: Lutterworth, 1945).

9. G. Brendler, *Martin Luther: Theology and Revolution*, trans. C. R. Foster (New York: Oxford University Press, 1991).

10. L. H. Waring, *The Political Theories of Martin Luther* (New York: Putnam's Sons, 1910).

11. K. Marx, *On Religion* (New York: McGraw-Hill, 1974), pp. 36–37.

12. V. Leppin, 'Luther and John Tauler: Some Observations about the Mystical Impact on Reformation Theology', *Theology and Life* 36 (2013), pp. 339–345; 'Mysticism in Martin Luther's Development and Thoughts', at *Oxford Research Encyclopedia of Religion* (Oxford University Press, 2016), <http://religion.oxfordre.com/view/10.1093/acrefore/9780199340378.001.0001/acrefore-9780199340378-e-260>.

13. R. Bainton, *Here I Stand* (repr., Oxford: Lion, 1987), p. 141; A. MacIntyre, *A Short History of Ethics: A History of Moral Philosophy from the Homeric Age to the Twentieth Century*, 2nd edn (London: Routledge, 1998), p. 266.

14. K. Holl, *What Did Luther Understand by Religion?*, trans. F. W. Meuser and W. R. Wietzke (Philadelphia: Fortress, 1977); W. Quanbeck, 'The Confessions and Their Influence upon Biblical Interpretation', in J. Reumann (ed.), *Studies in Lutheran Hermeneutics* (Philadelphia: Fortress, 1949), p. 182; D. Nineham, *The Use and Abuse of the Bible: A Study of the Bible in an Age of Rapid Cultural Change* (London: SPCK, 1978), p. 264.

15. R. D. Preus, 'Luther and Biblical Infallibility', in J. D. Hannah (ed.), *Inerrancy and the Church* (Chicago: Moody Press, 1994), pp. 99–142.

16. R. Marius, *Martin Luther: The Christian between God and Death* (Cambridge, MA: Harvard University Press, 1999), p. xii.

always a Christian and a pastor first, a man who knew nothing about Descartes'
revolution or Newton's, Germany as it would later be forged by Bismarck,
Tridentine Catholicism, or even the International Council for Biblical Inerrancy
(though he did on many occasions appeal to the concept, if not the language, of
biblical inerrancy).[17] He had a remarkably high sense of his calling as a doctor
of the church; but in the midst of the battles he insisted, 'I did nothing; the
Word did everything.'[18] His last words, scrawled on a piece of paper beside his
deathbed, half in German, half in Latin, read, 'We are beggars, that is true.'[19]
The battle today and always is to let Luther speak for himself. As a man, he was
strong and weak at the same time. He was plagued with constipation, gout and
kidney stones. On top of these he endured crushing bouts of depression
and despair, his *Anfechtungen*. But he also transcended his own time as a man of
tenacious courage, seeking faithful discipleship in the light of the word which
God has spoken and which centres on a precious saviour. His theology was
deeply interwoven with his life and, if it is to be properly understood, needs to
be read alongside it. When that is done, it becomes clear that while our questions
may not have been his questions, his legacy continues to be relevant though five
centuries have passed since it all began.

---

17. E.g. M. Luther, *Ad dialogum Silvestri Prieratis de potestate papae responsio* (1518)
    WA 1:647.22–24; *Proceedings at Augsburg* (1518) *LW* 31:282 = *WA* 2:21.5–6; *Grund
    und Ursach aller Artikel Martin Luthers, so durch römische Bulle unrechtlich verdammt sind*
    (1521) *WA* 7:315.35–38; *Sermons on the Psalms of David* (1526) *LW* 13:393 = *WA*
    19:300.19–21; *Lectures on 1 Timothy* (1528) *LW* 28:239 = *WA* 26:19.31–33; *Lecture
    on Psalm 45* (1532) *LW* 12:242 = *WA* 40/2:531.30–34; *Genesis Lectures* (1535–45)
    LW 1:122 = *WA* 42:92.25–26 (on Gen. 2:21).

18. The most detailed studies of Luther's *Doktoratsbewußtein* ('doctor consciousness')
    remain Hermann Steinlein, *Luthers Doktorat: Zum 400 jährigen Jubiläum desselben 18/19
    Oktober 1912* (Leipzig: Deichert, 1912); and Brian Gerrish, 'Doctor Martin Luther:
    Subjectivity and Doctrine in the Lutheran Reformation', in P. N. Brooks (ed.),
    Seven-Headed Luther: Essays in Commemoration of a Quincentenary 1483–1983 (Oxford:
    Clarendon Press, 1983), pp. 2–11. The quote comes from the second invocavit
    sermon preached upon his return from the Wartburg in March 1522, *LW* 51:77 =
    WA 10/3:19.2–3.

19. Written half in Latin, half in German: 'Wir sind Bettler. Hoc est verum.' Recorded
    in Luther's *Table Talk* as no. 5468 (16 February 1546) *LW* 54:476 = *WATr* 5:168.35
    cf. no. 5677 in *WATr* 5:318.2–3.

Miner's son, monk, magister

Martin Luder was born on 10 November 1483 in the north-eastern German town of Eisleben. The aspirations of his father, Hans, who managed a copper mine, led him to arrange for Martin's education first at the Cathedral School at Magdeburg and then at the University of Erfurt. The plan was that he would pursue a career in the law and so, after matriculating in 1501, he began the preparatory studies. He completed his BA in 1502 and his MA in 1505. However, Hans Luder's plans were undone when Martin was caught in the midst of a thunderstorm while travelling near the town of Stotternheim. When one bolt of lightning struck terrifyingly close to him, Luther cried out to the patron saint of miners and travellers in distress: 'Help me, St Anne, I will become a monk.' Others might later have dismissed the vow, but Luther's conscience could not. As he explained,

> Later I regretted that I had made the vow, and many tried to dissuade me. But I persevered, and the day before St Alexis's day I invited some of my very best friends to a farewell celebration, in the hope that the following day they would escort me into the monastery . . . And my father was angry about my vow, but I persisted in my determination. I thought I would never leave the monastery. I was quite dead to the world until God thought the time was right, and Squire Tetzel provoked me and Dr Staupitz incited me against the Pope.[20]

By now the surname Luder had been Latinized to Lutherus (from which would come Luther), a standard conceit of the Renaissance scholar. The story of Martin Luther the conscientious and troubled monk is well known. He was troubled by his own sinfulness and unworthiness, and sadly the monastic regime did not help. This would remain his burden right until the time of his 'Reformation discovery':

> Though I lived as a monk without reproach, I felt that I was a sinner before God with an extremely disturbed conscience. I could not believe that he was placated by my satisfaction. I did not love, yes, I hated the righteous God who punishes sinners, and secretly, if not blasphemously, certainly murmuring greatly, I was angry with God.[21]

20. M. Luther, *Table Talk* 4707 (July 1539), *WATr* 4:440; English translation I. Siggins (ed.), *Luther* (Edinburgh: Oliver & Boyd, 1972), pp. 36–37.

21. M. Luther, 'Preface to the Complete Edition of Luther's Latin Writings' (1545) *LW* 34:336–337 = *WA* 54:185.21–25.

The religious life did not bring peace but instead new opportunities for despair as Luther came to realize that he was alone in this experience. Nevertheless, it was in the monastery at Erfurt that Luther encountered Johann von Staupitz (1460–1524). Staupitz was a scholar as well as the Vicar General of the Observant Augustinian friars in Germany. He directed Luther's life in the monastery, became his father confessor, nurtured his love for Scripture and pointed him to the wounds of Christ.[22] Luther testified to this again and again. He wrote to Staupitz in September 1523, just over a year before the latter's death: 'it was through you that the light of the gospel first began to shine out of the darkness into my heart'.[23] He would tell those gathered at table ten years later, 'I got nothing from Erasmus. I got everything from Dr Staupitz.'[24]

It was most likely soon after Luther's ordination as a priest in April 1507 that Staupitz arranged for him to begin the formal graduated process of theological education. He began his studies under the theologians and philosophers of the University of Erfurt. However, in 1508 he was called by Staupitz to the relatively new University of Wittenberg to lecture in Moral Philosophy for a term while the usual lecturer was preparing for his doctoral examination. Staupitz was the dean of the Wittenberg theology faculty that year and so most likely took direct responsibility for Luther's continuing theological education while he was there.[25] Luther received his *Baccalaureus Biblicus* while at Wittenberg on 9 March 1509, which conferred responsibility to teach briefly on select biblical texts. Also while there, he received his *Baccalaureus Sententiarius*, which required him to lecture on Peter the Lombard's *The Sentences*, the standard theological text in late medieval scholasticism. He did not have time to deliver even the first of these lectures in Wittenberg before he was recalled to Erfurt to complete his studies there. Nevertheless, despite objection from the scholars at Erfurt, it was at Wittenberg that Luther was received as a Doctor of Theology on 19 October 1512. He began lecturing there as Professor of Bible (succeeding Staupitz himself) almost immediately afterwards.

---

22. M. Luther, *Table Talk* 526 (Spring 1533), *WATr* 1:245.11–12 = *LW* 54:97; *Table Talk* 1490 (April–Mary 1532), *WATr* 2:113.15–17. D. C. Steinmetz, *Luther and Staupitz: An Essay in the Intellectual Origins of the Protestant Reformation* (Durham, NC: Duke University Press, 1980).

23. M. Luther, 'To Johann von Staupitz, from Wittenberg, September 17, 1523', *LW* 49:48 = *WABr* 3:155.6–7.

24. M. Luther, *Table Talk* 173 (Feb–March 1532), *WATr* 1:80.6–7.

25. M. Brecht, *Martin Luther: His Road to Reformation 1483–1521*, trans. J. L. Schaaf (Philadelphia: Fortress, 1985), p. 92.

Right from the start Luther decided to do things differently. He lectured directly on the text of Scripture, rather than working his way through one of the great tomes of scholastic theology or even the *Glossa Ordinaria*. When he began lecturing on the Psalms for the first time, in 1513, he provided his students with a printed copy of the text with wide margins in which they could take their notes. Analysis of these lectures, the *Dictata super Psalterium*, reveals that when Luther began teaching at Wittenberg he was still very much a medieval exegete, adjusting but not abandoning the standard allegorical interpretation of biblical texts. Yet as this series of lectures progressed, Luther's approach to the Old Testament underwent a change. Particularly later in the series, greater place was given to the original historical context, as the 'faithful synagogue' was given voice.[26] Even more importantly, the focus of his exposition was increasingly on Christ. In one sense, such a 'Christological concentration' lay entirely within the range of medieval approaches to biblical interpretation.[27] After all, his preface to these lectures had insisted that 'Every prophecy and every prophet must be understood as referring to Christ the Lord, except where it is clear from plain words that someone else is spoken of.'[28] However, Luther's application of this principle took a new turn, insisting that the prophetic reference to Christ is the proper starting point for biblical exposition. As early as his exposition of Psalm 4 he commented,

> Christ is the Head of all saints, the Fountain of all, the Source of all rivers, of whom all partake, and 'from His fullness all have received'. From this it follows that 'in the roll' (that is, in the chief sense) 'of the book', that is of the entire Scripture and especially of the Psalms, 'it is written concerning him'. And as all His saints flow from Him like rivers, so Scripture, being similarly constituted and thus representing Him with His saints, speaks of Him in the sense of the first source.[29]

For Luther, the prophetic sense of Scripture (its reference to Christ) *was* the literal sense of Scripture, from which each other level of meaning must flow. God intended all Scripture to speak of his Son. Much is often made of Luther's fascination with the tropological (or moral) sense of Scripture. However, even this was understood by Luther with reference to Christ, as he explained when

---

26. J. S. Preus, 'Old Testament Promissio and Luther's New Hermeneutic', *Harvard Theological Review* 60 (1967), pp. 145–161.

27. A. E. McGrath, *Luther's Theology of the Cross* (Oxford: Blackwell, 1985), p. 81.

28. M. Luther, *First Lectures on the Psalms* (1513–16), *LW* 10:7 = *WA* 55/1:6.25–8.1.

29. *First Lectures on the Psalms*, *LW* 10:52 = *WA* 3:46.17–23.

he reached Psalm 72: 'So it is with all the works and ways of God: every one of them is Christ literally, and faith in him morally.'[30]

Luther's 'Reformation discovery' was in fact the result of a series of shifts in thinking like this arising from his study of the text of the Bible in preparation for his lectures. These were catalysed by pastoral issues such as the indulgence controversy and the sharp and unrelenting opposition of the Roman Catholic establishment. He came to see problems with scholastic theology and its dependence upon Aristotle, the significance of a distinction between law and gospel when reading the Scriptures, the centrality of the cross in all God's purposes, the critical nature of faith as trust and the futility of pursuing our own righteousness. Near the end of his life he would tend to telescope many of these developments into his critical engagement with Romans 1:6–17 as he commenced his second series of Psalms lectures in 1518 (NB *after* the Ninety-Five Theses):

> Meanwhile, I had already during that year returned to interpret the Psalter anew. I had confidence in the fact that I was more skilful, after I had lectured in the university on St. Paul's epistles to the Galatians, and the one to the Hebrews. I had indeed been captivated with an extraordinary ardour for understanding Paul in the Epistle to the Romans. But up till then it was not the cold blood about the heart, but a single word in Chapter 1 [:17], 'In it the righteousness of God is revealed', that had stood in my way . . . At last, by the mercy of God, meditating day and night, I gave heed to the context of the words, namely, 'In it the righteousness of God is revealed, as it is written, "He who through faith is righteous shall live."' There I began to understand that the righteousness of God is revealed by the gospel, namely, the passive righteousness with which merciful God justifies us by faith, as it is written, 'He who through faith is righteous shall live.' Here I felt that I was altogether born again and had entered paradise itself by open gates.[31]

Luther's burden was lifted by his realization that righteousness is a gift rather than an achievement, but that realization itself came on the back of a series of other realizations which freed him to look at the text of Scripture with fresh eyes.

---

30. *First Lectures on the Psalms, LW* 10:402 = *WA* 3:458.10–11. See Mark D. Thompson, *A Sure Ground on Which to Stand: The Relation of Authority and Interpretive Method in Luther's Approach to Scripture* (Carlisle: Paternoster, 2004), pp. 157–158 and the secondary sources cited there.

31. M. Luther, 'Preface to the Complete Edition of Luther's Latin Writings' (1545), *LW* 34:336, 337 = *WA* 54:185.21–25.

The indulgence controversy

In 1507, in an attempt to raise funds for the rebuilding of St Peter's in Rome, Pope Julius II had issued a plenary indulgence. The purchase of an indulgence certificate guaranteed the remission of time in purgatory on the authority of the Pope as the successor to Peter, the keeper of 'the keys of the kingdom of heaven' (Matt. 16:19, ESV). The indulgences were to be sold throughout Europe and in 1517 were vigorously promoted by Albrecht, Archbishop of Mainz (the neighbouring principality to Electoral Saxony, in which Wittenberg was located). Luther's pastoral concern for the congregation at Wittenberg under his care led him to speak out against not only the abusive sales tactics of the indulgence vendors, but also the theology which justified them. He preached against indulgences several times in 1516 and 1517.[32] Finally, he posted a notice of debate on the north door of the Castle Church on 31 October 1517.[33] It consisted of ninety-five theses, which spoke of the entire life of believers as one of repentance (thesis 1), insisted that the Pope has no power to remit any penalties beyond those imposed either at his own discretion or by canon law (thesis 5), decried the vendors' suggestion that the soul flees out of purgatory immediately the money clinks in the bottom of the chest (thesis 27) and stated that 'Christians should be taught that one who gives to the poor, or lends to the needy, does a better action than if he purchases indulgences' (thesis 43), and that the true treasure of the church is not a storehouse of surplus merit but 'the holy gospel of the glory and grace of God' (thesis 62).[34]

On 31 October Luther sent a copy of his theses to the Archbishop of Mainz, who first asked his own theological faculty for advice, but in the end did not wait for their report before forwarding the theses to Rome. It was not the first time in 1517 that the attention of the authorities had been drawn to Luther. Just

---

32. Sermons on 27 July and 31 October 1516 and 24 February 1517, *WA* 1:63–65, 94–99, 138–141.

33. There has been considerable historical debate about whether the theses were actually posted, and if they were, whether this was done some time after Luther sent them to the Archbishop of Mainz on 31 October. See Brecht, *Road to Reformation*, pp. 200–202. The evidence is not conclusive, though the report of Luther posting them on this date on the doors of the Church of All Saints (the *Schloßkirche*) goes back to Philip Melanchthon's preface to the second volume of Luther's complete works dated 1 June 1546. *CR* 6:161–162 (3478).

34. M. Luther, *Disputation on the Power and Efficacy of Indulgences* (1517), *LW* 31:25, 26, 27–28, 29, 31 = *WA* 1:233.10–11, 18–19; 234.29–30; 235.22–23; 236.22–23.

a month before, he had published a blistering attack upon scholastic theology and its enslavement to the philosophy of Aristotle. However, this time the interest stretched way beyond the narrow confines of the theological faculties of Europe. The Ninety-Five Theses were soon printed and distributed widely. We know that Erasmus of Rotterdam read them and sent them from Louvain to his friend Thomas More in England in early March 1518.[35] Luther continued to think and write on the issue, as is evident by his *Sermon on Indulgences and Grace*, preached in February 1518, and his steady work on his *Explanations of the Disputation Concerning the Value of Indulgences* from late 1517 until it was finally sent to the printer in August 1518.[36]

Johann Tetzel, the general subcommissary for the sale of indulgences in the ecclesiastical province of Magdeburg, defended a set of theses designed to justify the Roman position on indulgences in January 1518.[37] In April he did it again and also published a refutation of Luther's *Sermon on Indulgences and Grace*.[38] Tetzel seems, with some reason, to have seen Luther's campaign against indulgences as a personal attack. Meanwhile, the first official Catholic response to Luther came from Sylvester Mazzolini (Prierias), Master of the Sacred Palace in Rome. Perhaps earlier than anyone else, Prierias realized that the fundamental issue in this dispute was one of authority: the authority of the Pope and the authority of Scripture. He famously concluded, 'Whoever does not hold fast to the teachings of the Roman Church and of the Pope as the infallible rule of faith, from which even Holy Scripture draws its strength and authority, is a heretic.'[39]

35. D. Erasmus, 'To Thomas More' (5 March 1518), *Correspondence of Erasmus*, Vol. 5: *Letters 594 to 841*, trans. R. A. B. Mynors and D. F. S. Thomson (Toronto: University of Toronto Press, 1979), p. 327 (line 39).

36. M. Luther, *Ein Sermon von Ablaß und Gnade* (1517), *WA* 1:243–246; *Explanations of the Disputation Concerning the Value of Indulgences* (1518), *LW* 31:83–252 = *WA* 1:525–628.

37. These theses had been drawn up by Konrad Koch of Frankfurt, who had taken the name Wimpina. *D. Martini Lutheri Opera Latina Varii Argumenti ad Reformationis Historiam Imprimis Pertinentia*, ed. Heinrich Schmidt, 7 vols. (Frankfurt & Erlangen: Heyderi & Zimeri, 1865–73; hereafter *EA lat. var. arg.*), 1:296–305.

38. These theses can be found in *EA lat. var. arg.*, 1:306–312. Tetzel's refutation of Luther's sermon can be found in Valentin Gröne, *Tetzel und Luther*, 2nd edn (Soest: Nasse, 1860), pp. 219–234.

39. S. Mazzolini, *Dialogus Reverendi Patris Fatris Silvestri Prieriatis de Potestate Pape in Lutheri conclusiones* (1518), in *EA lat. var. arg.*, 1:344–377. For a discussion of this work and Prierias's insight, see H. A. Oberman, 'Wittenberg's War on Two Fronts:

Throughout this period Luther continued to teach. From March 1517 to April 1518 he lectured twice a week through the Epistle to the Hebrews.[40] From September 1518 until he left for Worms in June 1521, he lectured slowly through the Psalms for the second time, with quite a few interruptions.[41] He preached, never less than twice a week. He continued to write, with small pieces on the Ten Commandments, the confession of sins and the worthy reception of the Eucharist.[42] In the light of the brewing controversy, he was required to defend his theology before the triennial meeting of his Order in Heidelberg in April 1518. It was at that meeting he spoke about the theology of the cross and the way the cross changes our perspective on everything, especially keeping us from relying on our own prowess when it comes to the knowledge of God.[43] Luther received news that proceedings had begun against him in Rome in August and, following intervention by his protector, Elector Frederick the Wise of Saxony, Luther met with the papal legate, Cardinal Cajetan, in Augsburg in October. However, it soon became clear that Cajetan's only intention in meeting with Luther was to hear Luther recant. Luther refused to yield and the struggle between him and the papacy continued to escalate.[44]

Johann Eck and the Leipzig Disputation

The fiercest opponent of Luther throughout this period was undoubtedly Johann Maier of Egg an der Günz (known as Eck), Professor of Theology at the University of Ingolstadt. Eck had an enviable reputation as a debater and

---

What Happened in 1518 and Why', trans. A. C. Gow, in H. A. Oberman, *The Reformation: Roots and Ramifications* (Edinburgh: T&T Clark, 1994), pp. 117–148.

40. M. Luther, *Lectures on Hebrews* (1518), *LW* 29:109–241 = *WA* 57/3:1–238.

41. M. Luther, *Operationes in Psalmos* (1518–21), *WA* 5 (Pss 1 and 2 are translated in *LW* 14:279–349).

42. M. Luther, *Eine kurze Erklärung der zehn Gebote* (1518), *WA* 1:250–256; *Instructio pro confessione peccatorum* (1518), *WA* 1:257–265; *Sermo de digna praeparatione cordis pro suscipiendo sacramento eucharistiae* (1518), *WA* 1:329–334.

43. M. Luther, *Heidelberg Disputation* (1518), *LW* 31:39–70 = *WA* 1:353–374. Knut Alfsvåg has put this insight well: 'One will . . . never find God as an extension of the seemingly good and beautiful; one can never build a consistent theology on one's experience of the world.' K. Alfsvåg, 'The Centrality of Christology: On the Relation between Nicholas Cusanus with Martin Luther', *Studia Theologica* 70, no. 1 (2016), p. 28.

44. M. Luther, *Proceedings at Augsburg* (1518), *LW* 31:261 = *WA* 2:7.22–26.

was fiercely ambitious. Upon reading the Ninety-Five Theses, he saw an opportunity to cast himself as a defender of orthodoxy by preparing to debate them.
He prepared an initial refutation of the theses, which he circulated privately. It
was entitled *Obelisks* after the little dagger symbols used to mark spurious
sections in classical literature. In due course Luther would respond with his own
Asterisks, also circulated privately at first. Asterisks were the critical marks used
to indicate the most important parts of ancient texts. Within a few months, due
not least to some provocation by Luther's colleague Karlstadt, Eck was calling
for a public disputation (though he named Karlstadt alone at first, Eck admitted
later that his real target had always been Luther). Eventually Leipzig would be
settled upon as the venue. Eck prepared a set of theses for his debate, insisting
on the supreme authority of the church and the Pope. Luther used whatever
spare time he had to prepare for the confrontation by reading extensively in the
Church Fathers and the more recent pronouncements of popes and councils.
Nevertheless, he was kept in the dark until the eleventh hour about whether he
would be allowed to debate.

The critical importance of this single disputation, and especially Luther's
preparation for it, is often overlooked. However, it was at this point that
Luther's opposition to the papacy took on a new intensity. In February 1519
he spoke of Rome as 'Babylon, from which (if anywhere) vomits forth the
devastation of Scripture and the church'.[45] Just a month later, again in private
correspondence, the criticism was even more severe:

> In addition to this, I am studying the papal decretals for my disputation. And,
> confidentially, I do not know whether the pope is the Antichrist himself or whether
> he is his apostle, so miserably is Christ (that is, the truth) corrupted and crucified by
> the pope in the decretals. I am extremely distressed that under the semblance of laws
> and the Christian name, the people of Christ should be so deluded. One day I shall
> copy my notes on the decretals for you, so that you, too, may see what it is to make
> laws regardless of Scripture, simply from the desire to exercise tyranny. I don't even
> mention the other works which are so very similar to those of the Antichrist and
> of which the Roman Curia has an overabundance. Daily greater and greater help
> and support by virtue of the authority of Holy Scripture wells up in me.[46]

Luther continued to struggle with the consequences of this assessment. In
this he had help from an unexpected quarter, the writings of the Czech heretic

---

45. M. Luther to G. Spalatin (24 February 1519), *WABr* 1:351.15–17.
46. M. Luther to G. Spalatin (13 March 1519), *LW* 48.114 = *WABr* 1:359.28 – 360.36.

Jan Hus, who had been condemned and executed a century before. Eck had
drawn attention to a similarity between some of what Luther was teaching and
the teaching of 'the Bohemian' in his *Obelisks*. Hus had advanced the argument
that papal primacy had been established not by divine law but by human law.
Honour and obedience were due to the Pope as a legitimate governing authority,
but his pronouncements could not bind the conscience and were not necessary
for salvation. Luther went further: any claim of the Roman church to the
contrary, to final authority in matters of faith and practice or superiority over
the other churches, was contrary not only to Scripture but also to its own
decretals. One of the most dramatic points in the disputation would be the
moment when Luther declared 'among the articles of John Hus or the Bohemians
are many plainly Christian and evangelical, which the universal church cannot
condemn'.[47] At that point Duke Georg of Saxony exclaimed, 'There's the
plague!'

As significant as the preparation for this debate was in providing Luther
with a deeper and more informed opposition to papal primacy as well as an
incentive to re-evaluate the teaching of Jan Hus, its most important contribution was in further sharpening Luther's understanding of the authority of
Scripture. In February 1519 Luther wrote to his friend Wilibald Pirkheimer
insisting, 'I will serve and acknowledge the authority and majesty of the
Supreme Pontiff, but I will not become a corrupter of Holy Scripture.'[48] In
the debate itself Luther would be immovable on the unique and final authority
of Scripture:

> No believing Christian can be coerced beyond Holy Scripture, which is the proper
> divine law, without access to new and proven revelation. By divine law we are
> forbidden to believe anything which is not established by divine Scripture or
> manifest revelation.[49]

What, then, of councils such as that which condemned Hus in 1415? When
Eck cited Augustine in support of the authority of all councils, Luther made
another comment which caused consternation far and wide.

---

47. M. Luther, *Disputatio I. Eccii et M. Lutheri Lipsiae habita* (1519), *WA* 2:279.11–13
(Bainton, *Here I Stand*, pp. 115–116).

48. M. Luther to W. Pirkheimer (20 February 1519), *WABr* 1:348.20–22.

49. *Disputatio I. Eccii et M. Lutheri Lipsiae habita* (1519), *WA* 2:279.23–26 (Bainton,
Here I Stand, p. 116, modified).

> Augustine's argument concerned Scripture, which is the infallible word of God.
> A council is a creature of this word: therefore injury is done to the word of
> God when these are brought alongside each other. A council can err . . .[50]

The implication was obvious and Luther would make it in his report to Elector
Frederick after the disputation: 'therefore one should believe more a layman
who has Scripture than the Pope and Council without Scripture'.[51] The issue
in the foreground of the Leipzig Disputation may well have been the authority
of the Pope and church councils. Yet in the course of dealing with this issue
Luther was forced to think through in greater detail the place of Scripture in
the determination of doctrine and Christian practice. One of the critical affirm-
ations of the entire Reformation – *sola scriptura*, Scripture alone as the final
authority for the Christian that stands above all others, theologians, popes, canon
law, the pronouncements of church councils – can be traced to this confrontation. At the time, though, Luther's assessment of the exercise was unremittingly
negative. 'It began badly and ended worse,' he wrote to Spalatin on his return.[52]

The break with church and empire

Leipzig clarified the depth of the rift that had opened up between Luther and
the Roman church. Rome was determined to stamp out this new heresy before
it took root, but a number of factors made that difficult. The advent of the
printing press had made a quick and wide dissemination of Luther's ideas
possible. In hindsight, this early adoption of the latest communication technology was a masterstroke, though it was hardly a calmly calculated strategy at
the time. The second major factor was the political situation in Europe in the
critical period 1518–21. Emperor Maximilian I was not well and was seeking to
secure the succession of his grandson, Charles of Spain. His chief rival was
Francis I of France. The new emperor would be elected by the seven prince
electors of the empire, one of whom was Duke Frederick of Saxony, Luther's
prince. Rome was keen to prevent the election of Charles and in a tense political
atmosphere every vote was courted. The papacy could not afford to press for
Luther's extradition to Rome and so offend the prince whose vote it was trying
to secure. So the opportunity to nip this in the bud was lost. In the end Charles

---

50. Ibid.
51. Luther and Karlstadt to Elector Frederick (18 August 1519), *WABr* 1:472.261–263.
52. Luther to Spalatin (20 July 1519), *LW* 31:325 = *WABr* 1:424.146–147.

was elected on 28 June 1519, just a few weeks before the Leipzig Disputation. The proceedings against Luther continued, but quietly, in Rome.

A year later Rome sensed the time to act had come. Eck had travelled to Rome in May 1520 and appears to have raised the temperature considerably. He wanted Luther condemned and he wanted the opportunity to publish that condemnation throughout Germany. Less than a month later, the papal bull *Exsurge Domine* was promulgated by Pope Leo X, on 15 June 1520. It condemned forty-one of Luther's theses and ordered that his writings be destroyed. Most important of all, it gave him sixty days to recant or face excommunication. Eck posted the bull in various cities throughout Germany but it only arrived in Wittenberg through a circuitous route on or around 10 October. In the interim Luther began to publish what would prove to be a series of enduring statements of Reformation theology.

In June his *Sermon on Good Works* was published as an answer to the charge that his theology had no place for good works and no incentive to godliness. Luther removed the distinction between religious good works and secular good works and gave a priority to faith:

> the whole of Scripture gives the name good, divine work to no work except to faith alone . . . In this faith all works become equal . . . For the works are acceptable not for their own sake but because of faith, which is always the same and lives and works in each and every work without distinction.[53]

In August he published *An Appeal to the Christian Nobility of the German Nation*. It was clear that news of the publication of the bull against him had destroyed any last hope that the Roman church might reform itself in the light of the teaching of Scripture. In such circumstances the Christian princes must take up their own responsibility to care for Christ's bride. They needed to tear down the three walls the papacy had built to protect itself from criticism and reform: the claim to supremacy over secular princes, the claim to be the sole authorized interpreter of Scripture and the claim to be the only body able to call a General Council of the church. Here was Luther's ferocious attack upon the entire concept of monarchical papalism: 'The time for silence is over, and the time for speech has come.'[54] It also set out an agenda for change: a return to apostolic simplicity, the removal of compulsory celibacy for the clergy, the suppression of Masses for the dead and so on, and the reform of education.

---

53. M. Luther, *A Treatise on Good Works* (1520), *LW* 44:26 = *WA* 6:206.26–27, 33, 35–37.
54. M. Luther, *An Appeal to the Christian Nobility of the German Nation* (1520), *LW* 44:23 = *WA* 6:404.11–12.

In October Luther published his *Prelude on the Babylonian Captivity of the Church*. In this highly significant work he dismantled the Catholic sacramental system that had bound Christian people to falsehood and priesthood and fear. With specific attention to the Eucharist, he challenged the sacrifice of the Mass (the suggestion that the Eucharist is a re-offering of the sacrifice Christ made to the Father on the cross), transubstantiation (the suggestion that in the prayer known as 'the Canon of the Mass' the substance of the bread and wine is transformed into the body and blood of Christ while the accidents remain the same), and the withholding of the cup from the laity (where the priests alone receive both elements). More generally Luther redefined the very notion of sacrament along New Testament lines and reduced the number of sacraments from seven to three and then eventually two (baptism and the Lord's Supper).

In November, as part of one last attempt to plead his case before the Pope, Luther published one of his best-loved works, *The Freedom of a Christian Man*. In this work he sought to explain as simply as possible the implications of his rediscovery of justification by faith for Christian living. The language was clear, memorable and direct, as these three snippets show:

> A Christian is a perfectly free lord of all, subject to none. A Christian is a perfectly dutiful servant of all, subject to all.
>
> One thing, and only one thing, is necessary for Christian life, righteousness and freedom. That one thing is the holy Word of God, the Gospel of Christ . . .
>
> Our faith in Christ does not free us from works but from false opinions concerning works, that is, the foolish presumption that justification is acquired by works.[55]

Christian freedom is not the opposite of humble service, either of God or of each other. Rather, it energizes such service. It is a real, royal and priestly freedom: real, not illusory; royal, in that the Christian is master of all things; and priestly, because every Christian has direct access to God through faith in Christ.

These four treatises are masterly presentations of the new teaching. They appeared in public just as in various cities across Europe Luther's works were being collected and burnt. So did another, his less-than-temperate response to *Exsurge Domine*, entitled *Against the Execrable Bull of Antichrist*. Luther believed he recognized the hand of Eck in the bull but insisted 'whoever wrote this bull,

---

55. M. Luther, *The Freedom of a Christian* (1520), *LW* 31:344, 345, 372–373 = *WA* 7:49.22–25, 50.33–35, 70.14–16.

he is Antichrist'.[56] The final flourish made clear he would not be cowed: 'Since they excommunicated me for the sake of their own sacrilege of heresy, so I excommunicate them for the sake of the sacred truth of God. Christ the Judge will see whose excommunication will stand. Amen.'[57] On the very day the bull's deadline for recantation expired, 10 December 1520, Luther joined some students who were burning books of the canon law (in the place of Luther's works) and burned his copy of the bull. On 3 January 1521, another papal bull, *Decet Romanum Pontificem*, made it official. Luther was now cut off from the church of God.

As an excommunicated heretic, Luther could now expect the secular authorities to act against him. Through a complex set of manoeuvrings, he was given the opportunity to appear before the Imperial Diet meeting at Worms in April 1521. Luther travelled to Worms, not as the conquering hero of later romanticized accounts, but as a man expecting his safe conduct to be violated (as Hus's had been a century before). Yet what he feared most was that he would not withstand the test. The day came and it was clear yet again that Luther would not be heard. A table piled high with his works stood before him. He was asked first to identify these works as his own and then to recant what was taught in them. In a masterstroke he divided the works into types, some of which were completely inoffensive, some of which were written in the heat of debate and some of which were simply expositions of biblical truth. He had found a way to be heard. His speech ended with a crescendo heard around the world:

> Unless I am convinced by the testimony of the Scriptures or by evident reason –
> for I can believe neither pope nor councils alone, as it is clear that they have erred
> repeatedly and contradicted themselves – I consider myself conquered by the
> Scriptures adduced by me and my conscience is captive to the Word of God.
> I cannot nor will not recant anything, since to act against conscience is neither
> safe nor sound.[58]

The official record does not record a final line in German, which Luther's supporters took down in haste: 'Here I stand, I cannot do otherwise. God help me. Amen.'[59] Luther was escorted from the hall. It had been a bold stand, but Luther knew what was at stake. When he returned to his room he shouted with elation,

---

56. M. Luther, *Adversus execrabilem Antichristi bullam* (1520), *WA* 6:598.10–11.

57. *Adversus execrabilem Antichristi bullam* (1520), *WA* 6:612.21–23.

58. 'Luther at the Diet of Worms' (1521), *LW* 32:112 = *WA* 7:838.4–8.

59. 'Worms', *LW* 32:112 = *WA* 7:838.9.

'I've come through, I've come through.'[60] An imperial edict making Luther an outlaw in the empire was published on 26 May 1521.

The Wartburg and beyond

There it all might have ended had not Luther's prince decided to protect him. Luther was squirrelled away in Wartburg castle, where he grew his hair and beard and was known as 'Knight George'. While there, in the space of just less than eleven weeks, he translated the entire New Testament into German using the Greek text published by Erasmus in 1519. He would work on revising it and producing prefaces for each book so that it was published in September 1522. One of these prefaces, the last in fact to be written before publication, contains Luther's famous description of true faith which struck so deep a chord in John Wesley centuries later:

> O it is a living, busy, active, mighty thing, this faith. It is impossible for it not to be doing good works incessantly. It does not ask whether good works are to be done, but before the question I asked, it has already done them, and is constantly doing them. Whoever does not do such works, however, is an unbeliever . . . Faith is a living, daring confidence in God's grace, so sure and certain that the believer would stake his life on it a thousand times. This knowledge of and confidence in God's grace makes men glad and bold and happy in dealing with God and with all creatures. And this is the work which the Holy Spirit performs in faith.[61]

However, while Luther was translating the New Testament, others were causing havoc back in Wittenberg. Iconoclastic riots had broken out as men like Karlstadt tried to pursue further reform by force. Luther grew anxious and wrote a number of tracts aimed at addressing the issues, but it was soon clear that the only hope of order lay with Luther's return. He returned in early March, re-tonsured himself, put on his cowl and preached each day. His appeal to persuasion rather than coercion as the principle of ministry remains powerful. 'When you have won the heart, you have won the man,' he insisted. Forced conformity is not genuine faith. What is more, the real work is something that only God can do through his Word:

---

60. Brecht, *Road to Reformation*, p. 461.
61. M. Luther, 'Preface to the Epistle to the Romans' (1522), *LW* 35:370–371 = *WADB* 7:10.9–13, 16–19.

In short, I will preach it, teach it, write it, but I will constrain no man by force, for faith must come freely without compulsion. Take myself as an example. I opposed indulgences and all the papists, but never with force. I simply taught, preached and wrote God's Word; otherwise I did nothing. And while I slept, or drank Wittenberg beer with my friends Philip and Amsdorf, the Word so greatly weakened the papacy that no prince or emperor ever inflicted such losses upon it. I did nothing; the Word did everything.[62]

Regrettably Luther would not be as careful and irenic in his language when faced with peasants using his words to justify rebellion in 1525 or the continued resistance of Jews to the gospel (and indeed instances of counter-evangelism) in 1543.[63]

Over the next two decades Luther would continue to develop his theology in engagement with a range of opponents. In 1524 Erasmus of Rotterdam finally succumbed to pressure and produced a book against Luther and his theology. Erasmus chose to engage with Luther on the matter of the human will. It was to be, Luther's opponents hoped, the *coup de grâce* – Europe's leading intellectual demonstrating the foolishness of Luther's assertions. In reality Erasmus's work proved eminently forgettable, whereas Luther's response, *The Bondage of the Will*, remains one of his most significant theological contributions. In it he stressed the importance of assertions in theology, as opposed to the scepticism which Erasmus seemed at points to be espousing. 'A man must delight in assertions or he will be no Christian,' he insisted; but then he added, 'I am speaking . . . about the assertion of those things which have been divinely transmitted to us in the sacred writings.'[64] Luther was convinced there is a theological rather than rational or anthropological ground for Christian assertion. After all, he insisted, 'The Holy Spirit is no Skeptic, and it is not doubts or mere opinions that he has written on our hearts, but assertions more sure and certain than life itself and all experience.'[65]

Here too he spoke of an important distinction between the incomprehensibility of God and the clarity of his Word:

---

62. M Luther, 'Second Invocavit Sermon' (10 March 1522), *LW* 51:76, 77 = *WA* 10/3:16.12–13, 18.10 – 19.3.

63. M. Luther, *Against the Robbing and Murdering Hordes of Peasants* (1525), *LW* 46:49–55 = *WA* 18:357–361; *On the Jews and Their Lies* (1543), *LW* 47:121–306 = *WA* 53:417–552.

64. M. Luther, *The Bondage of the Will* (1525), *LW* 33:20 = *WA* 18:603.11–12, 14–15.

65. Ibid., *LW* 33:24 = *WA* 18:605.32–34.

God and Scripture are two things . . . That in God there are many things hidden,
of which we are ignorant, no one doubts . . . But that in Scripture there are some
things abstruse, and everything is not plain – this is an idea put about by the ungodly
Sophists.[66]

At first glance this might seem a naïve approach that ignores the difficulties of
Scripture. Yet Luther goes on to say,

I admit, of course, that there are many texts in the Scriptures that are obscure and
abstruse, not because of the majesty of their subject matter, but because of our
ignorance of their vocabulary and grammar; but these texts in no way hinder
a knowledge of all the subject matter (*omnium rerum*) of Scripture.[67]

In the end Luther saw that Erasmus's appeal to obscurity and uncertainty in
the biblical text raised far more problems than it solved: 'Christ has not so
enlightened us as deliberately to leave some part of his Word obscure while
commanding us to give heed to it, for he commands us in vain to give heed if
it does not give light.'[68] Luther advances the discussion by distinguishing
between two works of the Spirit of God: the external clarity of Scripture ('the
Word brought out into the most definite light', associated with its public nature
and the ministry of the Word); and its internal clarity ('the Spirit is required
for the understanding of Scripture', associated with the work of the Spirit in
the human heart).[69]

The main subject of the treatise, though, was Luther's assertion that human
will is bound by our sinfulness and blinded by the work of Satan. Only when
this is granted will we see the scope of God's provision for us in both the law
and the gospel:

it is Satan's work to prevent men from recognizing their plight and to keep them
presuming that they can do everything they are told. But the work of Moses or
a lawgiver is the opposite of this, namely, to make man's plight plain to him by means
of the law and thus to break and confound him by self-knowledge, so as to prepare
him for grace and send him to Christ that he may be saved.[70]

---

66. Ibid., *LW* 33:25 = *WA* 18:606.11, 12–13, 16–17.
67. Ibid., *LW* 33:25 = *WA* 18.606.22–24.
68. Ibid., *LW* 33:95 = *WA* 18:656.18–21.
69. Ibid., *LW* 33:28 = *WA* 18:609.4–14.
70. Ibid., *LW* 33:130–131 = *WA* 18:679.31–36.

Throughout his ministry Luther would insist that a proper distinction between law and gospel is essential if we are to understand the Scriptures.[71]

In the second half of the 1520s and into the 1530s, Luther was involved in debate with Zwingli and others over the Lord's Supper.[72] Luther saw no reason not to take the words of institution ('This is my body', 'This is the new covenant in my blood') literally. By the Word of God – and crucially not the words of the priest – this bread is also the body of Christ and this wine is also the blood of Christ. Obedience to the Word of God means taking these words literally, as Luther insisted against Zwingli at the Marburg Colloquy in October 1529. Zwingli tried unsuccessfully to convince Luther that these words were figurative rather than literal and that the elements represented Christ's body and blood and did not become them.[73]

Around the same time Luther also wrote against the Anabaptists, who rejected infant baptism and insisted on the baptism of believers only. He recognized their desire to distance themselves from the sacramental practice of the Roman church but argued that not everything under the papacy was unbiblical. He acknowledged he had no scriptural text that commanded the baptism of children, just as the Anabaptists had no scriptural text that commanded only the baptism of adults.[74] Yet he could point to Jesus' command to let the children come to him (Matt. 19:14), the baptism of entire households by the apostles (Acts 16:15), John's address to little children (1 John 2:12) and John the Baptist's response of faith in his mother's womb (Luke 1:41) as evidence that the baptism of infants was not incompatible with Scripture.[75] His argument, though, was not based on a war of texts, but rather on the priority of the promise and command of God over the human recognition of faith (whether in ourselves or in another). Not only does basing baptism on faith open us up to the uncertainty of human experience and human perception, he argued, it puts faith

---

71. *Freedom of a Christian Man* (1520), *LW* 31:348 = *WA* 7.23.29–30; *Enarrationes epistolarum et euangeliorum, quas postillas vocant* (1521), *WA* 7:502.34–35; *Bondage of the Will* (1520), *LW* 33:132 = *WA* 18:680.28–30; *Lectures on Galatians* (1535), *LW* 26:302 = *WA* 40/1:469.32 – 470.14.

72. M. Luther, *That These Words of Christ "This Is My Body" Still Stand Firm Against the Fanatics* (1527), *LW* 37:3–150 = *WA* 23:64–283; *Confession Concerning Christ's Supper* (1528), *LW* 37:161–372 = *WA* 26:261–509; *Admonition Concerning the Sacrament of the Body and Blood of Our Lord* (1530), *LW* 38:91–137 = *WA* 30/2:595–626.

73. *The Marburg Colloquy and the Marburg Articles* (1529), *LW* 38:15–89 = *WA* 30/3:110–171.

74. *Concerning Rebaptism* (1528), *LW* 40:258 = *WA* 26:169.31–33.

75. Ibid., *LW* 40:257 = *WA* 26:169.9–13.

(a gift from God) in the place of the Word of God and so is in fact idolatry.[76] In such cases baptism is transformed into a work of obedience rather than an embrace of the promise of God and the sign of the covenant.[77] Nevertheless, Luther showed more compassion than many towards those who differed from him on this subject:

> Still it is not right, and I truly grieve, that these miserable folk should be so lamentably murdered, burned and tormented to death. We should allow everyone to believe what he wills. If his faith be false, he will be sufficiently punished in eternal hell-fire.[78]

In the 1530s Luther was drawn into two controversies to do with the key Reformation doctrine of justification by faith alone. The Cordatus Controversy of 1536–7 concerned the place of repentance and good works. Conrad Cordatus, a student at Wittenberg, discerned a difference between his teachers. Melanchthon was beginning to sound too much like Erasmus with his emphasis on good works (in an attempt to counter what he saw as moral laxity), and was even reported to have spoken about the 'necessity' of repentance in justification. Luther was able to obtain at least temporary agreement by declaring that 'the law is good and necessary to this life toward its end. However, God saves a man through his mercy alone, without the law.'[79] Before this controversy was resolved, a former student, Johann Agricola, ignited another debate by denying the relevance of the law for the Christian. The gospel is all that is necessary to understand the profundity of sin and the necessity of grace. Through a series of sermons, disputations and his tract *Against the Antinomians*, Luther insisted upon the law as the necessary preparation for the gospel. 'How can one know what sin is without the law and conscience?' he asked. 'And how will we learn what Christ is, what he did for us, if we do not know what the law is that he fulfilled for us and what sin is, for which he made satisfaction?'[80]

For thirty-four years Luther exercised the office of doctor in the university and the church. Yet his contribution to the evangelical cause was not limited to the classroom, the pulpit and the writing desk. On 13 June 1525 Martin

---

76. Ibid., *LW* 40:252 = *WA* 26:164.39 – 165.5.
77. Ibid., *LW* 40:248–249 = *WA* 26:161.35–38.
78. Ibid., *LW* 40:230 = *WA* 26.145.22 – 146.2.
79. *Die Promotionsdisputation von Palladius und Tilemann* (1537), *WA* 39/1:209.22 – 210.2.
80. *Against the Antinomians* (1539), *LW* 47:113 = *WA* 50:473.6–10.

Luther had married Catherine von Bora, a former nun with whom he would have six children. Luther saw marriage as a godly enjoyment of life as God had created it. But it was more than that in his case. He was not of course the first of the evangelical pastors to marry – Karlstadt had married in 1522 and Zwingli had married in 1524. Yet given Luther's standing, his marriage was the highest possible endorsement of such arrangements and it can be fairly said that he and his Katy provided a model for the clergy family that had not existed before. Luther revelled in being 'entangled in the pigtails of my girl' and spoke of children as 'the sweetest pledges of married life . . . the best wool on the sheep'.[81]

In his later years Luther was the Protestant elder statesman, called upon for advice by princes as well as church leaders. His confessional advice to Philip of Hesse (in which he was joined by both Melanchthon and Bucer), that instead of the divorce he wanted in order to marry another woman he should just marry her and care for both wives, was a serious miscalculation that was misunderstood by just about everyone.[82] It was in fact during another diplomatic mission, this time involving a trip to Eisleben in order to broker an agreement between the Counts of Mansfield, that Luther fell seriously ill. He died following a series of heart attacks early in the morning of 18 February 1546.

Luther's legacy

Luther's legacy, in terms of both the life of the Christian churches and their teaching, is wide-ranging and extraordinary. His 'signature doctrines' may well have been the doctrine of the Word of God and justification by faith alone, but he made significant contributions to Christology, the doctrine of the church, the sacraments, the relationships of church and state, and so much more. His fresh insight and determined application of the teaching of Scripture inspired his contemporaries and Christians in the five centuries since. For all his flaws, he stands as one of the greatest figures of the Christian era. Yet near the end of his life, as others gathered his writings into collections and called on him to provide a preface, Luther gave a gentle warning. 'I would have been quite content to see my books, one and all, remain in obscurity and go by the board,' he said.

---

81. *Table Talk* 3456, *WATr* 3:321.
82. M. Brecht, *Martin Luther: The Preservation of the Church 1532–1546*, trans. J. L. Schaaf (Minneapolis: Fortress, 1993), pp. 205–215.

There should be less writing, and instead more studying and reading of the Scriptures
. . . it behoves us to let the prophets and apostles stand at the professor's lectern,
while we, down below at their feet, listen to what they say. It is not they who must
hear what we say.[83]

In the end, the legacy of Luther is the encouragement to sit humbly under
the teaching of God in his Scriptures, to be captured by them, and to stand with
him against every attempt to ignore, smother or overturn them.

Bibliography

Alfsvåg, K., 'The Centrality of Christology: On the Relation between Nicholas Cusanus
    with Martin Luther', *Studia Theologica* 70, no. 1 (2016), p. 28.
Bainton, R., *Here I Stand*, repr., Oxford: Lion, 1987.
Baum, W. et al. (eds.), *Corpus Reformatorum*, 101 vols. (Berlin/Leipzig/Zurich:
    Theologischer Verlag, 1834–).
Brecht, M., *Martin Luther: His Road to Reformation 1483–1521*, trans. J. L. Schaaf,
    Philadelphia: Fortress, 1985.
———, *Martin Luther: The Preservation of the Church 1532–1546*, trans. J. L. Schaaf,
    Minneapolis: Fortress, 1993.
Brendler, G., *Martin Luther: Theology and Revolution*, trans. C. R. Foster, New York:
    Oxford University Press, 1991.
Brinks, J. H., 'Luther and the German State', *Heythrop Journal* 39 (1998), pp. 1–17.
Correspondence of Erasmus, Vol. 5: *Letters 594 to 841*, trans. R. A. B. Mynors and D. F. S.
    Thomson, Toronto: University of Toronto Press, 1979.
Dumont, L., *German Ideology: From France to Germany and Back*, Chicago: University
    of Chicago Press, 1994.
Gerrish, Brian, 'Doctor Martin Luther: Subjectivity and Doctrine in the Lutheran
    Reformation', in P. N. Brooks (ed.), *Seven-Headed Luther: Essays in Commemoration
    of a Quincentenary 1483–1983*, 2–11, Oxford: Clarendon Press, 1983.
Gritsch, E. W., 'The Cultural Context of Luther's Interpretation', *Interpretation* 37 (1983),
    p. 276.
Gröne, Valentin, *Tetzel und Luther*, 2nd edn, Soest: Nasse, 1860.
Holl, K., *What Did Luther Understand by Religion?*, trans. F. W. Meuser and W. R. Wietzke,
    Philadelphia: Fortress, 1977 (1921).

---

83. 'Preface to the Wittenberg Edition of Luther's German Writings' (1539), *LW*
    34:283–284 = *WA* 50:657.1–2, 19–20, 28–30.

Knaake, J. K. F., G. Kawerau et al. (eds.), *D. Martin Luthers Werke, Kritische Gesamtausgabe: Briefwechsel*, 18 vols., Weimar: Hermann Böhlaus Nachfolger, 1930–85.

———, *D. Martin Luthers Werke, Kritische Gesamtausgabe: Die Deutsche Bibel*, 12 vols., Weimar: Hermann Böhlaus Nachfolger, 1906–61.

———, *D. Martin Luthers Werke, Kritische Gesamtausgabe: Schriften*, 66 vols., Weimar: Hermann Böhlaus Nachfolger, 1883–.

———, *D. Martin Luthers Werke, Kritische Gesamtausgabe: Tischreden*, 6 vols., Weimar: Hermann Böhlaus Nachfolger, 1912–21.

Leppin, V., 'Luther and John Tauler: Some Observations about the Mystical Impact on Reformation Theology', *Theology and Life* 36 (2013), pp. 339–345.

McGrath, A. E., *Luther's Theology of the Cross*, Oxford: Blackwell, 1985.

MacIntyre, A., *A Short History of Ethics: A History of Moral Philosophy from the Homeric Age to the Twentieth Century*, 2nd edn, London: Routledge, 1998.

Marius, R., *Martin Luther: The Christian between God and Death*, Cambridge, MA: Harvard University Press, 1999.

Marx, K., *On Religion*, New York: McGraw-Hill, 1974.

'Mysticism in Martin Luther's Development and Thoughts', in *Oxford Research Encyclopedia of Religion*, Oxford University Press, 2016, <http://religion.oxfordre.com/view/10.1093/acrefore/9780199340378.001.0001/acrefore-9780199340378-e-260>.

Nineham, D., *The Use and Abuse of the Bible: A Study of the Bible in an Age of Rapid Cultural Change*, London: SPCK, 1978.

Oberman, H. A., *Luther: Man Between God and the Devil*, trans. E. Walliser-Schwarzbart, New Haven: Yale University Press, 1989.

———, 'Wittenberg's War on Two Fronts: What Happened in 1518 and Why', trans. A. C. Gow, in H. A. Oberman, *The Reformation: Roots and Ramifications*, 117–148, Edinburgh: T&T Clark, 1994.

Parsons, M., 'The Apocalyptic Luther: His Noahic Self-Understanding', *JETS* 44, no. 4 (2001), pp. 627–645.

Pelikan, Jaroslav and Helmut T. Lehmann (eds.), *Luther's Works*, 55 vols. (St Louis: Concordia; Philadelphia: Fortress Press, 1955–86.

Preus, J. S., 'Old Testament Promissio and Luther's New Hermeneutic', *Harvard Theological Review* 60 (1967), pp. 145–161.

Preus, R. D., 'Luther and Biblical Infallibility', in J. D. Hannah (ed.), *Inerrancy and the Church*, 99–142, Chicago: Moody Press, 1994.

Quanbeck, W., 'The Confessions and Their Influence upon Biblical Interpretation', in J. Reumann (ed.), *Studies in Lutheran Hermeneutics*, 177–187, Philadelphia: Fortress, 1949.

Rupp, G., *Martin Luther: Hitler's Cause or Cure?*, London: Lutterworth, 1945.

———, *The Righteousness of God: Luther Studies*, London: Hodder & Stoughton, 1953.

Schubart, C., *Die Berichte über Luthers Tod und Begräbnis*, Weimar: Böhlau, 1917.

Siggins, I. (ed.), *Luther*, Edinburgh: Oliver & Boyd, 1972.

Steinlein, Hermann, *Luthers Doktorat: Zum 400 jährigen Jubiläum desselben 18/19 Oktober 1912*, Leipzig: Deichert, 1912.

Steinmetz, D. C., *Luther and Staupitz: An Essay in the Intellectual Origins of the Protestant Reformation*, Durham, NC: Duke University Press, 1980.

Thompson, Mark D., *A Sure Ground on Which to Stand: The Relation of Authority and Interpretive Method in Luther's Approach to Scripture*, Carlisle: Paternoster, 2004.

Treitschke, H. von, 'Luther und die deutsche Nation', *Preußische Jahrbücher* 52 (1883), pp. 469–486.

Waring, L. H., *The Political Theories of Martin Luther*, New York: Putnam's Sons, 1910.

Wiener, P. F., *Martin Luther: Hitler's Spiritual Ancestor*, London: Hutchinson, 1945.

2. HULDRYCH ZWINGLI: A TRULY QUINTESSENTIAL REFORMER

Joe Mock

Introduction

Despite a relatively short life of some forty-seven years, the Swiss Reformer Huldrych Zwingli (1484–1531) pioneered and played a pivotal role in establishing a Reformed church in Zurich and beyond. Since the formation of the *Zwingliverein* (Zwingli Association) in 1895 and the subsequent systematic publishing of his works, the role of Zwingli as a quintessential Reformer has been studied and analysed. The efforts of Zwingli were not confined to Zurich as he sought to encourage the establishment of Reformed churches in other cantons. For example, William Farel (1489–1565), who had been discipled by Zwingli, established the Reformed church in Geneva which, at the time, was not part of the Swiss Confederation. Zwingli's tireless efforts and his vision helped to establish Reformed churches even beyond the Swiss Confederation.[1] Zwingli's legacy had a significant impact on the church in England as well as the church in Scotland.[2] His vision

---

1. B. Gordon, *The Swiss Reformation* (Manchester: Manchester University Press, 2002), pp. 46–118.
2. Carrie Euler, *Couriers of the Gospel: England and Zurich 1531–1558* (Zurich: Theologischer Verlag Zürich, 2006); Duncan Shaw, 'Action, Remembrance and Covenant: Zwinglian

was supported, affirmed and carried on by his successor at Zurich, Heinrich Bullinger (1504–75).

However, Zwingli remains somewhat of an enigma to many, especially those in the English-speaking world. The term 'Zwinglian', for example, is often used with pejorative overtones. Zwingli is probably most remembered for his sharp difference with Martin Luther (1483–1546) over the vexed question of the presence of Christ's body in the Lord's Supper in their celebrated debate at the Colloquy of Marburg (1529). He is also remembered for his untimely death on the battlefield at Kappel am Albis in 1531. A recent study observed:

> Little read or studied today, the Zwingli of Reformation textbooks is repeatedly cast as Luther's foil and Calvin's forerunner, a humanist visionary of a Christian community, a drowner of Anabaptists and an iconoclast with a limited, symbolic theology of the Lord's Supper.[3]

Visitors to Zurich today will see the statue of his successor Bullinger on the side of the Grossmünster in a prominent position. While there is an image of Zwingli on the bronze doors of the Grossmünster that were installed as recently as 1935, the statue of Zwingli is just short of 100 m away, down next to the Wasserkirche adjacent to the Limmat River. This statue, with Zwingli standing with the Bible in his right hand and the sword in his left hand, nonetheless gives rise to two misrepresentations. When the statue was erected in 1884 (the quadri-centennial of Zwingli's birth), Alexander Schweizer, one of the ablest Swiss church leaders of the time, whose last public service was to deliver the Zwingli oration in the university (7 January 1884), protested against the sword and resigned from the monument committee. The first misrepresentation of the statue is to portray that, for Zwingli, church and state are not two separate communities (the sword representing the magistrate), but rather one and the same community under God's sovereign rule. This, patently, was not Zwingli's understanding of 'church and state', which actually mirrored the complementary roles of the prophets and the kings in the time of the Old Testament.[4] Second,

---

(note 2 *cont.*) Contributions to the Scottish Reformation Understanding of the Lord's Supper', in Alfred Schindler and Hans Stickelberger (eds.), *Die Zürcher Reformation: Ausstrahlungen und Rückwirkungen* (Bern: Verlag Peter Lang, 2001), pp. 303–316.

3. Luca Baschera, Bruce Gordon and Christian Moser, *Following Zwingli: Applying the Past in Reformation Zurich* (Farnham: Ashgate, 2014), p. 34.

4. W. P. Stephens, *Zwingli: An Introduction to His Thought* (Oxford: Clarendon Press, 1992), p. 123.

the statue reinforced the popular yet erroneous view that Zwingli died *fighting* on the battlefield (the sword representing a weapon in warfare). It is reported that, when told the news of Zwingli's death, Luther commented, 'All who take the sword die by the sword.' The reality is that as chaplain to the troops it was customary to carry a sword. G. R. Potter points out that, 'Like all other states, Zurich relied for its security upon the army. Military service was taken for granted; to be a citizen was also to be armed.'[5] What is not well known is that, as a concerned citizen of Zurich, Zwingli produced his *Plan for a Military Campaign* in 1524 as he contemplated the possibility of a pre-emptive strike against some of the surrounding cantons in order to preserve the Reformation in Zurich. Not surprisingly, in the year that celebrated Zwingli's own personal reform (2016), the Professor of Church History at the University of Zurich, Peter Opitz, proposed that this statue of Zwingli be removed.[6]

Zwingli was born on New Year's Day 1484, some seven weeks after Luther, at Wildhaus in the Toggenburg valley of eastern Switzerland. This is close to the borders with Liechtenstein and Austria and is now part of the Canton of St Gallen. After attending schools in both Basel and Bern he studied at the universities of Vienna and Basel. He was introduced to both humanist studies and scholastic theology according to the 'old way' (*via antiqua*). In true humanist tradition, he was instructed in Latin, Greek, philosophy, logic and rhetoric. Being thoroughly versed in Cicero, Virgil, Horace, Livy, Seneca, Caesar, Pliny, Aulus Gellius and Valerius Maximus, he admired the works of Lactantius (240–320) whom he regarded as the 'Christian Cicero'. He also immersed himself in the works of Aristotle, Plato, Thucydides and Homer. Zwingli was one of the earliest Reformers to study Hebrew. His personal copy of Johann Reuchlin's *De Rudimentis Hebraicis* (1506) reveals by virtue of its many annotations clear signs that it was well used. At the heart of humanism was a return to sources in the original languages (*ad fontes*). One of his fellow students at Basel was Leo Jud (1482–1542), who was later to be a close colleague of Zwingli both in Einsiedeln and in Zurich where he ministered as the pastor of St Peter's Church. One of Zwingli's teachers at Basel was Thomas Wyttenbach (1472–1526), who later became the Reformer of Biel. During his time at Basel he met Oswald Myconius (1488–1552), who was to write a biography of Zwingli (1536). He also made the acquaintance of Johannes Oeco-lampadius (1482–1531), who became Professor of Theology at Basel and who accompanied Zwingli at the Bern Disputation (1528) and the Marburg Colloquy

5. G. R. Potter, *Zwingli* (Cambridge: Cambridge University Press, 1976), p. 53.

6. 'Das Zwingli-Denkmal sollte man entfernen', Kommunikation in der Kirche, <https://www.ref.ch/kirche-kultur/das-zwingli-denkmal-sollte-man-entfernen/>.

(1529). Throughout his life, Zwingli was a fervent Swiss patriot. This was abundantly evident in his poem *The Ox* (1510), which, in similar vein to Orwell's *Animal Farm*, satirized the Swiss as a fat ox taking bribes from the leopard (France) and the lion (the Holy Roman Empire). Similar themes are found in *The Labyrinth* (1516). Although he nearly lost his life in the plague which severely affected Zurich in August 1519, Zwingli remained in Zurich to encourage and support his fellow Zurichers and thus demonstrated his pastoral heart for his people. Zwingli strove continuously for a united confederation of the Swiss cantons.

Road to reform

Although his writings did not indicate a fully Reformed position until 1522, Zwingli testified himself that, independently of Luther, he had turned to Christ and to Scripture in about the year 1516. This was during the time when he ministered at the Benedictine monastery at Einsiedeln, which was famous not only because of pilgrimages to its 'black Madonna' but also because of its extensive library which Zwingli made frequent use of. Zwingli had ample time here to read the works of Ambrose, Jerome and Chrysostom, among others. Indeed, he had begun his practice of avid reading during his first pastorate at Glarus, where the church boasted that it exhibited the relics of St Fridolin and St Hilary. Among the books he brought with him from Glarus to Einsiedeln were his own annotated volumes of Augustine, Cyril of Alexandria, Gregory of Nazianzus, Gregory of Nyssa and Origen.

This period in Zwingli's life also followed a sexual misdemeanour that he had to work through and which led him to meditate deeply on the grace and mercy of God. Moreover, still fresh in his mind were his deep reflections after he witnessed the deaths of thousands of young Swiss mercenary soldiers on the battlefields of Pavia (1512), Novarra (1513) and Marignano (1515) when he accompanied the troops from Glarus as their chaplain. The year 1516 was some two years before people in the Canton of Schwyz had even heard of Luther. It was also the year that Zwingli met Erasmus at Basel. In 1516 Erasmus had published his Greek New Testament, which was immediately read and reread by Zwingli and the Pauline epistles memorized. Indeed, Zwingli was one of the very first to obtain a copy of Erasmus's *Novum Instrumentum Omne* which had been published by Froben in Basel. He also closely studied Erasmus's *Annotations of the New Testament*. Zwingli thus testified:

> Before anyone in the area had ever heard of Luther, I began to preach the gospel of
> Christ in 1516 so that I never entered the pulpit without looking up the words which

were to be read in the mass that day and expounding them on the basis of scripture . . .
I started preaching the gospel before I had even heard Luther's name . . . Luther, whose
name I did not know for at least another two years, had definitely not instructed me.
I followed holy Scripture alone.[7]

In August 1518, independently of Luther, Zwingli preached vehemently
against the practice of indulgences that were being sold by the Franciscan monk
Bernhardin Samson:

Jesus Christ, the Son of God, has said, 'Come unto me all ye that labour and are heavy
laden, and I will give you rest.' Is it not then audacious folly and insensate rashness
to say, on the contrary, 'Buy letters of indulgence! Run to Rome! Give to the monks!
Sacrifice to the priests! And if thou doest these things, I absolve you from your sins'?
Jesus Christ is the only oblation, the only sacrifice, the only way![8]

Zwingli explained that he had been led to reform in his own life through his
study of Chrysostom, Augustine's tractates and Paul's epistles. Although he
repeatedly testified to his independence from Luther, even invoking God as his
witness, he did, nonetheless, admire Luther's courage in his stand against the
Pope at the Leipzig Disputation in 1519. He warmly referred to the fact that
Luther acted like a David against Goliath and like a Hercules 'who slew the
Roman boar'.

The marginal notes Zwingli wrote in his books before he came to Zurich
seem to indicate that he had independently come to a Reformed position.
Moreover, the absence of marginal notes in his personal copies of Luther's
books seems to point to the fact that he was not reliant on Luther.[9] However,
their significance is somewhat a matter of debate.[10] In several of his works in
the period 1521–27 Zwingli referred pointedly to his independence from Luther.

7. E. J. Furcha and H. W. Pipkin, *Huldrych Zwingli Writings*, trans. H. W. Pipkin (Allison
    Park: Pickwick Publications, 1984), pp. 116–117.

8. Jean Henry Merle D'Aubigné, *History of the Reformation in the Sixteenth Century, Part 1*
    (London: Whittaker & Co., 1842), p. 229.

9. W. P. Stephens, 'Zwingli and Luther', *Evangelical Quarterly* 71 (1999), pp. 51–65.
    However, for the dependence of Zwingli on Luther, see Martin Brecht, 'Zwingli
    als Schüler Luthers: Zu seiner theologischen Entwicklung, 1518–1522', *Zeitschrift
    für Kirchengeschichte* 96 (1985), pp. 301–319.

10. Ulrich Gäbler, *Huldrych Zwingli: His Life and Work* (Edinburgh: T&T Clark, 1986),
    pp. 34–36.

These works include *The Clarity and Certainty of the Word of God* (1522), *An Exposition of the Articles* (1523) and *A Friendly Exegesis* (1527). But he did acknowledge the influence of Erasmus and his Greek New Testament, and also of Wyttenbach who had led a disputation at Basel in 1515. Zwingli was also influenced by the reading of Erasmus's poem about Jesus, which led him to conclude that only Christ could mediate between God and humankind. Although Zwingli was later to be estranged from his erstwhile mentor Erasmus, who would destroy all the letters he had received from Zwingli, nonetheless, there are many elements in Zwingli's theology that point unmistakably to Erasmus's influence.[11] These include the differentiation between Creator and creature, the understanding of the spirituality of the believer in neo-Platonic terms and an emphasis on God's justice and mercy.[12]

Not only was Zwingli concerned for a Reformed faith in the heart of the individual but he also strove to make the Reformation in Zurich and beyond a social as well as political reformation. Zwingli's vision was for a Christian society that would be ruled by two God-ordained officers akin to the kings and the prophets of the Old Testament, *viz.* the magistrate and the pastor.[13] The key to reform in Zurich was Zwingli's powerful preaching coupled with his political acumen. The dynamics in Zurich in the early 1520s, *viz.* the roles of key individuals and groups, were skilfully portrayed in the play *Lucretia and Brutus* written by Bullinger (1526). This was a reworking of the story of Lucretia and Brutus as related by the Roman historian Titus Livy (59 BC–AD 17) in his *Ab urbe condita* which focused on ethical and political issues.[14] Zwingli expressed his desire for Reformed faith to bring social and political change in his *Divine and Human Righteousness* (1523). In particular, Zwingli tirelessly battled to overturn the lucrative mercenary service and the foreign pensions from foreign lords. Zwingli called for the rejection of mercenary service not only because of the influence of Erasmus's pacifism and because of the numbers of young Swiss men lost on the battlefield, but also because the money obtained gave rise to a series of social ills. However, this stance on the mercenary service was bitterly opposed

---

11. Christine Christ-von Wedel, *Erasmus of Rotterdam: Advocate of a New Christianity* (Toronto: University of Toronto Press, 2013), pp. 186–193.

12. Gottfried W. Locher, *Zwingli's Thought: New Perspectives* (Leiden: Brill, 1981), pp. 233–255.

13. Robert C. Walton, *Zwingli's Theocracy* (Toronto: University of Toronto Press, 1967).

14. Emidio Campi, 'Brutus Tigurinus: Heinrich Bullinger's Early Political Theological Thought', in Emidio Campi (ed.), *Shifting Patterns of Reformed Tradition* (Göttingen: Vandenhoeck & Ruprecht, 2014), pp. 35–55.

by the surrounding 'forest cantons' of Uri, Schwyz, Unterwalden, Zug and Luzern. Of Zwingli's Reformation in Zurich, Bullinger noted:

> He praised God the Father, and taught men to trust only in the Son of God, Jesus Christ, as Saviour. He vehemently denounced all unbelief, superstition and hypocrisy. Eagerly he strove after repentance, improvement of life and Christian love and faith. He insisted that the government should maintain law and justice, and protect widows and orphans.[15]

Zwingli declared, 'I do not deny, nay, I assert, that the teachings of Christ contribute very greatly to the peace of the state, if indeed they are set forth in their purity.'[16] Of particular note was the emphasis of being a gracious neighbour to others in view of the fact that God is gracious. In this connection, Zwingli underlined that the gospel 'fires people with love for God and for the neighbour'.[17] Brotherly love was a clear emphasis in his public preaching.[18] Hence, Zwingli ensured that the poor were properly cared for. In 1520 an 'Alms Statute' was enacted which was followed by the 'Poor Law' of 1525.[19] His vision was for a Reformed church and a Reformed society that would keep on being reformed (*semper reformanda*) through the ministry of the Word of God by the power of the Holy Spirit. This underlies his deliberate patience in bringing reform to Zurich step by step, much to the impatience and the annoyance of the Anabaptists. His method was not that of a fiery sermon followed by direct action. Rather, he chose to teach from Scripture and work through the process of public disputations as well as winning the support of the leading families of Zurich and the leaders of the various guilds.[20]

Zwingli has been wrongly accused of iconoclasm in Zurich. In point of fact, the iconoclasm of popular lore was a knee-jerk reaction by the people following

---

15. Hans J. Hillerbrand, *The Reformation in Its Own Words* (New York: SCM, 1964), p. 118.

16. Samuel Macauley Jackson, *The Latin Works and the Correspondence of Huldreich Zwingli Together with Selections from His German Works*, Vol. 1 (New York: G. P. Putnam's Sons, 1912), p. 267.

17. Ibid., p. 71.

18. Lee Palmer Wandel, 'Brothers and Neighbours: The Language of Community in Zwingli's Preaching', *Zwingliana* 17 (1988), pp. 361–374.

19. Lee Palmer Wandel, *Always among Us: Images of the Poor in Zwingli's Zurich* (Cambridge: Cambridge University Press, 1990).

20. Norman Birnbaum, 'The Zwinglian Reformation in Zurich', *Archives de sociologie des religions* 8 (1959), pp. 15–30.

a fiery sermon by Leo Jud in 1523 at St Peter's Church, across the Limmat from the Grossmünster. Zwingli, rather, sought to teach the people before taking any action: 'Let them first teach their hearers to be upright in the things that pertain to God, and they will immediately see all these objectionable things fall away ... Teaching should come first, and the abolition of images follow without disturbance.'[21] Images were then removed in an orderly fashion and not destroyed. They were either returned to their original donors or sold.[22]

W. Peter Stephens has aptly described Zwingli's *modus operandi* as follows:

> To misquote Chaucer, he taught and afterwards he wrought. Preaching and persuasion came first, whether by book, or sermon, or public disputation. The persuasion led to pressure from the people for change, and then – at least in many instances – there followed legislation and action.[23]

With this embracing method of reform it was not surprising that many of the changes that were introduced were long-lasting. For example, Zwingli had a strong aversion to any form of idolatry and although he himself was an accomplished musician he convinced Zurich's ruling council to remove the organs and choir singing from the Grossmünster and the other churches in Zurich. Singing was only reintroduced after 1598, while organs were only reinstalled towards the end of the nineteenth century.

Zwingli on the gospel and salvation

A brief summary of Zwingli's understanding of the gospel is found in Article 2 of *The Sixty-Seven Articles* (1523):

> The summary of the gospel is that our Lord Jesus Christ, true son of God, has made known to us the will of his Heavenly Father and has redeemed us from death and reconciled us with God by his guiltlessness.[24]

---

21. Samuel Macauley Jackson and Clarence Nevin Heller, *Commentary on True and False Religion: Zwingli* (Durham, NC: Labyrinth Press, 1981), pp. 330, 337.

22. Lee Palmer Wandel, *Voracious Idols and Violent Hands: Iconoclasm in Reformation Zurich, Strasbourg, and Basel* (Cambridge: Cambridge University Press, 1994), pp. 53–101.

23. W. P. Stephens, 'Zwingli's Reforming Ministry', *The Expository Times* 93 (1981), p. 8.

24. Furcha and Pipkin, *Zwingli Writings*, p. 14.

Zwingli's understanding of the gospel is further explained in section 7 of his *Commentary on True and False Religion* (1525) which was dedicated to King Francis I of France. In this work, Zwingli totally rejected salvation by works (the 'false' religion of Rome). In echoing Anselm (1033–1109), Abélard (1079–1142), Athanasius (296–373) and Irenaeus (130–202), he declared that, through God's love and mercy, in the name of Christ, there is forgiveness of sins through the death, resurrection and ascension of Christ. Hence the gospel is 'good news', in that 'This is the gospel, that sins are remitted in the name of Christ; and no heart ever received tidings more glad.'[25] He particularly emphasized the need for repentance, which is only possible through the election and mercy of God and the prior work of the Holy Spirit to convict men and women of sin through knowledge of the justice of God and the knowledge of self. There is an unmistakeable emphasis on *solus Christus* (Christ alone) as Zwingli asserted that 'Through Christ alone we are given salvation, blessedness, grace, pardon, and all that makes us in any way worthy in the sight of a righteous God.'[26]

Unlike Luther's gospel, which centred on justification by faith alone, Zwingli's gospel revolved around reconciliation to God and his will which is found only in Christ. Whereas Wittenberg emphasized law and gospel, Zurich emphasized election and covenant.[27] One further characteristic feature of the gospel that Zwingli proclaimed was the freedom it offers over against the burdens placed on the backs of believers by the traditions of the Roman church.[28] This explains his frequent reference to Matthew 11:28–30. Zwingli referred to reconciliation with God through the imputation of the righteousness of Christ to believers, enabling them to stand before God. This righteousness is not simply imputed, it is also imparted.[29] Zwingli referred to salvation as reconciliation with God in terms of God giving the believer 'all things' (*omnia bona*) or 'treasure' in Christ.[30] In other words, Zwingli viewed reconciliation with God through faith in Christ

---

25. Jackson and Heller, *Commentary on True and False Religion*, p. 119.

26. Ibid., p. 129.

27. Peter Opitz, 'The Swiss Contribution to the Reformation Movement', in Petra Bosse-Huber et al. (eds.), *Reformation: Legacy and Future* (Geneva: World Council of Churches, 2015), pp. 70–71.

28. Peter Opitz, 'Das Evangelium als Befreiung zum Vertrauen bei Huldrych Zwingli', in Ingold U. Dalferth and Simon Peng-Keller (eds.), *Gottvertrauen: Die ökumenische Diskussion um die Fiducia* (Freiburg: Herder, 2012), pp. 182–208.

29. Zwingli referred to both *Rechtmachung* and *Rechtwerdung* (Z, 5:625). W. P. Stephens, *The Theology of Huldrych Zwingli* (Oxford: Clarendon Press, 1986), p. 160.

30. See, for example, Article 20 of *The Sixty-Seven Articles*.

to mean being reconciled to the Creator, whom Zwingli described as 'the fountain and spring of all good'.[31] Years later, Calvin was to point out that, through the Spirit, the believer comes 'to enjoy Christ and all his benefits (*bonisque eius omnibus*)',[32] for Calvin also regarded God as the 'font of all good things'.[33] For Zwingli, saving faith results in union with Christ. The gospel also results in new life, which is why Zwingli constantly emphasized righteous living as evidence that one has saving faith. Significantly, following Athanasius, in Article 13 of *The Sixty-Seven Articles* he referred three times to the believer being deified or transformed into God through the working of the Holy Spirit.[34] He also referred to deification in section 6 of *The Commentary on True and False Religion*: 'To become one of us, therefore, He, great God that He is, just, holy, merciful, Creator, became man, that we through His fellowship might be raised to gods.'[35]

Sola scriptura (Scripture alone)

There could probably be no clearer demonstration of the primacy Zwingli placed on the Word of God than the first condition of peace which he insisted on after the First Kappel War of 1529, namely, freedom for the preaching of the Word of God. Furthermore, in 1526 Zwingli had demolished the stone altar in the Grossmünster and used the stonework for the floor of the chancel from where the Word of God was proclaimed and which was adjacent to where the communion table/baptismal font was located.[36] The intended symbolism of the priority of the Word of God was thus very powerful. Prior to that, in 1520 (prior to the Diet of Worms) Zwingli had convinced the Zurich Council to mandate that preaching was to be scriptural. The two disputations held in Zurich in 1523 were occasions when priority was given to the authority of the Word of

---

31. Jackson and Heller, *Commentary on True and False Religion*, p. 64.
32. John Calvin, *Institutes of the Christian Religion*, trans. F. L. Battles, ed. J. T. McNeill, Library of Christian Classics (London: SCM, 1961 [1559]), III.i.1.
33. B. A. Gerrish, *Grace and Gratitude: The Eucharistic Theology of John Calvin* (Minneapolis: Fortress Press, 1993), pp. 21–49.
34. Furcha and Pipkin, *Zwingli Writings*, pp. 57–58.
35. Jackson and Heller, *Commentary on True and False Religion*, p. 111.
36. In the Grossmünster the wooden lid on the baptismal font was used as the communion table and an open Bible was placed upon it. This indicated the intimate link between Word and sacrament.

God over against church tradition.[37] Indeed, at the First Disputation (29 January 1523) Zwingli made a point of encouraging the priests in Zurich to obtain their own personal copies of the New Testament and to read systematically through them.[38] The Zurich Council decreed at the First Disputation that 'the Council itself would be the final arbiter in matters of public religious discourse in Zurich. The principle of *sola scriptura* was now a matter of civil law.'[39] By the occasion of the Second Disputation (26–28 October 1523), it was the case that

> Those who did not base their speeches on Scripture were called to order by the
> presidents . . . Moreover, there is no mere quoting of scriptural texts. They are set
> in their context and examined in the original Hebrew or Greek in order to come
> to the true teaching of the Bible.[40]

In the Baden (1526) and the Bern (1528) Disputations Scripture was given priority over against the Church Fathers.[41] Although there is no doubt that Zwingli read the Scriptures with keen awareness of how the Church Fathers handled them,[42] nonetheless, he constantly gave priority to Scripture itself.

Zwingli underscored the authority of the Word of God in that it 'will as surely have its way as the Rhine, which you can stem for a while, but not stop'.[43] He set the absolute authority of the Word of God over against the tradition of the church.[44] Soon after the First Disputation, the New Testament was published

------

37. W. P. Stephens, 'Authority in Zwingli – in the First and Second Disputations', *Reformation and Renaissance Review* 1 (1999), pp. 54–71.

38. 'The First Zurich Disputation', in Leland Harder, *The Sources of Swiss Anabaptism: The Grebel Letters and Related Documents* (Scottdale: Herald Press, 1985), p. 202.

39. Arnold Snyder, 'Word and Power in Reformation Zurich', *Archiv für Reformationsgeschichte* 81 (1990), p. 267.

40. Stephens, 'Authority in Zwingli', p. 63.

41. I. Backus, *The Disputations of Baden, 1526 and Berne, 1528: Neutralizing the Early Church* (Princeton: Princeton Theological Seminary, 1993).

42. I. Backus, 'Ulrich Zwingli, Martin Bucer and the Church Fathers', in Irena Backus (ed.), *The Reception of the Church Fathers in the West: From the Carolingians to the Maurists* (Leiden: Brill, 2001).

43. W. P. Stephens, 'Zwingli', in David Bagchi and David C. Steinmetz (eds.), *The Cambridge Companion to Reformation Theology* (Cambridge: Cambridge University Press, 2004), p. 82.

44. Peter Opitz, 'The Authority of Scripture in the Early Zurich Reformation (1522–1540)', *Journal of Reformed Theology* 5 (2011), pp. 296–309.

in Swiss German (1524). The whole Bible was published by the printer Christoph
Froschauer in Swiss German in 1531. That the authority of Scripture was
integral to the Reformation in Switzerland was reflected in the fact that Bullinger
dedicated to King Henry VIII a work entitled *On the Authority of Holy Scripture,
Its Certainty, Trustworthiness and Absolute Perfection* (1538).

Although he made use of the Church Fathers, as can be witnessed by the
copious handwritten notes in his personal volumes of their works, as well as
intimate knowledge of the councils of the church, nonetheless, Zwingli constantly emphasized that 'the Fathers should give way to the Word of God and
not God's Word to the Fathers'.[45] Both the Fathers and the councils of the
church needed to be tested by Scripture, with Christ as the touchstone. This
indicates that, for Zwingli, it was not just *sola scriptura* (Scripture alone) but also
tota scriptura (all of Scripture with no 'canon within a canon') read from a
christoscopic perspective. From 1525 onwards Zwingli wrote about the one
covenant of God with his elect which links the Old and New Testaments. He
highlighted the significance of the *protoevangelium* of Genesis 3:15 in Article 6
of *The Sixty-Seven Articles* (1523) and particularly in his tome against the Anabaptists, *Refutation of the Tricks of the Catabaptists* (1527), but also in his *Commentary
on True and False Religion* (1525). It is probable that he did so in tandem with
Bullinger. Zwingli further declared that the Holy Spirit is the author of Scripture
which, therefore, can only be interpreted and understood correctly when the
Holy Spirit gives understanding. Because the Bible as a whole is the work of
one author, the Holy Spirit, rhetorical tools can be used to understand its
message. Zwingli applied rhetorical tools to interpret Scripture. He was particularly alert to the use made by the biblical authors of figures of speech such
as tropes, alloeosis, ellipsis, metathesis, hyperbole, prolepsis and synecdoche.[46]
However, Zwingli kept in tension the effort to master the languages and the
tools to interpret Scripture with the humility to come under the authority of
the Word and the leading of the Holy Spirit. For those passages regarded as
difficult to interpret he believed that Scripture interprets itself because it is
internally consistent. He also believed in the perspicuity or clarity of Scripture
(*claritas scripturae*) and that, of itself with the guidance of the Holy Spirit,
Scripture could lead to the truth. Reconsidering what Augustine wrote about
the significance of the creation of human beings in the image of God, Zwingli
concluded that the perspicuity of the Scriptures is linked to the fact that we

---

45. H. Wayne Pipkin, *Huldrych Zwingli Writings*, Vol. 2 (Allison Park: Pickwick
      Publications, 1984), p. 111.

46. Potter, *Zwingli*, p. 43.

are created in the image of God.[47] Because God is the author of Scripture he teaches the believer:

> No matter who a man may be, if he teaches in accordance with his own thought and mind his teaching is false. But if he teaches you in accordance with the Word of God, it is not he that teaches you, but God who teaches him . . . When I was younger, I gave myself overmuch to human teaching . . . But eventually I came to the point where, led by the Word and Spirit of God, I saw the need to set aside all these things and to learn the doctrine of God direct from his own Word.[48]

Zwingli further emphasized that the interpreting of the Scriptures belongs not to a select few but to any believer who has the Holy Spirit. Zwingli thus taught the priesthood of all believers, an emphasis which was taken up by Bullinger.[49] Indeed, as early as the First Disputation, Zwingli pointed out:

> The Scriptures are much the same everywhere, the Spirit of God flows so abundantly, walks in them so joyfully, that every diligent reader, in so far as he approaches with humble heart, will decide by means of the Scriptures, taught by the Spirit of God, until he attains the truth.[50]

Zwingli especially unpacked the perspicuity of Scripture in *The Clarity and the Certainty of the Word of God* (1522) which was a sermon preached at the Dominican monastery at Oetenbach. Zwingli's insistence that Scripture originates from God and that the believer is taught by God himself (*theodidacti*) led to him equating Scripture with the Word of God.[51] Stephens observed that, for Zwingli,

---

47. Opitz, 'Authority of Scripture', pp. 300–301.

48. From Zwingli's 'Of the Clarity and Certainty of the Word of God', in G. W. Bromiley, *Zwingli and Bullinger* (Philadelphia: Westminster Press, 1953), pp. 90–91.

49. Jon Delmas Wood, 'Bullinger's Model for Collective Episcopacy: Transformational Ministry in a Society Facing Final Judgment', in Luca Baschera, Bruce Gordon and Christian Moser (eds.), *Following Zwingli: Applying the Past in Reformation Zurich* (Farnham: Ashgate, 2014), pp. 81–105.

50. Samuel Macauley Jackson, *Selected Works of Huldreich Zwingli (1484–1531), The Reformer of German Switzerland* (Philadelphia: University of Philadelphia, 1901), p. 106.

51. Mark D. Thompson, 'Reformation Perspectives on Scripture: The Written Word of God', *Reformed Theological Review* 57 (1998), pp. 112–115. Zwingli's emphasis on the faithful preaching of the Word of God led Bullinger to declare in The Second Helvetic Confession (1566) that 'Preaching of the Word of God is the Word of

the order was the Spirit and then the Word.[52] In point of fact, Zwingli taught that the internal illumination of the believer is carried out by the triune God as the Father, the Son and the Holy Spirit work together as one in the Word.[53] In this connection, Zwingli stated: 'We ought to be taught by the word of God externally, and by the Spirit internally.'[54] Hence, with respect to the public preaching of the Word, Zwingli stated:

> In fact, speaking canonically or regularly, we see that among all peoples the outward preaching of apostles and evangelists or of bishops preceded faith, which nevertheless we refer to as being received by the Spirit alone . . . To whatever place, therefore, prophets or preachers of the word are sent, it is a sign of God's grace that he wishes to disclose the knowledge of himself to his elect; and to those whom it is denied, it is a sign of impending wrath.[55]

It is clear that preaching was given utmost priority by Zwingli for the role of ministers who are called to shepherd through preaching. The citation above indicates that he took a different view from Luther and his followers who taught that faithful preaching of the Word led to faith. Zwingli, on the other hand, insisted on the sovereignty of God in that God gives faith to the elect who then respond to the public preaching of the Word. Indeed, he deliberately pointed this out to Luther in his *A Friendly Exegesis* (1527).[56] It was, for him, always Spirit and Word in tandem, but with the prior role of the Spirit.

When Zwingli commenced his ministry at the Grossmünster in Zurich in January 1519 he preached consecutively (*lectio continua*) through the Gospel of Matthew. It may be that he was inspired to do so through his reading of Chrysostom.[57] He declared that he would preach 'the complete plain text without the accretions of scholastic interpretation'.[58] Over the years this was followed

---

(note 51 *cont.*) God' (*Praedicatio verbi Dei est verbum Dei*). See also Peter Opitz, *Ulrich Zwingli: Prophet, Ketzer, Pionier des Protestantismus* (Zurich: Theologischer Verlag Zürich, 2015), pp. 29–31.

52. Stephens, *Theology of Huldrych Zwingli*, p. 59.

53. Bromiley, *Zwingli and Bullinger*, pp. 79–80.

54. Jackson and Heller, *Commentary on True and False Religion*, pp. 331–332.

55. Account of the Faith (1530) – Fidei Ratio, *Z*, 6:2, 813.

56. *Z*, 5:591.

57. H. O. Old, *The Reading and Preaching of the Scriptures in the Worship of the Christian Church*, Vol. 4: *The Age of the Reformation* (Grand Rapids: Eerdmans, 2002), pp. 46–47.

58. Potter, *Zwingli*, p. 60.

by series on Acts, 1 and 2 Timothy, Galatians, 1 and 2 Peter, Hebrews, and so on. By all accounts Zwingli was a powerful preacher who challenged his flock.[59] In a work addressed to King Francis I of France, *Exposition of the Christian Faith*,[60] Zwingli outlined the basis of his preaching:

> This is a summary of my faith and preaching which I hold by the grace of God, and I stand ready to give an account of it to any man, for there is not one jot of my teaching that I have not learned from the divine Scriptures, and I advance no doctrine for which I have not the authority of the leading doctors of the Church, the prophets, apostles, bishops, evangelists and translators – those of old, who drank from the fountain-head in its purity.[61]

After the Zurich Council made the decision and set aside the necessary funds from tithes and other beneficiaries, in 1525 Zwingli set up a 'school', the *Prophezei* (1 Cor. 14:1), five days a week at the Grossmünster. This was probably modelled on the *Collegium Trilingue* in Louvain that had been inspired by Erasmus. Bullinger subsequently developed the *Prophezei* into the *Lectorium*, which functioned as a quasi-tertiary institution and which became the forerunner to the present University of Zurich. The Hebrew, Greek and Latin texts of the Old Testament, commencing with Genesis, were expounded in Latin before an exposition of the passage was given in German. The pivotal role of the *Prophezei* was to train the Zurich clergy to read the Scriptures in the original languages and then to expound them in the vernacular.[62] This was a direct application of Zwingli's sermon *The Shepherd* (1524). The *Prophezei* resulted in the publishing of some major commentaries and the publishing of the Zurich Bible in 1531.

Based on his affirmation of *sola scriptura* Zwingli set about attacking systematically the cult of the saints, indulgences, legalistic fasting, clerical celibacy, the mass, the papacy, episcopal authority, simony and the abuse of ecclesiastical tithes. He achieved this through a series of disputations where he put forward the clear teaching of Scripture over against the tradition of the church.

---

59. William Boekestein, *Ulrich Zwingli* (Holywell: EP Books, 2015), pp. 45–47.

60. Written in the summer of 1531 but published in 1536 by Bullinger.

61. 'Exposition of the Christian Faith', in Samuel Macauley Jackson, *Ulrich Zwingli on Providence and Other Essays* (Eugene: Wipf and Stock, 1999), p. 274.

62. Reita Yazawa, 'The Prophezei and the Lectorium: The Zurich Academy under the Leadership of Zwingli and Bullinger', *Stromata* 49 (2008), pp. 1–12.

Perhaps one of the toughest challenges he faced was with the Anabaptists and their biblicism. With respect to their approach to Scripture, Zwingli concluded that they 'prattle on the Spirit and negate Scripture'.[63] Led by Conrad Grebel, they complained that the reforms had not gone far enough. Zwingli wrote *The Office of the Preacher* (30 June 1525) specifically to counter the influence of the unauthorized preaching of the Anabaptists. He emphasized that only those authorized (called by God and the church) should preach and that they should be proficient in the biblical languages because, he underscored, without a thorough knowledge of Hebrew and Greek there could be no real knowledge of the contents of the Old and New Testaments.

Zwingli's difference with Luther concerning the presence of Christ's body in the Eucharist was rooted in their differing principles of interpretation. Leading up to the Colloquy of Marburg (1529) Zwingli wrote the following in response to one of Luther's sermons:

> Scripture is to be understood by faith alone; and to see whether faith is true, it must be tested only against Scripture, which is rightly understood by faith . . . so you see that one must have faith and Scripture side by side.[64]

Not surprisingly, comparisons were made between Zwingli and Luther with respect to their roles as prophetic preachers. Luther regarded Zwingli's death on the battlefield as divine condemnation of his teachings. Bullinger's sermon on the Feast of Charlemagne (28 January 1532) at the Grossmünster soon after he took up office as *Antistes* or chief minister was published as *Concerning the Office of the Prophet* (*De prophetae officio*). Bullinger defended Zwingli as a prophetic teacher and praised his rhetorical skills, his sermon delivery, his holy lifestyle, his exegetical acumen, his prophetic learning and his tireless resistance to all forms of wickedness.[65] Bullinger underscored that Zwingli placed the highest priority on the ministry of the Word of God in tandem with the role of the Holy Spirit. Citing Paul's admonition, he declared that 'the spirits of prophets are subject to the prophets'. This was a veiled criticism of Luther's reluctance to consider the teaching of his fellow Reformers.

---

63. *Z*, 6:1, 24.

64. *A Friendly Answer Concerning Luther's Sermon on the Enthusiasts* (1527), *Z*, 5:773, 774 – translation from Locher, *Zwingli's Thought*, p. 189, n. 206.

65. Daniël Timmerman, *Heinrich Bullinger on Prophecy and the Prophetic Office (1523–1538)* (Göttingen: Vandenhoeck & Ruprecht, 2015), pp. 181–197.

Solus Christus (Christ alone)

Christ was given unmistakeable priority by Zwingli in *The Sixty-Seven Articles*. Christ is the only way to salvation (Art. 3). Christ is the guide and captain promised by God (Art. 6), and all who live in him are members and children of God (Art. 8) with the consequence that it is impossible to do anything without Christ as head (Art. 9). Christ is the sole mediator between God and mankind (Art. 19) through whom God wants to give us all things (Art. 20). A summary of the gospel is found in Article 21: 'All things are given us through Christ alone.' Moreover, God alone remits sin through Jesus Christ (Art. 50) because Christ has borne all our pain and travail (Art. 54).

Leading up to the Colloquy of Marburg, Zwingli wrote the following to Luther in his *A Friendly Exegesis* (1527): 'This, I repeat, we believe in the son of God for with Jesus Christ is our acquittal, atonement, and remission of all sins; now, in fact, we know that he gives us all things with him and through him.'[66]

Sola gratia (grace alone)

Luther's personal journey to a Reformed faith through a series of personal struggles or crises (*Anfechtungen*) in seeking personal forgiveness of sins and peace with a righteous God has been well documented and studied. In Zwingli's case there was always a keen focus on the free grace of God upon his life in view of his sexual weakness while at Einsiedeln and other weaknesses. He never took God's free grace for granted. God's free grace and God's initiative to save the elect were in the background of all his works. It is most probable that Zwingli learned from Ambrose his grasp of grace and faith, and from Augustine a theocentric perspective of grace.

The sharp difference between Zwingli and Luther concerning the presence of Christ's body in the Eucharist is probably the best-known aspect of Zwingli and his ministry. Although the importance of Scripture was paramount in the Eucharist debate, for Zwingli the primary issue was to do with the connection between God's grace and the sacraments. Zwingli was adamant that no person nor anything in creation should usurp God's rightful place and role in the salvation of the elect. He rejected the notion that the sacraments are 'instruments of grace'. So he reacted to Luther's understanding of baptism in which the candidate for baptism 'may receive in the water the promised

---

66. *Z*, 5:715, 716.

salvation'.[67] Zwingli reacted even more strongly against how he perceived Luther to insist on the real presence of the body and blood of Christ in the Eucharist as essential if the sacrament is truly to offer Christ and his salvation.

Sola fides (faith alone)

From Erasmus Zwingli understood faith (*fides*) in terms of trust (*fiducia*). He was adamant in asserting that faith is a gift from God to the elect, for without election there would be no faith.[68] Zwingli declared: 'Faith is the sign of the election by which we obtain real blessedness.'[69] Zwingli's understanding of faith is reflected in Article 20 of *The Sixty-Seven Articles* (1523):

> Faith is nothing else than the certain assurance with which man relies on the merit of Christ . . . that man himself contributes nothing, but believes that all things are directed and ordered by God's providence, and this comes only from giving himself to God and trusting in him completely; that he understands in faith that God does everything, even though we cannot perceive it.[70]

Zwingli sees faith as directed both to God and to Christ:

> Faith is a matter of fact (*rem*), not of knowledge or opinion or imagination. A man, therefore, feels faith within, in his heart: for it is born only when a man begins to despair of himself, and to see that he must trust in God alone. And it is perfected when a man wholly casts himself off and prostrates himself before the mercy of God alone, but in such fashion as to have entire trust in it because of Christ who was given for us. What man of faith can be unaware of this? For then only are you free from sin when the mind trusts itself unwaveringly to the death of Christ and finds rest there.[71]

Zwingli could never be accused by the Church of Rome of antinomianism for he regarded that a person with true faith in the grace of Christ in the heart is never indifferent to sin. Such a living faith is necessarily expressed in love and good works.

---

67. The Large Catechism, IV.36.
68. 'On the Providence of God', in Jackson, *Zwingli on Providence and Other Essays*, pp. 197–198.
69. Ibid., p. 201.
70. Locher, *Zwingli's Thought*, p. 166.
71. Stephens, *Theology of Huldrych Zwingli*, p. 162.

Soli Deo gloria (glory to God alone)

Zwingli constantly criticized the hypocrisy of the papacy and, in particular, its failure to give glory to God. He reacted against anyone or anything that would take away God's glory. He opposed idolatry in any form. He removed the organ from the Grossmünster. He declared that linking the sacraments to salvation was a denial that salvation is wholly from God. Time and time again, Zwingli reiterated the providence of God and the election of men and women to salvation. He preached on 'The Providence of God' at the Colloquy of Marburg.

Because election underscores that salvation is wholly of and from God, Zwingli posited that some pagans might well be in heaven. He stated this in his *Exposition of the Faith* published after his death by his successor, Bullinger, in 1536. Luther reacted rather angrily to this and wrote his *Brief Confession Concerning the Holy Sacrament* (1544) in which he not only complained that Zwingli had gone against the articles agreed to at Marburg,[72] but also accused Zwingli of being a heathen for his view concerning the salvation of pagans such as Socrates. Luther's reaction demonstrated that he and Zwingli had subtle differences in their theology of God, Christ, Scripture, sacrament and faith. Although this is a controversial aspect of Zwingli's theology, he nonetheless declared that 'there is not one jot of my teaching that I have not learned from the divine Scriptures, and I advance no doctrine for which I have not the authority of the leading doctors of the church'.[73] Stressing the freedom of the Holy Spirit, Zwingli stated that for all the elect, both those who have heard the gospel and those who have not, their salvation is through Christ alone, through God's grace alone and through the work of the Holy Spirit. The salvation of each person points to glory given only to God.

Conclusion

Zwingli was truly a quintessential Reformer. He was pastor, fearless preacher, prophet, teacher and friend to many. He ministered effectively to those in the academy, those in leadership in society, the traders in a growing city economy and those who laboured in the fields. He fearlessly proclaimed the gospel and

---

72. In particular, Luther was referring to Articles 5 to 9 which deal with salvation.

73. W. P. Stephens, 'Zwingli and the Salvation of the Gentiles', in W. Peter Stephens (ed.), *The Bible, the Reformation and the Church: Essays in Honour of James Atkinson* (Sheffield: Sheffield Academic Press, 1995), p. 241.

trained many others to do so. He was proactive in applying the love of Christ and biblical principles in helping the weak in society, the marginalized and those who had fallen between the cracks. He upheld and promoted the five *sola*s as absolutely necessary for the life of the individual believer as well as for the church. In particular, he strongly emphasized *sola scriptura* in tandem with the work of the Holy Spirit in the individual and in the church. There was no 'Zwingli Bible' but a Swiss German Bible based on the highest scholarship on the biblical text in the original languages. This Bible paved the way for the church to keep on being reformed (*semper reformanda*).

Zwingli continues to be an example for us in the twenty-first century as to how we can be the elect of God in our contemporary world. His world was clearly different from ours. It would be inaccurate to use the terms 'church' and 'state' to describe Zwingli's society which was viewed as a single Christian body or *corpus christianum*.[74] Today, many societies oppose biblical standards, norms and lifestyle. Nonetheless, Zwingli inspires us to be the people of God who are Bible-based, Christ-centred and Holy Spirit-empowered as we minister to fellow believers as well as those who are spiritually lost, doing all to the glory of God. As we do this, we demonstrate we have true faith in our hearts.

Bibliography

D'Aubigné, Jean Henry Merle, *History of the Reformation in the Sixteenth Century, Part 1*, London: Whittaker & Co., 1842.

Backus, I., *The Disputations of Baden, 1526 and Berne, 1528: Neutralizing the Early Church*, Princeton: Princeton Theological Seminary, 1993.

———, 'Ulrich Zwingli, Martin Bucer and the Church Fathers', in Irena Backus (ed.), *The Reception of the Church Fathers in the West: From the Carolingians to the Maurists*, 627–660, Leiden: Brill, 2001.

Baschera, Luca, Bruce Gordon and Christian Moser, *Following Zwingli: Applying the Past in Reformation Zurich*, Farnham: Ashgate, 2014.

Birnbaum, Norman, 'The Zwinglian Reformation in Zurich', *Archives de sociologie des religions* 8 (1959), pp. 15–30.

Boekestein, William, *Ulrich Zwingli*, Holywell: EP Books, 2015.

Brecht, Martin, 'Zwingli als Schüler Luthers: Zu seiner theologischen Entwicklung, 1518–1522', *Zeitschrift für Kirchengeschichte* 96 (1985), pp. 301–319.

Bromiley, G. W., *Zwingli and Bullinger*, Philadelphia: Westminster Press, 1953.

---

74. Walton, *Zwingli's Theocracy*, p. xi.

Calvin, John, *Institutes of the Christian Religion*, trans. F. L. Battles, ed. J. T. McNeill, Library of Christian Classics, London: SCM, 1961 (1559).

Campi, Emidio, 'Brutus Tigurinus: Heinrich Bullinger's Early Political Theological Thought', in Emidio Campi (ed.), *Shifting Patterns of Reformed Tradition*, 35–55, Göttingen: Vandenhoeck & Ruprecht, 2014.

Christ-von Wedel, Christine, *Erasmus of Rotterdam: Advocate of a New Christianity*, Toronto: University of Toronto Press, 2013.

Euler, Carrie, *Couriers of the Gospel: England and Zurich 1531–1558*, Zurich: Theologischer Verlag Zürich, 2006.

Furcha, E. J. and H. W. Pipkin, *Huldrych Zwingli Writings*, trans. H. W. Pipkin, Allison Park: Pickwick Publications, 1984.

Gäbler, Ulrich, *Huldrych Zwingli: His Life and Work*, Edinburgh: T&T Clark, 1986.

Gerrish, B. A., *Grace and Gratitude: The Eucharistic Theology of John Calvin*, Minneapolis: Fortress Press, 1993.

Gordon, B., *The Swiss Reformation*, Manchester: Manchester University Press, 2002.

Harder, Leland, *The Sources of Swiss Anabaptism: The Grebel Letters and Related Documents*, Scottdale: Herald Press, 1985.

Hillerbrand, Hans J., *The Reformation in Its Own Words*, New York: SCM, 1964.

Huldreich Zwinglis sämtliche Werke (Berlin: Schwetschke; Leipzig: Hensius; Zurich: Berichthaus/Theologischer Verlag, 1905–1991).

Jackson, Samuel Macauley, *The Latin Works and the Correspondence of Huldreich Zwingli Together with Selections from His German Works*, Vol. 1, New York: G. P. Putnam's Sons, 1912.

———, *Selected Works of Huldreich Zwingli (1484–1531), The Reformer of German Switzerland*, Philadelphia: University of Pennsylvania, 1901.

———, *Ulrich Zwingli on Providence and Other Essays*, Eugene: Wipf and Stock, 1999.

Jackson, Samuel Macauley and Clarence Nevin Heller, *Commentary on True and False Religion: Zwingli*, Durham, NC: Labyrinth Press, 1981.

Locher, Gottfried W., *Zwingli's Thought: New Perspectives*, Leiden: Brill, 1981.

Old, H. O., *The Reading and Preaching of the Scriptures in the Worship of the Christian Church*, Vol. 4: *The Age of the Reformation*, Grand Rapids: Eerdmans, 2002.

Opitz, Peter, 'The Authority of Scripture in the Early Zurich Reformation (1522–1540)', *Journal of Reformed Theology* 5 (2011), pp. 296–309.

———, 'Das Evangelium als Befreiung zum Vertrauen bei Huldrych Zwingli', in Ingold U. Dalferth and Simon Peng-Keller (eds.), *Gottvertrauen: Die ökumenische Diskussion um die Fiducia*, 182–208, Freiburg: Herder, 2012.

———, 'The Swiss Contribution to the Reformation Movement', in Petra Bosse-Huber, Serge Fornerod, Thies Gundlach and Gottfried Locher (eds.), 67–76, *Reformation: Legacy and Future*, Geneva: World Council of Churches, 2015.

———, *Ulrich Zwingli: Prophet, Ketzer, Pionier des Protestantismus*, Zurich: Theologischer Verlag Zürich, 2015.

Pipkin, H. Wayne, *Huldrych Zwingli Writings*, Vol. 2, Allison Park: Pickwick Publications, 1984.

Potter, G. R., *Zwingli*, Cambridge: Cambridge University Press, 1976.

Shaw, Duncan, 'Action, Remembrance and Covenant: Zwinglian Contributions to the Scottish Reformation Understanding of the Lord's Supper', in Alfred Schindler and Hans Stickelberger, *Die Zürcher Reformation: Ausstrahlungen und Rückwirkungen*, 303–316, Bern: Verlag Peter Lang, 2001.

Snyder, Arnold, 'Word and Power in Reformation Zurich', *Archiv für Reformationsgeschichte* 81 (1990), pp. 263–285.

Stephens, W. P., 'Authority in Zwingli – in the First and Second Disputations', *Reformation and Renaissance Review* 1 (1999), pp. 54–71.

———, *The Theology of Huldrych Zwingli*, Oxford: Clarendon Press, 1986.

———, 'Zwingli', in David Bagchi and David C. Steinmetz (eds.), *The Cambridge Companion to Reformation Theology*, 80–99, Cambridge: Cambridge University Press, 2004.

———, *Zwingli: An Introduction to His Thought*, Oxford: Clarendon Press, 1992.

———, 'Zwingli and Luther', *Evangelical Quarterly* 71 (1999), pp. 51–63.

———, 'Zwingli and the Salvation of the Gentiles', in W. Peter Stephens (ed.), *The Bible, the Reformation and the Church: Essays in Honour of James Atkinson*, 224–244, Sheffield: Sheffield Academic Press, 1995.

———, 'Zwingli's Reforming Ministry', *The Expository Times* 93 (1981), pp. 6–10.

Thompson, Mark D., 'Reformation Perspectives on Scripture: The Written Word of God', *Reformed Theological Review* 57 (1998), pp. 105–120.

Timmerman, Daniël, *Heinrich Bullinger on Prophecy and the Prophetic Office (1523–1538)*, Göttingen: Vandenhoeck & Ruprecht, 2015.

Walton, Robert C., *Zwingli's Theocracy*, Toronto: University of Toronto Press, 1967.

Wandel, Lee Palmer, *Always among Us: Images of the Poor in Zwingli's Zurich*, Cambridge: Cambridge University Press, 1990.

———, 'Brothers and Neighbours: The Language of Community in Zwingli's Preaching', *Zwingliana* 17 (1988), pp. 361–374.

———, *Voracious Idols and Violent Hands: Iconoclasm in Reformation Zurich, Strasbourg, and Basel*, Cambridge: Cambridge University Press, 1994.

Wood, Jon Delmas, 'Bullinger's Model for Collective Episcopacy: Transformational Ministry in a Society Facing Final Judgment', in Luca Baschera, Bruce Gordon and Christian Moser (eds.), *Following Zwingli: Applying the Past in Reformation Zurich*, 81–105, Farnham: Ashgate, 2014.

Yazawa, Reita, 'The Prophezei and the Lectorium: The Zurich Academy under the Leadership of Zwingli and Bullinger', *Stromata* 49 (2008), pp. 1–12.

3. PHILIP MELANCHTHON: THE HUMANIST WHOSE *LOCI COMMUNES* SYSTEMATIZED LUTHERAN THEOLOGY

Dean Zweck

Melanchthon: enigmatic Reformer

Almost everyone who knows that there was a reformation in the church of the sixteenth century also knows that it began when a young monk called Martin Luther published the Ninety-Five Theses in 1517. Far fewer people have heard of his co-Reformer, Philip Melanchthon. One reason for this is that, in contrast to Luther, he was of a quiet and retiring disposition and until Luther's death in 1546 was content to labour unobtrusively and diligently at his side. He regarded himself as a 'quiet bird'[1] and steadfastly refused advancement or honours. He declined promotion to the degree of master, let alone doctor, of theology, and turned down positions that were offered him, including one at Cambridge.

Another reason Melanchthon is far less known and far less celebrated than Luther is that Lutherans do not quite know what to do with him. Going right back, even to his lifetime, there is a long history of ambivalence towards Melanchthon: his character, his place in Lutheran Reformation history and his legacy. This ambivalence seems to receive attention in just about everything

---

1. 'Ego sum tranquilla avis', in a letter to Bucer, 28 August 1544; cited in Vilmos Vajta (ed.), *Luther and Melanchthon in the History and Theology of the Reformation* (Philadelphia: Muhlenberg, 1961), p. 27.

written about him. One study of his life is aptly titled *Melanchthon: The Enigma of the Reformation* (R. Stupperich). Other descriptions in the titles of books or articles are illuminating: 'the Unknown Melanchthon' (also Stupperich), 'Reformer without Honor' (M. Rogness), 'The Quiet Reformer' (C. Manschreck), 'Controversial Reformer' (K. Hendel), 'Alien or Ally?' (F. Hidebrandt).[2] Luther, who held him in high esteem until the very end, addressed him as follows in two of his last letters (February 1546): 'To the man of outstanding learning, Mr. Philip Melanchthon, Master, theologian and servant of God, my dearest brother in the Lord', and 'To Philip Melanchthon, a most worthy brother in Christ'.[3] In his own lifetime he was acclaimed as the *Praeceptor Germaniae* (the Teacher of Germany), and yet he was denounced by some of his own students as a traitor to the Lutheran cause. His successor in Wittenberg, Leonhard Hutter, 'went so far as to tramp on his picture in public'.[4] Some more recent assessments, far from stomping on his image, applaud him as a worthy irenicist, 'the ecumenical voice of Lutheranism'.[5] Mostly forgotten and unknown for several centuries, Melanchthon enjoyed some popularity in North America in the nineteenth century among Lutherans who wanted to become more involved ecumenically in Protestant circles. Holding theological opinions and views that would have made Melanchthon turn in his grave, some lionized him to the extent of even naming a new church body for him: 'The Melanchthon Synod'.[6] Melanchthon is not without honour among Lutherans, and one piece of evidence for this is that in Australia a theological circle met in Adelaide for some years under his name: 'The Melanchthon Society'.

---

2. Robert Stupperich, *Melanchthon: The Enigma of the Reformation* (Cambridge: James Clarke, 2006 [1965]); Michael Rogness, *Philip Melanchthon: Reformer without Honor* (Minneapolis: Augsburg, 1969); Clyde L. Manschreck, *Melanchthon: The Quiet Reformer* (New York/Nashville: Abingdon Press, 1958); Kurt Hendel, 'Philip Melanchthon: Controversial Reformer', *Currents in Theology and Mission* 7 (1980), p. 53; Franz Hildebrandt, *Melanchthon: Alien or Ally?* (Cambridge: Cambridge University Press, 1946).

3. *LW* 50:293, 314.

4. Robert Kolb, 'Melanchthon: Reformer and Theologian', *Concordia Journal* 23 (1997), p. 309.

5. Eric W. Gritsch, 'Reflections on Melanchthon as Theologian of the Augsburg Confession', *Lutheran Quarterly* 12 (1998), p. 451.

6. The synod was short-lived: 1857–69. See Theodore G. Tappert, 'Melanchthon in America', in Vilmos Vajta (ed.), *Luther and Melanchthon in the History and Theology of the Reformation* (Philadelphia: Muhlenberg, 1961), pp. 189–198.

Melanchthon came to Wittenberg in 1518 as a brilliant young humanist to teach Greek and the classical authors at its fledgling university. He soon became devoted to Luther and Luther's theology, and within three years, at the age of twenty-five, published the first edition of his systematized compendium of Lutheran theology known as the *Loci Communes* ('theological commonplaces').

In this chapter we will look at how Melanchthon used his training in humanism and his intellectual giftedness and originality to systematize Luther's theology in a way that gained immediate admiration and widespread acclaim. In a concluding section we will reflect on the legacy of Melanchthon and his *Loci Communes*.

Melanchthon: humanist and theologian

Philip was the son of Georg Schwarzerd, a distinguished armourer, and his mother was the daughter of the mayor of Bretten, the small town where he was born in February 1497. His father died when he was ten, and his mother looked to her uncle, the eminent humanist and Hebraist Johannes Reuchlin, to oversee his education. He was an apt student, to say the least, graduating with a bachelor of arts degree in 1511 at Heidelberg, a lively centre of humanist learning. That university's regulations would not admit a fourteen-year-old to the next step, so he went on to study at Tübingen where he graduated as Master Philip in 1514 while aged sixteen. Under Reuchlin's guidance, Philip became a scholar of the new northern humanism and, typically, took on the more elegantly sounding Greek equivalent of his name: from Schwarzerd (meaning 'black earth') to Melanchthon. While still a student, he was apprenticed as a corrector to a printer called Thomas Anshelm, who by no coincidence was Reuchlin's publisher. Both his academic studies and his work as a manuscript editor enabled the young Melanchthon to become immersed in the classics, especially Aristotle. The publication of Erasmus's Greek New Testament in 1516 was a significant event that prepared Melanchthon for what was to come. Nominated by his great-uncle Reuchlin, he was accepted by the University of Wittenberg to be its first professor of Greek.

On 29 August 1518 the twenty-one-year-old Greek scholar delivered his inaugural lecture in Wittenberg. Addressing 'the youth of the Academy, on correcting the studies of youth', Melanchthon eruditely appealed for the new humanistic learning to be expanded and applied to all areas of learning, including theology:

> For it will be a diligent concern of mine to suggest the things that seem right for each subject. We have in hand Homer, and we have Paul's letter to Titus. Here you can see

how much a sense of appropriate language contributes to understanding the mysteries of sacred things; and also what difference there is between learned and unlearned interpreters of Greek.[7]

Two days later Luther wrote to his friend George Spalatin saying that young Melanchthon 'delivered an extremely learned and absolutely faultless address'.[8] Thus began a cordial relationship that endured. Melanchthon speedily and whole-heartedly embraced the evangelical theology of Luther, and within a short time he was lecturing not only on Homer but also on Titus. The following year, 1519, he gave lectures on both the Hebrew language and the Psalms. At Luther's suggestion he began expounding the letter to the Romans, and at the same time he was busy with the editing and printing of Luther's commentary on Galatians. These lectures, as we shall see, were the impetus for the famed *Loci Communes* of 1521. So popular was the book of the *Loci* that it went through eighteen editions in four years.[9] Two decades later Luther was still singing its praises:

> There's no book under the sun in which the whole of theology is so compactly presented as in the *Loci Communes* ... No better book has been written after the Holy Scriptures than Philip's. He expresses himself more concisely than I do when he argues and instructs. I'm garrulous and more rhetorical.[10]

In the meantime, Melanchthon, with some persuasion from his friends, had become married. Katherine was the daughter of the Wittenberg mayor, and theirs was a good and happy marriage. During these years Melanchthon toiled faithfully as a successful lecturer, theologian and quiet collaborator with Luther in various aspects of the reform movement, especially the church visitation (1527–8) and reform of church life in Saxony. He maintained an abiding interest in education and the reform of studies in schools and universities. In 1529 he participated alongside Luther in the Marburg Colloquy, at which early Reformers were attempting to resolve their differences, especially in regard to the teaching of Christ's presence in the Lord's Supper.

---

7. Ralph Keen (ed.), *A Melanchthon Reader*, American University Studies (New York: Peter Lang, 1988), p. 56.
8. *LW* 48:78.
9. Stupperich, *Melanchthon*, p. 51.
10. *Table Talk, LW* 54:440.

Melanchthon's hour truly came at Augsburg in 1530. Because Luther was under the ban of the empire, it was Melanchthon who headed the Lutheran theologians that were there to present their confession of faith before Emperor Charles V and the Diet (parliament) of the Holy Roman Empire; it was he who drafted the Augsburg Confession, drawing on the Schwabach and Torgau Articles that were to hand; and it was he who soon thereafter wrote the robust and fulsome Apology in response to the Roman Confutation.[11] Soon after the reading of the Confession, Luther penned these words: 'I am tremendously pleased to have lived to this moment when Christ, by his staunch confessors, has publicly been proclaimed in such a great assembly by means of this really most beautiful confession.'[12]

Melanchthon was no controversialist. Irenic by nature, he never went looking for trouble, and when it came he did not relish it. This is not to say that he was weak or a pushover. Luther knew his colleague well: 'Philip stabs, too, but only with pins and needles. The pricks are hard to heal and they hurt. But when I stab, I do it with a heavy pike used to hunt boars.'[13] There is irony in the fact that in pursuing peace and harmony Melanchthon actually became a controversial figure, because it was often in seeking a middle way that he incurred wrath and hostility from both sides. Although some of the controversial matters were brewing in Luther's lifetime, it was only after his death that they became major issues, making life very difficult for Melanchthon in the next fourteen years. Melanchthon died on 19 April 1560, tired of this life, and in some ways a broken man. His preference would have been to go through life as 'a quiet bird', but his theology and the tumultuous times in which he lived made of him an unwilling controversialist. Although his close friendship with Luther endured, his theology was shaped not only by Luther, but also by the thought-world and intellectual approach of northern humanism. It is not surprising that after the death of Luther, tensions between Luther's theology and his own would become serious cracks and fissures in the struggle between 'Philippists' and 'Gnesio-Lutherans'. Lutherans see it as a miracle of grace that the warring factions were able to overcome their differences and come to agreement in the *Book of Concord* of 1580.

---

11. Robert Kolb and Timothy Wengert (eds.), *The Book of Concord: The Confessions of the Evangelical Lutheran Church* (Minneapolis: Fortress, 2000), pp. 27–105 and 107–294.

12. *LW* 49:354.

13. *Table Talk, LW* 54:50.

Melanchthon and the *Loci Communes*: systematizing Luther's evangelical theology

Melanchthon arrived in Wittenberg as a humanist scholar, employed to teach Greek and the classical authors. He always remained committed and faithful to that calling. He remained a layperson and resisted Luther's intention of making him a preacher; he maintained a vital interest in the ancient languages, the classical authors and many other subjects; and he was actively involved in the renewal of university education along humanist lines. He was indeed a humanist and a polymath.

Melanchthon's initial focus in Wittenberg was, as one would expect, his scholarly work in the humanities. Within a short time he published two works that he had probably begun to compose in Tübingen, both of which soon gained attention in academic circles. The twin works were the *Rhetorices* and the *Dialectices*.[14] Rhetoric in the classical tradition is the art of speaking correctly and well, and it must be informed by knowledge. In particular, rhetoric needs to be accompanied by 'dialectic' – what we would describe as the ability to search out a particular topic and construct a lucid discussion on it that emphasizes what is important and gives a clear point of view. Using this method, Melanchthon especially emphasized the finding of material (*inventio*) and then summarizing one's view of it as 'commonplaces' or basic concepts: *loci communes*. These basic concepts are derived by discerning a common criterion that enables one to establish what needs to be emphasized in a given topic. Melanchthon probably derived the concept of *loci communes* from Erasmus (who, following Aristotle, used it in ethics), but the entirely original thing that Melanchthon did, as we shall see, was 'to carry over this device into the realm of theology in order to emphasise and explain the most important material'.[15]

This work on rhetoric and dialectic coincided with Melanchthon's rapid theological development after his arrival and settling in at Wittenberg. He was quickly won over to Luther's theology, and when only in his second year he accompanied Luther to the Leipzig debate where he acted as his assistant, especially in researching historical matters. In September of that same year, 1519, he defended his theses for the degree of bachelor in Bible (*baccalaureus biblicus*), and that qualified him to lecture in an exegetical way on the text of the

---

14. In Carolus Brettschneider (ed.), *Corpus Reformatorum*, Vol. 13 (Halle: Schwetschke & Son, 1846), pp. 413ff. and 507ff.

15. Stupperich, *Melanchthon*, p. 45.

Latin Bible (the Vulgate) – beyond what he was already doing with the letter to Titus as a teacher of Greek and grammar.

Luther soon set him to work expounding Paul's letter to the Romans, and this is where Melanchthon began to apply his rhetorical–dialectical method to identify and expound theological commonplaces for the benefit of his students. At that very time Melanchthon was also busy with the editing and printing of Luther's commentary on Galatians. This was for him a revelatory experience that enabled him to see this book as 'the cord of Theseus which leads one through the labyrinth of the entire Scripture'.[16] In essence, what Melanchthon discovered in a very personal way via Luther's exposition of Galatians was the Pauline doctrine of justification, which he then applied in his own work on Romans. With the doctrine of justification as the key, Melanchthon determined that the most important topics in theology are not what were to be found in the traditional theological tomes in use at that time, the *Sentences* of Peter Lombard and the *Summa* of Thomas Aquinas, but those found in Paul's own little 'summa' of theology, the letter to the Romans: sin, law and the gospel, especially grace and justification by faith.

His first brief effort was titled *Theologica Institutio* (theological instruction), but this served merely as a forerunner for a more extended treatment based on the letter to the Romans – not in the form of a commentary, but theological exposition in the form of 'commonplaces' (*loci communes*). This version, on Melanchthon's own testimony, was only 'a very rough treatment of the subject' for the benefit of his students. But then something went wrong: 'Someone – I don't know who – published it,' Melanchthon tells us.[17] It seems that the culprits were in fact his own students. Far from happy with this state of affairs, Melanchthon took it upon himself hastily to publish his own version:

> Now I cannot take back the little book . . . and so I thought it would be best to rework and revise it. For many places required more precise arguments and much of it needed revision . . .
>
> I here present the chief topics of Christian doctrine, so that the youth may know what they should especially look for in the Scriptures . . . I am not doing this to distract students away from the Scriptures into obscure and difficult arguments, but rather to attract them, if possible, to the Scriptures.[18]

---

16. Ibid.

17. Philip Melanchthon, *Commonplaces: Loci Communes 1521*, trans. and ed. Christian Preus (St Louis: Concordia, 2014), p. 20.

18. Ibid.

Furthermore, Melanchthon goes on to explain why he has departed from the traditional list of topics as found in the *Sentences* of Peter Lombard, passing over some ('we should adore the mysteries of divinity, not investigate them') to focus on the topics essential for saving Christian knowledge: sin, the law and grace.

> Does Paul, in his Epistle to the Romans, which he wrote as a summary of Christian doctrine, philosophize about the mysteries of the Trinity, the mode of the incarnation, active and passive creation? Certainly not! But what does he treat? Of course he treats the Law, sin and grace, the sole foundations for knowledge of Christ.[19]

If sin, law and grace are the chief topics of Romans, it was Luther who enabled Melanchthon to see them so clearly in the text. At this early stage of his theological development, Melanchthon himself testifies how he had been 'led by Luther into the profundities of Scripture', and especially by Luther's exposition on the Pauline doctrine of justification.[20] Christian Preus comments:

> It is hard to overstate Luther's influence on Melanchthon's *Loci Communes* of 1521. Melanchthon constantly refers to Luther. Even when he makes no explicit reference to Luther and his works, the stamp of Luther's theology is clearly imprinted. In fact, the *Loci Communes* is, in large part, a digest of the early Luther's theology: a strong condemnation of papal and Scholastic claims regarding the freedom of the will; the articulation of the Law as God's condemnation of the guilty sinner and of the Gospel as God's favor toward underserving sinners with no regard to human merit; the insistence that a Christian can be sure of his salvation; that the sacraments have been given for this assurance; a rejection of popes and councils as authoritative sources of doctrine; and the championing of Scripture as the pure and unadulterated Word of God.[21]

But neither was Melanchthon merely parroting or 'digest-ing' Luther. Melanch-thon's development of a characteristic way of ordering Luther's biblical theology according to common topics actually initiated a way of doing Lutheran theology that was to continue. Discernible in the *Loci* of 1521 are the beginnings of a systematizing of Luther's theology. At this initial stage it is a kind of 'topical'

---

19. Ibid., p. 25.
20. Stupperich, *Melanchthon*, p. 46.
21. Christian Preus, 'Introduction', in Melanchthon, *Loci Communes 1521*, pp. 13–14.

theology, not a comprehensive system of theology. However, by the time of the last edition of 1559, not only had the *Loci* expanded to be four times as long as the first edition, but in the process many more topics had been added, with the effect that the last edition is virtually a handbook of systematic theology (including also topics scorned and rejected in the first edition as scholastic sophistry).[22]

As one reads the *Loci*, it is surprising to see how soon and how far Melanchthon diverged from Luther's exegetical discussion of the biblical text of Romans. For example, in the *Loci* discussion on the topics of sin and the law, there is no attempt to follow the theological argument in Paul's letter, which ends with the conclusion that all people are without excuse because all are guilty of transgressing God's law – whether as Jews who received the law by special revelation, or as Gentiles who have the law written in their hearts. The *locus* on sin[23] is devoted almost entirely to a biblical defence of the doctrine of original sin. The *locus* on law,[24] having (somewhat incorrectly) stated that 'the Law is called the knowledge of sin' (Rom. 3:20), goes into a catalogue and discussion of various types of law: natural law, divine laws, counsels, monastic vows, judicial and ceremonial laws and human laws. There is virtually no discussion about how Paul understands 'law' in his letter to the Romans.

The third major topic in the 1521 *Loci* is 'The Gospel', and together with it 'Grace' and 'Justification and Faith'. Here one finds a fine and noble exposition of the gospel, one that would bring much comfort to sinners with terrified consciences, but again, there is no real attempt to enter into the world of the Romans text and to expound on gospel, grace, justification or faith in the way that Paul does, following his line of thought. In this way the text of the letter to the Romans, while providing the actual topics, functions more as pretext than text.

If, however, one accepts this way of doing theology, or can get used to it, the original appeal and popularity of the first edition of the *Loci* becomes entirely understandable. For people who had read only the medieval systems of Lombard or Thomas Aquinas, Melanchthon's clear, simple, biblical and pastoral exposition of these topics would have been a breath of fresh air. This, for example, is how he begins the *locus* on 'The Gospel':

---

22. Compare the table of contents in the first edition (pp. v–vi) with the one in the last. Philip Melanchthon, *The Chief Theological Topics: Loci Praecipui Theologici 1559*, trans. J. A. O. Preus, 2nd English edn (St Louis: Concordia, 2011).

23. Melanchthon, *Loci Communes 1521*, pp. 37–60.

24. Ibid., pp. 61–89.

Just as the Law is that by which correct living is commanded and sin is revealed, so the Gospel is the promise of God's grace and mercy, that is, the forgiveness of sin and the testimony of God's kindness toward us. By this testimony our souls are assured of God's kindness. By it we believe that all our guilt has been pardoned, we are strengthened to love and praise God, [and] to be happy and rejoice in him . . . Moreover, Christ is the guarantee of all these promises, and for this reason we should refer all the promises of Scripture to him.[25]

Not surprisingly, in the *locus* on 'Justification and Faith' Melanchthon echoes the language of Paul and the theology of Luther. It begins with these wonderful words:

We are justified, therefore, when having been put to death by the Law we are brought back to life by the word of grace that has been promised in Christ, that is, by the Gospel of the forgiveness of sins; when by faith we cling to this Gospel without doubting that Christ's righteousness is our righteousness, that the satisfaction of Christ is our expiation, and that the resurrection of Christ is ours; in short, when we do not doubt at all that our sins are forgiven and that God is now favorably disposed toward us and desires our good.[26]

A little further on, Melanchthon quotes Romans 4:5, 'Faith is accounted as righteousness to the one who believes', and also Genesis 15:6, 'Abraham believed God and it was accounted to him as righteousness', and highlights them: 'These two verses I especially want to recommend to you so that you may understand that faith is properly called righteousness.'[27] In the 1521 *Loci* Melanchthon does not use the word 'impute' or 'imputation' – that Christ's righteousness is imputed to those who believe – but clearly his theology of justification is heading in that direction, and that emphasis can be clearly seen in later editions of the *Loci*. For example, from 1555:

God forgives us our sins, and accepts us in that he imputes righteousness to us for the sake of the Son, although we are still weak and sinful. We must, however, accept this imputed righteousness with faith. So, now in this mortal life, that by

---

25. Ibid., p. 92.
26. Ibid., p. 115.
27. Ibid.

which we are pleasing to God is the righteousness of *Christ*, which is imputed to us.[28]

How then is faith related to justification? 'Faith is constant assent to God's every word, and it does not exist outside of God's Spirit renewing and enlightening our hearts.'[29] But faith is more than assent. 'Faith is nothing else than trust in God's mercy promised in Christ . . .'[30] Such faith is not dormant or passive,

> for when by faith we have tasted God's mercy . . . our souls cannot but love God
> in return and rejoice in him . . . [The converted mind] pours itself out for all its
> neighbours, serves them, makes itself available for their use, considers their needs
> its own . . . This is the efficacy of faith.[31]

Among the few remaining *loci*, all of which are treated far more concisely, the most important is the one on 'Signs', the term Melanchthon uses for the sacraments. Following Luther, Melanchthon does not understand 'sign' as mere symbol. Rather the 'sign' conveys and seals what is signified. Thus in baptism 'the function of this sign is to testify that you are crossing through death to life . . . Take heart and believe, for you have received the seal of God's mercy toward you.'[32] Similarly, 'participation in the Lord's Supper, that is, eating Christ's body and drinking his blood, is a sure sign of God's grace'.[33]

Melanchthon's legacy: the *Loci* as foundation for the systematic theology of Lutheran orthodoxy

The 1521 edition of the *Loci* was extraordinarily popular and widely acclaimed. It found its way to Italy where it appeared under an Italian title and was well received – even read in Rome 'with the greatest applause' – until a certain Franciscan monk worked out who the actual author was.[34] Melanchthon put

---

28. Philip Melanchthon, *Melanchthon on Christian Doctrine: Loci Communes 1555*, trans. Clyde L. Manschreck (Grand Rapids: Baker, 1965), p. 161.

29. Ibid., p. 119.

30. Ibid.

31. Ibid., pp. 138–139.

32. Ibid., p. 172.

33. Ibid., p. 182.

34. Manschreck, *The Quiet Reformer*, p. 88.

out a revised edition the next year, and kept editing and expanding the *Loci* right up until the year before he died. As it expanded to four times its original length, the *Loci* changed from being a guide to studying the Scriptures to a book of systematic theology. In Lutheran circles it was to become the university textbook that replaced Lombard's *Sentences*. There were three major periods in the publication of the *Loci*, marked by two major revisions, the first in 1535 and the second in 1543. In the last stage there was also a name change: from *Loci Communes* to *Loci Praecipui Theologici* (The Chief Theological Topics).[35]

Melanchthon's *Loci* became the foundation for Lutheran systematic theology in an extraordinarily direct way. Martin Chemnitz, who is widely regarded as the heir of Luther and therefore sometimes called 'the second Martin', based his own major theological work, the *Loci Theologici*, on Melanchthon's *Loci*.[36] The reason why is that as a young lecturer at the university in Wittenberg he used Melanchthon's *Loci* as his principle text and then for thirty years continued to study and lecture on it. The work published as his *Loci* is actually his lecture notes on Melanchthon's text as recorded by some of his students, Johannes Gasmer in particular, and then edited by Polycarp Leysner and Chemnitz's two sons. So it is that in the work you will first read Melanchthon's text of a particular *locus* and then Chemnitz's own exposition that often runs to many pages; for example, Melanchthon's *locus* on 'Grace and Justification' is two pages while Chemnitz's exposition runs to almost twenty-four pages. Scholars have not been able to discern whether the 1535 edition of Melanchthon's *Loci*, the one that appears in the published edition of Chemnitz's work, was in fact the one he used for his lecture notes or whether it was a much later edition, that of 1555.[37] Chemnitz's work, building on Melanchthon's, laid the foundation for the tradition of systematic theology that became the hallmark of Lutheran orthodoxy. Probably the most revered theologian of this tradition was Johann Gerhard (1582–1637), whose *Loci Theologici* fill nine volumes.[38]

This is not the place to critique Lutheran orthodoxy and the great tomes of theology that were produced in that period, following a tradition that clearly goes back to Melanchthon and the *Loci Communes* of 1521. Many would share Luther's enthusiasm for the original *Loci* and would concur with this tribute from one who translated them into English:

---

35. See footnote 22.
36. Martin Chemnitz, *Loci Theologici*, trans. J. A. O. Preus, 2 vols. (St Louis: Concordia, 1989).
37. See J. A. O. Preus, 'Translator's Preface', in ibid. 1:15.
38. Johann Gerhard, *Loci Theologici*, 9 vols. (Berlin: Schlawitz, 1863).

Philip Melanchthon's *Loci Communes* (*Common Topics*) of 1521 reflects the fusion of humanist and theologian. With the eloquence and philological acumen of a humanist, Melanchthon derides the inconsistencies and subtleties that he finds so objectionable in the writings of the Scholastics and arranges a summary of Christian theology in good, rhetorical fashion around clear and concise passages of Scripture. But with the fervor of a theologian, he takes the confession of Martin Luther as his own, parting ways with his humanist roots and insisting that canonical Scripture alone with its radical message of sin and grace, Law and Gospel, captivity and freedom, be the source and norm of a Christian's confession and life.[39]

But did Melanchthon remain steadfast in this endeavour? In some important respects, we would have to say that he did not. As successive editions of the *Loci* appeared, Melanchthon's criticism of scholasticism became muted. Instead, increasingly he reverted to the old scholastic categories and Aristotelian ways of thought that he had initially rejected in favour of guiding readers back into the Scriptures. 'The last thing I want to do is to draw anyone away from studying the canonical Scriptures with too long a writing,' he said in 1521,[40] but that is not the way it panned out. A slim biblical guide became a book of systematic theology more than three hundred pages long, and his successors in the period of orthodoxy ended up writing great, multiple tomes of theology that represented a new form of scholasticism rather than the deeply biblical theology of Martin Luther.

I think that there is a fundamental problem with Melanchthon's methodology that means the drift back into scholasticism was inevitable. The idea of setting up a theological topic and gathering around it various biblical texts that support and illustrate its doctrinal content means that the Bible can come to be used as a kind of storehouse of proof-texts. The theological topic sets the agenda, and the various biblical texts are not truly heard in their own right or in their own contexts, but rather as pieces of testimony or evidence for a particular doctrine. And here it is that we find the fundamental difference between Luther and Melanchthon as theologians. Luther was ever and always a biblical scholar, whereas Melanchthon, despite his knowledge and love of the Scriptures, increasingly became a systematic theologian.

The difference between the two Reformers is pervasive in their writings, but I would like to reflect on it from the perspective of the central doctrine of the

---

39. Christian Preus, 'Introduction', p. 1.

40. Melanchthon, *Loci Communes 1521*, p. 20.

Reformation: justification. I have already shown that Melanchthon's teaching on justification moved in a particular direction, with the result that forensic justification became a central fixture in his theology.[41] His use of the language of imputation and forensic pronouncement gives his doctrine a distinctive flavour compared with Luther's. Michael Rogness summarizes this difference well:

> By basing justification on a pronouncement from God about something outside of us, imputed to us, the whole process acquires a somewhat abstract coloring . . . This was certainly not the case with Luther. Justification, for him, was very concrete, a uniting of ourselves with Christ. Luther, of course, agreed in substance with the *imputatio* of Christ's righteousness, since it was his righteousness which God counted as ours, but he never used the word much himself. Whereas the two Reformers themselves never disputed each other's outlooks, scholars today are aware of this shade of difference, feeling that the church has neglected Luther's particular emphasis.[42]

Rogness (1969) seems to have anticipated what subsequently came strongly to the fore in the new Finnish interpretation of Luther. Tuomo Mannermaa and other Finnish Luther scholars[43] have carefully studied Luther's exegetical writings and have found there a depth and richness in his teaching on justification that is not reflected in subsequent Lutheran teaching, with its singular focus on imputed righteousness – that is, the teaching that God declares sinners to be righteous because the righteousness of Christ, obtained by his perfect obedience and sacrificial death for our sins, is imputed to us. While Luther does sometimes speak in that way, there is more to his teaching. Commenting on Galatians 2:16, 'yet we know that a person is justified not by the works of the law but through faith in Jesus Christ' (NRSV), Luther said that '[true faith] takes hold of Christ in such a way that Christ is the object of faith, or rather not the object, but, so to speak, *in ipsa fide Christus adest* – in faith itself Christ is present'.[44]

---

41. 'Forensic' in the sense of a law-court situation where the judge makes a pronouncement to clear the accused: 'Not guilty.'

42. Rogness, *Reformer Without Honor*, pp. 112–113.

43. See the essays by Tuomo Mannermaa and others in Carl Braaten and Robert Jensons (eds.), *Union with Christ: The New Finnish Interpretation of Luther* (Grand Rapids: Eerdmans, 1998).

44. *LW* 26:129.

The strength of Melanchthon's teaching on justification is that it magnifies the aspect of *pro nobis*, God for us. We come before God with nothing but our sin and wretchedness, but God comes in grace and blessing, and he imputes to us the righteousness of Christ, which we receive by faith. This is indeed pure gospel, but with this emphasis something important is lacking of Luther's biblical understanding, based especially on his exegesis of Paul's letters to the Galatians and Romans. This is the theology of not just 'for us' (*pro nobis*) but also 'in us' (*in nobis*). The righteousness of Christ, his work and his benefits cannot be separated from his person. When we believe 'that Christ has suffered for us and that for his sake our sin is forgiven',[45] we not only receive Christ's benefits, such as righteousness and eternal life, but we receive Christ himself. Luther said it so well: *in ipsa fide Christus adest* – in faith itself Christ is present. Thus, not only is justification an external pronouncement, but simultaneously there is a change, because, as St Paul wrote, 'it is no longer I who live, but it is Christ who lives in me' (Gal. 2:20, NRSV). With the emergence of the strongly forensic teaching on justification that was initiated by Melanchthon and became so dominant in the *Formula of Concord* and subsequent Lutheran orthodoxy, a central feature of Luther's biblical teaching on justification became neglected. And we are the poorer for it, because the teaching is not just Luther's, but that of Paul and the New Testament.

On the positive side, one of Melanchthon's enduring contributions to theology is the way he brought to prominence the biblical understanding of law and gospel, especially as we find that in the Pauline writings, teaching it in the *Loci* and all his writings with consistency and clarity. The law accuses us and convicts us of our sins, and the sweet comfort of the gospel is the sure and gracious promise that our sins are forgiven for Christ's sake. As Timothy Wengert has commented, 'Melanchthon puts the distinction between law and gospel at the heart of the theological enterprise.'[46]

Conclusion

It is good to let Melanchthon have the last word. In his last days he wrote down on a scrap of paper a couple of thoughts on why he did not fear death. In its

---

45. Melanchthon in the Augsburg Confession, Article 4, *The Book of Concord*, p. 40.
46. Timothy J. Wengert, *Philip Melanchthon, Speaker of the Reformation: Wittenberg's Other Reformer* (Farnham: Ashgate, 2010), p. 19.

own way, it is a humble and deeply personal reflection on his life's work, the troubles he had, and his own steadfast faith and hope.

On the left side he wrote:

> You will be redeemed from sin,
> and set free from cares and from the fury of theologians.

On the right side:

> You come to the light, and you will look upon God and his Son,
> you will understand the wonderful mysteries
> which you could not comprehend in this life:
> why we were so made, and not otherwise,
> and in what the union of the two natures in Christ consists.[47]

Bibliography

Braaten, Carl, and Robert Jensons (eds.), *Union with Christ: The New Finnish Interpretation of Luther*, Grand Rapids: Eerdmans, 1998.

Brettschneider, Carolus (ed.), *Corpus Reformatorum*, Vol. 13, Halle: Schwetschke & Son, 1846.

Chemnitz, Martin, *Loci Theologici*, trans. J. A. O. Preus, 2 vols., St Louis: Concordia, 1989.

Gerhard, Johann, *Loci Theologici*, 9 vols., Berlin: Schlawitz, 1863.

Gritsch, Eric W., 'Reflections on Melanchthon as Theologian of the Augsburg Confession', *Lutheran Quarterly* 12 (1998), p. 451.

Hendel, Kurt, 'Philip Melanchthon; Controversial Reformer', *Currents in Theology and Mission* 7 (1980), p. 53.

Hildebrandt, Franz, *Melanchthon: Alien or Ally?*, Cambridge: Cambridge University Press, 1946.

Keen, Ralph (ed.), *A Melanchthon Reader*, American University Studies, New York: Peter Lang, 1988.

Kolb, Robert, 'Melanchthon: Reformer and Theologian', *Concordia Journal* 23 (1997), p. 309.

Kolb, Robert and Timothy J. Wengert (eds.), *The Book of Concord: The Confessions of the Evangelical Lutheran Church*, Minneapolis: Fortress, 2000.

Manschreck, Clyde L., *Melanchthon: The Quiet Reformer*, New York/Nashville: Abingdon Press, 1958.

---

47. Cited in Stupperich, *Melanchthon*, p. 148.

Melanchthon, Philip, *The Chief Theological Topics: Loci Praecipui Theologici 1559*, trans. J. A. O. Preus, 2nd English edn, St Louis: Concordia, 2011.

———, *Commonplaces: Loci Communes 1521*, trans. and ed. Christian Preus, St Louis: Concordia, 2014.

———, *Melanchthon on Christian Doctrine: Loci Communes 1555*, trans. Clyde L. Manschreck, Grand Rapids: Baker, 1965.

Pelikan, Jaroslav and Helmut T. Lehmann (eds.), *Luther's Works*, 55 vols., St Louis: Concordia; Philadelphia: Fortress Press, 1955–86.

Preus, Christian, 'Introduction', in Philip Melanchthon, *Commonplaces: Loci Communes 1521*, trans. and ed. Christian Preus, St Louis: Concordia, 2014.

Rogness, Michael, *Philip Melanchthon: Reformer without Honor*, Minneapolis: Augsburg, 1969.

Stupperich, Robert, *Melanchthon: The Enigma of the Reformation*, Cambridge: James Clarke, 2006 (1965).

Vajta, Vilmos (ed.), *Luther and Melanchthon in the History and Theology of the Reformation*, Philadelphia: Muhlenberg, 1961.

Wengert, Timothy J., *Philip Melanchthon, Speaker of the Reformation: Wittenberg's Other Reformer*, Farnham: Ashgate, 2010.

4. JOHN CALVIN:
THE REFORMER AND THE NECESSITY OF REFORM

John McClean

John Calvin was a theologian, author, pastor, preacher and even a jurist, and in each of these roles he was self-consciously a Reformer. From 1533, following his spiritual awakening, Calvin was associated with reformist movements within the Roman church and gradually aligned openly with the Reformation.[1] His unexpected call to Geneva in 1536 overruled his desire to be a scholar and author and thrust him into the role of Reformer.

At the end of his career, bidding farewell to his colleagues in Geneva, he recalled that at first in Geneva he 'found almost nothing in it': apart from evangelical preaching 'there was no reformation'.[2] In January 1537 the Genevan preachers presented the Council with the *Articles Concerning the Organization of the Church* (henceforth, *Articles*), to which Calvin was presumably a significant contributor. They pleaded that 'it is not possible to reduce everything to good order in a moment, if only because the ignorance of the people would not allow it', but asserted that the moment had arrived when things could be consolidated so the church was better conformed to God's Word.[3]

---

1. B. Gordon, *Calvin* (New Haven: Yale University Press, 2009), pp. 33–46.
2. J. Calvin, 'Calvin's Farewell to the Minister of Geneva', in H. Beveridge (ed.), *Selected Works of John Calvin: Tracts and Letters*, repr. edn, 7 vols. (Grand Rapids: Baker, 1983), 7:385.
3. J. Calvin, 'Concerning the Organization of the Church and of Worship at Geneva Proposed by the Ministers at the Council', in J. K. Reid (ed.), *Calvin: Theological Treatises* (Louisville: Westminster John Knox, 2000), pp. 48–49.

The course of reform in Geneva was not smooth, and by April 1538 Calvin and Farel left Geneva. In the ensuing interlude in Strasbourg, Calvin's direction as a Reformer developed considerably. He learned a great deal about church order from Bucer and was also involved in the wider movement for church reform, including the colloquies of 1540–41 seeking reunion with Catholics.[4]

When Calvin returned to Geneva in September 1541 he had far greater freedom and was an emerging leader in the wider Reformation. He could insist that the church have a settled order as prescribed by Scripture. The Council agreed that Articles of church polity be drawn up.[5] These were soon presented as the *Ecclesiastical Ordinances* (henceforth, *Ordinances*).[6]

This chapter explores Calvin's understanding of 'reformation' through his programmatic treatise *The Necessity of Reforming the Church* (henceforth, *Necessity*).[7] Two years after Calvin's return to Geneva the Emperor Charles V called a diet in Speyer which he hoped would unite his forces to fight France, including some rapprochement with the Lutherans.[8] Bucer wondered about writing a letter to the emperor setting out the case for church reform and sought Calvin's advice. Calvin took on the task and completed the document, addressed to Charles and the other princes of the Holy Roman Empire, in time for the February diet. There is no evidence that the document gained any significant attention at the diet.[9] It did allow Calvin to set out the case for reform and his priorities, while he was still in the midst of reforming the church in Geneva. Beza considered it

---

4. See W. van't Spijker, 'Bucer's Influence on Calvin', in D. F. Wright (ed.), *Martin Bucer: Reforming Church and Community* (Cambridge: Cambridge University Press, 1994), p. 371; S. M. Manetsch, 'Is the Reformation Over? John Calvin, Roman Catholicism, and Contemporary Ecumenical Conversations', *Themelios* 36, no. 2 (2011), p. 189; C. Ocker, 'Calvin in Germany', in C. Ocker (ed.), *Politics and Reformations: Histories and Reformations* (Leiden: Brill, 2007), pp. 313–344.

5. 'Letter 76', in Beveridge, *Selected Works of John Calvin*, 4:276.

6. Reid, *Theological Treatises*, pp. 58–72.

7. The most commonly available edition of *Necessity* is found in Reid, *Theological Treatises*, pp. 184–216. This version gives only about a third of the original (see 'General Introduction', pp. 19–20). I will refer to the full version English translation published in H. Beveridge (ed.), *Calvin's Tracts Relating to the Reformation*, Vol. 1 (Edinburgh: Calvin Translation Society, 1844), pp. 123–234. Numbers in brackets refer to this edition.

8. See H. Kleinschmidt, *Charles V: The World Emperor* (Stroud: History Press, 2012), Kindle loc. 2404.

9. Manetsch, 'Is the Reformation Over?', p. 190.

one of the most important documents of the era.[10] *Necessity* provides an excellent
vantage point from which to consider Calvin's view of the Reformation.

Calvin and the Reformation

Calvin positioned himself as part of the Reformation. Although the diet was
concerned primarily with German issues and had no jurisdiction over the Swiss
churches, let alone France, Calvin saw himself as part of the same movement
as Luther and the Germans. He asked the emperor to accept his plea as if 'it
were pronounced by the united voice' of all concerned for reform (124). He
spoke for the movement which began when God raised 'Luther and others',
who 'held forth a torch to light us into the way of salvation' and also 'founded
and reared our churches' (125).

Reid (ignoring the *prima facie* addressees of the document – the emperor and
the princes) classifies *Necessity* as an apologetic which makes 'the case for the
Reformed faith' and seeks to convince churches of Switzerland, Germany and
elsewhere to work on Calvin's proposal.[11] In fact, *Necessity* is more properly
apologetic than Reid suggests since Calvin repeatedly summarized and addressed
criticisms of the Reformers. He also presented the case for urgent change:

> the question is not, whether the church labors under diseases both numerous and
> grievous . . . but whether the diseases are of a kind the cure of which admits not
> of longer delay, and as to which, therefore, it is neither useful nor becoming to await
> the result of slow remedies (125).

The need for church reform was self-evident; his task was to make the case that
it could not be delayed.

Calvin presented reformation as a matter of piety and public concern. God
was dishonoured by a church unreformed and the people were not served. He
admitted that the Reformation had upset Europe, bringing dissension and
church division. He argued, though, that the Reformers addressed obvious
wrongs in the church and the accusation they were trouble-makers was unfair,
like Ahab calling Elijah the disturber of Israel. Like Elijah, the Reformers were
required to act for God's glory. They had sought agreement, not division; their
opponents created the conflict (184).

---

10. Reid, *Theological Treatises*, p. 183.
11. Reid, 'General Introduction', in *Theological Treatises*, p. 15.

Towards the end of the document, Calvin dealt with more particular criticisms. One was that the Reformation had produced no fruit in Christian lives. The criticism, as he framed it, admitted that the church had been corrupt but asserted this could not be remedied, so the Reformation had been pointless: 'in probing sores which are incurable, we only enlarge the ulcer.' His response was that 'the restoration of the church is the work of God' and did not depend on human hopes and opinions. This was the reason they pushed on in the face of difficulty and opposition. The Reformers were bound to 'rush forward through the midst of despair', since the Lord required that the gospel be preached. Like Paul, the Reformers planted and watered; growth would come from God. Even if there was no obvious fruit, still reformation was required. Calvin also objected to the assessment that there had been no fruit. There had been outward changes which were to be desired (such as the end of idolatry). What was more, there were people who could testify they had learnt 'to worship God with a pure heart ... to invoke him with a calm conscience ... and [had been] furnished with true delight in Christ' (200).

It was not that the Reformation side was unblemished. There were those associated with it who perverted the gospel by indulging their passions. Calvin accused his opponents of exacerbating the problem by stopping the spread of the truth and prohibiting Protestants from establishing properly administered churches. With some ferocity, he turned the accusation back on his opponents, enumerating multiple shocking failures of discipline in the Roman church (201–209). He asserted that 'our disorder, such as it is, will be found at all events somewhat more orderly than the kind of order in which they glory' (206).

A further charge was that Protestantism was schismatic. Calvin again likened the Reformers to the prophets and apostles who stood against a false church. He insisted that they 'neither dissent from the church, nor are aliens from her communion'. The question, of course, was what constituted the church? Here Calvin applied the 'marks of the church'. Rome claimed the name of church but the true church had Christ as its head, and Christ was present by the gospel.

> Our adversaries, therefore, if they would persuade us that they are the true church, must, first of all, show that the true doctrine of God is among them; and this is the meaning of what we often repeat, that is, that the uniform characteristics of a well-ordered church are the preaching of sound doctrine, and the pure administration of the sacraments (213–214).

Since Rome could not claim to be the church in these terms, the Reformers were not guilty of breaking unity with the church. It was a common faith based on true doctrine which united Christians to Christ and so was the basis for unity in the church (211–218).

In reply to the accusation that the Reformers had no right to act, Calvin offered two points. First, the Pope had been asked to act: 'Luther himself humbly besought the pontiff that he would be pleased to cure the very grievous disorders of the church.' The problems were clear and demanded action, and the Pope was in a position to act. 'He now talks of impediments. But if the fact be traced to its source, it will be found that he has all along been, both to himself and to others, the only impediment.' On this basis Calvin rejected the idea that reform could wait until an ecumenical council (220–222). Second, the need for reform was urgent. Calvin made this point in a forceful passage.

> At the time when divine truth lay buried under this vast and dense cloud of darkness; when religion was sullied by so many impious superstitions; when by horrid blasphemies the worship of God was corrupted, and his glory laid prostrate; when by a multitude of perverse opinions, the benefit of redemption was frustrated, and men, intoxicated with a fatal confidence in works, sought salvation anywhere rather than in Christ; when the administration of the sacraments was partly maimed and torn asunder, partly adulterated by the admixture of numerous fictions, and partly profaned by traffickings for gain; when the government of the church had degenerated into mere confusion and devastation; when those who sat in the seat of pastors first did most vital injury to the church by the dissoluteness of their lives, and, secondly, exercised a cruel and most noxious tyranny over souls, by every kind of error, leading men like sheep to the slaughter; then Luther arose, and after him others, who with united counsels sought out means and methods by which religion might be purged from all these defilements, the doctrine of godliness restored to its integrity, and the church raised out of its calamitous into somewhat of a tolerable condition. The same course we are still pursuing in the present day (144–145).

Worship and doctrine: the focus of reformation

Against this background, *Necessity* focused on a clutch of interrelated issues. Its central thesis was that there were two things which made for genuine Christianity – knowledge of how God is to be worshipped and clarity about the source of salvation. These, Calvin said, 'comprehend' the whole substance of Christianity. He went so far as to assert that 'all our controversies concerning doctrine relate either to the legitimate worship of God, or to the ground of salvation' (146). Much of the document outlines the case for reforming church worship and doctrine, and giving an agenda for this reform. Secondarily, he turned to the sacraments and the government of the church (126).

Calvin began with worship. One of the major themes in his theology was that true knowledge of God is grounded in and directed towards the worship of God.[12] On the one hand, piety teaches religion; on the other, it is only when people 'establish their complete happiness' in God that they 'give themselves truly and sincerely to him' – that is, genuine religion feeds piety.[13] This virtuous cycle highlights the centrality of worship, or piety. For Calvin, the recognition of and right response to God was the central calling of human life. So it is no surprise that he gave worship the priority.

Worship is founded on the recognition that God is 'the only source of all virtue, justice, holiness, wisdom, truth, power, goodness, mercy, life and salvation'. This drives a double response: believers thank and glorify God for everything good and they rely on him for all things. Worship consists of such adoration and prayer; ceremonies are secondary aids to this heart response. From another perspective, worship is 'self-abasement' – 'denying self' and living a life of mortification and vivification, 'trained to obedience and devotedness to [God's] will, so that his fear reigns in our hearts, and regulates all the actions of our lives'. For Calvin, worship is turning to God in adoration and prayer with obedience (127).

Calvin then argued that we must follow God's rule for worship. This established God's authority and protected the church from wandering – 'such is our folly, that when we are left at liberty, all we are able to do is to go astray'. To add to God's word in the matter of worship always promotes vain 'will worship'. The term is taken from Colossians 2:23 where it translates *ethelothreœskia*, which could be translated 'self-willed worship' or 'self-imposed worship' (128–129).

Consistent with the secondary place he gave to ceremonies and his insistence on simplicity, Calvin had relatively little to say about required changes in the form of worship, apart from stripping away illegitimate additions. The first priority was to instruct people in and convince them of 'the doctrine of the spiritual worship of God'. Worshippers must understand God and his blessings and promises, and respond to them with conviction. The conduct of worship is related to a preaching and teaching ministry which proclaims God's glory, makes known his perfections, extols his benefits and calls people to 'reverence

---

12. See J. Beeke, 'Calvin on Piety', in D. K. McKim (ed.), *The Cambridge Companion to John Calvin* (Cambridge: Cambridge University Press, 2004), pp. 125–152.

13. John Calvin, *Institutes of the Christian Religion*, trans. F. L. Battles, ed. J. T. McNeill (Philadelphia: Westminster, 1960), I.ii.1.

his majesty, render due homage to his greatness, feel due gratitude for his mercies, and unite in showing forth his praise'. This proclamation and praise gives rise to dependent prayer and trains worshippers in proper self-denial and obedience (146–147).

Calvin tackled questions of statues and images and asserted, from the Scriptures and from the Church Fathers, that any veneration was idolatry, while also describing the foolish superstitions which accompany such veneration. On relics he commented that 'it is almost incredible how impudently the world has been cheated' (150). He then turned to some specific issues of practice which needed reform. The Reformers rejected the doctrine of the intercession of the saints and 'brought men back to Christ', to call on the Father through him. They also taught Christians to pray with confidence to Christ and with understanding. Calvin's argument, in summary, was that we should call only on God, that there is only one Mediator and that Christ promises that all we ask in his name we will receive. Reform would teach people these truths and ensure that believers knew what they were asking of God in their private prayers, while public prayer was 'framed so as to be understood by all' (154–159).

The concerns about worship in *Necessity* were reflected in Calvin's work in Geneva. When he first arrived public worship was being reformed, primarily by Farel, though with Calvin's support.[14] Clerical attire was simplified, services and preaching were moved to the French vernacular and the extra medieval 'sacraments' were eliminated. Manetsch summarizes:

> Public worship in reformed Geneva was simpler and less ornate than in the medieval church. Gone were the processions, the incense, the candles and acolytes, the monastic choirs, and the melodious organs. Instead, the reformers created a liturgy that gave priority to public prayers, the proclamation of the Word of God, and a cappella singing of the Psalter.[15]

During the Strasbourg years, Bucer had a notable influence on Calvin's practice of worship. Calvin used Bucer's liturgy in French with the congregation there and he explained that for the Genevan liturgy he 'took the form of Strasbourg, and borrowed the greater part of it'.[16] He offered a strikingly simple

---

14. Gordon, *Calvin*, pp. 71–72.

15. S. M. Manetsch, *Calvin's Company of Pastors: Pastoral Care and the Emerging Reformed Church, 1536–1609* (Oxford: Oxford University Press, 2013), pp. 19–20.

16. W. D. Maxwell, *An Outline of Christian Worship: Its Developments and Forms* (Oxford: Oxford University Press, 1936), pp. 113–115, shows the close parallel between the

service: a call to worship from Psalm 124:8, a confession of sin and a prayer for pardon, a psalm, the prayer for illumination, the Scripture reading, the sermon, a long prayer of intercession with a paraphrase of the Lord's Prayer, the Apostles' Creed recited and a final blessing. Compared with the medieval service, the congregation was highly involved. They were addressed at almost every point, they were expected to understand all that took place and they were required to sing and recite together. All of this was to encourage heartfelt engagement.

Calvin greatly valued the power of song to stir the heart. Introducing the liturgy he writes, 'we know by experience that singing has great power and vigor to move and inflame men's hearts.'[17] The Ten Commandments and the Creed were sung on Communion Sundays. For more than twenty years he pursued the project of producing a full metrical psalter.[18]

The second area of necessary reformation which Calvin identified was that the church needed to teach the doctrine required for salvation. He outlined three key areas. First, people must be aware of 'individual wretchedness' produced by sin. Depravity, Calvin said, is rooted in original sin but each person needed to recognize his or her own guilt and total helplessness. Second, people must understand the fullness of redemption provided in Christ. He is 'the only priest who reconciles us to the Father' and his death is the only sacrifice which expiates sin and acquires 'a true and perfect righteousness'. Believers must not be allowed to think they contributed some part to their salvation but must acknowledge that it is all of Christ. Recognizing total helplessness and Christ's sufficiency led to the final element of resting entirely and confidently in Christ (133).

Calvin showed how Rome had obscured these truths. Both the theologians and the preachers often seemed to reduce original sin to 'bodily appetite and lust' with no awareness of 'inward depravity of soul'. From this there was a doctrine of free will which gave people false confidence in their ability, rather than looking for the work of the Spirit (134–135).

German Strasbourg liturgy, the French Strasbourg liturgy and Calvin's 1542 Geneva liturgy. See also J. W. Montgomery, 'The Celebration of the Lord's Supper According to Calvin', in J. W. Montgomery, *Christ as Centre and Circumference: Essays Theological, Cultural and Polemic* (Eugene: Wipf and Stock, 2012), pp. 301–303.

17. F. L. Battles (trans), 'John Calvin: The Form of Prayers and Songs of the Church, 1542: Letter to the Reader', *CTJ* 15, no. 2 (1980), p. 163.

18. A. Heron, 'Shaping the Worship of the Reformed Church in Geneva: Calvin on Prayer and Praise', *HTS Teologiese Studies* 68, no. 1 (2012), p. 2.

The central dispute, he said, was whether justification was by faith or by works. Calvin was clear that good works were required and were accepted by God and rewarded by him; but they did not reconcile sinners to God, acquire eternal life, remove guilt or provide the grounds of salvation. Rome held that humans were tainted and weakened but, aided by God's grace, were able to contribute something to salvation. The Reformers taught that sinners had 'no ability whatever to act aright' and were only able to turn to God by the work of the Spirit.

For Calvin, Rome's teaching led people to 'plume themselves on the merit of works' and fed their pride and self-confidence. The Reformers insisted that a person was righteous before God 'because God, without any respect to works, freely adopts him in Christ, by imputing the righteousness of Christ to him, as if it were his own'. They insisted, with Paul, that salvation is all of God in Christ, with no contribution from the believer. They also rejected the Roman teaching of the need for continued confession of and satisfaction for the sins of Christians: 'we acknowledge no other satisfaction than that which Christ accomplished, when, by the sacrifice of his death, he expiated our sins.' This included a rejection of the doctrine of works of supererogation.

The Reformers valued the good works which result from justification and held that they were rewarded on the basis of God's pardon and adoption:

> as we said of man, so we may say of works: they are justified not by their own desert, but by the merits of Christ alone; the faults by which they would otherwise displease being covered by the sacrifice of Christ.

The third, and related, way in which Rome corrupted the gospel was that it denied assurance, holding that believers 'ought to be perpetually in suspense and uncertainty' about their salvation. This, Calvin pointed out, was an obvious correlate of the doctrine of justification by works – thus suggesting an indirect rebuttal of the Roman view of justification (135–137).

How did Calvin seek to establish proper doctrine in Geneva?

One of Calvin and Farel's first actions was to ensure that the services in Genevan churches were preaching services. Once he returned to Geneva, Calvin's *Ordinances* outlined a plan of two preaching services each Sunday at each of the city churches, and preaching services early in the morning on three weekdays. By 1561 there were thirty-three preaching services in Geneva each week – eleven on Sunday, and twenty-two weekday services.[19]

---

19. Manetsch, *Calvin's Company of Pastors*, pp. 148–149.

Geneva also adopted a confession and a catechism to establish sound doctrine. The *Instruction et confession de foy* was published in early 1537 and published in Latin the following year as *Catechismus, sive christiana religionis institutio*, suggesting that it was used for instruction.[20] It is, in effect, a *précis* of the first edition of the *Institutes*.[21] The shorter *Confession de la foy* seems to have been abstracted from the *Catechismus* and to have served as the confession to which the people of Geneva were expected to subscribe.[22]

The *Confession* begins with a commitment to Scripture alone: 'we desire to follow Scripture alone as rule of faith and religion' (Art. 1). It strikes Reformation notes, even when addressing non-controversial doctrines. For instance, the article on theology proper affirms one God who is worshipped and 'in whom we are to put all our confidence and hope', in contrast to putting hope in or worshipping any other thing (Art. 2); and the article on the law states that there is one Lord and Master whose will, expressed in the commandments of the law, is the 'perfection of justice' and must be followed while no other good works are to be invented (Art. 3). It works through Reformation soteriology – the totality of sin (Art. 4 & 5) and salvation provided fully in Christ (Art. 6), including righteousness (Art. 7) and regeneration (Art. 8). Article 10 affirms that all these benefits come from God's grace to sinners, not because of any human worthiness or merit, though works done in Christ are 'pleasing and agreeable' to God since they come from the Spirit. Article 11 affirms that salvation is received by faith. The next articles (Art. 12–16) deal with worship, asserting that prayer is only to God through Christ and with understanding, and giving a Reformation view of the two sacraments. The final articles deal with the ordering of the church (Art. 17–20) and the magistrates (Art. 21).[23] The *Catechismus* includes an exposition of the Apostle's Creed to cover the content of the Christian faith and an exposition of the Ten Commandments and the Lord's Prayer. It also includes discussion of Christian hope, the ministry and excommunication.

Calvin produced a new French catechism in Strasbourg, and a similar one for Geneva in 1542.[24] These are more like Luther's 1529 *Small Catechism* since they take the Apostles' Creed, the Ten Commandments and the Lord's Prayer

---

20. F. L. Battles, *John Calvin: Catechism 1538* (Pittsburgh: Pittsburgh Theological Seminary, 1976).

21. I. J. Hesselink, *Calvin's First Catechism* (Louisville: Westminster John Knox, 1997), p. 41.

22. Reid, *Theological Treatises*, pp. 25–33.

23. Ibid., pp. 26–33.

24. Ibid., pp. 88–139.

as a framework and use a question-and-answer format.[25] The soteriology which Calvin stressed in *Necessity* is covered in the first section. Heron gives the following summary:[26]

1. 'Of the Faith' (Q. 1–131) – an introduction, interpretation of the Apostles' Creed, Faith, Justification, Good Works and Penitence.
2. 'Of the Law' (Q. 132–232) – interpretation of the Ten Commandments, the Command of Love and the Uses of the Law.
3. 'Of Prayer' (Q. 232–295) – interpretation of the Lord's Prayer, general teaching on prayer.
4. 'Of the Sacraments' (Q. 296–373) – instruction on the proper way to worship God on the basis of his Word, ministry, Sacraments, church discipline.

These catechisms were tools for ministry. The *Articles* called for 'a brief and simple summary of the Christian faith, to be taught to all children'. Parents were to 'exercise pains and diligence that their children learn this summary and that they present themselves before the ministers at the times appointed'.[27] One of Calvin's conditions for returning to Geneva was that catechizing be enforced.[28] The *Ordinances* provided for teaching the catechism to children in all three city churches at midday every Sunday, and every school and household was to ensure that children attended. The Council and ministers exhorted fathers to instruct their children as well as to ensure they attended sermons and catechism classes. At times the Consistory disciplined parents for their failure on this score.[29] Calvin and his colleagues valued family instruction, but held that the pastors also had a key role to oversee and supplement catechesis in the family.[30] Children had to recite the sum of the catechism and make a profession of faith before they were admitted to the Lord's Supper.[31] The catechism itself was a teaching

---

25. W. Greef, *The Writings of John Calvin: An Introductory Guide* (Louisville: Westminster John Knox, 2008), pp. 116–117.
26. A. Heron, 'Calvin and the Confessions of the Reformation', *HTS Teologiese Studies* 70, no. 1 (2014), p. 3.
27. Reid, *Theological Treatises*, p. 54.
28. R. M. Kingdon, 'Catechesis in Calvin's Geneva', in J. Van Engen (ed.), *Educating People of Faith* (Grand Rapids: Eerdmans, 2004), p. 303.
29. Manetsch, *Calvin's Company of Pastors*, pp. 267–271.
30. Kingdon, 'Catechesis', p. 300.
31. Reid, *Theological Treatises*, pp. 62, 69.

manual and curriculum as well as a confession of faith for ministers in Geneva and students at the Academy.

The sacraments

In *Necessity* Calvin turns from worship and doctrine, the soul and life of religion, to the sacraments and the government of the church which provide its body or structure. Some of his concerns about the sacraments had already surfaced in his discussion of worship; similarly, his discussion of true doctrine highlighted the need for an effective preaching ministry.

Calvin complained that Rome ignored the distinction between what God has instituted and ceremonies devised by humans by adding to the two sacraments instituted by Christ. The sacraments alone were instituted by God to seal on the hearts of believers God's favour, to offer them Christ and testify to all God's spiritual gifts. No human ceremony had the right to do this, only those of divine appointment (165–166).

The sacraments themselves had also been corrupted, though Calvin differentiated between levels of corruption. Baptism was obscured by additions so that 'scarcely a vestige' remained, but the very form of the Supper had been changed. It had become 'a theatrical exhibition' in which the people were effectively excommunicated and the priest claimed to offer a sacrifice for sins. Calvin responded that Christ never called the Supper a sacrifice. Worse, this sacrifice was superstitiously applied to procure grace for the living and the dead. So, 'the efficacy of Christ's death has been transferred to a vain theatrical show, and the dignity of an eternal priesthood wrested from him to be bestowed upon men' (137–138).

Calvin complained that priests consecrated both sacraments with unintelligible words which resembled magic incantation, and communicated nothing of the promises and commands given by Christ. All attention was directed to the signs, not to Christ. Connected to this practice, Calvin pointed out, was the teaching of *ex opere operato*: that the sacraments would convey grace if mortal sin did not obstruct them. He also objected to the superstitious use of the reserved host, reminding his readers that the blessing of the Supper came from hearing the words of promise that people share in the body and blood of Christ as they eat and drink. Along with all of this, religious rites were sold for gain (139–140).

When Calvin laid out a programme for the reformation of the sacraments, he first insisted that the celebration of the sacraments should include the ancient custom of an explanation which directs people's confidence to Christ. The additions to it had to be removed to return it to the original simplicity of the apostles (165–166). The Lord's Supper required greater reform. The doctrine of the mass as a sacrifice had to be denied, including any extension of the expiation of sins in the mass to the dead. The Reformers rejected the doctrine of transubstantiation and the reservation of the host. In practice they restored regular communion in both kinds and removed the many extra ceremonies, some of which 'savored too much of Judaism', others of which 'ill accorded with the gravity' of the Supper and some of which were treated superstitiously. These doctrines, and the practices related to them, diverted faith from Christ to the elements themselves (167–169).

Calvin's concern for the sacraments was evident in his work in Geneva. The *Articles* express a desire for weekly communion which would bring great comfort since by it 'we are really made participants of the body and the blood of Jesus, of his death, of his life, of his Spirit and of all his benefits'. It would also stir the church to praise God for his grace and encourage all to live in Christian unity. Recognizing that weekly celebration brought the risk that 'this sacred and so excellent mystery [might] be misunderstood', the *Articles* proposed monthly services in each of the city churches, arranged so that communicants could attend each one if they desired. The distribution of the bread and wine was to be given to the ministers and a liturgy would be provided. The major concern was for church discipline to prevent the Supper being desecrated 'by those coming to it and communicating, who declare and manifest by their misconduct and evil life that they do not at all belong to Jesus'.[32]

The *Ordinances* also regulated the sacraments. Baptism was to be administered during a preaching service and only by ministers or their assistants. It should take place at the front of the church 'in order that there be better hearing for the recitation of this mystery and practice of baptism'. Godparents were to be known to the church or 'men of faith and of our communion' so they would be able to instruct children in the faith.

The *Ordinances* still insisted that the Lord's Supper 'was instituted for us by our Lord to be frequently used'. However, Calvin now accepted that the scheme in the *Articles* would not prevail in Geneva and proposed quarterly communion in each city church on a pattern in which there would be at least one communion service in the city each month, including in each church at Easter, Pentecost and Christmas. (Even this pattern was not accepted by the Council and the final outcome was simply quarterly communion.)[33] As in baptism, the Lord's Supper

32. Ibid., p. 50.
33. Maxwell, *Christian Worship*, p. 117; Manetsch, *Calvin's Company of Pastors*, p. 127.

was to be served from a table beside the pulpit at the front of the church so that it was easily seen and better understood. The week before a communion service, an announcement was to be made so that children and newcomers to the city could be examined and approved to receive the Supper.

Introducing the 1542 version of the liturgy, Calvin outlined the concerns which guided his approach to the sacraments, especially a determination that the sacraments be clearly explained. The medieval practice 'is a perverse custom' which 'profanes' the sacraments and promoted superstition. In fact, the sacraments were properly consecrated 'by the word of faith when it is declared and received'. This was Jesus' own pattern: he did not address the bread and wine but the disciples.[34]

The order itself was simple with the expected emphasis on explanation. The baptismal service began with a single question to the parents: 'Do you offer this infant for baptism?' (Answer 'We do indeed'), and then offered a lengthy explanation of baptism signifying remission of sins and the gift of the Spirit, and of the basis of infant baptism. There followed a prayer which concluded with the Lord's Prayer.[35] Parents then made promises: to instruct the child in the faith as summarized in the Apostles' Creed as well as teaching him or her the Scriptures, and to exhort the child to keep the law, loving God and neighbour. The child was then baptized in the name of the Father, Son and Spirit. The minister was given one clear, positive instruction:

> The whole is said aloud, and in the common tongue, in order that the people who are present may be witnesses to what is done (for which purpose it is necessary that they understand it), and in order that all may be edified by recognising and calling to mind the fruit and use of their own Baptism.

The instructions note that there are other ancient ceremonies often included in baptism; but they lack biblical authority and have been the cause of superstition, so they have been removed. The goal was that 'there might be nothing to prevent the people from going directly to Jesus Christ'.[36]

The Supper was a similarly unadorned service, following the 'Liturgy of Word' of the regular Sunday service. After the Apostles' Creed, the minister was to give the words of institution, an excommunication of unworthy

---

34. Battles (trans), 'Form of Prayers and Songs of the Church', pp. 161–162.
35. Heron, 'Shaping', p. 4, notes that the address is five times longer than the prayer and comments that 'Calvin was not Cranmer!'
36. Beveridge, *Selected Works of John Calvin*, 2:113–118.

communicants, a call to self-examination and an encouragement to come to the table for all who have the testimony of the Spirit. The explanation made clear that self-examination is not seeking perfect righteousness but, 'on the contrary, by seeking our life in Christ, we confess that we are in death'. The sacrament is

> a medicine for the poor spiritual sick, and . . . all the worthiness which our Saviour requires in us is to know ourselves, so as to be dissatisfied with our vices, and have all our pleasure, joy and contentment in him alone.

There is an exhortation to believe the promises in Christ, including the promise that communicants share in his body and blood; and a call to gratefulness for 'the infinite goodness of our Saviour, who displays all his riches and blessings at this table, in order to dispense them to us'. The minister was then to distribute the bread and cup to the people as they came forward, while singing a psalm or hearing Scripture read. The service finished with a prayer of thanks and the blessing. The form finished with a brief apologetic for those offended by the simplicity of the service, arguing that the changes from the mass had not removed the sacrament but rather had 'restored it to its integrity'.[37]

The government of the church

The final area in which Calvin called for reform was that of church government. He complained that the office of pastor had been corrupted. Pastors should edify the church by teaching sound doctrine, but instead bishops hardly taught at all and operated as secular princes while the lower clergy offered superstitious ceremonies. Both were likely to sell their office for others to fill.

> The spiritual government which Christ recommended has totally disappeared, and a new and mongrel species of government has been introduced, which, under whatever name it may pass current, has no more resemblance to the former than the world has to the kingdom of Christ (140).

His criticism was comprehensive. The problem was not that some bishops and priests failed in their duties; the failure was so general it had become the rule. Even if priests were to follow what was expected of them, they would offer superstitious ceremonies, not teaching. The corruption of their lives

---

37. Ibid., 2:119–122.

only further undermined their ministry. Candidates for ordination were not examined for their life and doctrine; instead, clergy were appointed at a price or through nepotism or worse! To cap all this off, rather than acting as ambassadors for God through preaching his Word, the clergy had 'a most cruel tyranny' over the souls of the people, reinforced by the church's claim to infallibility (141–143).

In the government of the church the first step in reformation was to return to the ancient practice that all who held a pastoral office were examined to ensure they would teach sound doctrine. Calvin applied Gregory's maxim 'those who abuse privilege deserve to lose privilege' directly to the Roman hierarchy, asserting that if they wished to remain bishops they should change the ministry entirely. He dismissed concerns about the form of the ordination service, stating that the Reformation churches followed the simple biblical practice of laying hands on the candidate (170–175).

One of Calvin's great occupations in Geneva was recruiting and training pastors. As Manetsch has highlighted, 'the long-term success of his religious program depended in large part on the company of reformed ministers who worked alongside Calvin'.[38] Initially he was unhappy with his associates. He wrote to Oswald Myconius in Lucerne explaining that he needed Pierre Viret to remain in Geneva since 'our other colleagues are more a hindrance than a help to us. They are proud and self-conceited, have no zeal, and less learning.'[39] Viret was recalled to Lausanne and did not move to Geneva until 1559. Calvin did, however, recruit a formidable group of preachers and pastors: Nicolas des Gallars, Michel Cop, François Bourgoing, François Morel, Raymond Chauvet, Nicolas Colladon and, most especially, Theodore Beza, were all part of 'an impressive group of talented and well-educated French ministers who shared his reformed commitments'.[40] The *Ordinances* give some detail about both the process and the requirements for selecting ministers. Candidates were to be examined by the ministers on their doctrine, their ability to preach and their life. The ministers would then recommend a candidate to the Council for appointment. As well as recruiting these French preachers, the Academy served to train a new generation.

Calvin was equally concerned with continued oversight of the clergy: 'as it is necessary to examine the ministers well when they are to be elected, so also it is necessary to have good supervision to maintain them in their duty'. This was

---

38. Manetsch, *Calvin's Company of Pastors*, p. 1.

39. Beveridge, *Calvin's Selected Works*, 4:303.

40. Manetsch, *Calvin's Company of Pastors*, p. 40.

the role of the *Congregations* in which the ministers, teachers and some interested laity met to discuss the interpretation of Scripture. The *Ordinances* instituted this weekly gathering 'for conserving purity and concord of doctrine'.[41] Each Friday morning one minister offered a commentary on the appointed text, followed by discussion and the opportunity for private correction if necessary.[42] The ministers, including those from the rural churches, also met in private every three months for the *Ordinary Censure* to deal more directly with their lives as well as any disharmony in the company. Traditionally, this concluded with a shared meal of soup as a sign of their continued fellowship. The *Ordinances* provided a list of faults which were not to be tolerated in a minister (beginning with heresy, schism, rebellion against ecclesiastical order and blasphemy, and running through to forbidden and scandalous games, dances and similar dissoluteness, and crimes), as well as those which, in the first instance, could be dealt with by brotherly admonition (strange interpretations of Scripture, doctrines or practices, laziness in ministry, slander, avarice and too great parsimony, quarrels and contentions). The records of the Consistory show that pastors were corrected and even disciplined on this basis.[43]

Calvin considered that this fraternal pastoral discipline was important for the church. When he heard that the ministers of the Pays de Vaud (centred on Lausanne) had been prohibited from such meetings by the Council of Bern, because they were too divisive, Calvin wrote to Wolfgang Musculus in Bern stressing their value. He admitted the risk of conflict, but advised that it could be ameliorated. Overall, these meetings were 'an excellent institution'. Pastors who were prone to be lazy were spurred to study, and the exchange of views helped them to avoid false teaching. 'The less the interchange of opinion, the greater will be the danger from pernicious dogmatisms. The slothful will sleep undisturbed; many will somehow or other grow godless, or become degenerate.'[44]

Calvin's concern for a well-ordered pastorate was in part because that provided proper discipline for the whole church. Most of the explicit discussion in *Necessity* is about clerical discipline, but at points he reminded the princes that this was a precursor for a wider discipline, one which was sorely needed. According to ancient synods, the task of a bishop, with assistance from the

---

41. Reid, *Theological Treatises*, pp. 59–60.
42. Manetsch, *Calvin's Company of Pastors*, pp. 134–135.
43. Reid, *Theological Treatises*, p. 61; Manetsch, *Calvin's Company of Pastors*, pp. 127–128.
44. Beveridge, *Selected Works of John Calvin*, 5:264–265.

presbyters, was to feed the people by preaching and the sacraments and to curb 'clergy and people by holy discipline' (218–219).

In practice in Geneva, church discipline was a large part of Calvin's reformation. The *Articles* highlighted to the Council the need for church discipline following Christ's directions (Matt. 18) and the apostolic pattern (1 Tim. 1; 1 Cor. 5). Discipline ensured that Christ was not 'blasphemed and dishonoured', sinners were led to repentance and others were encouraged to live godly lives. They recommended that the Council appoint elders to assist with this discipline.[45] The *Ordinances* presented a detailed plan for the appointment of elders and a set of regulations for ecclesiastical discipline.[46]

The right of the church to exercise discipline was a continuing point of contention between the Company of Pastors and the Council until 1555, particularly when the Council was dominated by Calvin's political opponents.[47] Throughout these years, Calvin persisted in claiming the right of the church to exercise discipline, including excommunication.

The other area of church government is that of church laws. Calvin judged that the laws of Rome brought a 'hard and iniquitous bondage' which had 'enthralled the souls of the faithful', especially when they sought to regulate the inner life. Laws had multiplied into a confusing 'labyrinth'; 'some of them seem framed for the very purpose of troubling and torturing consciences'. These were enforced as if they were 'the whole substance of piety', while violation of God's own law was treated lightly (144).

Calvin noted that the Reformers retained church laws which were not problematic for consciences and served good order. He refused, however, to accept that such laws could not be reformed, especially when they intruded on freedom of conscience. He particularly contested three rules – restrictions on eating meat, the requirement for clerical celibacy and the need for auricular confession. Calvin admitted that each of these was ancient, but asserted that none was the settled view of the early church and each brought spiritual damage, binding consciences unnecessarily and, in the case of celibacy and confession, requiring an impossible standard (176–183).

Calvin recognized the role of church law – hence the *Articles* and the *Ordinances*. Both of these were simple compared with canon law and were concerned

---

45. Reid, *Theological Treatises*, pp. 49–53.

46. Ibid., pp. 63–64, 70–71.

47. W. G. Naphy, *Calvin and the Consolidation of the Genevan Reformation*, 2nd edn (Louisville: Westminster John Knox, 2002), pp. 184–207; W. Monter, *Calvin's Geneva* (Eugene: Wipf and Stock, 2012), pp. 64–89.

with the external operations of the church.[48] They provided the structures for church discipline, but little of the content. Calvin's church discipline has become notorious, and no doubt there were moments when the Consistory in Geneva overstepped the bounds. There were times when laws regulated life beyond the limits of Scripture, as when the Council ruled on what names could be given to children – banning popular options in favour of biblical names. (This law produced riots in the city.)[49] Nevertheless, it is important to note Calvin's espoused view of discipline. Rather than impose church laws, he sought to apply biblical law to individuals and to do so with fatherly care, aiming for the good of the person and the church. He argued that even in the extreme cases of excommunication, discipline should be applied with 'a rule of moderation'.[50] In his view this was a biblical and evangelical discipline, radically different from the laws of Rome.

Conclusion

Necessity shows Calvin's ability as theologian and rhetorician to convey a vision for reform. His arguments are compelling and his urgency is forceful. The work in Geneva showed his ability to implement the vision. B. B. Warfield commented that Calvin's career as a reformer 'was the work of an idealist become a practical man of affairs'.[51] This chapter illustrates this combination. Calvin's basic convictions about reform seem to have remained consistent as he worked with considerable patience to see it realized in Geneva.

Calvin's vision of reform rested on several interrelated theological convictions: God deserves all glory for his majesty and mercy, humans are sinners who depend fully on Christ alone for salvation, and salvation cannot be earned by works but should lead to works. On this basis, the church exists to know and live for God through his salvation and is fed by preaching and sacraments which share Christ and his promises. For this the church requires faithful pastors who will proclaim the gospel of salvation in Christ and the glory of God, and lead

---

48. See S. M. Johnson, 'The Sinews of the Body of Christ: Calvin's Concept of Church Discipline', *WTJ* 59, no. 1 (1997), pp. 91–92.

49. J. Witte, *From Sacrament to Contract: Marriage, Religion and Law in the Western Tradition*, 2nd edn (Louisville: Westminster John Knox, 2012), p. 182.

50. J. Calvin, *Institutes of the Christian Religion*, trans. F. L. Battles, ed. J. T. McNeill, Library of Christian Classics (London: SCM, 1961 [1559]), IV.xii.8.

51. B. B. Warfield, *Calvin and Augustine* (Philadelphia: P&R, 1974), p. 15.

the church in adoration and prayer. Pastors must teach and model godly living, springing from salvation, and lead the church to live that way. Calvin held that the medieval church had obscured and corrupted every element of this, and so his programme for reform was to see each element restored in unadorned simplicity. In this, he understood himself as part of a wide reformation which served God's people and glorified God.

Bibliography

Battles, F. L., *John Calvin: Catechism 1538*, Pittsburgh: Pittsburgh Theological Seminary, 1976.

Battles, F. L. (trans.), 'John Calvin: The Form of Prayers and Songs of the Church, 1542: Letter to the Reader', *CTJ* 15, no. 2 (November 1980), pp. 160–165.

Beeke, J., 'Calvin on Piety', in D. K. McKim (ed.), *The Cambridge Companion to John Calvin*, 125–152, Cambridge: Cambridge University Press, 2004.

Beveridge, H. (ed.), *Calvin's Tracts Relating to the Reformation*, Vol. 1, Edinburgh: Calvin Translation Society, 1844.

———, *Selected Works of John Calvin: Tracts and Letters*, repr. edn, 7 vols., Grand Rapids: Baker, 1983.

Calvin, J., *Institutes of the Christian Religion*, trans. F. L. Battles, ed. J. T. McNeill, Library of Christian Classics, London: SCM, 1961 (1559).

———, *Institutes of the Christian Religion*, trans. F. L. Battles, ed. J. T. McNeill, Philadelphia: Westminster, 1960.

Gordon, B., *Calvin*, New Haven: Yale University Press, 2009.

Greef, W., *The Writings of John Calvin: An Introductory Guide*, Louisville: Westminster John Knox, 2008.

Heron, A., 'Calvin and the Confessions of the Reformation', *HTS Teologiese Studies* 70, no. 1 (2014). Art. 2084, 5 pages, <http://dx.doi.org/10.4102/hts.v70i1.2084>.

———, 'Shaping the Worship of the Reformed Church in Geneva: Calvin on Prayer and Praise', *HTS Teologiese Studies* 68, no. 1 (2012). Art. 1350, 8 pages, <http://dx.doi.org/10.4102/hts.v68i1.1350>.

Hesselink, I. J., *Calvin's First Catechism*, Louisville: Westminster John Knox, 1997.

Johnson, S. M., 'The Sinews of the Body of Christ: Calvin's Concept of Church Discipline', *WTJ* 59, no. 1 (1997), pp. 87–100.

Kingdon, R. M., 'Catechesis in Calvin's Geneva', in J. van Engen (ed.), *Educating People of Faith*, 294–231, Grand Rapids: Eerdmans, 2004.

Kleinschmidt, H., *Charles V: The World Emperor*, Stroud: History Press, 2012.

Manetsch, S. M., *Calvin's Company of Pastors: Pastoral Care and the Emerging Reformed Church, 1536–1609*, Oxford: Oxford University Press, 2013.

————, 'Is the Reformation Over? John Calvin, Roman Catholicism, and Contemporary Ecumenical Conversations', *Themelios* 36, no. 2 (2011), pp. 185–202.

Maxwell, W. D., *An Outline of Christian Worship: Its Developments and Forms*, Oxford: Oxford University Press, 1936.

Monter, W., *Calvin's Geneva*, Eugene: Wipf and Stock, 2012.

Montgomery, J. W., 'The Celebration of the Lord's Supper According to Calvin', in J. W. Montgomery, *Christ as Centre and Circumference: Essays Theological, Cultural and Polemic*, Eugene: Wipf and Stock, 2012.

Naphy, W. G., *Calvin and the Consolidation of the Genevan Reformation*, 2nd edn, Louisville: Westminster John Knox, 2002.

Ocker, C., 'Calvin in Germany', in C. Ocker (ed.), *Politics and Reformations: Histories and Reformations*, 313–344, Leiden: Brill, 2007.

Reid, J. K. (ed.), *Calvin: Theological Treatises*, Louisville: Westminster John Knox, 2000.

Spijker, W. van't, 'Bucer's Influence on Calvin', in D. F. Wright (ed.), *Martin Bucer: Reforming Church and Community*, 32–44, Cambridge: Cambridge University Press, 1994.

Warfield, B. B., *Calvin and Augustine*, Philadelphia: P&R, 1974.

Witte, J., *From Sacrament to Contract: Marriage, Religion and Law in the Western Tradition*, 2nd edn, Louisville: Westminster John Knox, 2012.

5. SALVATION ACCOMPLISHED: HEINRICH BULLINGER ON THE GOSPEL

Martin Foord

The story of the Reformation cannot properly be told without mentioning Heinrich Bullinger (1504–75). Unfortunately, today he is still something of an unsung Reformation hero. Bullinger is too often seen as simply the consolidator of Zwingli's reform programme in Zurich. But Bruce Gordon believes Bullinger 'was of seminal importance to both the European Reformation and the development of the Reformed tradition'.[1] Why so? First, Bullinger exerted enormous influence through his networking. He was at the centre of an extensive communications system spread throughout Europe.[2] Where Calvin's extant letters number some 4,300, Bullinger's are over 12,000. He was 'one of the most widely consulted figures of the age'.[3] Second, Bullinger was theologically influential via his prolific writings. He wrote more than Luther and Calvin combined![4]

---

1. B. Gordon, 'Heinrich Bullinger', in Carter Lindberg (ed.), *The Reformation Theologians: An Introduction to Theology in the Early Modern Period* (Oxford: Blackwell, 2002), p. 170.

2. B. Gordon, *The Swiss Reformation* (Manchester: Manchester University Press, 2002), p. 348.

3. B. Gordon, 'Introduction: Architect of the Reformation', in Bruce Gordon and Emidio Campi (eds.), *Architect of the Reformation: An Introduction to Heinrich Bullinger, 1504–1575* (Grand Rapids: Baker Academic, 2004), p. 17.

4. Victor Shepherd, 'Heinrich Bullinger, Reformer (1504–1575)', *Touchstone* 23, no. 1 (2005), p. 28.

Bullinger produced commentaries on many books of the Bible. His work *On the One and Eternal Testament or Covenant of God* (1534) was the first to address the principial nature of the covenant in biblical theology. It had a remarkable impact on the Reformed tradition.[5] Bullinger's largest work of systematic theology, the *Decades* (1549–51), had a wide-ranging impact being translated into German, Dutch, French and English. It especially influenced England. In 1586 Archbishop John Whitgift decreed that all lower clergy read and be examined on Bullinger's *Decades* in his province of Canterbury.[6] Furthermore, Bullinger authored the most widely received confession amongst the sixteenth-century Reformed communities, the Second Helvetic Confession (1566). This Swiss pastor was an indispensable figure in the sixteenth-century Reformation. This chapter will examine how Bullinger's influence is stamped even on the Reformation doctrine of the gospel.

The reformation of the gospel

Whatever else the Reformation achieved, it was a revolution in the doctrine of the gospel. That is why the Reformers initially called themselves 'evangelicals' years before being named 'Protestants'.[7] 'Evangelical' indicated something about their beliefs: the gospel (*evangelium*) was central to their reading of Scripture and their theology as a whole. Given this, it is striking that so little research has been given to the Reformers' understanding of the gospel. Much ink has rightly been spilt over the Reformers' understanding of justification by faith alone and the supreme authority of Scripture alone. However, we fail to grasp Reformation theology properly without an attentiveness to the Reformation gospel.

The magisterial Reformation resulted in the formation of two traditions: Lutheran and Reformed. The Lutheran tradition arose from the influence of

---

5. See Charles S. McCoy and J. Wayne Baker, *Fountainhead of Federalism: Heinrich Bullinger and the Covenantal Tradition* (Louisville: Westminster John Knox, 1991); J. Wayne Baker, 'Heinrich Bullinger, the Covenant, and the Reformed Tradition in Retrospect', *The Sixteenth Century Journal* 29, no. 2 (1998), pp. 359–376.

6. D. MacCulloch, 'Heinrich Bullinger and the English Speaking World', in Emidio Campi and Peter Opitz (eds.), *Heinrich Bullinger, Life – Thought – Influence: Zurich, Aug. 25–29, 2004, International Congress Heinrich Bullinger (1504–1575)*, Vol. 2 (Zurich: Theologischer Verlag, 2007), p. 932.

7. D. MacCulloch, *Reformation: Europe's House Divided, 1490–1700* (London: Penguin, 2003), p. xx.

one central person: Martin Luther. On the other hand, the Reformed tradition developed from a number of key figures, such as Huldrych Zwingli (1484–1531), Martin Bucer (1491–1551), Heinrich Bullinger (1504–75), Johannes Oecolampadius (1482–1531), Wolfgang Musculus (1497–1563) and John Calvin (1509–64). The two traditions had much common theological ground and so are both rightly called evangelical or Protestant. But differences between them became important enough to ensure their official separation. By the close of the sixteenth century the Lutheran and Reformed traditions had crafted separate confessions which set their own distinct standards of doctrinal orthodoxy.

The Lutheran and Reformed confessions contained doctrines of the gospel with much in common. But there were also subtle differences. As we will see, Heinrich Bullinger played a decisive role in the Reformed confessional understanding of the gospel. However, in order to understand the nuances of his position, it needs to be compared and contrasted with the medieval Catholic and Lutheran doctrines of the gospel. To these we now turn.

The medieval Catholic gospel

The genre of systematic theology reveals something of the medieval church's understanding of the gospel. Systematic theology seeks to summarize and elucidate the principal doctrines of the entire Christian faith. The chief textbook of systematic theology in the high and late medieval era was Peter Lombard's *Four Books of Sentences.*[8] And the dominant genre of systematic theology in this same era was the commentaries that numerous theologians wrote on the Lombard's *Sentences.*[9] Peter Lombard included a brief discussion of the gospel at the close of his third book (III.40). Hence further reflection on the gospel can be found in the many *Sentences* commentaries that examine this section.

---

8. Philipp W. Rosemann, *The Story of a Great Medieval Book: Peter Lombard's Sentences*, Rethinking the Middle Ages (New York: Oxford University Press, 2007); Philipp W. Rosemann, *Peter Lombard*, Great Medieval Thinkers (Oxford: Oxford University Press, 2004); Marcia Colish, *Peter Lombard*, Studies in Intellectual History, 2 vols. (Leiden: Brill, 1994).

9. For more on the commentaries, see G. R. Evans, *Mediaeval Commentaries on the Sentences of Peter Lombard: Current Research*, Vol. 1 (Leiden: Brill, 2002); Philipp W. Rosemann (ed.), *Mediaeval Commentaries on the Sentences of Peter Lombard*, 3 vols. (Leiden: Brill, 2015), Vols. 2 and 3.

What do we discover about the gospel in the medieval *Sentences* tradition? There appears to be a common understanding of the gospel and its relationship to the law (amidst differences).[10] The gospel was seen fundamentally as the 'new law' (*lex nova*).

The gospel was 'new' in a salvation-historical sense. Medieval theology (generally) divided salvation history into three basic stages. The first era of 'natural law' was the period prior to the giving of Torah at Sinai. The second epoch of the 'old law' began with the delivery of the Torah for Israel. And the third age of the 'new law' was inaugurated with the coming of Christ.

If 'new' referred to an era of salvation history, 'law' related to administration. The category of 'law' concerned the way God's people were governed. The 'old law' arranged Israel's life. Christ gave a 'new law' as a way to govern God's new people, the church. Hence, the 'new law' contained, amongst other things, moral instruction. This was particularly seen in the Sermon on the Mount.[11] The 'new law' (or gospel) also supplied seven new sacraments, as opposed to the plethora of sacraments in the 'old law'. The seven sacraments provided grace (or spiritual power) to obey the moral teaching of the new law and so merit salvation. Thus, the medieval gospel (new law) was distinguished from the law (old law) by salvation history and content.[12]

---

10. It would probably be impossible to consult all the *Sentences* commentaries because a vast minority are available in modern critical editions; the majority exist as medieval manuscripts in variegated locations. The commentaries by the following authors that discuss *Sentences* III.40 have been consulted for this chapter: Stephen Langton, Alexander of Hales, Richard Fishacre, Albert the Great, Bonaventure, Thomas Aquinas, Robert Kilwardby, Durandus of St Porçaine, Richard of Middleton, John Duns Scotus, Peter Aquila, William de la Mare, Henry of Gorkum, Denys the Carthusian, Gabriel Biel and Jan Hus.

11. For example, Bonaventure, *Bonaventurae Doctoris Seraphici Opera Omnia*, 10 vols. (Quaracchi: Collegium S. Bonaventurae, 1882), 3:885 col. 2; Duns Scotus, *Opera Omnia* (Civitas Vaticana: Typis Polyglottis Vaticanis, 1950), 10:346.48–57; Denys the Carthusian, *Doctoris Ecstatici D. Dionysii Cartusiani Opera Omnia*, 44 vols. (Monstrolii: Typis Cartusiae S. M. de Pratis, 1896), 23:644D col. 2 – 645A col. 1.

12. For further discussion on this, see Martin Foord, '"A New Embassy": John Calvin's Gospel', in Michael Parsons (ed.), *Aspects of Reforming: Theology and Practice in Sixteenth Century Europe* (Carlisle: Paternoster, 2014), pp. 139–140.

The confessional Lutheran gospel

Martin Luther's discovery of justification by faith alone went hand in hand with a new understanding of the gospel as well as the law/gospel distinction.[13] Where the medieval understanding of law (old law) and gospel (new law) were of the same kind (they were both law), Luther came to see them as radically opposed in kind: the law commanded and the gospel promised. For Luther, the law demanded works whereas the gospel promise could only be received by faith. As Luther said in his 1535 Galatians commentary:

> For this I must consult the Gospel and listen to the Gospel, which does not teach me what I should do – for that is the proper function of the Law – but what someone else has done for me, namely, that Jesus Christ, the Son of God, has suffered and died to deliver me from sin and death. The Gospel commands me to accept and believe this, and this is what is called 'the truth of the Gospel'.[14]

And because no-one could follow the law perfectly, Luther believed its function was to drive sinners to the gospel.

But, second, where the medieval distinction between law and gospel was salvation historical (the law was confined to the OT and the gospel was confined to the NT), Luther maintained that law and gospel were found in both Testaments: 'Here we must point out that the entire Scripture of God is divided into two parts: commandments and promises.'[15] In other words, Luther's understanding of law and gospel was also hermeneutical.[16] One must be aware if the part of Scripture one was reading was law or gospel, and not confuse the two.

Controversy soon arose amongst Luther's followers over the relationship of repentance to the gospel. Did the call to repentance belong to law or gospel? Luther's close colleague Philipp Melanchthon began to teach that repentance was included in the gospel.[17] He claimed this from the second edition onwards of his influential systematic theology, the *Loci communes*:

13. Bernhard Lohse, *Martin Luther's Theology: Its Historical and Systematic Development* (Edinburgh: T&T Clark, 1999), p. 267.

14. Luther, *Lectures on Galatians (1535)*, 2:4–5, *WA* 40:168.20–26; *LW* 26:91.

15. Luther, *The Freedom of the Christian*, *WA* 7:52.24–25; *LW* 31:348.

16. R. Kolb, *Martin Luther: Confessor of the Faith*, Christian Theology in Context (Oxford: Oxford University Press, 2009), pp. 50–55.

17. It seems that Melanchthon's position developed out of the so-called Antinomian controversy with Johannes Agricola. For this controversy, see Timothy J. Wengert,

> Christ defines the gospel in the final chapter of Luke, as plainly as an artist, when he commands [his disciples] to teach 'repentance and forgiveness of sins' in his name [Luke 24:47]. Therefore, the gospel is the preaching of repentance and promise.[18]

Other thinkers such as Erasmus Sarcerius (1501–59), Johann Spangenberg (1484–1550), Victor Strigel (1524–69), Paul Crell (1531–79) and Christoph Pezel (1539–1604) followed Melanchthon.

However, another stream of thinkers, such as Matthaeus Judex (1528–64), Matthias Flacius Illyricus (1520–75) and Johann Wigand (1523–87), opposed Melanchthon's position. They argued that if the gospel called people to repentance, which was a work, then justification would not be by faith alone. Hence, it was law not gospel that demanded repentance. When Christ in Luke 24:47 told his disciples to preach 'repentance and forgiveness of sins', they read this as a preaching of *both* law (repentance) and gospel (forgiveness).

This debate was resolved for the Lutheran tradition in the *Formula of Concord* (1577). The authorized confessions of Lutheranism were collected into the *Book of Concord* (1580), of which the *Formula of Concord* was one. The official Lutheran position on the relationship of repentance and gospel was defined in Article 5 of the *Formula*. It addressed the controversy in these words:

> Whether the gospel is properly only a preaching of the grace of God, which announces to us the remission of sins, or whether it is also a preaching of repentance, rebuking the sin of unbelief, as one which is not rebuked by the Law, but only by the Gospel.[19]

The *Formula* answered the question by giving two definitions of the gospel. The first meaning of 'gospel' was the 'entire teaching of Christ'. When understood this way, the gospel is 'a proclamation of both repentance and the

---

(note 17 *cont.*) *Law and Gospel: Philip Melanchthon's Debate with John Agricola of Eisleben over Poenitentia*, Texts and Studies in Reformation and Post-Reformation Thought (Grand Rapids: Baker Academic, 1997).

18. Philip Melanchthon, *Philippi Melanchthonis Opera Quae Supersunt Omnia*, Corpus Reformatorum (Halis Saxonum: Apud C. A. Schwetschke et Filium, 1854), 21:734.

19. *The Formula of Concord* V.1, in Irene Dingel (ed.), *Die Bekenntnisschriften der Evangelisch-Lutherischen Kirche: Herausgegeben im Gedenkjahr der Augsburgischen Konfession 1930*, 13th edn (Göttingen: Vandenhoeck & Ruprecht, 2010), 790.10–16; P. Schaff, *The Creeds of Christendom*, Vol. 3, *The Evangelical Protestant Creeds*, 1876 repr. edn (Grand Rapids: Baker, 2007), p. 126.

forgiveness of sins'.[20] The *Formula* finds this usage of 'gospel' in Mark 1:15 and
Acts 20:24:

> 'The time has come,' [Jesus] said. 'The kingdom of God has come near. Repent and
> believe the good news [gospel]!' (Mark 1:15)[21]

> [21]I [Paul] have declared to both Jews and Greeks that they must turn to God in
> repentance and have faith in our Lord Jesus . . . [24]However, I consider my life worth
> nothing to me; my only aim is to finish the race and complete the task the Lord Jesus
> has given me – the task of testifying to the good news [gospel] of God's grace.
> (Acts 20:21, 24)

But the *Formula* affirms a second meaning of 'gospel' and it is the 'proper'
or 'special' (*proprie*) definition. This understanding of the gospel is 'the delightful
proclamation of the grace and favour of God, won through Christ's merit'.[22]
It conveys to law-breaking sinners what a person 'ought to believe', namely that
Jesus Christ has made satisfaction for sins and obtained forgiveness and perfect
righteousness 'without any merit of the sinner'.[23] This second understanding
of the gospel does *not* contain a call to repentance, which the *Formula* states in
uncompromising terms:

> We reject, therefore, as a false and perilous dogma, the assertion that the Gospel
> is properly a preaching of repentance, rebuking, accusing and condemning sins,
> and that it is not solely a preaching of the grace of God. For in this way the Gospel
> is transformed again into Law, the merit of Christ and the Holy Scriptures are
> obscured . . .[24]

So the theological reason why repentance is not a call of the 'proper' gospel is
because it made repentance a work the sinner must do to obtain salvation. Thus,

---

20. *The Formula of Concord* V.6, in Dingel, *Die Bekenntnisschriften*, 791.5–17.
21. All Scripture quotations in this chapter are from the NIV.
22. *The Formula of Concord* V.6, in Dingel, *Die Bekenntnisschriften*, 791.29–31; R. Kolb
    and T. Wengert (eds.), *The Confessions of the Evangelical Lutheran Church* (Minneapolis:
    Fortress, 2000), p. 500.
23. *The Formula of Concord* V.5, in Dingel, *Die Bekenntnisschriften*, 791.5–17; Schaff,
    Evangelical Protestant Creeds, p. 127.
24. *The Formula of Concord* V neg. 1, in Dingel, *Die Bekenntnisschriften*, 792.34–41; Schaff,
    Evangelical Protestant Creeds, p. 130.

the work of repentance would add to Christ's merit. Justification would not be because of Christ alone through faith alone. Hence, the 'proper' doctrine of the gospel, in the Lutheran tradition, does not call its hearers to repentance. Repentance must be a command of the law.

Bullinger and the confessional Reformed gospel

When we turn to the Reformed tradition of the sixteenth century we discover a variety of positions on the gospel. For example, Theodore Beza had similarities with the Lutheran tradition.[25] And Wolfgang Musculus believed the gospel had three basic 'parts': repentance, faith and obedience.[26] However, a group of Reformed thinkers, such as Martin Bucer, Johannes Oecolampadius, John Calvin, Zacharias Ursinus and Heinrich Bullinger, shared a similar understanding of the gospel. Heinrich Bullinger would ensure it became confessional.

The Reformed tradition did not develop one set of official confessions like the Lutheran *Book of Concord*. Rather, a variety of confessions were formally accepted by the different geographic Reformed communities. The chief confessions are shown in Table 1. The Second Helvetic Confession was also endorsed by the Reformed churches of France (1571), Hungary (1567), Poland (1571 and 1578) and Scotland (1566). Thus, it was the most widely accepted Reformed confession in the sixteenth century. Two Reformed confessions address the doctrine of the gospel. The first is the Heidelberg Catechism which contains a simple abridgement.[27] The other is Heinrich Bullinger's Second Helvetic Confession which includes a fuller description.[28] The two accounts are in agreement. We now turn to Bullinger's explanation of the gospel in the Second Helvetic Confession.

---

25. Theodore Beza, *Confessio Christinae Fidei* (Genevae: Excudebat Eustathius Vignon, 1576), pp. 56–72; Theodore Beza, *Confession de la foy chrestienne* (À Genève: Par Jacques du Pan, 1563), pp. 81–100; Theodore Beza, *The Christian Faith*, trans. James Clark (Lewes: Focus Christian Ministries Trust, 1992), pp. 40–49.

26. Wolfgang Musculus, *Loci Communes Theologiae Sacrae, Iam Recens Recogniti & Emendati* (Basileae: Ex Officina Heruagiana: per Eusebium Episcopium, 1567), pp. 373–374.

27. 'The Heidelberg Catechism', Question 19, in Schaff, *Evangelical Protestant Creeds*, p. 313.

28. If the Heidelberg Catechism is included.

Table 1: Chief confessions of Reformed communities

Name	Date	Reformed community
Gallic Confession	1559	France
Scots Confession	1560	Scotland
Belgic Confession	1561	The Lowlands
Heidelberg Catechism	1563	The Palatinate
Thirty-Nine Articles	1563	England
Second Helvetic Confession	1566	Swiss cantons, Palatinate

The Second Helvetic Confession on the gospel

Bullinger had addressed the gospel as a topic in his two earlier systematic theologies: *Decades* (1549–51) and *Summary of the Christian Religion* (1556).[29] He also presented a doctrine of the gospel in the introduction to his Matthew commentary, complete with an exposition of the word's meaning in classical Greek literature, the Hebrew Old Testament and the New Testament.[30] However, the Second Helvetic Confession represents Bullinger's mature thought.

Two meanings

The gospel is addressed in Article 13 of thirty in the Second Helvetic Confession.[31] In it, Bullinger believes there are two meanings of the gospel. The two are distinguished by salvation history. The first concerns promise, the second fulfilment.

The first meaning relates to the gospel's existence in the Old Testament era. Bullinger explained that the gospel existed in the Old Testament as 'evangelical promises'. The first evangelical promise was Genesis 3:15, 'The seed of the women will crush the serpent's head'.[32] The Reformers regularly appealed to this

---

29. Bullinger, *Decades* 4.1; Bullinger, *Summary of the Christian Religion* 6.23. The latter work was originally published in German as Heinrich Bullinger, *Summa Christenlicher Religion* (Zürych: Christoffel Froschauer, 1556). The Latin edition soon appeared as Heinrich Bullinger, *Compendium Christianae Religionis Decem Libris Comprehensum* (Tiguri: Apud Froschoverum, 1556).

30. Heinrich Bullinger, *In Sacrosanctum Iesu Christi Domini Nostri Evangelium Secundum Matthaeum Commentariorum Libri XII* (Tiguri: Apud Froschoverum, 1542), 1b–3a. Author's translation.

31. The Latin text used here is Schaff, *Evangelical Protestant Creeds*, pp. 237–306. An English translation is located in ibid., pp. 829–909.

32. Bullinger, 'The Second Helvetic Confession', 13.1, ibid., p. 260.

verse as the original gospel promise from as early as the first Reformation system of theology, Philipp Melanchthon's *Loci communes* (1521).[33] Bullinger's further examples of evangelical promises include:

> In your seed all nations will be blessed (Gen. 22:18).

> The sceptre will not be removed from Judah, until Shiloh comes (Gen. 49:10).

> The Lord will raise up a prophet from among [their] brothers (Deut. 18:18).[34]

Bullinger clarified that some Old Testament promises referred simply to temporal matters such as Israel inheriting Canaan and their victories against enemies in war.[35] However, he claimed that other Old Testament promises involved 'heavenly and eternal issues' like the forgiveness of sins and eternal life. Why does Bullinger need to make this point? Many medieval Catholic doctors held that the Old Testament promises related only to temporal matters. Thus, they concluded that the gospel was not 'literally' found in the Old Testament. These medieval theologians argued that the gospel could only be found in the Old Testament when the promises were interpreted 'spiritually' (or symbolically).[36] Hence, in the Second Helvetic Confession Bullinger seeks to clarify that the gospel indeed exists literally in the Old Testament. It is in promise form (*modus*) which is precisely what the New Testament teaches (Rom. 1:2; 1 Pet. 1:10).[37]

The second and proper meaning of the gospel, for Bullinger, focuses on fulfilment.[38] It is the message that

> God has now fulfilled what he promised from the beginning of the world,
> and has sent, indeed given, to us his only Son and in him [we have been

---

33. Philipp Melanchthon, *Loci communes* (1521), *Quid Evangelium*, in Melanchthon, *Philippi Melanchthonis Opera Quae Supersunt Omnia* (Halis Saxonum: Apud C. A. Schwetschke et Filium, 1854), 21:141.56a.17–19.

34. Bullinger, 'The Second Helvetic Confession', 13.1, in Schaff, *Evangelical Protestant Creeds*, p. 260.

35. Bullinger, 'The Second Helvetic Confession', 13.2.

36. For example, see Bonaventure, *In Tertium Librum Sententiarum* XL.ii.con, in Bonaventure, *Bonaventurae Doctoris Seraphici Opera Omnia*, 3:888–889.

37. Bullinger, 'The Second Helvetic Confession', 13.2, in Schaff, *Evangelical Protestant Creeds*, pp. 260–261.

38. Ibid., 13.3.

given] reconciliation with the Father, forgiveness of sins, all fullness and eternal life.[39]

There are several noteworthy points here. First, this second understanding of the gospel did not exist in the Old Testament. It is a *new revelation*. Bullinger states that it was 'first' preached by John the Baptist, then Christ, and afterwards by the apostles and their successors. Thus, the second meaning of the gospel speaks of something altogether new which cannot be found in the Old Testament. Second, the New Testament gospel message includes the element of *fulfilment*. It fits into a larger narrative from which it cannot be divorced. Third, the gospel is a message about salvation fully *accomplished*. In Christ's person and work is 'all fullness'. The medieval Catholic gospel did not make a distinction between salvation accomplished and applied. For Rome, human works contributed to a person's final salvation (even if they were Spirit-produced) and so were included in the gospel message. But for Bullinger, the gospel was a message of redemption accomplished only, not redemption applied. Emphasizing salvation accomplished by Christ (*solo Christo*) helped highlight that humans could not contribute to their salvation (*sola fide*). This in turn accentuated God's grace (*sola gratia*) in salvation.[40]

Given that for Bullinger the gospel was a message of fulfilment, the historical accounts by the evangelists which narrate this are fittingly named 'gospel'. He says:

> Therefore, the history described by the four evangelists, which explains how these
> things [reconciliation, forgiveness, fullness and eternal life] were done or fulfilled
> in Christ, what he taught and did, and that they who believe in him have all fullness,
> this [history] is rightly called the gospel.[41]

Moreover, Bullinger claimed that the preaching and writings of the apostles, when they convey how the Father gave the Son, in whom are 'all of life and salvation', are also 'rightly called the gospel'.[42]

---

39. Ibid.
40. Bullinger emphasizes this particularly in *Summary of the Christian Religion*
    6.18, in Bullinger, *Compendium Christianae Religionis Decem Libris Comprehensum*,
    93a.
41. Bullinger, 'The Second Helvetic Confession', 13.3, in Schaff, *Evangelical Protestant
    Creeds*, p. 261.
42. Ibid.

Bullinger finishes his article on the gospel with two points. First, the Spirit works through the preaching of the gospel in people's hearts, something the law was unable to do.[43] So the New Testament calls the ministry of the gospel simply 'the Spirit' (2 Cor. 3:6). And second, against the Roman Catholic objection that the Reformation gospel was a recent invention by the Reformers, Bullinger claims it is 'the most ancient of all in the world' because it originated in God's eternal counsel (2 Tim. 1:9–10).[44]

Repentance

Does Bullinger include the call to repentance in the gospel? Yes, in the following article (14) on repentance: 'The gospel has the doctrine of repentance joined to it.'[45] Bullinger justifies this affirmation with the much-used Luke 24:47: 'In my name must repentance and forgiveness of sins be preached to all nations.'[46] In his commentary on this verse Bullinger is clear:

> Next, in these two headings, repentance and the forgiveness of sins, is summed up or is contained the whole preaching of the Gospel, so that you will rightly define the gospel to be the preaching brought forth from heaven which announces to all humans repentance and forgiveness of sins in the name of Christ.[47]

Bullinger explicitly retains repentance in the gospel in his *Decades* and *Summary of the Christian Religion*.[48] Furthermore, early Reformed thinkers like John Calvin, Wolfgang Musculus, Pierre Viret and Zacharias Ursinus all include repentance in the gospel.[49]

---

43. Ibid., 13.4.

44. Ibid., 13.5–7, p. 262.

45. Ibid., 14.1.

46. Ibid. Author's translation.

47. Heinrich Bullinger, *In Luculentem et Ss. Evangelium D. N. Jesu Christ Secundum Lucam Commentariorum Lib. IX* (Tiguri: Apud Christ. Froschoverum, 1546), p. 146.

48. Heinrich Bullinger, *The Decades of Heinrich Bullinger: The Fifth Decade*, trans. H. I., 4 vols. (Cambridge: The Parker Society, 1852), IV.i., p. 35; Bullinger, *Summa Christenlicher Religion*, 6.18.93a–b.

49. John Calvin, *Institutes of the Christian Religion*, trans. F. L. Battles, ed. J. T. McNeill, Library of Christian Classics (London: SCM, 1961 [1559]), III.iii.1; Musculus, *Loci Communes Theologiae Sacrae, Iam Recens Recogniti & Emendati*, pp. 20, 373–374; Pierre Viret, *Instruction chrestienne en la doctrine de la Loy et de l'Evangile* (À Genève: Par Jean Rivery, 1564), 14.1, p. 67; Zacharias Ursinus, *The Commentary of Dr Zacharias Ursinus*

But how can Bullinger keep repentance in the gospel without compromising justification by faith alone? Would not repentance become a work that contributes to salvation? No, because repentance is *evidence* of justification, not a means to justification. Repentance is not an instrument of salvation, but a thankful *response* for salvation. Bullinger says: 'Similarly, the gospel preaches repentance to all who are born again ... that after grace received they should conduct themselves as true sons of God.'[50]

Bullinger is unyielding that Christ alone has accomplished the fullness of salvation and that no other human works contribute to it. However, he also believes that repentance must be included in the gospel, otherwise there is no formal connection between the gospel and a resulting Christian lifestyle. The inclusion of repentance ensures that the gospel renews lives.

Conclusions

The Lutheran and Reformed traditions both affirm in their confessions a 'proper' gospel that preaches salvation because of Christ alone by grace alone through faith alone. However, as we have seen, there are differences between the two traditions. Both the *Formula of Concord* and the Second Helvetic Confession affirm two meanings of the gospel. However, despite common ground, the meanings in each do not exactly match. The confessional Reformed gospel places greater emphasis on salvation history, of promise and then fulfilment in Christ. Moreover, a stark difference between the two traditions is the inclusion or not of repentance in the 'proper' gospel. For the Lutherans, repentance turned the gospel into law. For Bullinger, it safeguarded the transformation of Christian lives.

A celebration of the Reformation gospel

Having examined Heinrich Bullinger's doctrine of the gospel against the backdrop of medieval Catholicism and Lutheranism, it is worth reflecting on why this topic is so important.

First, the gospel can never be assumed. The old adage is critical: the first generation discovers the gospel, the second assumes it and the third loses it. One sign the gospel has become assumed in our own time is that most systematic

---

on the *Heidelberg Catechism*, trans. G. W. Williard (Columbus: Scott & Bascom, 1852), 19.1, pp. 101–102.

50. Bullinger, *Compendium Christianae Religionis Decem Libris Comprehensum*, 93b.

theologies do not contain a formal topic on the gospel itself. They may contain explanations of various parts of the gospel, such as the atonement or the resurrection. But the gospel as a theological doctrine in its own right (evangeliology) is regularly absent. This was not so in the systems of theology produced in the sixteenth century. The Reformers were right to explore the theological anatomy of gospel.

Second, too often people think the Reformers understood the gospel as simply justification by faith alone, or that justification by faith alone was the very centre of their theology.[51] The case of Bullinger proves this to be false. In the confessional Reformed tradition, the gospel focuses on 'Christ alone' accomplishing salvation in fulfilment of the Old Testament (*solo Christo*). When this message is unpacked, justification by faith alone (*sola fide*) follows naturally, itself a part of the gospel. But the gospel can be preached without mentioning justification by faith alone. 'Faith alone' serves to safeguard 'Christ alone'. 'Faith alone' clarifies that the gospel is salvation accomplished, not salvation applied.

Moreover, if the gospel focuses on salvation accomplished by Christ in fulfilment of the Old Testament, then the four Gospels themselves have a crucial significance in the life of the church. That is why the Reformers wrote commentaries on them and preached their way through them. We must eschew the common notion that the Reformers were too focused on Paul at the expense of Jesus in the Gospels.

Third, Bullinger reminds us that the gospel calls people not simply to faith but also to repentance (Acts 14:15). The Roman Catholic Church contended that 'faith alone' would lead to licentiousness. Including repentance in the gospel protects against this. But when repentance is preached without the gospel, the result is legalism. The proper place for repentance is in the gospel.

Finally, the gospel, as Bullinger said, is indeed 'glad and happy tidings' for believers.[52] It is ultimately a message about God the Father himself. Christ's accomplished work superlatively reveals the kind of love that characterizes God: grace (*sola gratia*). Such gracious love is fathomless, such that it becomes the believer's greatest treasure. And, as Jesus says, 'where your treasure is, there your heart will be also' (Matt. 6:21).

---

51. For example, 'The traditional view, fostered by the Reformers and perpetuated by generations of Protestants, is that "justification by faith" is the key to Paul's theology', Gordon D. Fee, *God's Empowering Presence: The Holy Spirit in the Letters of Paul* (Peabody: Hendrickson, 1994), p. 11.

52. Bullinger, 'Second Helvetic Confession', 13.3, in Schaff, *Evangelical Protestant Creeds*, p. 857.

Bibliography

Baker, J. Wayne, 'Heinrich Bullinger, the Covenant, and the Reformed Tradition in Retrospect', *The Sixteenth Century Journal* 29, no. 2 (1998), pp. 359–376.

Beza, Theodore, *The Christian Faith*, trans. James Clark. Lewes: Focus Christian Ministries Trust, 1992.

———, *Confessio Christinae Fidei*, Genevae: Excudebat Eustathius Vignon, 1576.

———, *Confession de la foy chrestienne*, À Genève: Par Jacques du Pan, 1563.

Bonaventure, *Bonaventurae Doctoris Seraphici Opera Omnia*, 10 vols., Quaracchi: Collegium S. Bonaventurae, 1882.

Bullinger, Heinrich, *Compendium Christianae Religionis Decem Libris Comprehensum*, Tiguri: Apud Froschoverum, 1556.

———, *The Decades of Heinrich Bullinger: The Fifth Decade*, trans. H. I., 4 vols., Vol. 4, Cambridge: The Parker Society, 1852.

———, *In Luculentem et Ss. Evangelium D. N. Jesu Christ Secundum Lucam Commentariorum Lib. IX*, Tiguri: Apud Christ. Froschoverum, 1546.

———, *In Sacrosanctum Iesu Christi Domini Nostri Evangelium Secundum Matthaeum Commentariorum Libri XII*, Tiguri: Apud Froschoverum, 1542.

———, *Summa Christenlicher Religion*, Zürych: Christoffel Froschauer, 1556.

Calvin, John, *Institutes of the Christian Religion*, trans. F. L. Battles, ed. J. T. McNeill, Library of Christian Classics, London: SCM, 1961 (1559).

Carthusian, Denys the, *Doctoris Ecstatici D. Dionysii Cartusiani Opera Omnia*, 44 vols., Monstrolii: Typis Cartusiae S. M. de Pratis, 1896.

Colish, Marcia, *Peter Lombard*, Studies in Intellectual History, 2 vols., Leiden: Brill, 1994.

Dingel, Irene (ed.), *Die Bekenntnisschriften der Evangelisch-Lutherischen Kirche: Herausgegeben im Gedenkjahr der Augsburgischen Konfession 1930*, 13th edn, Göttingen: Vandenhoeck & Ruprecht, 2010.

Evans, G. R., *Mediaeval Commentaries on the Sentences of Peter Lombard: Current Research*, Vol. 1, Leiden: Brill, 2002.

Fee, Gordon D., *God's Empowering Presence: The Holy Spirit in the Letters of Paul*, Peabody: Hendrickson, 1994.

Foord, Martin, '"A New Embassy": John Calvin's Gospel', in Michael Parsons (ed.), *Aspects of Reforming: Theology and Practice in Sixteenth Century Europe*, 138–149, Carlisle: Paternoster, 2014.

Gordon, B., 'Heinrich Bullinger', in Carter Lindberg (ed.), *The Reformation Theologians: An Introduction to Theology in the Early Modern Period*, Oxford: Blackwell, 2002.

———, 'Introduction: Architect of the Reformation', in Bruce Gordon and Emidio Campi (eds.), *Architect of the Reformation: An Introduction to Heinrich Bullinger, 1504–1575*, 17–32, Grand Rapids: Baker Academic, 2004.

———, *The Swiss Reformation*, Manchester: Manchester University Press, 2002.

Knaake, J. K. F., G. Kawerau et al., *D. Martin Luthers Werke, Kritische Gesamtausgabe: Schriften*, 66 vols., Weimar: Hermann Böhlaus Nachfolger, 1883–.

Kolb, R., *Martin Luther: Confessor of the Faith*, Christian Theology in Context, Oxford: Oxford University Press, 2009.

Kolb, R. and T. Wengert (eds.), *The Confessions of the Evangelical Lutheran Church*, Minneapolis: Fortress, 2000.

Lohse, Bernhard, *Martin Luther's Theology: Its Historical and Systematic Development*, Edinburgh: T&T Clark, 1999.

McCoy, Charles S. and J. Wayne Baker, *Fountainhead of Federalism: Heinrich Bullinger and the Covenantal Tradition*, Louisville: Westminster John Knox, 1991.

MacCulloch, D., 'Heinrich Bullinger and the English Speaking World', in Emidio Campi and Peter Opitz (eds.), *Heinrich Bullinger, Life – Thought – Influence: Zurich, Aug. 25–29, 2004, International Congress Heinrich Bullinger (1504–1575)*, Vol. 2, 891–934, Zurich: Theologischer Verlag, 2007.

———, *Reformation: Europe's House Divided, 1490–1700*, London: Penguin, 2003.

Melanchthon, Philipp, *Philippi Melanchthonis Opera Quae Supersunt Omnia*, Corpus Reformatorum, Vol. 21, Halis Saxonum: Apud C. A. Schwetschke et Filium, 1854.

Musculus, Wolfgang, *Loci Communes Theologiae Sacrae, Iam Recens Recogniti & Emendati*, Basileae: Ex Officina Heruagiana: per Eusebium Episcopium, 1567.

Pelikan, Jaroslav and Helmut T. Lehmann (eds.), *Luther's Works*, 55 vols., St Louis: Concordia; Philadelphia: Fortress Press, 1955–86.

Rosemann, Philipp W., *Peter Lombard*, Great Medieval Thinkers, Oxford: Oxford University Press, 2004.

———, *The Story of a Great Medieval Book: Peter Lombard's Sentences*, Rethinking the Middle Ages, New York: Oxford University Press, 2007.

———, (ed.), *Mediaeval Commentaries on the Sentences of Peter Lombard*, 3 vols., Leiden: Brill, 2015.

Schaff, P., *The Creeds of Christendom*, Vol. 3: *The Evangelical Protestant Creeds*, 1876 repr. edn, Grand Rapids: Baker, 2007.

Scotus, Duns, *Opera Omnia*, Civitas Vaticana: Typis Polyglottis Vaticanis, 1950.

Shepherd, Victor, 'Heinrich Bullinger, Reformer (1504–1575)', *Touchstone* 23, no. 1 (2005), pp. 28–31.

Ursinus, Zacharias, *The Commentary of Dr Zacharias Ursinus on the Heidelberg Catechism*, trans. G. W. Williard, Columbus: Scott & Bascom, 1852.

Viret, Pierre, *Instruction chrestienne en la doctrine de la Loy et de l'Evangile*, À Genève: Par Jean Rivery, 1564.

Wengert, Timothy J., *Law and Gospel: Philip Melanchthon's Debate with John Agricola of Eisleben over Poenitentia*, Texts and Studies in Reformation and Post-Reformation Thought, Grand Rapids: Baker Academic, 1997.

6. MARTIN BUCER:
THE CATHOLIC PROTESTANT

Stephen Tong

Introduction

Martin Bucer died in Cambridge on 28 February 1551 at the age of fifty-nine. He was a religious refugee, did not speak English and did not appreciate the English climate or cuisine.[1] Before coming to England, Bucer already considered himself a feeble old man. Beset with many illnesses, including chronic coughing, rheumatism, lithiasis, intestinal ailments and leg ulcers, he complained that his 'bowels are in an obstinate state'.[2] Despite these setbacks, Bucer had been Regius Professor of Divinity at Cambridge University since December 1549.[3] And in combination with Peter Martyr Vermigli, the Italian Reformer who was Regius Professor of Divinity at Oxford (1549–53), Bucer exercised a significant

---

1. H. Robinson (ed.), *Original Letters Relative to the English Reformation*, 2 vols. (Cambridge: Parker Society, 1847), 2:550–551; H. J. Selderhuis, *Marriage and Divorce in the Thought of Martin Bucer*, ET (Kirksville: Thomas Jefferson University Press at Truman State University, 1999), pp. 126–127; D. MacCulloch, *Thomas Cranmer: A Life* (New Haven/London: Yale University Press, 1996), pp. 469–471.
2. Robinson, *Original Letters*, 2:548.
3. All official communication at the two universities was conducted in Latin during this period.

influence upon the evangelical character of the Church of England during
the reign of Edward VI (1547–53).[4] Bucer's reputation should not be confined
to the British Isles, however. Although he spent most of his life as a minister
in Strasbourg, his continual correspondence allowed him to maintain close
ties with Martin Luther in Wittenberg, Ulrich Zwingli in Zurich (until his death
in 1531) and John Calvin in Geneva. Through these letters we see that Bucer
was not just abreast of the latest Protestant issues; he was intimately involved
in shaping them. Yet until recently, English-speaking scholars have viewed
Bucer not as playing a role on centre stage, but rather as a Reformer in the
wings.[5]

A few contributing factors to this academic trend must be pointed out. First,
it is possible that his being dislocated from his pastoral ministry in Strasbourg
removed Bucer from the popular mind. Also, unlike his close friend Thomas
Cranmer, Archbishop of Canterbury, who had a spectacular martyr's death,
Bucer died as an academic in an unremarkable way. After this, Lutheran influences infiltrated Strasbourg and obscured his legacy there.

It is primarily through his writing that Bucer's memory has survived. In 1577
Conrad Hubert, his secretary, published many of Bucer's works for an English
audience in a single Latin volume under the title *Martini Buceri Scripta anglicana
fere omnia*. Other Elizabethan and Stuart divines also posthumously published
some sections of Bucer's works for varying polemical, ecclesiastical and theological purposes.[6] However, these reprints never made the same impression in
England as the works of Calvin and Heinrich Bullinger, Zwingli's successor
in Zurich, who were both still alive when Elizabeth acceded to the throne in 1558.

The bulk of Bucer's writing survives in manuscript form, mainly preserved
in either the city archives of Strasbourg or the Parker Library of Corpus Christi
College, Cambridge. But even these repositories present certain practical
problems. Bucer's original manuscripts are nigh on impossible to decipher. His

---

4. For a full discussion, see C. Hopf, *Martin Bucer and the English Reformation* (Oxford:
Blackwell, 1946). See also MacCulloch, *Thomas Cranmer*; N. Scott Amos, *Bucer,
Ephesians and Biblical Humanism: The Exegete as Theologian* (Cham: Springer, 2015);
M. Greschat, *Martin Bucer: A Reformer and His Times*, ET (Louisville: Westminster,
2004), pp. 227–250.

5. D. C. Steinmetz, *Reformers in the Wings* (Grand Rapids: Baker, 1981), pp. 121–132.

6. For instance, John Milton took extracts from *De Regno Christi* and published Bucer's
Judgement Concerning Divorce (1644). Hopf, *Martin Bucer*, pp. 33–34; K. Gunther,
Reformation Unbound: Protestant Visions of Reform, 1525–1590 (Cambridge: Cambridge
University Press, 2014).

handwriting and 'Latin style is notoriously difficult and unattractive'.[7] Moreover, Bucer's prose is overly verbose and lacks the succinct punch of Luther's scatological wit. This is perhaps why very little has been translated into modern English compared with Luther, Calvin and Bullinger.[8] As a result, only a limited circle of interested scholars has bothered to access Bucer's writing. However, recent efforts have gone some way to alleviate this situation.[9]

This chapter seeks primarily to introduce Bucer to those who may never have heard of the Strasbourg Reformer. It will roughly follow the chronology of Bucer's life in order to set the context in which to consider the more salient theological issues raised by his ministry and thought. We will begin with an overview of his early influences, focusing particularly on Bucer's relationship with Luther. The bulk of this chapter will deal with the twenty-five years Bucer spent as a minster in Strasbourg. During this time he wrote extensively on the sacraments and ecclesiology, and travelled widely to pursue his goal of bringing visual unity to the church. Finally, we will consider Bucer's time in England, when he had a direct influence on the fledging evangelical movement there.

Early life and education

Bucer was born on the festival day of St Martin, 11 November 1491, in Sélestat.[10] This town was part of the former German Holy Roman Empire and is now located in the modern region of Alsace, France, west of the River Rhine and 50 km south of Strasbourg. It was a region famous for its wine; Martin came from a family of coopers. This placed the Butzers[11] at the bottom of the pecking

7. E. A. Livingston, *Oxford Dictionary of the Christian Church*, 3rd edn (Oxford: Oxford University Press, 1997), p. 246.

8. Modern editions and translations of Bucer's works appear in Latin, German, French and English. See bibliography for a full list.

9. Greschat's 1990 work stands as the definitive biography. The last English biography of Bucer was produced in 1931 by Hastings Eells. David Wright's essay, 'Martin Bucer 1491–1551: Ecumenical Theologian' (in D. Wright [ed.], *Common Places of Martin Bucer* [Appleford: Sutton Courtenay Press, 1972], pp. 15–71), also furnishes a great deal of insight. The biographical details of this chapter are largely based on Greschat's work, and supplemented by Wright and MacCulloch.

10. Greschat, *Martin Bucer*, pp. 1–20.

11. 'Butzer' is how the Reformer spelt his surname when writing in German. Modern scholars have tended to accept the Latinized version used throughout this chapter.

order in their local winegrowers' guild, and the family did not enjoy full citizenship in Sélestat. The arbitrary nature of the family income meant that young Martin grew up 'in rather pitiful economic conditions'.[12] Martin's father, Claus, relocated to Strasbourg in 1501 and was granted citizenship there in December 1508 (Martin remained in Sélestat). Very little is known about Martin's mother. According to tradition her name was Eva, and she worked as a midwife. The only certain fact is that she died before her husband, since according to the Strasbourg archives Claus Butzer was remarried by 1538 to Margaretha Windecker.

The limited finances of the Butzer family did not impede Martin's education. He was able to attend Sélestat's prestigious Latin school because it often reduced its tuition fees for poor students. Thus Martin received an excellent foundation in Latin, Greek and Aristotelian logic. His teachers were devotees of the latest intellectual and philosophical trends of late medieval/early modern humanism emanating from the French scholar Jacques Lefèvre. This early exposure to humanism had a profound impact on Martin's intellectual, moral and spiritual formation. Bucer would later translate humanism's emphasis on moral and ethical change into a spiritual pursuit founded on sound theological reasoning.

After his preliminary schooling, Martin entered the Dominican monastery at the behest of his grandfather in 1507. The Sélestat monastery had been recently reformed according to the Observant movement, and offered an avenue for social advancement. After an initial probationary year, Bucer professed the perpetually binding vows of poverty, chastity and obedience, at the age of fifteen. Bucer would later reject his theological origins, especially the wellspring of Dominican theology, Thomas Aquinas. Part of the reason was because he never abandoned his interest in humanism.[13]

On 31 January 1517, Bucer matriculated at the University of Heidelberg to study theology as a Dominican. During this time, his interest in Erasmus turned to enthralment. The Dutchman's erudite scholarship, 'aesthetically sophisticated' use of Latin and biblical focus excited Bucer's imagination.[14] The budding German theologian, now in his mid-twenties, was captivated by Erasmus's concept of 'Christian philosophy'. This vision encouraged a form of piety characterized by humility and neighbourly love as outlined in the Bible. It was a scriptural faith that eschewed any reliance on ritual or ceremonial devotion.

---

12. Greschat, *Martin Bucer*, p. 11.
13. J. Rott (ed.), *Correspondance de Martin Bucer*, 5 vols. (Strasbourg: Brill, 1979), pp. 42–58.
14. Greschat, *Martin Bucer*, p. 25.

The combination of intellectual inquiry and biblical faith was quickly becoming a hallmark of Bucer's life.

Bucer and Luther

Things changed drastically for Bucer on 26 April 1518. Luther had been invited to present his theology to the General Chapter of the Augustinians at Heidelberg by his academic mentor, Johannes von Staupitz.[15] Bucer attended, and recorded his recollections in a letter to his Sélestat friend, Beatus Rhenanus.[16] The key aspect that Bucer took away from this initial meeting was Luther's insistence on the doctrine of justification by faith alone. On top of that, Bucer discovered to his delight that Luther was in almost total agreement with Erasmus. The significant difference in Bucer's mind was that Luther was actually willing to say what he believed, whereas Erasmus merely implied. Luther agreed to meet privately with Bucer the following day for what the Dominican monk-in-training described as 'a supper rich with doctrine rather than with dainties'. The upshot was that he deemed Luther a 'real authentic theologian'.

This meeting was a turning point for Bucer. But he did not receive Luther's theology uncritically.[17] Even at this early stage, as evidenced by his correspondence with Rhenanus, Bucer and Luther held divergent views on how to treat the Old Testament law. Whereas Luther emphasized the role of the law in exposing human sinfulness, thereby underlining our inability to earn salvation, Bucer considered the law from the perspective of one who had been saved, and thus had been given the gift of the Holy Spirit.[18] With a renewed heart filled by the Spirit, the Christian is able to live in obedience to the law and fulfil its demands on the merit of Christ, in whom the Christian's only hope for salvation is founded. This synergy of gospel and law, quite distinct from Luther's thinking, reflected Bucer's guiding principle that doctrine should issue into ethics.

---

15. A. Pettegree, *Brand Luther: How an Unheralded Monk Turned His Small Town into a Center of Publishing, Made Himself the Most Famous Man in Europe – and Started the Protestant Reformation* (New York: Penguin, 2015), pp. 94–95.

16. P. Smith (ed.), *Luther's Correspondence and Other Contemporary Letters*, 2 vols. (Philadelphia: Lutheran Publication Society, 1913), pp. 81–83.

17. W. Pauck, *Heritage of the Reformation*, 2nd edn (Oxford: Oxford University Press, 1961), pp. 73–84.

18. W. P. Stephens, *The Holy Spirit in the Theology of Martin Bucer* (Cambridge: Cambridge University Press, 1970).

As Bucer's theological and intellectual convictions drew closer to Luther and Erasmian humanism, his life was increasingly under threat. At the same time as Luther was taking his stand against papal authority at the Diet of Worms (1521), those opposed to reform within the Dominican Order were setting their sights on the young academic from Sélestat. Quite aware of the danger that might befall him, Bucer sought the aid of those he knew who had influence within ecclesiastical circles. (In fact, Bucer had established a network of like-minded contacts while studying at Heidelberg by writing letters and through personal visits, perhaps in anticipation of such circumstances.) On 29 April 1521, Bucer was released from his monastic vows on the grounds of having taken them before he was of age. This was just in the nick of time, since his opponents had sent a warning to Rome in an attempt to stop Bucer leaving the Dominicans.

After leaving Heidelberg, Bucer took refuge in Ebernburg Castle, situated high above the Nahe River in modern-day Rhineland and a day's ride from Worms. Thus he entered the entourage of the imperial knight Franz von Sickingen. Other reform-minded thinkers were already safely housed in the castle, including Johannes Oecolampadius. Bucer spent the next two years closely associated with Sickingen. He travelled widely, developing secretarial and diplomatic skills in the process. Somewhere in the midst of his busy schedule Bucer found time to meet and marry Elisabeth Sibereisen, a former nun, in mid-1522 while spending six months as pastor of the town parish of Landstuhl.

In late 1522, Bucer was en route to Wittenberg via Strasbourg. The intention was to leave his new bride with his parents while he pursued a year's further study at the University of Wittenberg. The couple travelled through Wissembourg, a town in the north-eastern corner of Alsace. The town's priest, Heinrich Motherer, was already engaged in reforming the parish and was eager to enlist the aid of Bucer. He must have been very persuasive because Bucer postponed his plans for study and agreed to stay on for six months as Motherer's chaplain.

Through this ministry, Bucer's profile as a public proponent of evangelical theology quickly became conspicuous. Beginning with 1 Peter, then moving on to the Gospel of Matthew, Bucer preached every day, and twice on Sundays and holy days.[19] It was an opportunity to vent his spleen about the monastic orders:

> There isn't anything spiritual about them and even a touch of natural human decency in them . . . [they] conduct themselves as unbridled and reckless lords . . . sell the body

---

19. R. Stupperich (ed.), *Martin Bucers deutsche Schriften*, 17 vols. (Gütersloh: Gütersloher Verlagshaus, 1960), 1:69–147. Bucer compiled a compendium of his preaching agenda in a document written in Strasbourg, 1523, entitled *Summary*.

and blood of Christ and mumble or wail their way through the Psalms, without
understanding a word . . . [while] they suck the marrow out of the poor man's bones
and ravish his wife and daughters . . . all unbelief, sin, disgrace and complete doom
ensues from them.[20]

Such open defiance of Rome had its consequences. Although the town
council unofficially supported Bucer, external political pressure and changing
military circumstances throughout the empire did not help his cause. Sickingen's
forces were overcome in 1523, leaving Bucer without any real political or military
protection. On 20 May 1523, Bucer and Motherer left Wissembourg secretly
with their pregnant wives.

Growing in stature

As Martin Greschat puts it, Bucer arrived in Strasbourg in mid-May 1523 as 'a
penniless priest, excommunicated and persecuted because of his marriage and
his agitational preaching'.[21] The Alsatian city had traditionally been neither the
wealthiest nor the politically most important free city in Imperial Germany. But
with a population of about 25,000 it was almost certainly the largest. Its Latin
name, *Argentoratum*, 'the City of Silver', was a fitting allusion to Strasbourg's
increasing wealth. And by the time Bucer arrived, it had become a significant
economic and cultural centre placed at a major European crossroads between
Italy and the Rhine Valley.

The Reformation already had a foothold there via the preaching of Matthew
Zell, the pastor of the cathedral congregation, which regularly drew crowds of
up to a thousand from all social backgrounds. And it was thanks to him that
Bucer was given an opportunity to preach every day (in Zell's house). Wolfgang
Capito was another hugely influential Strasbourg theologian and churchman.
As he was a prominent aristocrat, Capito's conversion in 1523, which was accom-
panied by his marriage, taking citizenship and preaching in German, caused
quite an impression.

Bucer's preaching, at first in Latin, then soon in German, also attracted large
crowds. However, his popularity did not result in security. The city council
was wary of providing refuge for a married, excommunicated priest who had
associated with the disgraced Sickingen. Bucer was made to wait nearly eighteen

---

20. Ibid., quoted in Greschat, *Martin Bucer*, p. 43.
21. Greschat, *Martin Bucer*, p. 47.

months before it granted him citizenship on 22 September 1524.[22] By this time, Bucer had already been installed as preacher for the parish of St Aurelien in the north-western outskirts of the city. That the parish was mostly filled with small urban farmers says less about Bucer's popular appeal than it does about the hunger for gospel preaching within Strasbourg. Judging by Bucer's later work, we can speculate that this appointment was formative for the budding theologian. A continual theme in his writings was a concern for the most vulnerable in society, and he urged social leaders (pastors and secular rulers) to exercise social justice according to biblical principles in response to God's mercy shown to sinners.[23]

We do not know when Bucer first repudiated transubstantiation, but soon after his arrival in Strasbourg he entered a debate over the Lord's Supper with Conrad Treger, the prior provincial of the Augustinian order.[24] Since late medieval devotion centred on the Mass, nothing signalled the disjunction between Roman Catholicism and Protestantism more than the difference in understanding and practice of the Lord's Supper. Abstract theological argument was accompanied by practical action. Bucer simultaneously began drawing up a new liturgy, which abolished former rituals, liturgical garments and the altar.[25] Liturgical innovation was not a secondary thought for Bucer. Like Luther and Zwingli, Bucer saw the transformation of public worship as an essential expression of their theological understanding. Thus sacramental theology and practice became a shibboleth for Protestants throughout the early modern period. This, however, did not mean that all Protestants agreed.

The Anabaptist presence in Strasbourg from the early 1520s threatened to destabilize Bucer's reform programme. Although the radical movement did not present a unified bloc, Anabaptists generally distinguished themselves by denying infant baptism. Broadly speaking, Bucer appeared to share many of their theological concerns: emphasis on the Spirit, God's election and ecclesiastical discipline.[26] However, Bucer abhorred the Anabaptist streak of anarchy as well as their desire to establish spiritual communities separate from the world. He

---

22. The political situation in Strasbourg was complex. Greschat provides a clear discussion of it and its role in ecclesiastical and doctrinal reform, ibid., pp. 47–77.

23. M. Bucer, 'De Regno Christi', in W. Pauck (ed.), *Melanchthon and Bucer* (London: SCM, 1969), pp. 306–315.

24. C. Augustijn, P. Fraenkel and M. Lienhard (eds.), *Martini Buceri opera Latina*, 5 vols. (Leiden: Brill, 1982–), 1:3–58; Stupperich, *Martin Bucers deutsche Schriften*, 2:15–173.

25. Stupperich, *Martin Bucers deutsche Schriften*, 1:185–278.

26. Greschat, *Martin Bucer*, pp. 69–70; Wright, 'Ecumenical Theologian', pp. 29–32.

saw this as another form of monasticism. Bucer also detected a deficiency in their Christology, which demoted Christ's role in salvation to a mere cipher. But rather than express outright condemnation that commonly resulted in corporal punishment in Roman Catholic and Protestant centres, Bucer invited his radical opponents to debate their theology openly. Such public disputes often achieved little. But in Hesse in 1538, hundreds of Anabaptist dissenters rejoined the Church of Hesse after hearing Bucer expound the Scriptures. Bucer's methods were an inspired combination of his humanist education and theological conviction to love all people. Reasoned theological argument, it was believed, could heal the wounds of a fractured church and bring stray sheep back into the fold.

Bucer applied this attitude to the tensions within the mainstream Protestant camp. This is not the place to delve into the interesting and complex debate between Luther and Zwingli, which culminated at the Marburg Colloquy (1529).[27] It is enough to agree with Martin Greschat: Bucer was a Zwinglian in his exegetical understanding of a spiritual presence in the Lord's Supper; he could not understand why Luther placed so much emphasis on the external, physical objects.[28] Unlike Zwingli, however, Bucer was able to compromise with Luther, as we will see. The Strasbourg Reformer derived much from both Wittenberg and Zurich, but in regard to theology and churchmanship he was certainly his own man. We are unable here to give a full account of Bucer's sacramental theology, which reflected his handwriting: indecipherable to the naked eye, but hugely rewarding upon closer inspection. However, it is worthwhile pausing to consider some of the nuances in his thought.

Sacramental theology

Against Roman Catholic doctrine, Bucer contended that the Lord had instituted only two sacraments for use in the church: baptism and the Lord's Supper.[29] And as with the rest of his theology, Bucer understood these within the matrix of the Holy Spirit. The physical elements are of no value in and of themselves. It is only when the Spirit affects the believer's heart by the Word that the sacraments take on any spiritual significance. Hence the sacraments are effective only

---

27. H. A. Oberman, *Luther: Man Between God and the Devil*, trans. E. Walliser-Schwarzbart (New Haven: Yale University Press, 1989), pp. 226–245.

28. Greschat, *Martin Bucer*, p. 74.

29. He did query whether or not laying on of hands was to be considered a sacrament. See Bucer, 'De Regno Christian', pp. 239–240.

for those who possess the indwelt Spirit of God. Bucer's interpretation therefore denied the sacraments any role in salvation. Only those who are already saved benefit from baptism or communion; true sacramental participation issues only from true faith.

The sacraments, according to Bucer, should be understood as signs and seals of faith.[30] Infant baptism signifies our initial washing in Jesus' blood. Communion reminds us of our continual need for repentance as beloved sinners. Both sacraments also act as seals of faith on the heart of the believer. This is possible only because the Spirit applies the promise of redemption to the participant through faith in God's Word. This pertains equally to infants who are baptized as to adults who take the Lord's Supper. The elect are always children of grace, even before they become fully cognizant of it.

From this perspective, the very earthy experiences of washing and eating resonate with deep spiritual significance. Indeed, they are an act of grace on the part of God. They are not dependent on the quality of faith or the worthiness of the participant. For the sacraments are effective only when faith is enlivened by the Spirit and combined with the Word. Thus the Spirit enables an elect believer to receive Christ through the physical elements of water, bread and wine. To put it another way, the sacraments provide a tangible means of being incorporated into Christ as members of his body (*Corpus Christi*).

This ecclesiological dimension was key for Bucer. He argued that infant baptism incorporates one into the kingdom of heaven, and communion celebrates the spiritual unity of the church through the sharing of one loaf of bread and one common cup. In his advice to the English church, particular emphasis was placed on the regular celebration of the sacraments in the corporate context of the entire community of saints.[31] The physical gathering of God's people to witness and participate in the sacraments is important. Sacramental participation is more than a confirmation of individual faith; it is an edifying experience for the whole church.

Searching for concord

By emphasizing the role of the Spirit, Bucer stood between Wittenberg and Zurich. For him, the sacraments were more than an act of remembrance. The

---

30. Wright, *Common Places of Martin Bucer*, pp. 285–312; E. C. Whitaker (ed.), *Censura, in Martin Bucer and the Book of Common Prayer* (London: The Alcuin Club, 1974), pp. 16–80.
31. Bucer, 'De Regno Christi', pp. 225–240; Whitaker, *Censura*, pp. 38–40, 44, 82–86.

Lord's Supper could not be downgraded as merely memorial (not that Zwingli espoused this understanding either). But neither were the bread and wine the physical embodiment of Christ in either a transubstantiated (Roman Catholic) or consubstantiated (Lutheran) way. To be sure, Christ was bound to the sacraments in a sacramental way. That is to say, God the Holy Spirit is present, for Christ remains seated in glory at the right hand of the Father. Bucer's original conception of a 'real presence' was later given full liturgical expression for the Church of England in the 1552 edition of the Book of Common Prayer.

Despite holding an idiosyncratic view, Bucer was always concerned about the divergence of positions regarding the sacraments amongst fellow Reformers. For Bucer was a peace-broker at heart. This was another way in which the Strasbourg Reformer stood apart from the often cantankerous and uncompromising Luther as well as other belligerent Protestants from Switzerland. Bucer firmly believed that a full reformation of the visible church, that is, a defeat of Roman Catholic error, would only occur if all Bible-believing Protestants presented a united front. Hence he continually sought for Protestant unity, especially on the delicate issue of the sacraments.

Achieving this goal entailed a willingness to accommodate the weaker brother. The visible body of Christ can abide with imperfect understandings about the sacraments as long as they 'do not overturn a child-like faith in God'.[32] Bucer typically justified this by appealing to the Spirit. The elect are unified by a common fellowship in the Spirit, who grants salvation. The Spirit also works to sanctify the believer, but the completion of this work comes at a different speed for each person. So until full spiritual perfection is obtained by all on the Final Day, external differences will persist and need to be tolerated.

An opportunity for Protestant unity presented itself in the mid-1530s. Luther had invited south German theologians to Eisenach to discuss the delicate issue of the Lord's Supper.[33] But owing to his ill-health, the meeting was moved to Luther's house in Wittenberg. Going into these discussions, which resulted in the Wittenberg Concord (1536), Bucer's reputation amongst both the Lutherans and the Swiss was not good. He had repeatedly tried to synthesize the sacramental views of Luther and Zwingli to no avail since the 1520s.

It is a testament to Bucer's quality as a statesman, and to his willingness to compromise where possible, that the Wittenberg Concord was agreed upon. From Bucer's perspective, the outcome was a positive one. He had conceded

---

32. Stupperich, *Martin Bucers deutsche Schriften*, 4:4. Quoted in Greschat, *Martin Bucer*, p. 75.

33. Greschat, *Martin Bucer*, pp. 132–142.

to Luther that participants receive more than the physical objects of bread and wine. But he stood his ground by insisting that Christ is present only in a spiritual sense. Thus the bread and wine bind the believer to Christ in a 'sacramental' way. The most contentious issue between Luther and Bucer was the question of who received Christ in the sacraments. Luther's understanding was that since Christ was embodied in the consecrated bread and wine, even unbelievers – the unrighteous (*impii*) – eat the body of Christ. Against this, Bucer insisted that because the Spirit lived only in the elect, Christ could be received only by the righteous – who were in fact unworthy (*indigni*) – during sacramental participation (including infant baptism). Of course it is not our responsibility to discern who is or is not elect. That is the role of the Spirit, who alone knows our hearts.

Despite finding common ground with Luther, Bucer struggled to convince others of the theological integrity of this document. Although he managed to obtain the signatures of his Strasbourg colleagues, the Concord was not accepted in other southern German towns, and was roundly rejected in Switzerland.

Another opportunity for a Protestant consensus on sacramental theology appeared once Bucer was in England. In 1549, Calvin composed the *Consensus Tigurinus*, or Zurich Consensus. The document contained twenty-six articles expounding the Reformed view of the Lord's Supper. Its theology was acceptable to Bullinger. Thus the Reformed churches finally had a formalized agreement on the Lord's Supper that was distinct from both Lutheranism and Roman Catholicism. Bucer's influence on its formulation is clear. The *Consensus* emphasized the role of the Spirit in combination with the Word; that only the elect can access the spiritual benefits of the Lord's Supper; and that we are to look beyond the physical to the concrete promises of Scripture as signified by communion. In essence, Calvin stated what Bucer had been arguing for some time: the Lord's Supper is a principle means of leading us to Christ by faith.

Ecclesiology

Theology was not an abstract way of thinking for the Strasbourg Reformer. As Bucer's sacramental theology demonstrated, theology had a practical bearing on the operations of the visible church. At all times, theology needed to edify the church. Bucer's ecclesiology therefore framed the physical activities of Christians within the limits of scriptural authority. From this, he derived a definition of the church that was commonly held among sixteenth-century Reformers. The two key markers of the 'True Church' were faithful preaching and a godly administration of the sacraments. Bucer added a third mark, discipline, which was not universally endorsed as necessary for the True Church to exist. These three marks were designated as Word ministries, and were the responsibility of ordained ministers.

Those who exercised an official Word ministry were answerable to God for the salvation of their congregations. When ordained ministry was viewed through such an eternal perspective, it was natural for Bucer to endorse discipline as a key marker of the church. At its most harsh, ecclesiastical discipline excluded someone from taking communion. It effectively meant that the recalcitrant was no longer a member of Christ's body and could not participate in the spiritual life of the church. Hence it was only to be enforced on those who obstinately refused to repent from serious and habitual sin, or in cases where reconciliation within the congregation was not forthcoming. Thus an essential task of the pastor is continually to call for repentance, so that the body of Christ is not continually harmed. Again, Bucer's influence on the 1552 Prayer Book can be detected when one considers the prefatory rubrics to the communion service.

Bucer's mature ecclesiology was expressed in his 1536 work *The True Care of Souls*.[34] This great pastoral treatise revealed the inherent tension within evangelical ecclesiology regarding the visible embodiment of the invisible, spiritual fellowship of believers. In *The True Care of Souls*, Bucer defined the church as an invisible body of believers, elected by God and united by the Holy Spirit. The Spirit's role is essential to the creation of the church, since it is only by the Spirit's power that one can understand Scripture and thus come to faith in Jesus (in itself a gift of the Spirit). However, Bucer also understood that while the church is truly spiritual in nature, it also has a temporal manifestation.

One goal of Bucer's ecclesiology, therefore, was to give the spiritual church a recognizable form. This meant having a structure that enabled the Word ministries to prosper. He was content to continue the threefold ecclesiastical structure inherited from Roman Catholicism, but he reinvested the offices of bishop, pastor and elder with a renewed scriptural warrant for the care of souls. The terminology of 'shepherd' and 'flock' was constantly invoked. He implored ministers to seek the 'lost sheep' through unashamed evangelism. After all, Jesus had promised that the elect would recognize his voice.[35] Similarly, ministers were to do everything in their power to rescue those who had fallen away, the stray sheep. Maintaining discipline under the authority of God's Word was a further

---

34. M. Bucer, *Concerning the True Care of Souls* (Edinburgh: Banner of Truth, 2009 [1536]).

35. Ibid., pp. 75–90; cf. John 10.

key in protecting the flock from wolves and providing an environment in which to flourish.

Bucer also endorsed the responsibility of secular leaders in helping to establish the church and promote the gospel. Ideally the state should act to protect and promote the gospel, while Word ministries remain the sole charge of ordained men. Since God gave all rulers their authority, submitting to them was another way of upholding the created order that reflected God's sovereignty. Hence, the visible church should cooperate with the state wherever possible. In doing so, the church obeys God's commandments while simultaneously witnessing to God's love for sinners.

These ecclesiological principles were displayed throughout Bucer's career. His first treatise, *That No One Should Live for Himself* (1523), cast a vision of God's kingdom as 'an earthly community of love'.[36] His final masterpiece echoed and amplified this concept. *De Regno Christi* (1551) was a gift for the English king Edward VI.[37] It provided him with a comprehensive ecclesiological blueprint to implement throughout his realms to the glory of God and for the benefit of his subjects. The godly magistrate was tasked with the responsibility of making Christ-like love normative for his society, for Bucer argued that faith is made complete only when the Spirit-filled believer acts in love to worship God and serve his or her neighbour.

Marriage was conceived as a wonderful reflection of this principle. Curbing sexual immorality was only one aspect of Christian marriage for Bucer. The greater purpose was to provide a social context in which to mirror God's affection. Thus he encouraged all eligible people to marry if possible – including clergy, which flew in the face of centuries of Roman Catholic dogma.

Paradoxically, Bucer used the standard of reciprocal love to propose radical ideas about divorce.[38] He wrote, '[t]here is no true marriage without a true assent of hearts between those who make the agreement'.[39] If the ideal of mutual love was not being met, it was permissible to file for divorce. As perplexing as this may be for some modern evangelicals, Bucer's intention was to eliminate sin. He theorized that a husband sinned against his wife if he did not love her fully by putting her needs before his own. No woman should be denied the

---

36. Stupperich, *Martin Bucers deutsche Schriften*, 1:50. Quoted in Wright, 'Ecumenical Theologian', p. 21.
37. Bucer, 'De Regno Christi'.
38. Wright, *Common Places of Martin Bucer*, pp. 403–428; Bucer, 'De Regno Christi', pp. 315–328.
39. Bucer, 'De Regno Christi', p. 325.

opportunity to enter and enjoy a 'true' marriage. Therefore divorce was permissible in some cases. It might be helpful to remember that Bucer lived in a time when concubines and mistresses were an unofficial part of life for both secular and ecclesiastical leaders (in the Roman Catholic Church).

Be that as it may, Bucer's views on marriage and divorce led to awkward situations. In 1538, he gave confidential advice to Philip, the Landgrave of Hesse, regarding his desire to take a second wife and form a bigamous marriage. Philip received it as positive affirmation, even though Bucer did not explicitly endorse this course of action (Luther and Melanchthon had given similar counsel).[40] When this became public in the early 1540s, Bucer's reputation took a significant blow along with the Protestant cause in Germany. In the meantime, however, Bucer continued to strive towards the goal of bringing visual unity to the church.

Ecumenical Reformer

Bucer believed in the catholic church – that is, in the universal fellowship of believers referred to by the Apostles' Creed. This doctrine lay behind his efforts in seeking agreement across the confessional divides of early modern Europe. And he was willing to travel great distances to make this happen. It has been estimated that he covered 12,000 km on horseback across paths that can hardly be described as roads between 1534 and 1539.[41] This was no easy feat; one did not travel for pleasure in early modern Europe. Having a reputation as an evangelical only increased the risk when travelling through Roman Catholic territories. In comparison, Bullinger never left Zurich; Melanchthon was a very cautious traveller; and Luther's movements were heavily restricted.

We have already noted Bucer's ecumenical desires in relation to Luther. More controversially, Bucer entered into dialogue with Roman Catholics between 1539 and 1541 in an attempt to establish a national church council for Germany.[42] Bucer attended colloquies at Leipzig (1538–9), Frankfurt (1539), Hagenau (1540), Worms (1540) and Regensberg (1541), often arriving in disguise. The Strasbourg Reformer was perhaps overly naïve in his attempts to bring together a national concord. Very limited doctrinal agreement was ever achieved

---

40. Oberman, *Luther*, pp. 284–289.

41. Greschat, *Martin Bucer*, pp. 129–132, at 131.

42. D. Wright (ed.), *Martin Bucer: Reforming Church and Community* (Cambridge: Cambridge University Press, 1994), pp. 107–121.

throughout this series of discussions, the major sticking points being the sacraments, papal authority and justification by faith.

Having failed at Regensberg, Bucer returned to a plague-stricken Strasbourg. Just about every home lost a family member at this time. The Bucer household lost nine: Martin's wife, Elisabeth; three children; two infant daughters; and three domestic servants.[43] As was the custom, he quickly remarried. His second wife, Wibrandis, was the widow of Wolfgang Capito, who had also fallen victim to the plague in 1541. Incidentally, this was Wibrandis's fourth marriage to a Reformer, and she outlived them all.

Despite his failure, Bucer's reform-minded ecumenical efforts had not gone unnoticed. In 1542 the Archbishop of Cologne, Hermann von Wied, invited Bucer (and Melanchthon) to assist him in reforming that city. Hermann's reformation ultimately amounted to nothing. He was excommunicated by Pope Paul III and died a Lutheran in 1552. The one concrete result was to produce a new Protestant liturgy. The *Consultatio* was a collaborative effort between Melanchthon and Bucer, who both took inspiration from other Reformed rites. Bucer had the crucial role of composing both the baptismal and communion services. The *Consultatio* shared the same fate as the Cologne reformation. It had been printed only for private use and was never given official backing by the city authorities. It did, however, have a life outside Germany. The liturgy was published in England in 1545 (Latin), 1547 and 1548 (English) as *A Simple and Religious Consultation*. Cranmer made extensive use of it when drawing up the original Book of Common Prayer (1549). Thus Bucer's influence on the English church was pronounced even before he set foot there.

However, not all Reformers were enamoured of Bucer's conciliatory attitude. For one, it provoked the ire of Bullinger, who wrote numerous letters decrying Bucer's 'union efforts'.[44] Bucer's negative reputation within Zurich circles followed him to England.[45] Of particular concern was the apparent theological flexibility displayed by the Strasbourg Reformer. It was a valid criticism from an outsider's perspective. Bucer's sacramental theology did undergo subtle shifts through time as his relationship with Wittenberg waxed and waned. What Bullinger and others may not have realized was that Bucer's principle of neighbourly love, as based on the standard of Christ, determined his approach in all matters of theological discussion. This enabled the Strasbourg Reformer to realize points of similarity with his opponents and broker compromise where possible. But it never came

---

43. Greschat, *Martin Bucer*, pp. 201–202.

44. Pauck, *Heritage*, p. 95.

45. Robinson, *Original Letters*, 1:37–38; 2:650–651, 678–679; Hopf, *Martin Bucer*, pp. 12–13.

with total concession. In all his ecumenical dealings, Bucer never surrendered allegiance to the church's foundational doctrine of justification by faith alone.

Exile

In April 1549, Bucer was forced to travel once more. The political and military victory of Charles V over the Schmalkaldic League (the politico-military forces of the Protestant princes) in 1548 was decisive. The peace imposed upon the German Empire, known as the Augsburg Interim, was unacceptable for evangelicals like Bucer. In theory, Protestants were given the freedom to worship according to their conscience. In reality, this Roman peace was unpalatable for convinced evangelicals. The city council manoeuvred against Bucer to minimalize the continuing presence of the Reformation. In the end, Bucer was cast out from Strasbourg. After twenty-five years of ministry, he sneaked away under the cover of darkness with his dear friend Paul Fagius, who was appointed Hebrew lecturer at Cambridge later that year.

What can be said of Bucer's failed attempts to implement his own ecclesiological ideas?

It has been argued elsewhere that Calvin managed to realize Bucer's ecclesiological vision more fully in Geneva.[46] Calvin had found refuge in Strasbourg between 1538 and 1541. This was a formative and fruitful time for the younger Reformer. The second, and much expanded, edition of his *Institutes* was published in 1539. And he accompanied Bucer to Hagenau in 1540 and Regensberg in 1541. Of course, Calvin was an independent and original theologian, but one can trace much of his thinking back to Bucer. It is not for nothing that Calvin has been called a 'Bucerian'.[47]

We should also turn to England under Edward VI to see how Bucer's theology was received.

Bucer in England

It was no small decision for Bucer to leave Strasbourg and make the arduous journey to England. He was old, stricken by various ailments and had to leave

---

46. Pauck, *Heritage*, pp. 64–69, 85–100; B. Gordon, *Calvin* (New Haven: Yale University Press, 2009), pp. 82–102.

47. Wright, 'Ecumenical Theologian', p. 17.

behind his wife and family. Twelve days later (18 April) the two refugees, Bucer and Fagius, arrived to a warm welcome and the personal hospitality of the Archbishop of Canterbury. They stayed with Cranmer for six months at Lambeth Palace. The Englishman was delighted finally to meet the Alsatian face to face, having shared correspondence with him over the past eighteen years. Moreover, the significance of Cranmer's plans to host a General Council of Protestant theologians to counter the Council of Trent (1545–63) would not have been lost on the very model of an ecumenical Reformer.[48]

Bucer's impact was immediate. A most ambitious undertaking was a collaborative project between Fagius, Bucer and Cranmer: a new Bible translation with commentary. The project soon fell by the wayside, however, partly due to Fagius's death in mid-November 1549.[49] Although Cranmer was relatively new to translation work, such an endeavour was bread and butter for the two Germans. Bucer's formidable abilities as an exegete were well founded, with his having published a myriad of commentaries on Old and New Testament books in the 1520s and 1530s.[50] His mastery of both Greek and Hebrew can be attributed to his early education. Within a year of being in England, Bucer was passing this on to a new generation of students at Cambridge. His lectures there often drew capacity audiences. And Bucer's presence in the university left a deep impression on the hearts and minds of many who would later effect evangelical reform in the English church, two of the more prominent figures being the future Archbishops of Canterbury Matthew Parker and Edmund Grindal.[51]

The greatest collaboration between Bucer and Cranmer, however, was in the area of liturgical reform. Compulsory use of the Book of Common Prayer was officially set from Whitsunday, 9 June 1549, but both men knew that this was only one step towards attaining a full reformation in England. Bucer's treatise on ordination, *De ordinatione legitima*, written at Lambeth, formed the basis for

---

48. MacCulloch, *Cranmer*, pp. 392–395.

49. The surviving fragments of this project are known as the 'Croydon Commentary' in MS 104, Corpus Christi College, Cambridge. A modern edition is H. Vogt (ed.), *Martin Bucer und Thomas Cranmer: Annotationes in octo priora capita evangelii secundum Matthaeum, Corydon 1549* (Frankfurt: Athenäum Verlag, 1972). See also A. Null, *Thomas Cranmer's Doctrine of Repentance: Renewing the Power to Love* (Oxford: Oxford University Press, 2000).

50. Amos, *Exegete as Theologian*; Greschat, *Martin Bucer*, pp. 81–83.

51. P. Collinson, 'The Reformer and the Archbishop: Martin Bucer and an English Bucerian', *Journal of Religious History* 6, no. 4 (1971).

the 1550 Ordinal.[52] Cranmer's adaptation developed Bucer's ideas for the English context and was subsequently inserted into the second Prayer Book of 1552. This, too, was a by-product of Bucer's influence.

In 1550, both Bucer and Peter Martyr were asked to provide their opinion on the first edition of the Prayer Book. Martyr's notes have not survived, but Bucer's are now known as the *Censura*. Bucer's detailed analysis of the entire liturgy focused attention on the Lord's Supper. It was clear that he wanted to help create a more robustly evangelical liturgy. He criticized the use of the Homilies, demanding that better, more authentic preaching of the gospel should take place instead of merely reading out a standardized text, even if these sermons were theologically sound. Although Cranmer did not incorporate Bucer's comments wholesale, the second edition of the Book of Common Prayer – the most conspicuously evangelical liturgy the Church of England would ever see – effectively sealed the coffin of official Roman Catholic worship in England during the life of Edward VI.

Bucer never saw his proposals for reform as outlined in both *De Regno Christi* or the *Censura* come to fruition. He was already old and feeble before taking up his post at Cambridge, and the king's gift of an Alsatian tiled stove to warm his house in Trinity College, where the Grand Court stands today, did little to stave off the inevitable. The news of Bucer's death was attended by a large out-pouring of grief. A crowd of 3,000 attended his funeral, including the university dignitaries, town mayor and other civil representatives.[53] The king himself made an entry in his personal journal noting these events.[54] Bucer had clearly won a reputation as a leading evangelical scholar and Reformer. This was ironically consolidated during the next reign.

In 1556, the Roman Catholic monarch of England, Queen Mary (1553–58), exhumed Bucer's remains from Great St Mary's Church, located in the centre of Cambridge. His bones were chained to a stake in the town marketplace and burnt along with any available works of the German theologian.[55] It was a symbolic act of ecclesiastical retribution and excommunication. Though it was not just a victory for Roman Catholics in England; for, as we have seen, Bucer was an international figure.

---

52. Whitaker, *Censura*, pp. 176–183.

53. Hopf, *Martin Bucer*, pp. 28–31. The estimated population size of Cambridge in 1550 was 25,000.

54. W. K. Jordan, *The Chronicle and Political Papers of King Edward VI* (New York: Cornell University Press, 1966), pp. 53–54.

55. The remains of Paul Fagius were also subjected to this treatment.

Queen Elizabeth I overturned the unceremonious treatment of Bucer's remains by a formal act of rehabilitation on 22 July 1560. Visitors to Great St Mary's can still view a brass plaque where his original grave lay that commemorates Bucer's life and ministry.

Conclusion

John Bradford, one of Bucer's Cambridge disciples, was awaiting his martyrdom in 1555 when he gave this advice to his alma mater: 'Remember the readings and preachings of God's prophet and true preacher, Martin Bucer.'[56] Considering the Alsatian's widespread impact on the evangelical movement of Germany and England, it is somewhat surprising that Bradford's advice has not been heeded in the modern church. For Bucer's impact continues to be felt, indirectly perhaps, but felt nonetheless. Those who subscribe to an evangelical faith that broadly accords with Calvin's theology, or to the historic and orthodox Anglican formularies established by Cranmer, are indebted to the Strasbourg Reformer. It is on this basis that we should remember Bucer, a true catholic Protestant.

Bibliography

Amos, N. Scott, *Bucer, Ephesians and Biblical Humanism: The Exegete as Theologian*, Cham: Springer, 2015.

Augustijn, C., P. Fraenkel and M. Lienhard (eds.), *Martini Buceri opera Latina*, 5 vols., Leiden: Brill, 1982–.

Bucer, M., *Concerning the True Care of Souls*, Edinburgh: Banner of Truth, 2009 (1536).

———, 'De Regno Christi', in W. Pauck (ed.), *Melanchthon and Bucer*, London: SCM, 1969.

Collinson, P., 'The Reformer and the Archbishop: Martin Bucer and an English Bucerian', *Journal of Religious History* 6, no. 4 (1971), pp. 305–330.

Gordon, B., *Calvin*, New Haven: Yale University Press, 2009.

Greschat, M., *Martin Bucer: A Reformer and His Times*, ET, Louisville: Westminster, 2004.

Gunther, K., *Reformation Unbound: Protestant Visions of Reform, 1525–1590*, Cambridge: Cambridge University Press, 2014.

Hopf, C., *Martin Bucer and the English Reformation*, Oxford: Blackwell, 1946.

---

56. A. Townsend (ed.), *Writings and Remains of John Bradford* (Cambridge: Parker Society, 1848), p. 445.

Jordan, W. K., *The Chronicle and Political Papers of King Edward VI*, New York: Cornell University Press, 1966.

Livingston, E. A., *Oxford Dictionary of the Christian Church*, 3rd edn, Oxford: Oxford University Press, 1997.

MacCulloch, D., *Thomas Cranmer: A Life*, New Haven/London: Yale University Press, 1996.

Null, A., *Thomas Cranmer's Doctrine of Repentance: Renewing the Power to Love*, Oxford: Oxford University Press, 2000.

Oberman, H. A., *Luther: Man between God and the Devil*, trans. E. Walliser-Schwarzbart, New Haven: Yale University Press, 1989.

Pauck, W., *Heritage of the Reformation*, 2nd edn, Oxford: Oxford University Press, 1961.

Pettegree, A., *Brand Luther: How an Unheralded Monk Turned His Small Town into a Center of Publishing, Made Himself the Most Famous Man in Europe – and Started the Protestant Reformation*, New York: Penguin, 2015.

Robinson, H. (ed.), *Original Letters Relative to the English Reformation*, 2 vols., Cambridge: Parker Society, 1847.

Rott, J. (ed.), *Correspondance de Martin Bucer*, 5 vols., Strasbourg: Brill, 1979.

Selderhuis, H. J., *Marriage and Divorce in the Thought of Martin Bucer*, ET, Kirksville: Thomas Jefferson University Press at Truman State University, 1999.

Smith, P. (ed.), *Luther's Correspondence and Other Contemporary Letters*, 2 vols., Philadelphia: Lutheran Publication Society, 1913.

Steinmetz, D. C., *Reformers in the Wings*, Grand Rapids: Baker, 1981.

Stephens, W. P., *The Holy Spirit in the Theology of Martin Bucer*, Cambridge: Cambridge University Press, 1970.

Stupperich, R. (ed.), *Martin Bucers deutsche Schriften*, 17 vols., Gütersloh: Gütersloher Verlagshaus, 1960.

Townsend, A. (ed.), *Writings and Remains of John Bradford*, Cambridge: Parker Society, 1848.

Vogt, H. (ed.), *Martin Bucer und Thomas Cranmer: Annotationes in octo priora capita evangelii secundum Matthaeum, Corydon 1549*, Frankfurt: Athenäum Verlag, 1972.

Whitaker, E. C. (ed.), *Censura, in Martin Bucer and the Book of Common Prayer*, London: The Alcuin Club, 1974.

Wright, D., 'Martin Bucer 1491–1551: Ecumenical Theologian', in D. Wright (ed.), *Common Places of Martin Bucer*, 15–71, Appleford: Sutton Courtenay Press, 1972.

Wright, D. (ed.), *Common Places of Martin Bucer*, Appleford: Sutton Courtenay Press, 1972.

———, *Martin Bucer: Reforming Church and Community*, Cambridge: Cambridge University Press, 1994.

7. THOMAS CRANMER:
THE REFORMATION IN LITURGY

Tim Patrick

Introduction

Thomas Cranmer, Archbishop of Canterbury under Henry VIII, Edward VI and Mary I, was the central ecclesiastical figure of the English Magisterial Reformation. Working closely with the kings, Henry's vicegerent Thomas Cromwell, and other English and European Protestants, he oversaw a thorough reshaping of English theology and church life that in some ways paralleled, and in others overlapped, the developments on the Continent. Cranmer's planned reforms were near comprehensive; he drove projects aimed at renewing everything from the Canon Law to the Articles of Religion, and from the accessibility of vernacular Bibles to the weekly teaching from parish churches. However, he is perhaps best known for his revision of the Church's liturgies and creation of the Book of Common Prayer (BCP).[1]

The various merits of the BCP are well known and oft repeated, and among the most lauded is the fact that, since its second edition of 1552, it has provided a great continuity with ancient liturgical traditions, while at the same time

---

1. Where 'Church' is capitalized, the reference is particularly to the Church of England or the Anglican Church. When it is not, it refers to either the local church or the church universal, the distinction being clear from context.

unashamedly communicating an unambiguously Protestant theology. With his book, Cranmer masterfully engineered some unprecedented movements in the underlying doctrine of the realms he served, while at the same time controlling the surface disturbances to weekly corporate worship such that it was not entirely dislocated from the past, but remained familiar in many ways. As much as all this is important and true, to emphasize only this aspect of Cranmer's reform of the liturgy would actually be to miss a main focus of the work, and one of the enduring legacies of the BCP.

Cranmer's reasons for reforming the liturgy

The most direct way to come to an understanding of Cranmer's primary purposes and achievements in the BCP is to consider the 'Preface' that he prepared for it in 1549, which remained unchanged through to the Prayer Book's final 1662 version – although there it is presented as an essay entitled 'Concerning the Service of the Church'.[2] The 'Preface' runs to 1,000 words and can helpfully be thought of as having two roughly equal and complementary parts, the first outlining some of the problems that Cranmer saw in England's late medieval Catholic worship, and the second explaining how the BCP addresses them.

Three issues were identified in the first half, and there was, in fact, one more flagged in the second half. One problem was the unintelligibility of the divine service when conducted in Latin, a practice that directly contradicted Paul's requirements for Christian gatherings (in 1 Cor. 14). The simple solution provided by Cranmer was to have a service book in the vernacular, something quite consistent with the Protestant priority of furnishing the people with Bibles translated into their own tongue. Another problem was the set of overly complicated rules that made preparing a service unnecessarily laborious for the clergy. Cranmer famously captured the issue by saying that 'many times there was more business to find out what should be read, than to read it when it was found out'.[3] This was remedied by the provision of a comprehensive BCP that supplied all that the clergy needed for the regular and pastoral services of the Church, apart from the Bible, laid out straightforwardly so that it was

---

2. J. Ketley, *The Two Liturgies, AD 1549 and AD 1552: With Other Documents Set Forth by Authority in the Reign of King Edward VI* (Cambridge: Cambridge University Press, 1844), pp. 17–19.

3. Ibid., p. 18.

very simple to use. Savings in costs to each parish – which would normally be required to provide its own liturgical resources – was also noted as an additional benefit of this two-book-only system. A third issue was the great diversity of service orders across the realm, with numerous variations arising from places like Salisbury, Hereford, Bangor, York and Lincoln. Although it is not clear that this was a pressing concern of the local peoples, it was certainly an obstacle to the uniform imposition of reform throughout the realms: from the passing of the first Act of Uniformity in 1549, every parish under the supreme headship of the king was required to use the BCP, which had been based on the Salisbury liturgy.[4]

While all three of these matters were well addressed by the new BCP, it was another problem that opened and dominated the 'Preface': the abandon-ment of the ancient tradition of reading through the whole Bible once each year in public worship. According to Cranmer, the intention of this disused practice was that the clergy should 'be stirred up to godliness themselves, and be more able also to exhort others by wholesome doctrine, and to con-fute them that were adversaries to the truth'.[5] However, he went on to lament that

> these many years passed, this godly and decent order of the ancient fathers hath bee
> so altered, broken, and neglected, by planting in uncertain stories, Legends, Responds,
> Verses, vain repetitions, Commemorations, and Synodals, that commonly when any
> book of the Bible was begun, before three or four chapters were read out, all the rest
> were unread.[6]

The reality of the situation of which Cranmer despaired can easily be demon-strated by considering some of the popular medieval lectionaries and their prescribed readings. Prior to the Reformation, two types of lectionaries were commonly used in English churches: the Temporale and the Sanctorale.[7] The Temporale divided the year into five liturgical seasons – Christmas, Epiphany, Easter, Ascension and Whitsunday – and it prescribed the scriptural text for each Sunday, mostly drawing from the Gospels. For all the strengths that this annual

---

4. 2–3 Edward VI c. 1, reproduced in G. L. Bray (ed.), *Documents of the English Reformation* (Cambridge: James Clarke & Co., 1994), pp. 266–271.

5. Ketley, *Two Liturgies*, p. 17.

6. Ibid.

7. H. L. Spencer, *English Preaching in the Late Middle Ages* (Oxford: Clarendon, 1993), p. 24.

cycle brought in terms of repeatedly focusing congregations on the advent, death and resurrection of Christ, its weakness was that it would recycle the same texts of Scripture year after year, while at the same time never directing the church to any others. Certainly the ancient tradition of reading the whole Bible in a year could not be maintained by following the Temporale alone.

The Sanctorale was also an annualized calendar, but its purpose was to list all of the Church's Saints' Days and Red Letter Days. What was particularly striking about the Sanctorale was how crowded it could be. For example, in the version printed as 'The Kalender' in the Matthew's Bible of 1537, around 90% of all the days in the year were commemorative days.[8] The problem with this was that on those days (or the adjacent Sunday when the saints of the week could also be celebrated), the set readings tended not to come from the Bible, but from one of the popular medieval hagiographies, such as William Caxton's *Legenda Aurea* or John Mirk's *Liber Festivalis*. Consequently, the cult of the saints that had infused much of the life of the medieval church brought a significant disruption to the continuous public reading of the Bible.[9] It was in this context that Cranmer's first purpose for the BCP was to establish it as the *channel through which the whole Scripture could be delivered to the gathered people of God, essentially uninterrupted*. To put it another way, Cranmer did not view his work on the reform of the liturgy as an end in itself, but rather as the means by which the entirety of the Bible would be returned to the centre of the public life of the Church.

Of course, this intention marries perfectly with the English Protestants' long efforts to have native-language Bibles brought to the people. Although William Tyndale never lived to see his translations of the Scriptures accepted by the crown, it was only one year after his death that the aforementioned Matthew's Bible was given royal privilege. Prepared by John Rogers, who would become the first of the Protestant martyrs under 'Bloody' Mary, Matthew's Bible was, in fact, the earliest compilation of all of Tyndale's translations, completed by the addition of the Psalter, Writings, Prophets and Apocrypha from Miles Coverdale's Bible of 1535.[10] Matthew's Bible proved too confrontational in its paratextual materials to receive a long circulation, but two years after its publication, the Great Bible – the text of which also owed a great deal to Tyndale –

---

8. *Matthew's Bible, 1537 Edition* (Peabody: Hendrickson, 2009), *ii^r–*iii^v.

9. See P. Brown, *The Cult of the Saints: Its Rise and Function in Latin Christianity* (London: SCM, 1981).

10. D. Daniell, *The Bible in English* (New Haven: Yale University Press, 2003), pp. 157, 190–197.

was coming off the presses, and in 1538, Henry's second set of Royal Injunctions required that his clergy

> shall provide on this side the feast Easter next coming (06 April 1539) one book of the whole Bible of the largest volume, in English, and the same set up in some convenient place within the said church that you have cure of, whereas your parishioners may most commodiously resort to the same and read it.[11]

The *lectio continua*

While this level of access to the Bible was unprecedented, Cranmer's intention was never just that parishioners should be able to peruse it at their leisure. Rather, as already noted, his 'Preface' to the BCP reveals that his great desire was for them to hear it read aloud in its entirety each year. To understand better how the BCP facilitated that, it is necessary to look at a part of it that is often ignored today, but which was absolutely critical both to it and to Cranmer's overall project of liturgical reform: its new lectionaries.[12]

As a solution to the great problem of the abandonment of orderly Bible reading, the BCP 'Preface' explains:

> And for a readiness in this matter, here is drawn out a Kalendar for that purpose, which is plain and easy to be understanded; wherein (so much as may be) the reading of holy scripture is so set forth, that all things shall bee done in order, without breaking one piece thereof from another.[13]

This 'Kalendar of Lessons' was paired with a 'Table of Psalms'; and together, these mapped out a plan for daily churchgoers to hear the New Testament read out three times each year, the Old Testament once and the Psalms monthly, and all in their right sequence.[14] There were still some intrusions into this pattern for commemorative days, but in Cranmer's system the alternative texts accounted

---

11. Bray, *Documents*, p. 179.

12. Cf. H. O. Old, *The Reading and Preaching of the Scriptures in the Worship of the Christian Church*, Vol. 4: *The Age of the Reformation* (Grand Rapids: Eerdmans, 2002), pp. 148, 151.

13. Ketley, *Two Liturgies*, p. 18.

14. Only Isaiah was not given in sequence, but instead offered as the readings for Advent.

for only around 50 of the 1,400 annual readings.[15] If the lectionary were followed, this would equate to greater than 96% of the readings in annual church services being focused on the seriatim proclamation of the Scriptures. This restored *lectio continua* was prepared for use with 'Matins' and 'Evensong' (as 'Morning Prayer' and 'Evening Prayer' were still known in 1549), and together these three resources opened the first BCP, both highlighting and manifesting Cranmer's stated priority of delivering all of the Bible to all of the people of the realm. Not counting the different prefatory materials, the lectionaries and 'Morning Prayer' and 'Evening Prayer' remained in first place through to the 1662 BCP – and thus retain their prime position in Anglican liturgy even today.[16] This means that, technically, for more than four and a half centuries, any Anglican who has attended properly conducted daily divine services should have been exposed to six public chapter-long sequential readings of the Bible each day, and to an annual cover-to-cover diet of Scripture. If the maxim *Lex orandi, lex credendi* is applied to the Anglican Church, it is incontrovertibly clear that its beliefs are centred on the Bible.

As encouraging as it is to recognize this purpose of the BCP, some short-comings in the project can be found when turning to consider the finer details of Cranmer's lectionaries. While these neither alter the intention, nor significantly reduce the overall value of his work, they are nonetheless real and do give rise to some serious questions.

Cranmer had been working on smaller parts of his liturgical reform project for some time prior to 1549 when he compiled his efforts into the single volume of the BCP. His *Litany* of 1544 and *Order of the Communion* of 1548 are well known, and manuscript evidence shows that he was also following Cardinal Quiñones in his labours to revise divine service, including the lectionaries, as early as the late 1530s. Progress in this enterprise has been well traced by Geoffrey Cuming, who makes some interesting observations regarding the development of Cranmer's three draft calendars.[17] In particular, Cuming notes

---

15. Old, *Reading and Preaching*, p. 155.

16. G. J. Cuming, 'The Office in the Church of England', in Cheslyn Jones, Geoffrey Wainwright and Edward Yarnold SJ (eds.), *The Study of Liturgy* (London: SPCK, 1978); p. 392 rightly says, 'The orderly reading of Holy Scripture remains the chief function of the office.'

17. G. J. Cuming, *The Godly Order: Texts and Studies Relating to the Book of Common Prayer* (London: SPCK, 1982), pp. 1–25. For a comparison of the lectionaries in 1549, 1552 and 1661, see F. E. Brightman, *The English Rite, Being a Synopsis of the Sources and Revisions of the Book of Common Prayer*, Vol. 1 (London: Rivingtons, 1915), pp. 46–125.

that while Cranmer's earliest version accounted for every book of the Bible, including the Apocrypha, the second and third drafts (although we cannot be certain of the chronology of their production) show a number of omissions, as does the final 'Kalendar of Lessons' in the 1549 BCP. Following Cuming, these are shown in Table 2.

Table 2: Chapters omitted from Cranmer's early calendars

	Table of Lessons for Scheme B (Second? Draft Calendar)	Calendarium secundum (Third? Draft Calendar)	Kalendar of Lessons, 1549 BCP
Genesis	10, 36	10	10
Exodus	25–31, 36–39	25–31, 36–39	25–31, 36–39
Leviticus	1–17, 21–27	1–17, 21–27	1–17, 21–27
Numbers	1–9	1–9	1–9
Joshua	13–19, 21	13–19	13*
1 Kings	6–7	6–7	Nil
Esther	12	Nil	10⁺–16†
Song of Songs‡	?	?	Whole book
Jeremiah	13–14, 16–17, 19, 24, 32, 34–35	13–14, 16–17, 19, 24, 32, 34–35	Nil
Ezekiel	Whole book	1, 4, 7, 10–11, 23–24, 27, 38–48	1, 4–5, 8–13, 15–17, 19–32, 35–48
1 and 2 Chronicles	Whole of both books	Whole of both books	Whole of both books
3 and 4 Esdras‡	?	?	Whole of both books
Prayer of Manasseh‡	?	?	Whole book
1 and 2 Maccabees	Whole of both books	Whole of both books	Whole of both books
Revelation‡	?	?	2–18, 20–21

* This chapter is, in fact, found in the 'Kalendar' as presented in Ketley, *Two Liturgies*, p. 24.

† Here, ch 10⁺ refers to the extension of ch. 10 found as part of the Apocryphal addition to the book of Esther. The canonical part of ch. 10 is not missing in the Great Bible, as it was appended to the end of ch. 9 (para. G), although, confusingly, the contents page of the same did indicate that Esther has ten chapters. See *The Byble in Englyshe* (1540) ✠ iv', fo.cxii', online at 'Great Bible, 1540', Internet Archive, <https://archive.org/stream/GreatBible1540>; accessed 23 November 2016.

‡ Cuming does not note the absence of Song of Songs, 3 & 4 Esdras, the Prayer of Manasseh or Revelation from the 1549 BCP 'Kalendar'. In the 1549 'Kalendar', the three chapters of Revelation that are supplied are done so in connection with Saints' Days: ch. 19 for All Saints' Day (1 Nov.) and chs. 1, 22 for St John's Day (27 Dec.); Ketley, *Two Liturgies*, p. 28.

The Apocryphal Scriptures

Before commenting on the significance of these omissions, it is necessary to give some consideration to the fact that the Apocrypha is present in all iterations of Cranmer's lectionary. Despite the protests of Jerome, the Latin Vulgate – which was the sole sanctioned Bible of the Roman Catholic Church during the medieval period – had always carried the books of the Apocrypha within the Old Testament, and although the Protestants strongly rejected their canonicity (because of both the support the books gave to the doctrine of Purgatory and their dubious provenance), they nonetheless maintained them within the covers of their Bibles.[18] Indeed, for the English, it was not until the revision of the Articles of Religion in 1563 that the books of the Old Testament and Apocrypha were explicitly named by the Church for the purpose of distinguishing them from each other.[19] This was in response to the Council of Trent, which had formally classified the Apocrypha as Scripture in 1546.[20]

All of this highlights something of enormous significance for the Reformation that is not often enough recognized. Despite the fact that *sola scriptura* was a unifying doctrine for the different groups of early Protestants, there was some continuing ambiguity among them regarding the canon of Scripture. That is, while the importance of 'Scripture alone' was not contentious, what exactly ought to be regarded as Scripture was. It is well known that there were, at times, disagreements about the status of some of the books of the New Testament; for example, James, which Luther famously described as 'an epistle of straw' in his 1522 'Preface to the New Testament', and Revelation, about which Zwingli had concerns.[21] Revelation was particularly contentious. It was the only New

---

18. The common understanding of Jerome's view was put in the prefaces to the Apocrypha in several of the early printed English Bibles and then, in 1563, also included in Article 6 of the Thirty-Eight Articles. See e.g. *Matthew's Bible*, Apocrypha iv; *Byble in Englyshe*, Apocrypha iv; Bray, *Documents*, p. 288. However, for the possibility that this may not, in fact, have been Jerome's position, see his *Apology Against Rufinus*, Book 2, ch. 33, in P. Schaff and H. Wace (eds.), *Nicene and Post-Nicene Fathers: Second Series*, Vol. 3, *Theodoret, Jerome, Gennadius, Rufinus: Historical Writings, etc.* (Peabody: Hendrickson, 1994), pp. 516–517.

19. Bray, *Documents*, pp. 287–288.

20. *The Canons and Decrees of the Sacred and Œcumenical Council of Trent* (London: C. Dolman, 1848), pp. 17–19.

21. I. Backus, *Reformation Readings of the Apocalypse: Geneva, Zurich, and Wittenberg* (Oxford: Oxford University Press, 2000).

Testament book for which Calvin produced no commentary and Erasmus produced no paraphrase.[22] Yet it was regarded as the climax of, and key to, the biblical story for the likes of John Foxe. While Foxe is best known for his martyrology, he also produced important works on the Apocalypse, which can be understood as his *explanation* of church history, with *Acts and Monuments* serving as the companion *record* of that history.[23]

The status of the Apocrypha was also in transition and it remained unclear in England even after the 1563 Articles of Religion had made plain that the Apocryphal books could not be taken as authoritative in matters of doctrine. This is evidenced by the fact that even the officially sanctioned Second Book of Homilies of 1563 could refer to Apocryphal text as Spirit-inspired Scripture.[24] In the context of such ambiguity, the incorporation of the Apocryphal books in the first BCP 'Kalendar' would only have reinforced the historically established view that they were as much a part of the Scriptures as anything else heard as readings during 'Matins' and 'Evensong'. Indeed, for the very astute sixteenth-century English churchgoer, the immediate question may well not have been: Why is the Apocrypha heard in church services? but rather: Why have the end of Esther, 3 and 4 Esdras, the Prayer of Manasseh and the Maccabean histories been *excluded* from the lectionaries, especially given that they are present in the lectern Bible? It is a good question without any simple or satisfying answer. It could be conjectured that once Esther chapters 10+–16 are severed from the canonical chapters of the book and parked in the intertestamental space with the rest of the Apocrypha, they become hard to reintroduce as a stand-alone set of readings. Also, 3 and 4 Esdras and the Prayer of Manasseh were counted as Apocryphal even in the Vulgate and so had no tradition of being counted fully canonical. And finally, 2 Maccabees was the Apocryphal book most strongly opposed by the Protestants because of its

---

22. For more on Erasmus's views, see I. Backus, 'The Church Fathers and the Canonicity of the Apocalypse in the Sixteenth Century: Erasmus, Frans Titelmans, and Theodore Beza', *The Sixteenth Century Journal* 29, no. 3 (1998), pp. 651–665.

23. R. Bauckham, *Tudor Apocalypse* (Oxford: Sutton Courtenay Press, 1978), pp. 83–84, 87–88.

24. G. L. Bray, *The Book of Homilies: A Critical Edition* (Cambridge: James Clarke & Co., 2015), pp. 383, 385. The Apocrypha is quoted extensively in the Second Book of Homilies, with B. M. Metzger, *An Introduction to the Apocrypha* (New York: Oxford University Press, 1957), p. 191, saying, 'Nineteen of the Homilies contain about eighty quotations from and references to all the books of the Apocrypha except the two books of Esdras and II Maccabees.'

endorsement of salvific prayers for the dead.[25] But of course, these reasons for the exclusion of these chapters are mostly just speculative, and there is no clear evidence that such explanations were ever advanced to any inquirers.

Omissions from the new lectionary

As interesting as Cranmer's use of the Apocrypha might be, an equally pressing issue for the twenty-first-century Anglican inheritors of the BCP concerns the exclusion of some accepted canonical Scriptures from the lectionary, especially given Cranmer's stated commitment to restoring the seriatim reading of the whole of the Bible to the heart of the liturgy. On this matter, the BCP itself does state of the Old Testament that 'certain books and chapters, which be least edifying, and might best be spared, and therefore left unread' have not been included, and of the New, that all is present 'except the Apocalypse, out of the which there be only certain Lessons appointed upon divers proper feasts'.[26] However, these statements amount to little more than an acknowledgment that the 'Kalendar' is incomplete after all, and they do not much satisfy as any sort of thoroughgoing explanation for the omissions. It is again possible to speculate on the more specific reasons why particular parts of the Old Testament were considered 'least edifying'. Perhaps the genealogy of Genesis 10 was considered too dry, Song of Songs too erotic, Leviticus 1–17 functionally redundant and Ezekiel 35–48 too abstract or other-worldly. But not only are these explanations mere guesswork, taken together they at best form only an *ad hoc*, disunited and inconsistent answer to the question that generates as many problems as it solves. For example, if the genealogy of Genesis 10 was indeed excluded because it was hard to understand how it could build up the church, what of the rest of the genealogies that remained in Cranmer's programme? And if Leviticus 1–17 was considered to focus too much on law and not enough on grace, what of the other legalistic sections of the Pentateuch? All in all, there does not seem to be any obvious, overarching explanation that makes consistent sense of Cranmer's omissions from the Old Testament.

There are, however, more historically plausible reasons for leaving most of the book of Revelation out of the New Testament readings. As noted above, there was significant disagreement over the importance of this book, to say

---

25. T. R. C. Patrick, 'The Purging of Purgatory and the Exclusion of the Apocrypha during England's Reformation' (paper, in preparation).

26. Ketley, *Two Liturgies*, p. 22.

nothing of the range of different interpretations, the latter no doubt affecting the former. But the understanding of Revelation was far more than an academic question; it had significant political and social implications. Among those who championed a more apocalyptic reading of Revelation in the early- to mid-1500s were some of the Anabaptists, those more radical Reformers who, among their various beliefs, did not accept that princes were head of the church in their dominions. This particular belief, however, was central to the entire English Reformation as it was crystallized in the doctrine of the Divine Right of Kings that allowed the English Church to break away from the authority of Rome. In the worst cases, the radicals could even go so far as to reject obedience to the state altogether in favour of a more immediately realized eschatological kingdom. This occurred most catastrophically in Münster, Germany, in 1534–5, when a group of Anabaptists attempted to establish a 'new Jerusalem' through acts of ethnic cleansing, the imposition of polygamy and complete rejection of recognized authorities who ended up besieging and eventually taking the town.[27] The whole experiment was considered to be so dangerously anarchic that in 1535, Henry issued the proclamation 'Ordering Anabaptists to Depart the Realm', which required compliance within twelve days or penalty of death.[28] In Richard Bauckham's analysis, the events of Münster thoroughly tainted not only the Anabaptist movement in England, but especially its eschatology.[29] Given all of this, Cranmer's omission of much of Revelation from his 'Kalendar' makes far more immediate sense than his exclusion of parts of the Old Testament. Even so, it is still a somewhat inadequate explanation given that the new lectionary did not avoid all of the Bible's eschatology, and it still does not finally resolve the greater question: Why did Cranmer find it theologically tolerable to exclude *any part* of the canon at all?

Two competing theological paradigms

A part of the answer might be found in the fact that within the Reformation movement, there was a clash of paradigms. That is, not only was there a

---

27. For an account, see N. Cohn, *The Pursuit of the Millennium*, rev. and expanded edn (London: Mercury Books, 1970), pp. 261–271; or G. H. Williams, *The Radical Reformation*, 3rd edn (Kirksville: Truman State University Press, 2000), pp. 553–588.

28. P. L. Hughes and J. F. Larkin (eds.), *Tudor Royal Proclamations*, Vol. 1: *The Early Tudors (1485–1553)* (New Haven: Yale University Press, 1964), pp. 227–228.

29. Bauckham, *Tudor Apocalypse*, p. 39.

disconnect between the new Protestant way of understanding the Christian faith and that of the Catholics, but even within the Protestant movement, two different core ideas were being championed together. The first idea was the doctrine of justification by grace through faith alone; the second was the primacy of Scripture for establishing doctrine.[30] Luther had made a strong connection between the two, seeing his doctrine of justification as the key that unlocked the whole of God's Word. For him, justification by faith was the Bible's own primary integrating truth that controlled the interpretation of all of its parts. But, returning to a point made above, to some extent this strong conviction depended on what was recognized as constituting the canon of Scripture – hence part of the Reformers' concerns with the Apocrypha and Luther's concerns about the book of James, the latter issue being ultimately grounded in the fact that it seemed difficult to square the teaching of that book with the 'law vs grace' theological paradigm. These types of concerns expose what is often observed nowadays: that despite Luther's convictions, there are still many texts of Scripture that do not make ready sense when read through the sole interpretive lens of justification by faith. Could it have been that Cranmer's decision to exclude certain parts of the Bible from his lectionary was one way of dealing with some instances of that problem? Although today's evangelicals would find such an approach to the Scriptures completely unacceptable, it may have been more so in a time when the Protestant canon was still being settled. As uncomfortable as it may feel to suggest that the architect of Protestant Anglicanism could employ such a method, the fact remains that for all the good he did in delivering so much Scripture to the people, for some reason Cranmer did choose to cut back from including the entire Bible in his otherwise largely restorative lectionary.

That Cranmer felt the tension between championing the set of core Protestant doctrines while at the same time letting the full voice of Scripture be freely heard is evident in another part of his BCP liturgies: what might today be called 'the ministry of the Word'. For Cranmer, there were two critical components to the regular ministry of the Word. As seen above, the first was that it presented (almost) the entire canon of Scripture in its right order, and the second was that it communicated this just through reading. But in prioritizing these things, Cranmer's liturgies could have risked allowing the general populace to interpret what they heard from the Scriptures too freely, perhaps even latching on to, and

---

30. For the priority of the doctrine of justification in Henry VIII's time, see D. B. Knox, *The Doctrine of Faith in the Reign of Henry VIII* (London: James Clarke & Co., 1961).

making determinative, some parts of the readings that did not quickly square
with the incoming Protestant theological paradigm. Cranmer's solution to this
potential problem was to ensure that not only were the Scriptures read aloud
to all the people, but that they also came with official and binding interpretations.
The people could have the Bible, so long as they understood it a certain way.
This is part of Cranmer's main point throughout his famous 'Preface' to the
Great Bible of 1540, the first half of which argued strongly that the Bible should
be read by all, and the second half of which tempered this by underscoring
that it should not be freely interpreted by all. Quoting Gregory of Nazianzus,
Cranmer wrote:

> 'It is not fit,' saith he [Gregory], 'for every man to dispute the high questions
> of divinity, neither is it to be done at all times, neither in every audience must
> we discuss every doubt; but we must know when, to whom, and how far we ought
> to enter into such matters.
>
> 'First, it is not for every man, but it is for such as be of exact and exquisite
> judgements, and such as have spend their time before in study and contemplation;
> and such as before have cleansed themselves as well in soul and body, or at the least,
> endeavoured themselves to be made clean.'[31]

This sentiment is magnified in the 'Preface' to the 1543 revision of the large
catechism of Henry's reign entitled *A Necessary Doctrine and Erudition for
Any Christian Man*, or more commonly just the *King's Book*. In it is the explicit
conviction that

> [God] hath ordered some sort of men to teach other, and some to be taught . . . it
> must be agreed then, that for the instruction of this part of the church, whose office
> is to teach other, the having, reading, and studying of holy scripture, both of the
> Old and New Testament, is not only convenient, but also necessary: but for the other
> part of the church, ordained to be taught, it ought to be deemed certainly, that the
> reading of the Old and New Testament is not so necessary for all those folks, that of
> duty they ought and be bound to read it . . . Consonant whereunto the politic law of our
> realm hath now restrained it from a great many,[32] esteeming it sufficient for those so

---

31. G. L. Bray, *Translating the Bible, from William Tyndale to King James* (London: The
    Latimer Trust, 2010), p. 87.
32. In 1543, an Act of Parliament restricted commoners from reading the Bible on pain
    of imprisonment: *The Statutes of the Realm*, Vol. 3 (London: Dawsons of Pall Mall, 1817),
    pp. 894–897; and in 1546 Henry banned the printing of Bibles and required that all

restrained to hear and truly bear away the doctrine of scripture taught by the preachers, and so imprint the lessons of the same, that they may observe and keep them inwardly in their heart, and as occasion serveth express them in their deeds outwardly.[33]

The idea that the Scriptures were to be heard but not interpreted or distilled into doctrine by the common people had at least two concrete expressions in the Edwardian and Elizabethan Churches. The first was that, in addition to the Bible, each parish in the realms was required to obtain an English translation of Erasmus's *Paraphrases* on the Gospels and this was to be made readily accessible to the people.[34] Erasmus had famously clashed with Luther over the doctrine of free will and was not a Protestant *per se*, but he was nonetheless highly regarded by many in the reform movements. He was, after all, the producer of the Greek New Testament from which many of Europe's vernacular translations would be made. Additionally, he had also championed the *ad fontes* method of Renaissance humanism which served to refocus theological studies on the original meaning of the Scriptures, rather than on the more abstract medieval debates. Erasmus's *Paraphrases* was a running commentary on the text of the New Testament and was considered to be particularly sympathetic to the Protestant agenda. Nicholas Udall, the chief translator of the *Paraphrases*, wrote in his 'Preface' that Erasmus

> bryngeth in and briefly compriseth the pith of all the mynds & menynges of all the good Doctours of the churche, that ever wrote in justificacion of feith, in honouryng God onely, in repentaunce and puritie of a Christen mannes lyfe, in detesting of imagerie and corrupte honouryng of Sainctes, in openyng and defacyng the tyrannie, the blasphemie, Hypocrisie, the ambicion, the usurpacion of the See of Rome . . . in teachyng obedience of the people towardes their rewlers and Governours.[35]

---

unauthorized versions be recovered and burned: J. R. Dasent (ed.), *Acts of the Privy Council of England*, Vol. 1: *AD 1542–1547* (London: Eyre and Spottiswoode, 1890), p. 107.

33. C. Lloyd, *Formularies of Faith Put Forth by Authority during the Reign of Henry VIII* (Oxford: Clarendon, 1825), pp. 217–218. Cf. the similar sentiment in Edward's Injunctions of 1547, Bray, *Documents*, p. 250.

34. Bray, *Documents*, pp. 250, 337; cf. 253, 339: all clergy who under Edward held a Bachelor of Divinity, and under Elizabeth held a Master of Arts, were to own Erasmus's *Paraphrases* on the entire New Testament.

35. Quoted in J. N. Wall, 'Godly and Fruitful Lessons: The English Bible, Erasmus' Paraphrases and the Book of Homilies', in John E. Booty (ed.), *The Godly Kingdom of Tudor England* (Wilton: Morehouse-Barlow Co., 1981), pp. 82–83.

By royal injunction, these clearly Protestant readings of the Bible became the sanctioned and mandated interpretation. Of course, given the fact that reading from the *Paraphrases* was not part of any of Cranmer's liturgies, and that in the sixteenth century many people in England could not read for themselves anyway, the reality may have been that relatively few people were directly shaped by Erasmus's book.

The Homilies and the prioritization of doctrine

However, the second clear way that the Protestant theological paradigm was established against any alternative interpretation of the Scriptures or the faith was through the provision of homilies that were to be delivered from the pulpit by the clergy as part of the regular liturgy. Although 'Morning Prayer' and 'Evening Prayer' provided only for the Scripture readings from the lectionaries, the 'Order for the Lord's Supper' in Cranmer's BCPs also included a sermon or homily.[36] (Interestingly, Cranmer's *Order of Communion* of 1548 contained neither Scripture readings nor provision for preaching, which again demonstrates that providing a ministry of the Word was a distinctive purpose of the BCP.) It is important to recognize that the BCP rubrics assume that sermons and homilies are distinct from each other. A 'sermon' was an original composition prepared and delivered by a licensed preacher, of which there were relatively few in England during Cranmer's episcopate – far fewer than parish priests.[37] A 'homily', on the other hand, referred to one of the twelve doctrinal set-pieces that had been published as a book in July 1547 and which were to be the mainstay of weekly pulpit teaching in Cranmer's model of church.[38] The five opening homilies in this First Book of Homilies are commonly recognized as mapping out both the shape and the content of England's Protestant doctrine – it was these five that Cranmer had translated into Latin and sent out to the Continental Reformers.[39]

---

36. Ketley, *Two Liturgies*, p. 79.

37. See the ninth of Henry's Second Royal Injunctions and the tenth of Edward's in Bray, *Documents*, pp. 181, 251, for the tight control on licensing under those kings.

38. Ibid., p. 256.

39. J. Griffiths (ed.), *The Two Books of Homilies Appointed to Be Read in Churches* (Oxford: Oxford University Press, 1859), p. viii. Some scholars consider that it was the first six homilies that covered essential doctrines, e.g. A. Null, 'Official Tudor Homilies', in Peter McCullough, Hugh Adlington and Emma Rhatigan (eds.), *The Oxford Handbook of the Early Modern Sermon* (Oxford: Oxford University Press, 2011), p. 354.

The homilies in the second half of the book – perhaps apart from the ninth, which dealt with a more pastoral issue – then addressed the behavioural requirements for Christian believers. It is easy to understand how having the same doctrinal homilies repeatedly rehearsed, Sunday by Sunday, in all of England's churches would aid in setting the theological paradigm for the nation, irrespective of which Scriptures were read aloud in church services. Thus the pattern that Cranmer had set up in the BCP was for Scripture to be heard but doctrine to be preached, with the hope that the hearers would associate the two. In the words of the 'Preface' to the *King's Book*, it was expected that the parishioners would 'truly bear away the *doctrine of scripture taught by the preachers*, and so imprint the lessons of the same'.[40] The first Protestant archbishop ensured that the doctrine of Scripture would be clearly expounded from the pulpit when the first homily, 'A Fruitful Exhortation to the Reading of Holy Scripture', was read. But in setting up the liturgy so that it was the Homilies that were preached, he left little possibility that the Scriptures that were read from the lectern would also be expounded. It seems likely that he believed that for his day, the Protestant theological paradigm needed to be communicated at all costs.

Cranmer's liturgical programme in today's Anglican churches

It is worth reflecting briefly on the way that Cranmer's liturgical programme has been altered by many of today's Anglican churches. Sadly, there are some that have altogether abandoned the Reformation's high view of Scripture and have either drifted backwards towards a form of Roman Catholicism, or else forwards into a theologically liberal progressivism. But there are even many evangelical Anglican churches that have changed the way they use the BCP and conduct the ministry of the Word. Unlike Cranmer, who placed the public reading of the entire Scripture at the core of his regular liturgies, many of today's Anglicans who share his theological convictions do not share his method, and have abandoned the lectionary and elevated the preaching of an originally composed expository sermon to primary place in the church services.

Of course, there are some very good things about this shift. Most obviously is that, when they are done well, expository sermons allow the unique contribution of each part of the Bible to be heard. They make it possible for God's will to be expounded on those topics that do arise in the Scriptures, but that are not captured anywhere in an unchanging homiliary. Furthermore, expository

---

40. Lloyd, *Formularies of Faith*, p. 218 (emphasis added).

preaching makes possible doctrinal refinement as that becomes necessary in the light of the church's ever-improving understanding of the Bible. Expository preaching places the Word of God itself over the doctrinal formulations of the church. This is something that cannot happen when a fixed set of homilies is all that is preached.

This development is, in fact, in line with what Edmund Grindal, Elizabeth's second Archbishop of Canterbury, was very eager to progress during the Church of England's settlement in the second half of the sixteenth century. Despite the fact that the 1559 revision of the BCP maintained the pattern of Word ministry found in the Edwardian Prayer Books, and that in its revision of the Articles of Religion, the convocation of 1563 reaffirmed the doctrine of the First Book of Homilies and added the Second Book of Homilies with the intention that both be read in parish churches, Grindal moved in another direction.[41] With the rise of Puritanism in the Elizabethan period came the advent of 'prophesyings', which were essentially unsanctioned workshops for the training of young preachers; and although he sought their regulation, Grindal was in favour of them.[42] He envisaged a time when the Church would no longer rely on the Books of Homilies, but would instead have fresh biblical sermons each week, potentially leading to a greater alignment between what was read and what was preached in the church services.

Grindal thus saw the Homilies as serving an interim purpose, but not fulfilling the ideal of parish ministry. He wrote to the Queen, 'If every flock might have a preaching Pastor, which is rather to be wished than hoped for, then were reading of homilies altogether unnecessary.'[43] Elizabeth, however, was of a

---

41. See Article 35 of the Thirty-Nine Articles, Bray, *Documents*, pp. 305–306; and cf. p. 342 for the 27th of Elizabeth's 1559 Injunctions, which acknowledged the continuing lack of preachers in the realms.

42. A good introduction to the Prophesyings and their historical setting can be found in I. Morgan, *The Godly Preachers of the Elizabethan Church* (London: Epworth, 1965), pp. 68–74. Grindal's conflict with Elizabeth is detailed in P. Collinson, *Archbishop Grindal 1519–1583: The Struggle for a Reformed Church* (London: Jonathan Cape, 1979), pp. 233–252; and J. Strype, *The History of the Life and Acts of the Most Reverend Father in God, Edmund Grindal* (Oxford: Clarendon, 1821), pp. 325–336, 343, 348–356.

43. Strype, *Grindal*, p. 565, where it is also seen that Grindal was additionally of the view that it was *never* the intention that the homilies would be enduringly preached in the churches of England. An important work arguing this point is P. E. Hughes, 'Preaching, Homilies, and Prophesyings in Sixteenth Century England', *Churchman* 89, no. 1 (1975), pp. 7–32. Cf. Old, *Reading and Preaching*, p. 152.

different view. She well knew how difficult and important it was to maintain religious uniformity, and therefore social cohesion, in her realms, and was not of the view that England needed more preachers, with differing views on the different texts of Scripture. She believed, in fact, that just three or four preachers would be adequate for all of England![44] The disagreement escalated to the point where Grindal boldly rejected the Queen's call to support her position and was consequently suspended and sequestered. Had he not died in his isolation, it is likely that Elizabeth would have eventually also deprived him of his office. The vision for more widespread preaching continued, however, under Grindal's successor, Archbishop Whitgift, and has since then been realized – as the great number of expository preachers in today's Anglican churches testifies.[45]

As welcome as this development may be, the shifts by evangelicals away from Cranmerian liturgical practices are not universally positive or without risk. In some ways, the abandonment of the lectionaries makes a great deal of practical sense, since twice-daily church attendance has become a thing of the past and expository preaching has become more of the norm. Any church that followed the lectionaries today would offer its members only one out of the fifteen sets of readings prescribed for each week in its public services, and this would make it impossible progressively to teach through the books of the Bible as they were read. But the great danger in separating the lectionaries from the liturgies is that something considerably less than the whole counsel of God may end up being offered through the weekly services and annual cycles of the church. And if church members do not hear all of the Scriptures read through in the public services, they may only occasionally, if ever, encounter them all. Additionally, without the structured guidance of the lectionary, it is possible that there may be no thoughtful rationale developed for choosing the different texts to have read and preached in each week's church services. Indeed, it seems that the Reformation heritage of many evangelical Anglicans can often lead them to default simply to following the likes of Luther and Tyndale in prioritizing the exposition of Paul's writings, which make up only around 5.5% of the canon. This could be to prioritize the presentation of theological convictions, as Cranmer did through the prescription of the First Book of Homilies, but

---

44. Strype, *Grindal*, p. 329.

45. R. B. Bond, *Certain Sermons or Homilies (1547) and a Homily against Disobedience and Wilful Rebellion (1570): A Critical Edition* (Toronto: University of Toronto Press, 1987), pp. 11–12; E. Cardwell (ed.), *Documentary Annals of the Reformed Church of England*, Vol. 2 (Oxford: Oxford University Press, 1844), pp. 201–206, 306–310.

without his check of ensuring that the entire Scripture is at least regularly heard by the gathered churches.

Cranmer's liturgies were revised three times after his death, resulting in the BCP of 1662 which is still in use and authoritative for much of the Anglican world today. It has been supplemented by local, modern service books, and there will no doubt be continuing development and refinement of the liturgies for as long as the Anglican Church has a viable ministry.[46] All of this is as it should be and expresses the modern recognition that *ecclesia semper reformanda est*. But reforming must always be done with a view to recapturing more of the substance of the historic faith, not to replacing it; to renewal, restoration and revival, not to redefinition. Cranmer reformed the Church of England by returning it to the Scriptures and by returning the Scriptures to its liturgies. As the Church that he established continues to move forward in the post-Reformation – and now the post-Christendom – age, it is well worth recalling his deep commitment to placing not just the doctrine of the Word of God, nor just parts of the Word of God, but the entirety of the Word of God, at the very centre.

Bibliography

Backus, I., 'The Church Fathers and the Canonicity of the Apocalypse in the Sixteenth Century: Erasmus, Frans Titelmans, and Theodore Beza', *The Sixteenth Century Journal* 29, no. 3 (1998), pp. 651–665.

———, *Reformation Readings of the Apocalypse: Geneva, Zurich, and Wittenberg*, Oxford: Oxford University Press, 2000.

Bauckham, R., *Tudor Apocalypse*, Oxford: Sutton Courtenay Press, 1978.

Bond, R. B., *Certain Sermons or Homilies (1547) and a Homily against Disobedience and Wilful Rebellion (1570): A Critical Edition*, Toronto: University of Toronto Press, 1987.

Bray, G. L., *The Book of Homilies: A Critical Edition*, Cambridge: James Clarke & Co., 2015.

———, *Translating the Bible, from William Tyndale to King James*, London: The Latimer Trust, 2010.

——— (ed.), *Documents of the English Reformation*, Cambridge: James Clarke & Co., 1994.

---

46. Some of the modern efforts at revising the lectionary are briefly outlined in W. K. L. Clarke, 'The Lectionary', in W. K. Lowther Clarke and Charles Harris (eds.), *Liturgy and Worship: A Companion to the Prayer Books of the Anglican Communion* (London: SPCK, 1950), pp. 296–301.

Brightman, F. E., *The English Rite, Being a Synopsis of the Sources and Revisions of the Book of Common Prayer*, Vol. 1, London: Rivingtons, 1915.

Brown, P., *The Cult of the Saints: Its Rise and Function in Latin Christianity*, London: SCM, 1981.

The Canons and Decrees of the Sacred and Œcumenical Council of Trent, London: C. Dolman, 1848.

Cardwell, E. (ed.), *Documentary Annals of the Reformed Church of England*, Vol. 2, Oxford: Oxford University Press, 1844.

Clarke, W. K. L., 'The Lectionary', in W. K. Lowther Clarke and Charles Harris (eds.), *Liturgy and Worship: A Companion to the Prayer Books of the Anglican Communion*, 296–301, London: SPCK, 1950.

Cohn, N., *The Pursuit of the Millennium*, rev. and expanded edn, London: Mercury Books, 1970.

Collinson, P., *Archbishop Grindal 1519–1583: The Struggle for a Reformed Church*, London: Jonathan Cape, 1979.

Cuming, G. J., *The Godly Order: Texts and Studies Relating to the Book of Common Prayer*, London: SPCK, 1982.

———, 'The Office in the Church of England', in Cheslyn Jones, Geoffrey Wainwright and Edward Yarnold SJ (eds.), *The Study of Liturgy*, London: SPCK, 1978.

Daniell, D., *The Bible in English*, New Haven: Yale University Press, 2003.

Dasent, J. R. (ed.), *Acts of the Privy Council of England*, Vol. 1: *AD 1542–1547*, London: Eyre and Spottiswoode, 1890.

Griffiths, J. (ed.), *The Two Books of Homilies Appointed to Be Read in Churches*, Oxford: Oxford University Press, 1859.

Hughes, P. E., 'Preaching, Homilies, and Prophesyings in Sixteenth Century England', *Churchman* 89, no. 1 (1975), pp. 7–32.

Hughes, P. L. and J. F. Larkin (eds.), *Tudor Royal Proclamations*, Vol. 1: *The Early Tudors (1485–1553)*, New Haven: Yale University Press, 1964.

Ketley, J., *The Two Liturgies, AD 1549 and AD 1552: With Other Documents Set Forth by Authority in the Reign of King Edward VI*, Cambridge: Cambridge University Press, 1844.

Knox, D. B., *The Doctrine of Faith in the Reign of Henry VIII*, London: James Clarke & Co., 1961.

Lloyd, C., *Formularies of Faith Put Forth by Authority during the Reign of Henry VIII*, Oxford: Clarendon, 1825.

Matthew's Bible, 1537 Edition, Peabody: Hendrickson, 2009.

Metzger, B. M., *An Introduction to the Apocrypha*, New York: Oxford University Press, 1957.

Morgan, I., *The Godly Preachers of the Elizabethan Church*, London: Epworth, 1965.

Null, A., 'Official Tudor Homilies', in Peter McCullough, Hugh Adlington and Emma Rhatigan (eds.), *The Oxford Handbook of the Early Modern Sermon*, 348–365, Oxford: Oxford University Press, 2011.

Old, H. O., *The Reading and Preaching of the Scriptures in the Worship of the Christian Church*,
    Vol. 4: *The Age of the Reformation*, Grand Rapids: Eerdmans, 2002.

Patrick, T. R. C., 'The Purging of Purgatory and the Exclusion of the Apocrypha during
    England's Reformation' (paper, in preparation).

Schaff, P. and H. Wace (eds.), *Nicene and Post-Nicene Fathers: Second Series*, Vol. 3: *Theodoret,
    Jerome, Gennadius, Rufinus: Historical Writings, etc.*, Peabody: Hendrickson, 1994.

Spencer, H. L., *English Preaching in the Late Middle Ages*, Oxford: Clarendon, 1993.

The Statutes of the Realm, Vol. 3, London: Dawsons of Pall Mall, 1817.

Strype, J., *The History of the Life and Acts of the Most Reverend Father in God, Edmund Grindal*,
    Oxford: Clarendon, 1821.

Wall, J. N., 'Godly and Fruitful Lessons: The English Bible, Erasmus' Paraphrases and the
    Book of Homilies', in John E. Booty (ed.), *The Godly Kingdom of Tudor England*, Wilton:
    Morehouse-Barlow Co., 1981.

Williams, G. H., *The Radical Reformation*, 3rd edn, Kirksville: Truman State University
    Press, 2000.

8. KATHERINE ZELL: THE VARIED MINISTRIES OF ONE REFORMATION WOMAN

Jane Tooher

'May your meeting with this remarkable lay theologian and church mother be as much fun as mine has been!'[1]

Background and early life

There were a number of remarkable women who lived during the Reformation, and Katherine Zell was one of them.[2] This chapter will look at some of the ways Katherine used the opportunities God gave her. In the way she made the most of these, Katherine serves as an example and an encouragement to Christians today, whether we are male or female, clergy or lay. We will interact with three of Katherine's writings, in which her character and priorities are clearly revealed.

Katherine Schütz was born sometime between 1497 and 1498 in Strasbourg to a respected carpenter named Jacob Schütz and his wife Elisabeth Gerster.[3] She was their fifth child, and after her they would have four more. Although her education was not nearly as extensive as that of some of her more famous

---

1. Elsie McKee, *Katharina Schütz Zell*, 2 vols. (Leiden: Brill, 1999), I:xviii.
2. E.g. Katherine von Bora, Wibrandis Rosenblatt, Argula von Grumbach, Elisabeth Cruciger, Marie Dentière, Olympia Fulvia Morata, Lady Jane Grey and Anne Askew.
3. See McKee for suggestions on why at times after her marriage Katherine is referred to as Katherine Schütz and at other times as Katherine Zell: McKee, *Katharina Zell*, I:xiv–xv.

Reformation contemporaries, it did provide her with a good foundation which would serve her well in years to come. Clare Heath-Whyte notes that Jacob and Elisabeth encouraged Katherine and her siblings to think for themselves, and we definitely see evidence of this ability later in Katherine's life.[4]

Unlike some of the other women we read about from the period, Katherine was never a nun, and so had never been a 'religious professional' in any sense. However, even as a child, she had a sincere and earnest faith, dedicating her life to the church at the age of ten. Though Katherine would never take formal religious vows, this did not stop her contemplating a life of celibacy rather than following the usual expectation of married life. A life of singleness, she believed, would enable her to live in service of God and the church. So, although her family was not poor, Katherine trained in tapestry; this would have been a way for her 'to contribute to her own support, as single women like the beguines had long done'.[5] McKee suggests that the household in which Katherine was raised 'was strongly influenced by a flourishing late medieval piety which may have had an increasingly lay orientation'.[6] This helps to explain Katherine's choice to pursue a life of devotion to the church, but without being cloistered in a convent.

Strasbourg was a key Reformation city, and so Katherine was extremely fortunate to have lived there. It was a free imperial and a sizeable trade city, with a population of approximately 20–25,000 people, and it had developed into an important centre for the printing industry, enabling Protestant tracts and books to be quickly and easily distributed, including works by Martin Luther and Philip Melanchthon.[7] Political and cultural factors had combined to allow greater religious freedom in Strasbourg than in many other European cities. As a result, Strasbourg became a safe haven for religious exiles, including a number of key Reformation thinkers who were experiencing difficulty at home. Calvin famously spent time in exile there between 1538 and 1541. It also attracted those commonly referred to today as the Radical Reformation – Anabaptists and others. Katherine would be exposed, over time, to the breadth of theological beliefs within Protestantism.

---

4. Clare Heath-Whyte, *First Wives' Club* (Farington: 10Publishing, 2014), p. 90.
5. The beguines were a lay Christian order active in northern Europe in the two centuries prior to the Reformation. McKee, *Katharina Zell*, I:11.
6. Ibid., I:12.
7. Geoffrey R. Elton (ed.), *The New Cambridge Modern History*, Vol. 2: *The Reformation 1520–1559* (Cambridge: Cambridge University Press, 1962), p. 107.

Katherine and Matthew: a gospel partnership

'Mrs Zell, the founding mother of all vicars' wives . . . .'[8]

Matthew Zell (1477–1548) may not be a familiar name to many today; however, during the mid- to late sixteenth century he was celebrated as one of the four male pioneers for the Reformation in Strasbourg. The others were Wolfgang Capito (1478–1541), Martin Bucer (1491–1551) and Caspar Hedio (1494–1552). Though Bucer would in time become the best known of the four, Matthew Zell's contribution should not be overlooked. In contrast to the woman he would eventually marry, Matthew received many years of formal education, studying at universities in Mainz, Erfurt and Freiburg im Breisgau, and culminating in becoming the rector of the University of Freiburg in 1517–18. Since his passion was preaching, he chose not to pursue doctoral studies in theology, but rather in 1518 he became priest of St Lawrence chapel, a side chapel located at the north end of Strasbourg's cathedral.

Luther's works first appeared in Strasbourg in 1519 and by 1521 Zell was preaching Reformed doctrines.

> His eloquence and his attacks on abuses swelled the congregation, and when the authorities forbade him the use of the stone pulpit in the great nave . . . the gild [*sic*] of carpenters made him a wooden pulpit from which he preached to congregations which numbered over 3000.[9]

The cathedral canons may have refused him permission to use the stone pulpit, but the city council made it possible for him still to preach in the nave of the cathedral, which had room for many more people than the side chapel. After he had finished, this portable wooden pulpit could be removed and stored in a safe place.[10] In November 1523, Zell was joined by fellow Reformer Hedio, who was appointed the cathedral's main preacher.[11] With both Zell and Hedio preaching Reformed doctrines, it is not surprising that Strasbourg soon became known as a city from which the Reformation had spread through the preaching

---

8. Ibid., p. 109.
9. Ibid., p. 107.
10. McKee, *Katharina Zell*, I:40.
11. R. W. Heinze, *Reform and Conflict: From the Medieval World to the Wars of Religion, AD 1350–1648*, The Baker History of the Church, ed. T. Dowley (Grand Rapids: Baker, 2005), p. 139.

of the Word of God, not simply by a decision of the magistrates or the local prince.

Katherine had read and been influenced by Luther's tracts, and she was also a regular member of Matthew Zell's congregation, where her convictions were strengthened by his strong biblical preaching. At 6 am on 3 December 1523, Matthew and Katherine were married by Martin Bucer. This was a brave move, since, as Matthew had been ordained a priest, he was expected to remain celibate and now faced the threat of excommunication by the local bishop. Theirs was one of the earliest high-profile clergy marriages. Bucer had married Elisabeth Silbereisen a year before and Martin Luther would not marry Katherine von Bora for another two years, in 1525. The Zell wedding began a gospel partnership that is clearly demonstrated in Katherine's writings. They would have only two children, both of whom would tragically die in infancy. This put Katherine in a rather unique situation: she was married to a prominent Reformer, and came into close contact with many other Reformers; and she also was not occupied with the responsibilities of raising children and daily managing a large household.

Katherine was known for showing hospitality on both a small and a large scale. Sometimes it was to prominent personalities associated with the Reformation. Huldrych Zwingli and Johannes Oecolampadius stayed at the Zells' home for two weeks on their way to Marburg in 1529,[12] and Calvin visited their home during his stay in Strasbourg in 1538.[13] At other times, care was shown to those who were not as well known and were in fact shunned by society. Felix Ambrosiaster had been one of the chief magistrates before he was diagnosed with leprosy and so was isolated, required to live in a quarantine area without contact with family and friends. Katherine, however, visited him frequently. She also visited her nephew who had syphilis, and this at times involved a lot of care for him.[14]

Katherine's Christian concern and care were not restricted to those with whom she agreed. It was offered as well to some of the Radical Reformers. She worked with Lucas Hackfurt to distribute aid relief to refugees who had flocked into Strasbourg following the Peasants War in 1525.[15] After the Marburg Colloquy, when Luther separated himself decisively from Zwingli and other Swiss Reformers, Katherine wrote to him pleading for him to unite because love was above all else. Luther responded on 24 January 1531, 'For you know that love must go before

---

12. McKee, *Katharina Zell*, I:80.

13. Roland H. Bainton, *Women of the Reformation in Germany and Italy* (Minneapolis: Augsburg, 1971), p. 64.

14. Ibid., pp. 68–71.

15. Ibid., p. 63.

everything, except God, who is over all, even above love itself. Wherever God and His word dwell, there love will have the upper hand next to God.'[16] Later she would visit Melchoir Hoffman, who had famously spoken of Strasbourg as the location of the New Jerusalem, when he was imprisoned in 1533.[17] Her consistent emphasis was on the brotherliness of Christians which could be extended even to those with whom one might disagree. She believed she was called to love all Christians. Love had a priority over theological agreement, something that marked out her ministry as somewhat different from that of Bucer in Strasbourg.

Katherine's ministries included writing, and in the rest of this chapter we will focus on three of her written works: two letters, one to the women of Kentzingen and the other a public letter defending her husband; and her exhortation delivered at Matthew's funeral in January 1548. These three pieces of writing from her own hand clearly display Katherine's priorities and convictions as a Reformation woman.

Letter 1: 'To the suffering women of the community of Kentzingen, who believe in Christ, sisters with me in Jesus Christ' (22 July 1524)[18]

Although she had written to select people before this date, this is the earliest of Katherine's public letters that has survived.[19]

> It apparently became known and appreciated over a fairly wide region of Germany and German Switzerland. It was reprinted by Philip Ulhart in Augsburg in November 1524 and received favourable comment in the chronicle by Johannes Kessler of Saint Gall not long after. The author sent a copy to Martin Luther, which may be the letter later owned by his correspondent Felicitas von Selmenitz.[20]

The people of Kentzingen accepted Protestant teaching largely through the preaching of Jacob Otter. However, those in authority, both religious and civil,

---

16. M. Luther to K. Zell, 24 January 1531, in M. A. Currie (ed.), *The Letters of Martin Luther* (London: Macmillan, 1908), p. 261.
17. Bainton, *Women of the Reformation*, p. 64.
18. Elsie McKee, *Katharina Schütz Zell, Church Mother: The Writings of a Protestant Reformer in Sixteenth-Century Germany* (Chicago: University of Chicago Press, 2006), pp. 50–56.
19. Ibid., p. 47.
20. Ibid., p. 49.

did not join them, and so soldiers were summoned to the city. Otter was forced to flee before troops arrived. As a sign of solidarity, one hundred and fifty male citizens went with him, but now that the soldiers were in control, the men were not allowed to return to their homes. That is when they sought protection for four weeks in Protestant Strasbourg, housed and fed by the Zells and other Reformers.[21]

Since the men could not return to their homes, it is easy to assume they were the only ones suffering in this situation, or else that they were the main ones who suffered. This is where Katherine's letter helps us. The women and children back in Kentzingen did not just suffer because their husbands and fathers were not with them, they also suffered persecution from the soldiers, which is why Katherine wrote an open letter to the wives. The letter clearly demonstrates her Protestant convictions.

Katherine wrote to comfort these women in the suffering they were experiencing, and to encourage them to keep growing in their trust in God. The means Katherine recommended was continuous meditation on God's Word. In keeping with this, she used Scripture extensively throughout her letter in order to encourage them. Every couple of sentences has Bible references that demonstrate that Katherine had both a broad knowledge of the Word of God and a firm grasp of deep theological truths taught in the Scriptures. These truths include the unity that Christians have in Christ; the purpose of suffering and discipline for the children of God; predestination; the primacy of the believer's relationship with Jesus Christ above any earthly relationship, including the relationship to one's spouse; and faith being the work of the Spirit in the life of the believer.[22]

MacCulloch notes, 'It is perhaps significant that the model of faithfulness in the Christian life in the literature and discourse of Protestant churches swapped gender, shifting from the Blessed Virgin Mary to the literally patriarchal Abraham.'[23] We see this in the Kentzingen letter, as Katherine urges these women to be encouraged by the example of Abraham. Her main concern is not to ensure they follow Mary or other female examples of faith, but something of much more significance: that they grow in their faith in God, no matter the gender of the person who is their example. Since these women were facing possible imprisonment and the threat of death at the hands of their persecutors,

---

21. McKee, *Katharina Zell*, I:2.

22. McKee, *Church Mother*, pp. 50–52.

23. D. MacCulloch, *Reformation: Europe's House Divided, 1490–1700* (London: Penguin, 2003), p. 649.

if they were to persevere through these trials and temptations they would need to keep looking to God and trust his Word. Katherine urged them not to let 'the invincible word of God go out of your heart, but always meditate on that word'.[24] This meant taking God at his word, believing his promises and responding to them with obedience, as Abraham before them had done:

> Take on you the manly, Abraham-like courage while you too are in distress and while you are abused with all kinds of insult and suffering. When you may meet with imprisonment in towers, chains, drowning, banishment, and such like things; when your husbands and you may be killed, meditate then on strong Abraham, father of us all [cf. Rom. 4:16].[25]

Katherine signed off the letter by making clear the connection she had to these women because of Christ, saying that she was the 'wife of Matthew Zell, preacher of the word of God to the Christian community in Strasbourg, your fellow sister in Christ'.[26]

Letter 2: 'Katharina Schütz's apologia for Master Matthew Zell, her husband, who is a pastor and servant of the Word of God in Strasbourg, because of the great lies invented about him' (early September 1524)[27]

The marriage of the clergy was one of the most obvious of the religious and social changes brought about by the Reformation. As soon as an ordained man was publicly married, it was clear to all that he had broken canon law. At times a reforming priest might be so guarded in his teaching that it was not entirely clear whether he opposed the teaching of Rome or not, but his marriage left no doubt. It was most obviously a rejection of clerical celibacy and the suggestion that the clergy were a different class of people, somehow more holy than ordinary Christian men and women. It was also a celebration of marriage and an affirmation that marriage and family life were appropriate contexts in which to live a life consecrated for God's use. The laity who were married were not somehow less in God's eyes, nor had they settled for something less than true

---

24. McKee, *Church Mother*, p. 50.
25. Ibid., p. 51.
26. Ibid., p. 56.
27. Ibid., pp. 62–82.

discipleship. Nevertheless, some of the laity needed to be convinced that clergy should be allowed to marry (a famous example of this was Queen Elizabeth of England, who considered it distasteful and even suspicious).[28] The attitude to those women who married priests was diverse. Some priests married women with whom they had long cohabited, housekeepers who were little more than concubines, and so these women became more respectable in the eyes of many laypeople after a legalized union. However, respect for the canon law lingered in many places and, according to canon law, a woman who married a priest was complicit in something illegal and indeed immoral. Respectable women who did so were sometimes treated as if they were common prostitutes. Katherine, as the first respectable woman in Strasbourg to marry a priest, faced criticism from amongst the laity as well as from the church.[29]

Clerical marriage also carried huge theological significance for Protestant leaders. It was a practical example of justification by faith and the priesthood of all believers, and, more importantly, it made clear that Scripture, not the canon law, was the ultimate authority in matters of faith.[30] Katherine valued her own marriage for all these reasons, and criticism of it mattered enormously. Initially she replied to such criticism with private letters, to a bishop and to others. However, when the opposition increased, she wrote a defence of both her husband and the idea of clerical marriage more generally. McKee suggests that the beginning of this letter is 'one of the most creative sixteenth-century examples of a layperson's arguments for public speech'.[31]

Katherine's personal defence is critically important because it shows that the women concerned were not merely passive participants in this new social order. Courage was required by both partners. Many laywomen like Katherine were acting deliberately and conscientiously, expressing the deep convictions of their faith. They, and not just the men who married them, faced insult and disapproval both in the church and in wider society. However, they did not all write letters defending their actions. Katherine's letter is a rare example of a public defence made by a prominent Reformer's wife and so has a particular significance. It is also a great example of a layperson writing largely to educate other laypeople, urging them not to return to the Roman church.

Katherine's letter was published as a pamphlet, most likely in early September 1524, by Wolfgang Köpffel. On 10 September 1524, the city council confiscated

---

28. MacCulloch, *Reformation*, p. 270.
29. McKee, *Church Mother*, pp. 57–58.
30. McKee, *Katharina Zell*, II:15–16.
31. McKee, *Church Mother*, p. 59.

copies that were circulating in Strasbourg and forbade Katherine from publishing it. In the delicate situation in which they found themselves, they did not wish for libellous attacks on the Roman clergy.[32]

Katherine began her letter by identifying her intended audience: 'all the elect who love the godly truth'.[33] She insisted that she wrote because it was her 'duty'.[34] Yet she also acknowledged that some of her other writings, which she had not been allowed to publish, might have been more use to them, since this one was focused more on her own husband. She wrote about 'he who is now and has for a long time been maligned with such great lies'.[35] These lies motivated her to write because, first, some people had heard them and were then filled with doubt and fear; and, second, Matthew was innocent.

Her argument for Matthew's innocence did not arise from the fact that she was his wife. Rather she sought a weightier argument that would be more persuasive with her audience. This man was a fellow Christian, her brother and neighbour, and all Christians are bound to defend their neighbour since we are all members of the body of Christ. We must stand with our fellow Christians when they are suffering. Katherine recognized that if she simply defended him on the premise that he was her husband, that would be simply an expression of human love. Yet defending him as a fellow Christian was a case of acting in accordance with the Word of God.[36]

Katherine made clear that Matthew did not know she had written the letter and that, if he had known, he would not have allowed her to publish it. Matthew would have insisted on Jesus' command to bless those who persecute you and the fact that God is the avenger. This passing comment from Katherine gives us a glimpse into the health of their relationship, the amount of freedom she enjoyed within her marriage and how she had been encouraged to develop an independent mind. Despite knowing what Matthew thought, Katherine was nevertheless convinced of the need to write because she believed her excessive patience about the situation had resulted in both good and bad people becoming suspicious and believing that she (and Matthew) was guilty. She believed some had interpreted her patience in not defending herself as an admission of guilt: even she realized she had been wrong to marry someone who was ordained. Some in Strasbourg were returning to their traditional Roman conviction that

32. Ibid., p. 62.
33. Ibid., p. 63.
34. Ibid.
35. Ibid.
36. Ibid., p. 64.

clerical marriage was wrong, and in that light the Roman clergy looked especially spiritual.[37]

Katherine insisted that if the lies people were believing and spreading had had a negative impact only on this couple, Katherine and Matthew, she would have been willing to suffer the fallout silently and not write in their defence. Yet precisely because people were believing these lies and some were being drawn back to Roman beliefs and practice, she felt she had to write. Katherine wanted people to be instructed in the truth and to recognize and protect themselves from the children of the devil, rather than just trust what they said. She was convinced that God's Word is powerful. It had created heaven and earth and all the creatures, and it was the means by which lost sheep are found, nourished and guarded from error.[38]

Katherine reminded her readers that this plan of God causes anguish for the devil, who therefore sends his children, his messengers, with a different message, one which has some partial truth to it in order to be attractive enough for people to accept. These messengers of Satan spread false rumours about God's messengers, saying how wicked they are. Yet they cannot prove what they say from Scripture at all, and so what they say lacks ultimate authority. Those who believed their lies were in danger of forfeiting their salvation, whilst God's servants would enter the Promised Land.[39]

Katherine's Protestant convictions are crystal clear. She constantly returned to Scripture to argue her case, citing the Bible throughout her letter, and she stated that the false teachers and defamers of the Strasbourg preachers were the ones who did not and could not argue their case from Scripture. Yet she indicated that she also wrote for them, since they had sinned publicly. Taking Timothy as her model, she wrote publicly so that they might be ashamed of themselves. She recognized that God might yet choose to give them grace so that they also might be saved. Here again is evidence of the depth of her grasp of Protestant theological principles.[40]

Katherine's defence of Matthew was not just for his sake, but for the sake of many good-hearted people. She also defended Luther and the many other Protestant preachers who served the gospel. She noted the persuasive power and potentially far-reaching effects of evil teaching, both inside and outside Strasbourg, and called those responsible poison brewers. She put it to her

---

37. Ibid.
38. Ibid., pp. 65–67.
39. Ibid., p. 67.
40. Ibid., p. 68.

opponents that if the teaching of Luther and his followers was false, why had they been unable to show that from Scripture itself?[41]

Among those who were attacking the Protestant preachers, she noted three whom she viewed as particularly dangerous. She did not hold back in saying what she thought of them. The first was Johannes Cochlaeus, the Catholic polemicist whose attack on Luther and his theology suggested that Luther's convictions arose from his inability to keep his vow of chastity. Katherine played on the word 'Cochlaeus', which sounds like the German word for 'cooking spoon'. His so-called wisdom made him act like a spoon that makes a lot of noise in an empty pot. Yet the spoon was made of such weak material that it could barely stir a bowl of liquid food for a child. She reminded her readers to protect themselves from false prophets who enter the church in sheep's clothing but are in fact wolves.[42]

Another wolf, one she considered even more dangerous than Cochlaeus, was Conrad Treger. Katherine's description of him makes clear how dangerous she viewed him to be:

> I and all Christians may call him a dog and evil worker who tramples God's vineyard with his feet and a rapacious wolf, yes, a father of all wolves, and a thief and murderer who comes to strangle and kill [cf. Phil. 3:2; Jer. 12:10; John 10:1, 10]. Therefore I warn not only an honourable Confederation about him, but all those who seek to be saved, for he is an enemy of the cross of Christ, whose end is damnation.[43]

Katherine's critique of Treger then became even stronger, highlighting how significant this issue was for her. She described him as more than a wolf, more like the fourth beast that Daniel wrote about, a dragon, and it was this she wanted to communicate to him. Treger had written a book, and Katherine made it clear that she wanted to respond to it herself, rather than the Protestant clergy being distracted from much more important work by the need to respond. Treger and his book were not worth their precious time. They were better being ceaselessly busy preaching the Word of God to the lambs entrusted to them, and they should not be distracted from this task. Katherine would serve them by answering the charges herself.[44]

---

41. Ibid., p. 69.
42. Ibid., p. 70.
43. Ibid.
44. Ibid., p. 71.

She then exhorted all Christians to keep the promise they had made to God in their baptism: 'not to allow this poison spewer to corrupt them, but . . . remain with the wholesome, life-teaching of Christ Jesus, who alone is our wisdom, righteousness, sanctification, and redemption'.[45] Here again Katherine's Reformed convictions are evident, with her challenge to Christians to take responsibility themselves for their relationship with God.

The third and final wolf Katherine decided to name was Thomas Murner. Katherine was convinced he was full of pride and a desire to be well known, and so she ironically declared that she would repay him in the manner he would appreciate most, by speaking about him in her letter. In the end Katherine argued that all three 'wolves' had much in common: they mounted straw arguments, invented many lies, wrote books that deafened people, fought against the faith, continued to pursue wealth and sensual pleasure, and railed against the gospel which would cut off their access to these things. That is why they fought against clerical marriage, despite what Katherine insisted were clear and bright grounds in Scripture.[46]

Katherine was convinced that people in the ecclesiastical hierarchy had two principal reasons for arguing against clerical marriage. The first was financial greed. If a priest married, he would be acting like any other honourable citizen. There was no tax on a legal union like this, since God had given it to the priest freely. However, if the only option open to a priest who could not keep his vow of celibacy was to keep a mistress, or even a number of mistresses, he would need to seek the permission of his bishop and pay a concubinage fee of around one and a half to two gulden a year, whether he was rich or poor.[47] Katherine insisted that this practice was against all teaching of Scripture, as fornicators will be shut out of the kingdom of God. In contrast, God had given marriage as a gift and it was plainly suited to clergy. The Roman clergy wanted to condemn the gift, keep it from as many as possible and make any priests who had already married suffer. In doing so, Katherine concluded, they conspired against God.[48]

The second reason Katherine outlined for official resistance to clerical marriage was that, should priests normalize and legalize their conjugal arrangements, they would have to choose one woman and give up the others. A priest

---

45. Ibid., p. 72.

46. Ibid., p. 73.

47. Steven Ozment, *The Reformation in the Cities: The Appeal of Protestantism to Sixteenth-Century Germany and Switzerland* (New Haven: Yale University Press, 1975), p. 60.

48. McKee, *Church Mother*, pp. 73–74.

would not be able simply to get rid of one woman if she displeased him and choose another, as he did with prostitutes. If he had a legal union, any other sexual liaison would be adulterous, and legal action could be taken against him. How much more preferable to allow to continue the current state, in which those who were not legally married might have mistresses, and the clergy turned a blind eye to each other's behaviour. Katherine insisted that such behaviour was completely against God's design and the justification of it perverse. The Holy Spirit made clear through the apostle Paul that marriage helped to prevent fornication (1 Cor. 7:2) and that those who forbade marriage were from the devil, since they did not receive God's good gift with thanksgiving (1 Tim. 4:1–3). She asked, 'Does God not know better than the devil what is good?'[49] The prohibition of marriage came from the devil, while marriage came from God.

Katherine's argument for the goodness of marriage led her to consider children. Legitimate children inherited when their parents died. The offspring of an illegitimate union often got thrown out when their parents died and relations took the inheritance. She acknowledged that some women and children provided for themselves well when the priest – their partner and father – died. But there was no guarantee. These women and children were not protected.[50]

Not only did Katherine challenge clergy not wanting clerical marriage, she also challenged some of the laity who rejected it. Like the clergy, she argued, they too rejected clerical marriage for selfish gain. Once a priest was married, some would be cut off from the priest's property, and others would lose what they had gained from the priest's non-legal sexual relations.[51]

Having argued why marriage was from God and consequently why forbidding it was from the devil, and along the way commenting on some of the evil practices the Roman clergy indulged in, Katherine then began a 'conversation' with her readers. She acknowledged that what she had said so far might have been a long excursus from her original intention in writing, but she also revealed that the excursus itself was not unintended. She imagined that some of her readers would think that it was not her business to speak about clerical marriages. In response she answered that it was entirely her business because she saw so many people trapped in bondage to sin by the devil.[52]

---

49. Ibid., p. 75.
50. Ibid., pp. 75–76.
51. Ibid., p. 76.
52. Ibid., pp. 77–82.

The next section of Katherine's letter is more personal testimony of her own marriage – why she chose to get married despite having previously determined to be celibate.

> With God's help I was also the first woman in Strasbourg who opened the way for clerical marriage, when I was then still not consenting or wishing to marry any man. However, since I saw the great fear and furious opposition to clerical marriage, and also the great harlotry of the clergy, I myself married a priest with the intention of encouraging and making a way for all Christians – as I hope has also happened. Therefore I also made a little book, in which I showed the foundation of my faith and reason for my marriage. For no one had in any way been able to perceive in me, by word or deed, that I wanted to be married. Therefore it seemed necessary to me to set out for honest people my apologia for so doing, as Peter teaches us [1 Pet. 3:15]. These reasons also moved my husband . . . He began such a marriage because he wanted very much to raise up God's honour, his own salvation, and that of all his brothers. For I can perceive in him no dishonourableness, no inclination toward lust or other such thing – for I am not gifted with either overwhelming beauty or riches or other virtue that might move one to seek me in marriage! Because of his behaviour in teaching and life, he has borne such envy from the godless that it is as if his body and life were given over to the birds in the air and worms on the earth – to say nothing about what people have done. And so I come again to my beginning, that is, to justify him. Such envy of him is so deeply rooted in the hearts of the godless that if they cannot discredit him in body, soul, and life, they do it through such great devilish lies invented and spoken about him and spread in all lands.[53]

Katherine knew the lies that had been spread about her and her marriage. Some had suggested she had run away from Matthew. Others whispered that Matthew had hanged himself over sorrow that he had married. Still others accused Matthew of seducing another woman in a garden. When these lies were not believed (Matthew was still alive and there was no other woman), others were invented. It was put about that Matthew had physically abused Katherine; that she had caught him having sexual relations with their maid and when she confronted him he hit her and chased her out of the house; that Katherine had fled their marital home, gone weeping to the city official and ended up staying at her father's home for eight days.

In answer to these lies, Katherine wrote that as God was her witness, she was not lying, and that since their marriage there had not been more than one

---

53. Ibid., pp. 77–78.

quarter of an hour when they were not together with each other. Matthew had never hurt her; they had no maid, only a young child as a servant; she had never found anything in Matthew that would make her suspect him of having such a relationship.[54]

Katherine was blunt about the way Matthew kept house before she became his wife.

> He behaved then just as pope and bishop want: those who forbid marriage that God commanded and permit harlots whom God forbade. That is also why I married him: having considered his life and that of others, I dared by God's grace and power to try to gain his soul and many others, as I hope I have done for God.[55]

Katherine's letter is a wonderful testimony to the changes in domestic life wrought by the Reformation. The corruption in this area within the structures of the Roman church was overturned by an appeal to the teaching of Scripture. As evidenced by Matthew and Katherine Zell, this brought powerful changes in their understanding of sexuality, sexual relations and marriage. Their decision to be married was not a flight from God's purpose and his call on their lives, but an embrace of the good things God has given. Far from it being something of which they should be ashamed, it was something for which to give great thanksgiving to God. It enabled a gospel partnership between these two Christian people which brought substantial benefit to many others and glory to God.

Letter 3: 'Lament and exhortation of Katharina Zell to the people at the grave of Master Matthew Zell, minister at the cathedral in Strasbourg, her upright husband, over his dead body' (11 January 1548)[56]

Matthew and Katherine had been married for twenty-four years when he died on 10 January 1548. Matthew's death came at a time when Protestant forces were being defeated and when Charles V would soon reintroduce Roman clergy and the beliefs and practices that went with them. Understanding this context helps us see why Katherine said what she did at his funeral. Sadly, by February 1550, half of the churches in Strasbourg had Roman clergy, including the cathedral.

---

54. Ibid., pp. 78–79.
55. Ibid., p.79.
56. Ibid., pp. 103–123.

The funeral was held the day after Matthew died. Bucer preached and then Katherine spoke. Throughout her eulogy she was very open about her grief at the death of her 'dearest treasure on earth'.[57] She first thanked the congregation for their love and faithfulness to Matthew as their shepherd. Then she exhorted them to remember the teaching and life example of Matthew, and also not to forget the exhortation and prayer they had just heard from Bucer. She asked the congregation not to be annoyed with her for speaking, and she made it clear that she was not trying to place herself in the office of preacher or apostle. Rather she likened herself to Mary Magdalene, who became a messenger of the risen Christ, and just as Mary had spoken, so Katherine also felt she could not restrain herself. This in fact came as a surprise to her, as she initially thought that she would not speak.[58]

Katherine described Matthew as upright, a servant of the Lord Jesus Christ who was simple, faithful and truthful. He believed and taught the Scriptures as the Word of God, practised no hypocrisy, loved and feared God, served others and highly valued love. Matthew was, she said, quick to forgive. He had ordered his household without pride or arrogance, and had led a simple, quiet, austere, disciplined life. He had been frugal in his use of food and drink, but had regularly opened his home for refugees, the poor, and good friends in the faith.[59]

She reminded those present that Matthew had begun to preach the gospel in Strasbourg after being influenced by Luther, and that Luther taught him how to teach rightly. She described herself as Matthew's 'helper according to my means and my ability: in his house and also in his office and service' during the previous twenty-four years.[60]

Interestingly, Katherine then went on to explain in more detail what Matthew actually did teach, by way of both reminding and exhorting his congregation. She did this by concisely explaining the story of salvation: that God became flesh to take away our sins by his body on the cross, and that this was God's eternal plan; that Jesus' resurrection shows his victory over Satan and death, and that Jesus is now seated at the right hand of the Father; that one day all shall bow and confess that Jesus Christ is God; and that in the meantime, repentance and forgiveness of sins should and must be preached in Jesus' name. Throughout all of this Katherine regularly appealed to the text of the Bible,

---

57. Ibid., p. 104.
58. Ibid.
59. Ibid., pp. 104–105.
60. Ibid., p. 106.

and she concluded, 'That is the sum of the teaching and preaching of my upright and now blessed husband, which all of you have heard from him up to his death, teaching against all sanctification by works and false worship.'[61]

Matthew had preached two days before he died, and Katherine showed that his mission on that day was the same as it had always been: to teach and comfort his people and to warn them against false teaching. When speaking in his sermon about Jesus he had been so distressed that he could barely speak from weeping. After this final sermon, he went and spent time with a close friend, having a good conversation about godly matters and death. He went to bed without any pain; however, in the night he had so much pain that Katherine knew they must prepare themselves for his death. Matthew then began to confess his sins and prayed the Lord's Prayer. He continued with many words and prayers until 4 am, and then felt completely well again. On the following day, Monday, he once again had good conversations with friends, and read and wrote into the night. Appropriately, the last thing he was writing was a sermon on John 8:51. He ate dinner, lay down to sleep and thanked God it was well with him. At 11 pm the pain in his chest came back. He got up, dressed himself and went into his study, where he experienced great distress, falling on his knees weeping and praying to God. Katherine said, 'And he said to me, "I know this is the illness of our dear Martin Luther; my end will be like his and I will accept his death as he did."'[62] Matthew continued to pray, then sat in his armchair and soon became silent. 'Thus with my words of lament and confession of faith, he expired in my arms between one and two in the morning.'[63]

This death scene is significant because Matthew died a 'good death' as Luther had, namely without a priest and without prayers to saints, only prayers to God. Luther's 'good death' had been quickly published and was very popular with Protestants as evidence that he had not died as a condemned man, claimed at the last by the devil.[64] The need for this kind of vindication of the Protestant cause explains Katherine's detailed account of what Matthew did when he thought his death was close. Katherine's concluding exhortation was that they must not quickly forget their faithful shepherd, warning them that Matthew was concerned that the gospel would be lost in Strasbourg soon after he died. He was not convinced that the next generation would remain faithful when the

---

61. Ibid., p. 107.

62. Ibid., p. 110.

63. Ibid., p. 111.

64. Ibid., p. 110; H. A. Oberman, *Luther: Man between God and the Devil*, trans. E. Walliser-Schwarzbart (New Haven: Yale University Press, 1989), p. 3.

persecution came, and for that reason Katherine focused her attention at the end on the young people listening. She ended her speech with an expanded version of the Lord's Prayer, followed by a section from a hymn.[65]

The remarkable testimony of Katherine Zell

These three snippets from Katherine Zell's life reveal a great deal about her. They provide evidence of her compassion and her generosity, as well as her steadfast faithfulness and loyalty to her husband. They reveal an astute mind and enormous courage. However, above all they give testimony to her deep grasp of the truths recovered at the time of the Reformation. Her commitment to the teaching of Scripture, to its life-changing power and to a life of repentance and faith lived in the light of a full and sufficient salvation won for us by Christ shines through these very different pieces as well as in the others which have survived. Katherine was a woman who knew the Lord and gave herself to serve him in the context in which he had placed her. Far from living in the shadow of the husband she loved so dearly, she worked alongside him as a partner in ministry, convinced, as the funeral oration she delivered makes clear, of the vision for clear and unambiguous teaching of the Scriptures reinforced by lives of love and grace.

Matthew's fear that the gospel would be lost in Strasbourg sadly seemed to be realized soon after his death. Four months later Emperor Charles V published the Augsburg Interim requiring all the imperial cities and territories that had adopted the Reformation to return to the Catholic church. As a result, within a year Martin Bucer and Paul Fagius were exiled, and while they overstayed the deadline by three weeks, they were hidden by Katherine Zell, defiantly Protestant to the end. Both Bucer and Fagius found refuge in England, thanks to the generosity of Archbishop Thomas Cranmer, but Katherine remained in Strasbourg, dealing with her grief by immersing herself in the study of the Bible.[66] Until her death on 5 September 1562, even in her final year of ill-health, she remained consistently what she had been since she had married Matthew, and what is demonstrated so fulsomely by her own writings – a Reformation woman who took every opportunity to live out the gospel that had gripped her life.

---

65. McKee, *Church Mother*, pp. 120–123.

66. Ibid., p. 76.

Bibliography

Bainton, Roland H., *Women of the Reformation in Germany and Italy*, Minneapolis: Augsburg, 1971.

Currie, M. A. (ed.), *The Letters of Martin Luther*, London: Macmillan, 1908.

Elton, Geoffrey R. (ed.), *The New Cambridge Modern History*, Vol. 2: *The Reformation 1520–1559*, Cambridge: Cambridge University Press, 1962.

Heath-Whyte, Clare, *First Wives' Club*, Farington: 10Publishing, 2014.

Heinze, R. W., *Reform and Conflict: From the Medieval World to the Wars of Religion, AD 1350–1648*, The Baker History of the Church, ed. T. Dowley, Grand Rapids: Baker, 2005.

MacCulloch, D., *Reformation: Europe's House Divided, 1490–1700*, London: Penguin, 2003.

McKee, Elsie, *Katharina Schütz Zell*, 2 vols., Leiden: Brill, 1999.

———, *Katharina Schütz Zell, Church Mother: The Writings of a Protestant Reformer in Sixteenth-Century Germany*, Chicago: University of Chicago Press, 2006.

Oberman, H. A., *Luther: Man between God and the Devil*, trans. E. Walliser-Schwarzbart, New Haven: Yale University Press, 1989.

Ozment, Steven, *The Reformation in the Cities: The Appeal of Protestantism to Sixteenth-Century Germany and Switzerland*, New Haven: Yale University Press, 1975.

PART 2

KEY DOCTRINES

9. SALVATION THROUGH CHRIST ALONE

Edward Loane

Occasionally there are stories in the newspapers or on current affairs programmes which relate the vandalism of some magnificent and flourishing trees. Not long before, they stood proudly displaying their grand foliage, but now, they are withered and dying. As the story unfolds, however, it becomes apparent that what at first may appear to have been random and unprovoked was actually calculated and deliberate. The sole beneficiaries of the trees' destruction are certain homes that now have dramatically improved views and commensurate property valuations. Generally, these stories are reported to evoke sympathy for the trees, but it is not difficult to understand the motivation of the beneficiaries, especially if they lived there before the obstruction grew. Perhaps they bought their house precisely because of the views, but over time the great attraction of the property had been completely corrupted. Similarly, those living in late medieval Europe unfortunately had the wonderful truth of the gospel obscured by numerous 'trees' that had grown up in the preceding centuries. At the heart of Christianity are the questions: How will God accept sinful humanity? On what grounds can humans relate to him? The gospel shows forth a magnificent vista: God himself, through Jesus Christ, makes acceptance and relationship possible. The sixteenth-century Reformers worked hard to clear away the corruptions so that the glorious truth of salvation through Christ alone could be seen in all its glory.

This chapter will explore what has been described as the 'center of the *solas* and Christian Theology'[1] – the doctrine of Christ *alone*. The obstacles that the Reformers came to realize were perverting this gospel truth will be discussed. These include the cult of saints, the treasury of merit, the sacramental system, purgatory and indulgences, as well as the offices and structure of the medieval church. The Reformers' arguments against such doctrines and their biblical theology of the sufficiency of Christ's work will then be demonstrated. Following this general outline of the subject, the nuances of the debate will be exposed through a study of an interaction between Jacopo Sadoleto and John Calvin. It was the great realization that Christ alone is all people need to come to God and to live with God that was the passion of the Reformers and the driving doctrine of the sixteenth-century Reformation.

Late medieval theological obstructions

There are several dangers in writing a summary of the theological scene at the turn of the sixteenth century. One of the foremost is to present the church's doctrine as a monolithic system that was universally agreed upon. Such a scenario could hardly be further from the truth. The church had numerous competing emphases and there was vigorous debate among theologians. For example, scholars often point to the competing emphases of the *via antiqua* – associated with Thomas Aquinas and John Duns Scotus – and the *via moderna* – associated with William of Ockham and Gabriel Biel. Moreover, what was understood by educated monks, bishops or noblemen was in stark contrast to the prevailing ignorance among the general population, including many ignorant priests. Nevertheless, it is important for us to grasp some of the barriers to people depending on Christ alone for their salvation. There was 'a Christological lacuna' in the soteriology of the late medieval period.[2] It is only in the light of this late medieval context that the profound insights of the Reformers will be adequately appreciated.

---

1. Stephen Wellum, '*Solus Christus*: What the Reformers Taught and Why
   It Still Matters', *The Southern Baptist Journal of Theology* 19, no. 4 (Winter 2015),
   p. 80
2. McGrath uses this expression for the *via moderna* but it is relevant more
   generally also. Alister E. McGrath, *Luther's Theology of the Cross: Martin Luther's
   Theological Breakthrough*, 2nd edn (Oxford: Wiley-Blackwell, 2011), p. 153.

Saints

The place of saints in late medieval religious practice was pervasive. From the time of the early church, those who had been martyred or had been especially devout were revered. This reverence developed from being an example to the faithful which was supposed to be emulated, to a cult of supernatural beings who could do miracles and, most importantly, intercede with God. Among the plethora of saints that were venerated, Christ's mother, Mary, was the subject of the most widespread adoration. In the fifteenth century, the Council of Basle affirmed that Mary had been born without sin – the immaculate conception. People were encouraged to pray to Mary and the other saints in order that, on account of their holy status, they might mediate for them. For example, when Martin Luther was knocked to the ground by a lightning strike in 1505, he prayed to St Anne for help and promised her he would become a monk. The special powers of saints meant that pilgrimages to various places were considered a significant way people could access grace.

Treasury of merit

The concept of merit was a theological touchstone in the centuries before the Reformation and was a cause of great controversy in the sixteenth century. The term describes the value of human effort that deserved divine remuneration and salvation. Theologians distinguished between 'condign' merit, which referred to God's goodness given because of human action, and 'congruent' merit, which referred to God's goodness given because of a third party's action.[3] Despite the distinction, the church maintained that grace was primary in both cases, either by the Holy Spirit's work in prompting action or because reward is gained without being earned by the receiver. The notion that particular works warranted divine favour, despite the caveat that grace was an essential aspect, led to the introduction of the doctrine of works of supererogation, which essentially referred to works over and above what was necessary. Some people, according to this teaching, were especially holy and they achieved an excess of divine remuneration. According to Clement VI's proclamation in 1343, this excess was stored in the treasury of merit which was controlled by the church and could be metered out at the discretion of church authorities. In other words, salvation was conceived a little bit like a bank where people deposited their merit to pay down their debt of sin. However, the saints had so much merit that their accounts were in surplus. The church functioned as an

---

3. Brian Brewer, 'Merit', in R. Ward Holder (ed.), *The Westminster Handbook to Theologies of the Reformation* (Louisville, KY: Westminster John Knox, 2010), p. 112.

accountant with the authority to shuffle this surplus towards the debts of others. Although the church claimed that such authority was given by Jesus in his declaration to Peter that he would be given the keys of the kingdom of heaven, predatory abuse of the system was soon widespread. One such abuse was the sale of indulgences.

Indulgences

The practice of granting indulgences had developed in the eleventh century and was intimately related to the sacrament of penance. The sacramental life of a Christian was the means by which he or she received God's grace. Baptism incorporated someone into the church and the mass nourished the soul. Penance was something of a fallback option to fix the situation when a person sinned after baptism. The person needed to be contrite and confess his or her sin to a priest, and would then be granted absolution and assigned a punishment to make satisfaction for the offence. According to Carter Lindberg, 'Through the sacrament of penance, the church provided not only the absolution of guilt but also the means for satisfying the socially disruptive and religiously offensive actions of persons.'[4] Indulgences essentially offered a person another avenue to make satisfaction for an offence, through either a pilgrimage or payment. Famously, Pope Urban II declared an indulgence for all who participated in the first crusade in 1095. Thomas Aquinas supported the concept of indulgences and argued that merits could be shared, such that indulgences could be procured on behalf of others, including those already dead and in purgatory.[5] By the sixteenth century, the sale of indulgences had become an integral way the church raised finances, and Pope Leo X declared an indulgence for those who supported the building of St Peter's in Rome. Steven Ozment makes the point that the purchase price of an indulgence was not onerous, never more than a week's wages, and theologically it was considered an almsgiving rather than a purchase.[6] There was, however, no limit to how many indulgences were purchased. Furthermore, they were unscrupulously marketed to capitalize not only on personal insecurities, but also on uncertainty about the state of loved ones. This is evident in Johann Tetzel's ditty 'As soon as the coin in the box rings, a soul from purgatory to heaven springs.'

---

4. Carter Lindberg, *The European Reformations* (Oxford: Blackwell, 1996), p. 73.
5. Mickey Mattox, 'Indulgences', in R. Ward Holder (ed.), *The Westminster Handbook to Theologies of the Reformation* (Louisville, KY: Westminster John Knox, 2010), p. 90.
6. Steven Ozment, *Protestants: The Birth of a Revolution* (New York: Doubleday, 1993), p. 13.

Purgatory

The doctrine of purgatory as a third destination for the dead, along with heaven and hell, had developed in the early Middle Ages and had become ubiquitous by the early sixteenth century. This doctrine was based on the notion that because very few people would be able to perform satisfactory penance in this life, there was a second chance after death to offer satisfaction for sin and become the righteous people God demands. Moreover, the living could assist those in purgatory not only through the purchase of indulgences, but also through prayers and the saying of mass on their behalf.[7] What the experience in purgatory actually entailed was somewhat ambiguous in the church's official teaching, which meant that popular sentiment ran wild with the horrors involved. Needless to say, the motivation to avoid and minimize this fate both for oneself and for loved ones was intense. It led to the development of private mass, in which a priest performed the sacrament by himself on behalf of another individual, either dead or alive. This was a way of 'contracting out' penance and it led to the proliferation of chantry priests who were employed from the income of a deceased person's estate for the purpose of offering mass on behalf of that person. For example, Henry VIII left £250 for 10,000 masses to be said for his soul. The quest to escape purgatory was pursued by late medieval people throughout life, and after it.

Mass

It is difficult to overstate the significance of the mass in medieval religious thinking. It occupied the central place in the church's liturgical experience and was theologically loaded with significance. The service was a recapitulation of Christ's offering of himself upon the cross to atone for sinful humanity. But it was not a mere reminder and proclamation of this event for the spiritual benefit of the congregation: the mass was itself a reoffering of Christ's sacrifice. The doctrine of transubstantiation maintained that in the service the bread and wine ceased to be bread and wine, but rather became the real body and blood of Christ. Indeed, the emphasis for regular people was on seeing the consecration take place. At this point bells were rung and candles lit. Only once a year, at Easter, did the congregation actually receive mass, and even then it was only 'in one kind' – the bread and not the wine.[8] Day in and day out,

---

7. Peter Marshall, 'Purgatory', in R. Ward Holder (ed.), *The Westminster Handbook to Theologies of the Reformation* (Louisville, KY: Westminster John Knox, 2010), p. 133.

8. Peter Marshall, *Reformation England, 1480–1642*, 2nd edn (London: Bloomsbury Academic, 2012), p. 5.

if there was a congregation, the priest stood with his back to them, offering the sacrifice of the righteous Christ as a propitiation on their behalf, perpetuating the events of Calvary through history. Stephen Wellum states, 'The Reformers, then, in affirming *Christ alone*, were predominantly opposing Rome's sacramental theology that undercut and compromised Christ's all-sufficient work.'[9]

Papacy

One of the great battles of the Reformation was about the role and authority of the Pope. The papacy had developed from the time of the early church, but after the fall of the western Roman empire in the fifth century, the Pope assumed greater temporal and religious authority throughout Europe. Alister McGrath stated, 'The Middle Ages had seen the political power of the church, and particularly that of the papacy, reach previously unknown heights.'[10] The titles that this office assumed were indicative of the place it had in the life of the church. For example, from the time of Gelasius I (late fifth century), the Pope had been known as the 'Vicar of Christ'. This meant he was considered the earthly representative of Christ or even the substitute for Christ on earth. In the fifteenth century, an increasingly popular title for the Pope was 'Pontifex Maximus' – supreme pontiff. The word 'pontiff' derives from two Latin words: 'I make' and 'a bridge'. The title thus implied that the Pope himself was the bridge between people and God. What this meant for people living in the early sixteenth century was that to be out of fellowship with the Pope necessarily entailed being out of fellowship with God. In a derivative sense, the same was true in relation to bishops and clergy, despite the widespread immorality and negligence of those exercising these offices. Bishops were understood to stand in apostolic succession and, as such, exercised apostolic authority. The clergy represented the people to God and God to the people, not only in the service of the mass, but also in their role of hearing confession and absolving sin. At every level, the church was structured as a mediator between people and God. Moreover, it offered salvation through its sacramental system and the widespread use of indulgences. The work of Christ was not explicitly denied by the late medieval church; however, numerous erroneous doctrines had grown up, such that Christ's work was obscured and its application to people was perverted. It was remedying this great corruption and cutting away all these obstacles that was at the very heart of all the Reformers' work.

---

9. Wellum, *'Solus Christus'*, p. 85.
10. McGrath, *Luther's Theology of the Cross*, p. 11.

Reformers' doctrine of Christ alone

Our earlier caveat about the danger of generalization must be reiterated as the Reformers' doctrinal emphases are explored in contradistinction to the theology of the late medieval church. Nevertheless, despite the fact that not all the Reformers arrived at exactly the same conclusion on every point of doctrine, the overriding emphasis was shared. This emphasis was centred on the perfect sufficiency of Christ's work for the salvation of sinners. As Johnson states, 'Christ is the hub around which the doctrines of the gospel revolve.'[11] When considering the other *sola*s of the Reformation, they cannot be divorced from their relation to Christ. 'Faith alone' refers to faith in Christ alone, rather than faith as a nebulous concept. 'Grace alone' refers to the kindness of God in achieving his salvific purposes through Christ alone, rather than through human effort. The Reformers emphasized that it was Christ's merit, sacrifice and satisfaction which is at the heart of salvation. Furthermore, they maintained that Christ alone was the mediator between God and humanity and, therefore, the place that late medieval theology had given to the church, the papacy and the saints was a sacrilege that undermined the heart of Christianity. Daniel Preus points out that Luther's attack on the papal office was not focused 'on greed, the luxury of the papal court, simony or the cost of indulgences, but on the fact that the flock of Christ [was] deprived of the gospel'.[12] This motivating factor was common to the Reformers of the sixteenth century as they proclaimed the biblical truths about Jesus Christ.

Christ's merit alone
Question 60 of the Heidelberg Catechism asks, 'How art thou righteous before God?' The Catechism's answer is that, even though I have grievously sinned, 'yet God, *without any merit of mine*, of mere grace, grants and imputes to me the perfect satisfaction, righteousness, and holiness of Christ ... if only I accept such benefit with a believing heart'.[13] This statement, probably written by Ursinus in 1563, reflects the Reformers' understanding of the place of human merit in salvation. Although late medieval theology claimed that human merit

---

11. Terry Johnson, *The Case for Traditional Protestantism: The Solas of the Reformation* (Edinburgh: Banner of Truth, 2004), p. 47.

12. Daniel Preus, 'Solus Christus', *Logia* 5, no. 3 (1996), p. 19.

13. Italics mine. 'Heidelberg or Palatinate Catechism, AD 1563', in Philip Schaff (ed.), *The Creeds of Christendom: With History and Critical Notes* (Grand Rapids, MI: Baker, 1983), pp. 326–327.

was primarily gracious, Luther came to see that these two concepts were antagonistic. He claimed, 'For there are not, and could not be, more than these two ways: the one which relies upon God's grace, and the other which builds on our own works and merit.'[14] For Luther, justification by faith was an unadulterated doctrine of grace because it shifted the focus away from all forms of self-salvation to Christ.[15] Likewise, Calvin wrote that 'merit' was an unscriptural and dangerous word that had done great damage to the world. He said, 'Surely, as it is a most prideful term, it can do nothing but obscure God's favour and imbue men with perverse haughtiness.'[16] In refuting the Roman church he stated that, although they professed the name of Christ, they 'strip him of his power and virtually trample him underfoot', because if you are engrafted into Christ through faith, 'you obtain not the opportunity to gain merit but all the merits of Christ, for they are communicated to you'.[17] This shift from salvation depending, even in a small measure, on human merit to depending entirely upon the merit of Christ was tremendously liberating. It was wholly 'congruent' merit, but the notion of the treasury of merit – accrued by saints and administered by the church – was completely undermined. Rather, the perfect righteousness of Christ was imputed graciously through faith.

Christ's sacrifice alone

The Reformers emphasized the uniqueness and perfect sufficiency of Christ's atoning sacrifice at Calvary. This was presented in contrast to the Roman teaching that the sacrifice was essentially recapitulated through the mass each time the ceremony was performed. The author of Hebrews states unequivocally that, in contrast to the old-covenant priesthood that repeatedly offered sacrifices for sin, Christ offered for all time one sacrifice for sin.[18] The late medieval doctrine of the mass was effectively a reestablishment of the old-covenant sacrificial system, albeit with Jesus being offered over and over rather than an animal. The Reformers found this to be at odds with the teaching of the New Testament and repugnant to the gospel. It undermined the sufficiency of what Christ had done on the cross if the sacrifice needed to be offered over and over.

----

14. Luther, *Against Hanswurst* 41:213; cited in Preus, 'Solus Christus', p. 19.

15. Robert Letham, *The Work of Christ*, Contours of Christian Theology, ed. Gerald Bray (Downers Grove, IL: InterVarsity Press, 1993), p. 189.

16. John Calvin, *Institutes of the Christian Religion*, trans. F. L. Battles, ed. J. T. McNeill, Library of Christian Classics (London: SCM, 1961 [1559]), III.xv.2.

17. Ibid., III.xv.4.

18. Heb. 10:11–12.

Calvin claimed that the mass was a blasphemy against Christ and suppressed his passion.[19] According to Hebrews, Christ was both the priest and the victim of this perfect sacrifice. Yet, as Calvin points out, the role that the Roman church assigned to priests offering mass undermined Christ's forever priesthood in the order of Melchizedek and was therefore blasphemous.[20] Furthermore, rather than being a memorial of Christ's perfect atoning work, the mass, according to Calvin, resulted in forgetfulness of Christ's death.[21] In contrast, the Reformers were adamant that Christ's sacrifice alone was God's means of achieving forgiveness and reconciliation. For example, Article XVII of the French Confession of Faith (1559) states,

> We believe that by the perfect sacrifice that the Lord Jesus offered on the cross, we are reconciled to God, and justified before him; for we can not be acceptable to him, nor become partakers of the grace of adoption, except as he pardons [all] our sins, and blots them out. Thus we declare that through Jesus Christ we are cleansed and made perfect; by his death we are fully justified, and through him only can we be delivered from our iniquities and transgressions.[22]

Christ's satisfaction alone
The Reformed understanding of the perfect sacrifice offered by Christ necessitated numerous revisions of late medieval systematic theology. The notion that Christ's satisfaction alone achieved reconciliation undermined the theological foundation of penance and indulgences. Humanity could not make satisfaction for their own sins. This was a revolutionary concept. Luther recalled about his understanding in 1512, 'When I became a doctor, I did not yet know that we cannot make satisfaction for our sins.'[23] Yet it was the way that satisfaction is achieved that was the catalyst for his Ninety-Five Theses. As David Steinmetz highlights, 'when we focus on the sacrament of penance, we are focusing on an issue central to Luther's new Reformation understanding of the gospel'.[24] The indulgences that Luther intended to dispute were not just those

19. Calvin, *Institutes*, IV.xvii.2–11.
20. Ibid., IV.xviii.2.
21. Ibid., IV.xviii.5.
22. 'The Gallican Confession, AD 1559', in Philip Schaff (ed.), *The Creeds of Christendom: With History and Critical Notes* (Grand Rapids, MI: Baker, 1983), p. 369.
23. Cited in McGrath, *Luther's Theology of the Cross*, p. 161.
24. D. C. Steinmetz, *Luther in Context*, 2nd edn (Grand Rapids, MI: Baker Academic, 2002), p. 10.

being sold by Tetzel, but also those gained by visiting relics. The Castle Church in Wittenberg was famous for its collection of relics and the most important occasion each year for their display was All Saints' Day, 1 November. Knowing that crowds would throng to the church the following day in order to 'make satisfaction' for their sins, Luther posted his theses on 31 October 1517.[25] When exactly Luther arrived at a settled position about the nature of Christ's satisfaction is a matter of debate, but certainly by the end of the decade he was espousing the Reformed position that he would hold consistently for the remainder of his life.[26] J. I. Packer states,

> Luther was the first theologian to give prominence to the thought that the satisfaction to God for sin which, as Anselm, had established, Christ rendered on our behalf on the cross, was penal and substitutionary in its nature . . . Luther saw that in Scripture satisfaction to God means satisfaction of the penal claims of divine law – that is, punishment vicariously borne.[27]

This theme of penal substitutionary atonement shaped Reformed theology. Calvin argues that this achievement is only possible because of Christ's divine and human natures. He states,

> Accordingly, our Lord came forth as true man and took the person and name of Adam in order to take Adam's place in obeying the Father, to present our flesh as the price of satisfaction to God's righteous judgment, and, in the same flesh, to pay the penalty that we had deserved. In short, since neither as God alone could he feel death, nor as man alone could he overcome it, he coupled human nature with divine that to atone for sin he might submit the weakness of the one to death; and that, wrestling with death by the power of the other nature, he might win victory for us.[28]

As we have noted above, late medieval theology did maintain that Christ made satisfaction for sin, but the issue was that this satisfaction was supplemented by human satisfaction through the doctrine of penance and, after death, in purgatory. Christ's propitiation on the cross was not enough and needed to be continually offered through the mass. The Reformers concluded that such

25. McGrath, *Luther's Theology of the Cross*, p. 24.
26. For more detail on the development of Luther's thinking, see ibid.
27. J. I. Packer, *Honouring the People of God: The Collected Shorter Writings of J. I. Packer* (Carlisle: Paternoster, 1999), p. 7
28. Calvin, *Institutes*, II.xii.3.

notions were contrary to the teaching of Scripture and corrupted the gospel. These achievements were Christ's alone. As Article 31 of the Thirty-Nine Articles states: 'The Offering of Christ once made is that perfect redemption, propitiation and satisfaction, for the sins of the whole world, both original and actual; and there is none other satisfaction for sin, but that alone.'

Christ's mediation alone

A further implication of the unique nature of Christ's person and work was a rediscovery of the biblical teaching that Christ is the sole mediator between God and humanity. First Timothy 2:5–6a makes clear that 'there is one God and one mediator between God and mankind, the man Christ Jesus, who gave himself as a ransom for all people'.[29] According to the Reformers, late medieval theology had corrupted this truth through its teaching on the mediatorial role of the church, the Pope and the saints. These barriers were not merely adiaphora, but so impacted the nature of God's relationship to the world that they were denounced, and in the case of the papacy, regularly declared to be Antichrist.

The church functioned as a necessary mediator between people and God, particularly in the emphasis on the sacraments which were purported to be essential for establishing and maintaining a relationship with God and which the church had sole authority to administer. The church had a monopoly on people's access to God. The Reformers repudiated this teaching and pointed to Christ as the perfect and only mediator. Calvin stated, 'the Romanists vex us today and frighten the uneducated with the name of the church, even though they are Christ's chief adversaries.'[30] The Reformers used the Bible to undermine the sacerdotal priesthood and, in contrast, argued for the priesthood of all believers. The truth that a sinner was justified by faith proved the church's teaching about rites and ceremonies to be false. Indeed, McGrath points out that Luther, as late as 1535, was still prepared to acknowledge the authority of the Pope, 'on the condition that he acknowledge in turn that a sinner had free forgiveness of sins through the death and resurrection of Jesus Christ, and not through the observance of the traditions of the church'.[31] Considering Luther's attack on the papal office during the previous fifteen years, this claim is a demonstration of how central justification by faith in the completed work of Christ was to his entire theological system. The church was not the mediator; Christ alone was.

---

29. All Scripture quotations in this chapter are from the NIV.

30. Ibid., IV.ii.4.

31. McGrath, *Luther's Theology of the Cross*, p. 28.

The office of the papacy was the subject of sustained critique by Reformers. This was not primarily on account of the immorality, corruption and worldliness that had become associated with the role, but rather was because of the obstacle the Pope had become to the gospel of Christ. Luther, in his early complaints, had been very deferential to papal authority. It was not long, however, before he was denouncing the Pope for standing in opposition to Christ. From 1520 onwards, Luther regularly referred to the Pope as the Antichrist prophesied in the New Testament. In 1545, Luther wrote an entire treatise entitled *Against the Roman Papacy, An Institution of the Devil*, which indicates how rotten he believed the office was. As Preus points out, his chief concern was that the Pope was denying people access to salvation which is found in Christ alone.[32] In a similar way, Calvin shows that biblically the Antichrist is marked by depriving God of his honour and taking it upon himself. 'Since, therefore, it is clear that the Roman pontiff has shamelessly transferred to himself what belonged to God alone and especially to Christ, we should have no doubt that he is the leader and standard-bearer of that impious and hateful kingdom.'[33] He goes on to say that the papal claims of authority are 'utterly ridiculous and stupid'.[34] The Reformers were convinced that the papacy was not merely superfluous to the prosperity of the church; rather it was carcinogenic, because it supplanted the role and office of Christ as the sole mediator.

The late medieval veneration and adoration of saints, and particularly of Mary, was another theological obfuscation that the Reformers sought to remedy. People were encouraged to seek refuge in the intercession of the saints and honoured them with a semi-divine status. Calvin castigates those who attempt to obtain God's benevolence by repeatedly thrusting forward 'the merits of the saints, and for the most part overlooking Christ', because they 'transfer to the saints that office of sole intercession . . . which belongs to Christ'.[35] He maintained that there was no basis for this practice in Scripture. Furthermore, he argued that the pursuit of the intercession of the saints led to people adopting 'a particular saint as a tutelary deity' in whom they put their trust. Some went so far as 'calling on the saints now not as helpers but as determiners of their salvation'.[36] Such notions are blasphemous and Calvin was clear that Christ

---

32. Preus, 'Solus Christus', p. 21.

33. Calvin, *Institutes*, IV.vii.25.

34. Ibid., IV.vii.26.

35. Ibid., III.xx.21.

36. Ibid., III.xx.22.

is the only way, and the one access, by which it is granted us to come to God
[cf. John 14:6], to those who turn aside from this way and forsake this access,
no way and no access to God remain; nothing is left in his throne but wrath,
judgment and terror.[37]

While the Reformers were unapologetic about their rejection of the inter-
cessory role of saints, they were equally adamant about the wonderfully liberating
news for individual Christians that intercession through Christ has been secured
and is a privilege to be enjoyed by all the faithful. As Calvin stated, 'Christ is
constituted the only Mediator, by whose intercession the Father is for us
rendered gracious and easily entreated.'[38] The system of invoking saints as
mediators was correct in its presupposition that humanity does need a mediator
to gain access to and relate to God; its error was in whom it believed that
mediator was. The gospel unequivocally declares that God himself has provided
the perfect and gracious mediator in Christ Jesus.

Christ alone in the Sadoleto and Calvin exchange

The contention over what Christ alone meant to the Reformers and their
Catholic opponents can be helpfully observed by examining the interchange
between the Bishop of Carpentras in southern France, Jacopo Sadoleto, and
the leading Reformer, John Calvin. Politics and religion were intimately woven
together for Geneva in the 1530s. The city had adopted the Protestant faith
under the leadership of Guillaume Farel, and in 1536, Farel convinced a reluctant
John Calvin, who was just passing through the city, to help establish the
Reformed faith in Geneva. Two years later both Farel and Calvin were expelled
from the city because of a disagreement with the civic authorities about discipline. With the city deprived of its reforming leaders, Sadoleto wrote a letter to
the Genevans early in 1539, imploring them to return to the Catholic church.
Sadoleto was a humanist Catholic who wanted to amend corruptions in the
church, but he held firmly to the authority of the church to establish doctrine
and to establish the means by which people might receive salvation. Sadoleto's
winsome letter spoke regularly of Christ alone, but his qualifications of this
doctrine provided Calvin with a clear opportunity to articulate the Reformed
position.

---

37. Ibid., III.xx.19.
38. Ibid.

Sadoleto opens his letter warmly articulating his intention in writing and confirming that 'above all things' he desires the salvation of the Genevans.[39] He goes on to make clear how Christ's work and salvation are intimately related.

> For [the hope of salvation], Christ, the herald of the true God, was once received by the world with such universal consent and eagerness; for this reason He is adored and worshipped by us, and truly acknowledged to be God, and the Son of the true God; because, when the minds of men were dead to Almighty God, in whom alone is life, and after living for a little time to the deceitful and fading pleasures of the world, were forthwith doomed utterly and in every part of their nature to destruction, He alone, ever since the world began, awoke them from the dead, that is, from this most fatal kind of death, and first Himself, choosing to be Himself our salvation and deliverance and truth, by submitting to death in the flesh, and shortly after resuming a life no longer mortal, taught and instructed us, by His own example, how, by a way very different from that to which we had been previously accustomed, we should die to this world and the flesh, and live thereafter to God, placing in Him our hopes of living well and happily forever.[40]

There is little in this statement that the Reformers would have objected to, and Sadoleto goes on to say explicitly that 'we all believe in Christ in order that we may find salvation for our souls'.[41] In the next paragraph, however, he makes clear he is saying something quite different from what the Reformers were claiming. He writes,

> We obtain this blessing of complete and perpetual salvation by faith in God alone and in Jesus Christ. When I say alone, I do not mean, as those inventors of novelties do, a mere credulity and confidence in God, by which, to the seclusion of charity and the other duties of a Christian mind, I am persuaded that in the cross and blood of Christ all my faults are unknown; this indeed is necessary, and forms the first access which we have to God, but it is not enough. For we must also bring a mind full of piety toward Almighty God, and desirous of performing whatever is agreeable to Him; in this, especially, the power of the Holy Spirit resides.[42]

---

39. Jacopo Sadoleto, 'Sadoleto's Letter to the Genevans', in John Olin (ed.), *A Reformation Debate* (Grand Rapids, MI: Baker, 1966), p. 31.
40. Ibid., p. 33.
41. Ibid., p. 34.
42. Ibid., p. 35.

In other words, while faith is essential for salvation, so are good works. Sadoleto makes clear that if people lapse into sin, they 'rise again with the same faith of the Church; and by whatever expiations, penances, and satisfactions, she tells us that our sin is washed away'.[43] This statement is a clear example of the church's belief that it had the authority to determine the grounds on which forgiveness might be achieved. Sadoleto then argues that the Genevans would be better served by following and believing the teaching of the Catholic church rather than recently proclaimed novelties, because it is only in fellowship with Rome that salvation may be found.

Calvin's reply to Sadoleto is a clear and biblical retort to this soteriology. Even though he had been expelled from the city, Calvin still wanted to defend the gospel that had been proclaimed there because of his 'paternal affection'.[44] After spending some time rebutting Sadoleto's understanding of the church, Calvin articulates Reformed soteriology. He maintains that a person must become aware of his or her utter helplessness because of personal sin, and then he writes,

> we show that the only haven of safety is in the mercy of God, as manifested in Christ, in whom every part of our salvation is complete. As all mankind are, in the sight of God, lost sinners, we hold that Christ is their righteousness, since, by his obedience, He has wiped off our transgressions; by his sacrifice, appeased the divine anger; by His blood, washed away our sins; by his cross, borne our curse; and by his death, made satisfaction for us. We maintain that in this way man is reconciled in Christ to God, by no merit of his own, by no value of works, but by gratuitous mercy. When we embrace Christ by faith, and come, as it were, into communion with Him, this we term, after the manner of Scripture, *the righteousness of faith*.[45]

---

43. Ibid., p. 37.

44. John Calvin, 'Calvin's Reply to Sadoleto', in John Olin (ed.), *A Reformation Debate* (Grand Rapids, MI: Baker, 1966), p. 51.

45. Ibid., pp. 66–67. Calvin makes an even more thorough articulation of this claim in the *Institutes*: 'We see that our whole salvation and all its parts are comprehended in Christ [Acts 4:12]. We should therefore take care not to derive the least portion of it from anywhere else ... If we seek redemption, it lies in his passion; if acquittal, in his condemnation; if remission of the curse, in his cross [Gal. 3:13]; if satisfaction, in his sacrifice; if purification, in his blood; if reconciliation, in his descent into hell; if mortification of the flesh, in his tomb; if newness of life, in his resurrection; if immortality, in the same; if inheritance of the Heavenly Kingdom, in his entrance into heaven; if protection, if security, if abundant supply

This statement is a beautiful articulation of the Reformed belief that salvation is the work of Christ alone. Calvin goes on to show that this doctrine leads not to licentiousness but to holiness. Furthermore, one by one he shows that on account of this doctrine the late medieval beliefs about penance and satisfaction, mass, auricular confession to a priest, praying to saints, purgatory, as well as the inflated authority of the church and Pope, are without value or scriptural basis.[46] In January 1540 Calvin's response was received by the Genevans, published and circulated. This step has been considered significant in the reconciliation of Calvin and the city.[47] In September 1541 he returned to Geneva where, until his death twenty-three years later, he exercised one of the most profound ministries of the sixteenth century.

Celebrating Christ alone today

Throughout this chapter we have highlighted the distinction between late medieval theology and the Reformation breakthrough that salvation is through Christ alone. While there is a debate over whether the Council of Trent (1546–63) is appropriately called a counter-Reformation or a Catholic Reformation, there is no doubt that it reaffirmed much of the theology that the Reformers had rejected.[48] For example, session 22 of the Council declared that 'the Sacrifice of the Mass is propitiatory for the living and the dead'.[49] Likewise, session 25 declared that 'there is a Purgatory, and that the souls there detained are helped by the suffrages of the faithful, but principally by the acceptable sacrifice of the altar', and this session also upheld 'the intercession and invocation of saints; the honour (paid) to relics; and the legitimate use of images'.[50] These were

---

(note 45 *cont.*) of all blessings, in his Kingdom; if untroubled expectation of judgment, in the power given to him to judge. In short, since rich store of every kind of good abounds in him, let us drink our fill from this fountain, and from no other.' Calvin, *Institutes*, II.xvi.19.

46. Calvin, 'Reply', pp. 69–73.

47. John Olin, 'Introduction', in John Olin (ed.), *A Reformation Debate* (Grand Rapids, MI: Baker, 1966), pp. 24–25.

48. See A. G. Dickens, *The Counter Reformation* (London: Thames & Hudson, 1968), p. 7.

49. *Canons and Decrees of the Council of Trent*, trans. H. J. Schroeder (Rockford, IL: Tan Books, 1978), p. 145.

50. Ibid., pp. 214, 216.

doctrines that the Reformers denounced because of their corruption of the truth that salvation is through Christ alone. They, however, remain the official position of the Roman Catholic Church today. The 'trees' that had grown up to block the majestic view of Christ's achievements have been given a protected status, and the foliage is denser than ever.

Before twenty-first-century Protestants get on their high horse, it is worth reflecting on the 'trees' that we allow to grow in just the same way. Society has become increasingly relativistic, and liberal Protestants are increasingly reluctant to claim there is only one way of salvation. Even evangelical Christians, who champion the Reformation doctrine of Christ alone, can fall into the trap of depending on someone or something other than Christ. This can be as diverse as the reputation of a church or denomination, to how regularly a quiet time is kept. The Reformation message is to depend upon Christ alone. It is possible to worship things other than Christ, from children to health and wealth. The Reformation message is to worship Christ alone. The reason why the residents who have trees blocking their views are indignant is because they know how wonderful the experience is that they are now missing out on. Their outrage leads them to do something about the situation. So it was for the Reformers, and so it should be for contemporary Christians. Anything that corrupts the glorious truth that salvation is through Christ alone must be repudiated. For, as Peter declared, 'Salvation is found in no one else, for there is no other name under heaven given to mankind by which we must be saved.'[51]

Bibliography

Brewer, Brian, 'Merit', in R. Ward Holder (ed.), *The Westminster Handbook to Theologies of the Reformation*, 112–113, Louisville, KY: Westminster John Knox, 2010.

Calvin, John, 'Calvin's Reply to Sadoleto', in John Olin, *A Reformation Debate*, 49–94. Grand Rapids, MI: Baker, 1966.

———, *Institutes of the Christian Religion*, trans. F. L. Battles, ed. J. T. McNeill, Library of Christian Classics, London: SCM, 1961 (1559).

Canons and Decrees of the Council of Trent, trans. H. J. Schroeder, Rockford, IL: Tan Books, 1978.

Dickens, A. G., *The Counter Reformation*, London: Thames & Hudson, 1968.

'The Gallican Confession, AD 1559', in Philip Schaff (ed.), *The Creeds of Christendom: With History and Critical Notes*, 356–382, Grand Rapids, MI: Baker, 1983.

---

51. Acts 4:12.

'Heidelberg or Palatinate Catechism, AD 1563', in Philip Schaff (ed.), *The Creeds of Christendom: With History and Critical Notes*, 307–355, Grand Rapids, MI: Baker, 1983.

Johnson, Terry, *The Case for Traditional Protestantism: The Solas of the Reformation*, Edinburgh: Banner of Truth, 2004.

Letham, Robert, *The Work of Christ*, Contours of Christian Theology, ed. Gerald Bray, Downers Grove, IL: InterVarsity Press, 1993.

Lindberg, Carter, *The European Reformations*, Oxford: Blackwell, 1996.

McGrath, Alister E., *Luther's Theology of the Cross: Martin Luther's Theological Breakthrough*, 2nd edn, Oxford: Wiley-Blackwell, 2011.

Marshall, Peter, 'Purgatory', in R. Ward Holder (ed.), *The Westminster Handbook to Theologies of the Reformation*, 133, Louisville, KY: Westminster John Knox, 2010.

———, *Reformation England, 1480–1642*, 2nd edn, London: Bloomsbury Academic, 2012.

Mattox, Mickey, 'Indulgences', in R. Ward Holder (ed.), *The Westminster Handbook to Theologies of the Reformation*, 89–90, Louisville, KY: Westminster John Knox, 2010.

Olin, John, 'Introduction', in John Olin (ed.), *A Reformation Debate*, 7–28, Grand Rapids, MI: Baker, 1966.

Ozment, Steven, *Protestants: The Birth of a Revolution*, New York: Doubleday, 1993.

Packer, J. I., *Honouring the People of God: The Collected Shorter Writings of J. I. Packer*, Carlisle: Paternoster, 1999.

Preus, Daniel, 'Solus Christus', *Logia* 5, no. 3 (1996), pp. 19–22.

Sadoleto, Jacopo, 'Sadoleto's Letter to the Genevans', in John Olin (ed.), *A Reformation Debate*, 29–48, Grand Rapids, MI: Baker, 1966.

Steinmetz, D. C., *Luther in Context*, 2nd edn, Grand Rapids, MI: Baker Academic, 2002.

Wellum, Stephen, '*Solus Christus*: What the Reformers Taught and Why It Still Matters', *The Southern Baptist Journal of Theology* 19, no. 4 (Winter 2015), pp. 79–107.

10. JUSTIFICATION BY FAITH ALONE[1]

Michael J. Ovey

Claim and counter-claim

I was very struck, in a set of discussions that I was forced to be involved in about three years ago, by the claim of some that actually the Reformation was all about the principle of the supremacy of Scripture and *nothing* else. I wanted to talk about justification. I wanted to talk about penal substitution too. Therefore, I wanted to talk about Reformation theology more broadly. Yet I was informed: 'No! That's not Reformation theology. The only point of the Reformation was the supremacy of Scripture.' It is that 'only point' that I want to contest.

The reason that I want to contest it is that if that is indeed *all* the Reformation was about, then sooner or later we will have to face the charge that, as Protestants, we are simply schismatic. After all, when you read the opening statements of various Roman Catholic articles of faith, whether it is the Catechism or the Council of Trent or whatever, you *will* find statements about scriptural authority. So if that is the case, why are we *not* under the jurisdiction of the bishop of

---

1. This chapter was delivered as a lecture at the 2016 Protestant Reformation Society Conference held in Oxford between 30 August and 1 September. We are grateful to all those involved for allowing us to reproduce it here.

Rome? Well, not least because the fundamental theological disagreement between us over what Scripture says and the false claims of Roman Catholicism about what Scripture says still lies between us on the issue of justification. I don't really see that Rome's fundamental position has changed. We may not be facing precisely the same fate from Roman Catholic theologians as our fore-bear Thomas Cranmer did outside Balliol College – it may well be much more polite – but the fundamental differences in various ways remain, judging by the most recent catechetical statements coming out of Rome.

So I want to oppose the notion that the Reformation was really *just* about the supremacy of Scripture, by saying that actually the Reformation was about Scripture *and* salvation. In fact, in terms of historical sequence, you would have to say that it was about salvation first, and then it became a dispute about Scripture. But it is both-and.

It is not wrong, of course, to say that the central part of the Reformation debate was about Scripture – of course it was. However, it was not the *only* thing. It is the combination of these two things that we have to bear in mind. The reason why that is so significant, quite frankly, is that this sooner or later will have an impact on what we think the gospel is and how we proclaim salvation today. We are therefore in Galatians 1 territory and there is no point beating around that particular bush, pretending that it is not so. We are talking about the content of the gospel: how a man, how a woman, how a child, finds peace with God. So that's the claim and counter-claim that I want to explore in this chapter.

The history

It is worth distinguishing between three different periods in the sixteenth century, then looking briefly at an important observation from Calvin, before explaining a little further the key doctrinal themes that emerge.

The via moderna

First of all, before Luther nails those theses to the door at Wittenberg, we are faced with the period of the *via moderna*, or, as we might say, the new perspective of its time, the modern way. The *via moderna* in late medieval Catholicism in Germany and elsewhere was, amongst other things, a reforming movement, seeking to clear up the morality of various parts of the Roman church. It was earnestly ethical and we misunderstand some of its concerns if we miss that. It was also a movement marked by a very high regard for divine sovereignty; paradoxically, we might want to say *too high* a regard for divine sovereignty, but that's a slightly different question. The big thing is that, as a movement, even from its start, the fears were that it was semi-Pelagian.

That was not a fear that surfaces for the first time with Luther. There were bellwethers who were sounding exactly that fear earlier on in the medieval period. Thomas Bradwardine, the Archbishop of Canterbury – one of our better ones – actually made that point in a very lengthy essay: 'The Cause of the City of God against the Pelagians.'[2] Technically, you might well say the soteriology of the *via moderna* is a semi-Pelagian heresy, since it is both God *and* human effort that sees us saved. We may well want to pick up that great motto of the *via moderna*: 'do what you can and God will do the rest'. In that sense it is a liberalizing movement. It's not asking for perfection. Of course it isn't. Do your best. Do your best and God will do the rest. It's meant to provide an incentive for holiness because it's saying you may not be able to keep all the laws in all their perfection, but do your best and God will do the rest.

Early Reformation

That was the theological environment against which Luther was reacting. He was trained in that way of thinking. It is intriguing that one of Luther's questions was, 'Is my best good enough?' It is worth remembering that at that point, he is not talking just about ethics. He is talking about doctrine. Luther's huge grasp of the issues from very early in the Reformation includes this observation that he is not talking just about ethics. There is a critical doctrinal question that lies at the heart of this, and the particular doctrine in question is the doctrine of salvation. It is not just ethics. If you want someone who sticks just with ethics, you have to go to Erasmus of Rotterdam from the same period. Erasmus was in some ways a much more congenial ethicist than Luther. When all is said and done, we have to admit that Luther had a stormy side to his temperament. Yet one of the key insights of the early Reformation is that the real problem with human works is that it is precisely our best that is our undoing. That is clear in the Heidelberg Disputation – and it became absolutely critical for Luther and his fellow Reformers in the 1520s and 1530s. Human works cannot save because we must face the judgment *of God*. And that God is the God whose judgment is perfect and pure, and he is too pure to look on our unholiness. That, as I say, is one of the great insights of Calvin,

---

2. T. Bradwardine, 'The Cause of God against the Pelagians', trans. P. L. Nyhus, in H. A. Oberman (ed.), *Forerunners of the Reformation: The Shape of Late Medieval Thought Illustrated by Key Documents* (London: Lutterworth, 1967).

Luther, Cranmer and the rest. It is surprising because we're so used to the accusation that the problem with Protestantism is that it is antinomian in various ways, that it almost inevitably leads to moral laxity. You can do anything you like because you know you will be forgiven. Of course there's that risk. But actually, if we look back at the core moves made at the time of the Reformation, there is this idea that God is too holy to look on *any* iniquity. That's the issue.

Trent

In 1545 Pope Paul III finally convoked the Council of Trent, which in various ways remains a definitional moment for Roman Catholic theology of the orthodox variety. Trent strongly adopted the position of the *via moderna*, and fairly uncritically. The fascinating thing that emerges from that, as you look at the Council of Trent therefore from 1546 onwards, as it is dealing with the doctrine of justification, is quite how non-catholic in the non-institutional sense it really is. It adopted the reformist movement of the *via moderna*. That's the choice that was made. One way of construing what was happening in Trent is to say that actually the Roman Catholic hierarchy was confronted with *two* reforming movements. One of these, culminating in the fifteenth century with Gabriel Biel and other theologians like him, was the *via moderna*: 'Do your best, God will do the rest.' The other reforming movement was the one that came through Luther and the other 'Protestants', which said that justification is the imputed righteousness of Christ as he keeps the law for us. It helps us to realize that they were both reforming movements. The tragedy of the Council of Trent, then, is that it chose the wrong reforming movement. But if you went back to 1200, you wouldn't have found the kinds of things that Gabriel Biel said and did in the 1450s and 1460s. In that sense, it was not a *catholic* council of the church because it selected *one* recent strand and it selected the wrong one.

So there in summary are the three major historical movements I wanted to talk about: the *via moderna* up to 1517/1518; the early Reformation as Luther started to articulate things and was joined by Calvin and eventually adopted in England; and then the Council of Trent and the counter-Reformation, which is still with us today in various forms.

Calvin

However, before we move on to talk further about the theological issues involved in the doctrine of justification as it was articulated in the Reformation, an important overarching paradigm is provided for us by what we find at the very beginning of Calvin's *Institutes*, where he wrote about the relationship between the doctrine of God and the doctrine of humanity.[3] Calvin insisted that these are related in many ways. It is a very profound point, because he was reminding us that if you do something to your doctrine of humanity, you *will* do something to your doctrine of God. Similarly, if you say something about your doctrine of God, that will have consequences for your doctrine of humanity. It really does matter. One way of thinking about the tragedies of England and the West over the last two hundred years is to realize that we didn't necessarily start off with atheism; we started off with an inflated opinion of humanity.

It is always worthwhile asking people about their doctrine of humanity as well as what they *think* their doctrine of God really is. If we say that the doctrine of humanity and the doctrine of God are linked, we are faced with the very real possibility that, if we have a big doctrine of humanity, we may be talking about God *sotto voce*. After all, who needs him? Similarly, if we have a smaller view of humanity – that is to say, if we don't say that humans are the most important entities in the universe – we may end up talking about God *magna voce* – and rightly so. The relationship is inverse: little humanity, big God; big humanity, little God. And that's the kind of framework that I want us to have in mind as we start to unpack the three major doctrinal areas I want to explore in terms of justification and the Reformation: humanity, God and the gospel.

The key doctrinal themes

Humanity

What are the kinds of common themes you see when it comes to the doctrine of humanity, both in the Continental Reformation and in Anglicanism? An important part of the background is a very famous image that comes from a sermon by the medieval theologian Gabriel Biel on the circumcision of Jesus (at least, that is the earliest appeal to the image I've been able to find). He gives us a description of what humans are like after the fall. 'We are like birds,' he says, 'who have stones attached to our feet that are too heavy to let us fly.'[4] On first hearing that, it sounds like a great picture of how hard it is to be a

---

3. John Calvin, *Institutes of the Christian Religion*, trans. Ford Lewis Battles, ed. John T. McNeill (Philadelphia: Westminster, 1960), I.i.1.

4. G. Biel, 'The Circumcision of the Lord', trans. P. L. Nyhus, in H. A. Oberman (ed.), *Forerunners of the Reformation: The Shape of Late Medieval Thought Illustrated by Key Documents* (London: Lutterworth, 1967), pp. 171–172.

human being who keeps God's law. It is hard, very hard. It sounds like a pretty pessimistic view of humanity.

Intriguingly, though, particularly in the sixteenth century, you find Reformed and Lutheran theologians saying that that is exactly the image that is wrong. Why? Because it is not bleak enough. In this image the bird is fundamentally intact. All that is wrong with the bird is the stones. It is a more victim-centred account of human nature. Poor old bird, all that's wrong is the stones. Martin Chemnitz, in his *Examination of the Council of Trent*, spends a certain amount of ink saying why this is wrong.[5] And it's wrong because it doesn't capture what our hearts are actually like. That image of the bird doesn't actually deal with the things that Jesus tells us about our hearts in Mark 7, does it? When you think of his depiction of the human heart at that point, you realize that actually this 'birds with stones' picture – for all its gravity and seriousness in saying we can't keep God's law perfectly – actually is still too optimistic. It's saying that there is *too much* that has survived the fall. It's saying that there are parts of me that are untouched by the fall.

One particular writer, contributing to recent debates on this issue from the New Perspective side, talks about how we can't say that there are some people who are good and then some people who are bad. Yes, absolutely. Then he says that the line between good and bad goes right down the middle of all of us.[6] At first hearing, you might think that that's quite a bleak view of human beings. But it's still too optimistic. It's actually still saying that there is a part of me that is still untouched by the fall. And that's simply not true. When you read Romans 1:18–32 and as you listen to what Jesus says about the condition of our hearts, you see that the problem is not the external things. The problem is my heart and what I do with all of my capabilities, all of my appetites, all of my desires, all of my intelligence. All of them are corrupted by the fall. Once you've acknowledged that, you realize that right *there*, from that simple account of humanity onwards, there is going to be a massive cleavage between those of us who say we are birds tragically weighed down by stones and needing someone to help us fly (and the ability to fly is still with us) and those of us who say, 'No. The trouble with sin is that it has clipped our wings off and we cannot fly.' There's

---

5. M. Chemnitz, *Examination of the Council of Trent: Part 1*, trans. F. Kramer (St Louis: Concordia, 1971), pp. 413, 481–482, 494–495.

6. N. T. Wright, *Surprised By Scripture: Engaging Contemporary Issues* (New York: HarperCollins, 2015), p. 115. At this point Wright is echoing not Scripture but A. Solzhenitsyn, *The Gulag Archipelago 1918–1958: An Experiment in Literary Investigation*, trans. T. P. Whitney (New York: Harper & Row, 1973), p. 168.

all the difference in the world between those two interpretations of humanity post-fall. What Luther and the other Reformers saw is that the reality of humanity as fallen has singularly significant consequences.

Fallen

First of all – and this is very clear in Luther, from the Heidelberg Disputation onwards, and is a thought taken up at various points by Calvin in the *Institutes* as well as in Homily 2 from the Anglican Book of Homilies on the corruption of humanity – the problem is our *good* deeds. There is a fascinating part within the Heidelberg Disputation where Luther recognizes that of course there are the evil things one does, but then there are the good things. 'The righteous man also sins while doing good,' Luther wrote.[7] Take my almsgiving, Luther would say. What's wrong with my almsgiving? The real pressing question is whether I do this because I love God or because I want eternal life. And all of us – particularly those of us who have been involved in ministry – know the stinging irony of that moment when you have been preaching Romans 3:24 and then go on to verse 27, saying, 'What becomes of boasting?' and you hear that little voice in the back of your mind saying, 'My goodness, I made that point well.' That's the reality. Part of the beauty and power of the Reformation account of the human heart is its realism. In that light, part of the problem with the Tridentine–*via modernist*–humanist account is that it is an unrealistic denial. It is a denial strategy that says I am not as bad as I might be.

Luther pointed out that finally we must face the problem that as religious people we do religious things because we love ourselves and not God and not our neighbours. Doesn't that ring true? It rings true not just because the Bible teaches us this (though that is completely sufficient), but because deep down it is echoed in the experience of every one of us. And of course at that point we realize yet another aspect of the offence of the cross and preaching it as it truly is. This takes us to two very important consequences.

Once we say that the problem is our good deeds, then, methodologically, we have to be revelation-dependent. My heart is so corrupt that I cannot be trusted to work out what God is like through natural revelation, whether that natural revelation is the testimony of the creation around me, or what my mind or intellect determines is my inner spiritual consciousness. When we are confronted with the ideas we normally associate with the much later German theologian Schleiermacher from 1797/8 onwards, who saw religion as about the internal yearnings of the human heart and the testimony of the human heart to what

---

7. M. Luther, 'The Heidelberg Disputation' (1518), in *LW* 31:60.

we see and hear about God, we have to say, 'No. That is precisely what religion must *not* be about.' And we must say this because the Reformers remind us that the problem is our goods deeds: our religiosity, our religious instincts. That is why we need revelation. Similarly, salvation must therefore be grace-dependent – in fact, dependent on grace *alone*. The problem is my good deeds. My good deeds are not in fact good deeds, and cannot be.

So on that account of fallen humanity alone, the seeds of so much else follow. This takes us directly to justification, of course. The *via moderna* approach of the Council of Trent spoke of justification as progressive, something that starts in this world and continues. It is important to recognize that this can still lay claim to being a grace-based account (though not a grace-*alone*-based account). You might say that you *attain* your status by grace but *maintain* your status by works enabled by grace. Where have you heard that before? You contribute as law-keepers. You do your best, God does the rest.

Does this subvert the principle of grace? Does it give us grounds for boasting? The classic answer of Canon XI of the Council of Trent's Decree on Justification is, in effect, 'No. It does not give us grounds for boasting because these are deeds that are wrought in the Spirit.' Final judgment is on the basis of the whole life lived; on the basis of your Spirit-wrought deeds. And if you cannot hear the contemporary echoes, then I will have to be even more explicit: in our time, this is the New Perspective.

What's wrong with it? My attempts to keep the law after my conversion. I was converted in 1975. I *know* I have not kept the law in all its entirety in the forty-one years since then. It is not just that the Prayer Book in Morning and Evening Prayer reminds me that I haven't. First John 1 tells me that if I say I haven't sinned, I have deceived myself and the truth is not in me. I suspect your testimony would be the same. And so the question arises, 'What happens to my post-conversion sin?' That is the unanswered question in the New Perspective. In terms of Tridentine Catholicism, of course, you would solve it by going back to a sacramental economy, to penance, absolution and the priestly administration of grace.

Justified

Catholicism spoke about justification as progressive, with us contributing in an ongoing way as we are enabled by the Spirit. The Reformation, in stark contrast, spoke about a justification that is decisive. There is a moment when we move from being under judgment to being justified. When was I justified? On a summer evening in 1975 when the minister of the church suggested we sing 'my chains fell off' one more time. I was justified then. I may not have understood everything I was entitled to say at that point; nevertheless, as I confessed how I had got things wrong to my heavenly Father, I was entitled to say, 'I am a justified sinner. I'm forgiven.' It was just as in the Luke 18 parable of the Pharisee and the tax collector: the tax collector went home justified. It was just as in Romans 4: Abraham was justified *before* the giving of the law. That is a temporal statement. There was a before and after. Before the giving of the law, Abraham could say that he was justified. Now, if we then say that we've got to wait for a second justification on the day of judgment, have we not simply undone Paul's argument in Romans 4, as the Reformers said? Luther, Calvin and the rest knew about the arguments about second justification because they had heard them all from their opponents. In response, they would point to passages like Romans 4 and Luke 18 and say that justification is a present reality. It is decisive.

As we look at Homily 3, 'A Sermon of the Salvation of Mankind by Only Christ Our Saviour from Sin and Death Everlasting' – one of the homilies you can't read enough, in my opinion – we find that the distinctive mark of Anglican, Lutheran and Reformed Reformers is exactly that Christ keeps the law for us as the new Adam.[8] If we wanted a connection with the early church at that point, the person to think of is Irenaeus of Lyon (c. AD 180) and his statement in *A Demonstration of the Apostolic Preaching* that Christ is the new Adam, through whose righteousness, his righteous obedience, Satan is conquered.[9] It is *his* obedience which is counted as *my* obedience. Luther, Melanchthon, Chemnitz, Calvin, Bucer, Cranmer, Hooker: Christ keeps the law for us. It is therefore an alien righteousness (Phil. 3:9), not a righteousness of our own (that's what Hooker keeps on stressing), but it belongs to Christ and is given through faith in union.[10] Just as a man and a woman marry and share, so too the human individual is united with Christ, his or her Saviour, in faith, and in that union he bears our guilt and we bear his righteous obedience.[11] So it is as if I washed the feet in John 13. That is counted to me. It is as if you welcomed the leper, and so on. It is impossible to state that without being both warmed and humbled

---

8. T. Cranmer, 'A Sermon of the Salvation of Mankind by Only Christ Our Saviour from Sin and Death Everlasting', in *Certain Sermons or Homilies Appointed to Be Read in Churches in the Time of Queen Elizabeth of Famous Memory* (London: SPCK, 1864), p. 21.

9. Irenaeus of Lyon, *The Demonstration of the Apostolic Preaching*, 31, Christian Classics Ethereal Library, <https://www.ccel.org/ccel/irenaeus/demonstr.iv.html>.

10. R. Hooker, 'A Learned Discourse of Justification', in *Of the Laws of Ecclesiastical Polity*, Books 1 to 4 (London: Dent & Sons, 1907), p. 21.

11. M. Luther, *The Freedom of a Christian* (1520), in *LW* 31:351.

simultaneously: warmed because we are overwhelmed by the generosity of our God, and humbled as we think about the difference between our own lives and the life of Jesus with which we are clothed. It is absolutely wonderful. And it is absolutely perfect.

Given the choice between being clothed with the perfect obedience of Christ or trying to manufacture my own continual *imperfect* obedience, the rational choice is alien righteousness. At least, it's the rational choice if I have a view of myself that I cannot keep the law. It is only if I have a bigger, more optimistic view of myself and other people that I start to think, 'Well, maybe I don't need the alien imputed righteousness, the perfect righteousness of the Lord Jesus Christ, because I already have something of my own.'

Responding

In terms of response to the call of God, the first huge question for many is about human freedom. Isn't that exactly what you hear as you try to explain the imputation of Christ's righteousness, as you talk about the irresistible calling of God, and so on? 'What about human freedom?' In the Council of Trent and in the *via moderna*, God's call is resistible. After all, I'm a bird with stones. That's all. But as a bird with stones I can still respond to whoever it is who wants to help me. I am fundamentally intact. My heart is intact. If, on the other hand, I say, 'I am dead in my sins and transgressions' (Eph. 2:1) – because of the world around me, because of the machinations of Satan and because I follow the desires of my own heart – then a positive response to God's call cannot be spontaneously generated by me. This follows as surely as night follows day. At that point, we are bound to realize that the entire account of conversion that is lurking there in the *via moderna* and the Council of Trent is an account of the resistible call with the human heart saying unaided, 'Yes, please'. However, the New Testament will not let us go there. Human freedom, in an important sense, has to be restricted precisely because God has to do it. This is what we find in Luther's *Bondage of the Will* (1525) which talks about the way my will is bound in sin and so God must do it.[12] This is what Calvin wrote about, particularly when he referred to the Holy Spirit. He described faith as the principal work of the Holy Spirit.[13] God must call sovereignly. So humanity is fallen, justified, and the call is irresistible to which the dead human soul responds. This is a very different account from that of Trent or the New Perspective.

---

12. M. Luther, *The Bondage of the Will* (1525), in *LW* 33:64–67.

13. Calvin, *Institutes (1559)*, III.i.4.

God

We have talked about the way the doctrine of God and the doctrine of humanity are intertwined. We have seen that the Tridentine–*via modernist* account of humanity is very different from the way the doctrine of justification is understood by the Reformers, who see as its background the biblical teaching on total depravity. What we're starting to see is that the *via modernist* account, the Tridentine account, the New Perspective account, has a far more optimistic view of what a human being is, and a very different view of the nature of human action from that of the Reformers.

Sufficient mercy

What about God? Following the logic of the Reformers, God is a God whose mercy is sufficient. His mercy is not just *efficient*, in the sense that it does something. God's mercy is *sufficient*, in the sense that it does everything that needs to be done. That's the critical thing. Put that way, isn't it ridiculous to think that God needs me to contribute to my salvation? Can't God complete the job himself? When put like that, it is a big question (and one with parallels elsewhere). God's mercy is sufficient for the salvation of sinners. Not just that: in the Reformers' account, God is a God of perfect justice. God is a God who is too pure to look on evil. So God does not simply overlook the evil that is done or the evil that compromises even my 'good' work. It is mercy, it is sufficient, and it does not vitiate God's character.

Perfect judge

It is vital that we see this, because so frequently the Reformation account is pictured as God just letting people off, as if he has somehow compromised his justice. No. God has insisted upon perfect justice, perfect righteousness, and he has found it *only* in the Lord Jesus. His mercy extends that obedience to our credit. That means that, in terms of the picture of God, God is free. On the Tridentine side of the equation, it is humanity that is free. We can resist God's call or accept God's call. But with the Reformers we must speak about the freedom *of God*. Romans 3:24 – God justifies *freely*.

The freedom of God

Now very frequently, and rightly, we want to say that God justifies us in the sense that we earn nothing – we need earn nothing. But the corollary of that is that God is under no obligation to us. God saved me when he didn't have to. That's what free justification means from the flipside. In that sense, as we talk about God's free justification (Rom. 3:24), we're actually talking about God's eternally free nature.

There are all kinds of theological things at stake there. One of the things that the sinful human heart longs to do is to bind God in one way or another, manufacturing rules for him. In its crudest form, that's magic. You might equally say that this is one of the problems with the sacramental economy of the late Middle Ages. It does not allow God to be free. It refuses to accept his freedom. Of course, sinful human beings are not going to be terribly pro-God's freedom, because if God is free, who knows what he might do? This finds expression in a very old poem:

> 'There is no God,' the wicked saith,
> 'and truly it's a blessing,
> for what he might have done with us
> it's better only guessing.'[14]

One of the things the Reformers force me to face up to in the account of justification, by the way they appeal to Romans 3:24, is the question, 'Do I want my God to be free?' Yet that freedom of God is incredibly good news because, to be honest, given the state of my heart, unless God is free there is no salvation for someone like me. Critical, and neglected in this discussion, is the freedom of God.

Gospel
Luke 24
Let's think about the gospel that flows out of this. One of the things that has intrigued me in recent years is a recollection that the evangelicalism in which I was reared, when it spoke about the great commission and God's plan for the church, would frequently refer to Matthew 28 – and rightly so. Luke 24 was much less to the fore as the emphasis was placed on mission, witness and obeying all that Christ commanded. However, as it happens, when we go back to the Reformers, frequently Luke 24 is much more in the foreground, especially its description of just what the content of the gospel is. The gospel is a preaching of 'repentance and forgiveness of sins in the name of the Lord Jesus Christ' to all nations. That's what the Bible is about, says the risen Jesus. And you find that in Melanchthon's *Apology for the Augsburg Confession*, you find it in our own Homily of Repentance, you find it in Calvin's *Institutes*, Book 3. Throughout each of

---

14. A. H. Clough, 'There Is No God, the Wicked Sayeth', from *Dipsychus*, <https://web.archive.org/web/20071124062834/http://whitewolf.newcastle.edu.au/words/authors/C/CloughArthurHugh/verse/misc/wickedsayeth.html>.

these and further afield in the Reformation, you will find this consistent theme: the gospel is repentance and forgiveness of sins in the name of the Lord Jesus Christ for all nations.

The reason why I think we must recapture this Reformation view just at the moment is because Matthew 28 doesn't talk explicitly about repentance. For various reasons, in our time that is a pretty serious lack, frankly. Not that the verse itself is defective, but in our context it doesn't teach everything that we need to be taught. We are living in a time when the gospel presentation is frequently put simply in terms of 'Christ is Lord'. The risk is that our culture, our time, hears that not as a call to repentance, as it might have been heard by someone in the first century reading Romans, but rather as an interesting piece of information on a par with 'Isn't it surprising that David Cameron won the last election? Oh, he is now the Prime Minister.' It's a piece of *information* about who happens to be in charge, not a *call* to my heart that says I have been a rebel and preferred my own way and have been spiritually complicit in Psalm 2's description of the assassination of the Messiah. I hear the news but not the summons to repentance.

To take an illustration from *The Lord of the Rings*, there is all the difference in the world between saying, 'Aragorn is the King of Gondor', and saying, 'I've been in rebellion against the king.' The first does not call for repentance. It does not even involve recognizing a need to repent. Yet the second does – and we do. In Acts, as we see Luke laying out what follows from Luke 24, we hear a message of repentance and forgiveness of sins for Jew and Gentile alike – whether it's the Jerusalemites, for their murder of the Messiah, or the Athenians for their idolatry. The God of Acts 17:30 calls on all people everywhere to repent. The reason why we need to recapture this is because the Reformers would say that is what the gospel is about, and it is what we in our time have lost. Furthermore, it is what, in terms of the Council of Trent and the *via moderna*, was being distorted in various ways.

So, from Luke 24, in terms of the Augsburg Confession, the *Institutes* and the Homily on Repentance, repentance is to do with contrition and faith in Christ. Contrition is a recognition that my sins deserve God's condemnation, and that means that there is a place for the preaching of the law. After all, the law teaches us that we are sinners amongst other things (Rom. 7). Just about everybody on the Protestant side in the sixteenth century was saying something like that, and those who weren't were held to account for denying it (e.g. Johann Agricola). We must preach the law. And we mustn't be choked off preaching the law by someone who says, 'You're just trying to make me feel guilty.' Yes, in an important sense, I am trying to make you feel guilty, because, unless you feel guilty, you will not seek salvation and forgiveness of sins in the name of Jesus

Christ. You will think you can do it yourself. I do no-one any favours when I refuse to make people feel guilty. The Reformers would say to us, 'You must recover the preaching of the law.' There are certainly times when we must preach gospel in a kind of full Lutheran sense, especially when legalism is a real danger. Yet there are just as certainly times when we must preach law. In the 1520s, 1530s and 1540s the Reformers would explain it in these terms: 'You must preach law to those who are convinced of their own righteousness.' Doesn't that describe the dominant attitude of the West?

I sometimes listen to BBC Radio 4. One of the things that soon becomes very clear about the British establishment is its sense of self-righteousness (I suspect the British are not alone in this). 'We're not racist. We're not this, that or the other. We have political correctness programmes to stamp out homophobic bullying in schools. We are righteous compared with previous generations.' At that point our culture is a culture that needs to recover the preaching of the law because it is a culture convinced of its own righteousness. That's going to be a huge challenge, but that's what the Reformers – and indeed the New Testament – would say to us.

They'd also say that you must not preach law only. Contrition without faith in Christ is an empty repentance. It's the repentance of Judas and the repentance of Cain. Contrition must be married to faith in Christ: that sense that he has promised mercy even to me, a sinner. So, then, we have repentance/contrition and faith in Christ – these two elements – and both of these are related to the forgiveness of sins in the New Testament. It is in the name of Christ because that is the only name through which forgiveness can be granted, because he alone has the perfect life with which to clothe us. So much follows from that account of the gospel: the uniqueness of Christianity, its orientation towards forgiveness (and not therapy or health, wealth and prosperity) and its emphasis on preaching law as well as gospel. That stands in contrast to the way repentance operates in Roman Catholic polemic.

Repentance in Roman Catholic polemic

In 1530 Johann Eck and other Roman Catholic theologians produced a refutation of the Augsburg Confession, which granted contrition as part of repentance but insisted that repentance also involves satisfaction.[15] However, the moment you've said that, you have implied that God's mercy is not sufficient because it must be supplemented by my meritorious acts. We then

---

15. 'Response to Article 12', *Confutatio Pontificia*, in J. M. Reu (ed.), *The Augsburg Confession: A Collection of Sources* (St Louis: Concordia, 1983), pp. 349–383.

return to a soteriology with a fundamentally semi-Pelagian structure in which it is not just God's mercy, but God's mercy plus my acts. That's what repentance is. That's when satisfaction creeps in so easily. If you're really repentant, you'll give £50 to WaterAid. It's so easy – even in our evangelical churches – to add in that sort of rider, if not explicitly, then sometimes implicitly. As we do that, we've stopped preaching law to bring people to a knowledge of their sins and we've started preaching law as the way that they can be saved. But that's not what it's for.

Significance

We began with a claim and counter-claim. The claim was that the Reformation was only about the supremacy of Scripture. We have been exploring the evidence that the Reformation was *not* just about the supremacy of Scripture. It certainly was about that. But it was always about more than that, not least because Scripture itself is about more than that. At the heart of the Reformation was a cluster of core convictions about salvation.

Safeguarding grace alone

Why were the Reformers so concerned about justification by faith? I think the reason is aptly summed up by the second-generation German Reformer Martin Chemnitz. In his *Examination of the Council of Trent*, he maintained that the reason why justification by faith is the hinge of true religion is because, unless you hold to justification by faith alone, anchored in and given content by the imputed righteousness of Christ, you will lose the doctrine of salvation by grace alone.[16] It's as straightforward as that. If we do not have justification by faith in the Christ whose righteousness is given to us, we will be left justifying ourselves and grace will not be alone.

I suspect the Reformers would say that one of our problems as evangelicals in the early twenty-first century is that we have been fooled by people who talk about the grace of God an awful lot but who have actually forgotten that the decisive point of difference between Trent and Calvin, between Trent and Chemnitz, was the grace of God *alone*. Is the grace of God sufficient? Or does it need to be supplemented by our religious effort? Unless we have the Protestant doctrine of justification by faith, grace will not be alone.

---

16. M. Chemnitz, *Examination of the Council of Trent*, pp. 501, 533.

What is the gospel?

With that comes the whole question of 'What is the gospel?' What is the good news that I'm going to proclaim? And in particular, as a practical point of application, may I say, 'I am a justified sinner now?' If I'm sincerely seeking after God at all, and I'm not able to say that I'm a justified sinner now, then I will be left saying that I've got to *do* something, whether that something is a good deed or a ritual. Think of the sects in recent times that have insisted on baptism administered specifically by them as the final step in someone's salvation. Think of the way variations of that move are played out in other places.

Eschatology

Once we've understood that idea of being a justified sinner now, we come to realize that the Reformers had a profoundly different eschatology compared with what we have seen in the *via moderna* or today in the New Perspective. The current jargon is that we must not over-realize or under-realize our eschatology. We keep wanting to talk about what God has started but not finished.

Yet in terms of eschatology, the Reformers would insist that justification is fully realized. I can say I am a justified sinner now, even though I cannot say that I am a perfected sinner now. My children are particularly clear on that particular point at the moment. I am not yet perfected and it would be an over-realized eschatology for me to claim that I was. But my point is that it would be an under-realized eschatology for me to say anything less than 'I am a justified sinner now'.

I must not overstate my perfection or sanctification. That's something that has begun but has not yet reached its end. But as we looked at the *via moderna*, we saw that the eschatological balance had gone the other way, vastly understating our justification. Our justification was treated just like our sanctification, as inaugurated but not perfected, as we looked forward to a second justification or final justification. Whether according to the *via moderna* or the New Perspective today, the decisive moment in your justification is seen as in the future because it is based on your whole life lived and your deeds wrought in the Spirit. So at that point, whereas Romans 4 tells us that we must say that justification is now, because that at least is realized, the Roman Catholic view at that point is an under-realized eschatology, speaking of justification as an as-yet-incomplete process.

Strangely though, when it comes to meritorious works, this view is in fact *over*-realized, because it says that the works I do can be meritorious, even if they are not perfected. That is a subtle form of over-realization, but it is still an over-realized eschatology, just as much as that of the person who says that when you become a Christian you will never know a day's sickness ever again. Yes, that will be true in eternity – gloriously true – but it is not true now, unfortunately. So, eschatologically, there are some huge things at stake in this doctrine in terms of what God *has* done and what he has started but not finished. The problem is that the *via moderna* reversed what the Bible teaches, and that is one of the things that the Reformers in their account of justification recovered.

Humanity and God

Our starting point for exploring the doctrinal entailments of justification by faith was that great Calvin quote about humanity and God. If we are thinking about the picture of God that emerges in the Reformation, it is, very decisively, that God is free and sovereign while humanity is bound by sin which compromises every one of our faculties. However, if we consider the *via moderna* and the Council of Trent, humanity is in a critical sense unbound and God is not sovereign, not truly free in the way that he administers his grace. Now, as you think about that, there is a last but very basic question: 'Is it good to have such a little picture of God?' No. That is the seductive thing about the *via moderna*, and Trent and its twentieth- and twenty-first-century descendants: they flatter us. At the end of the day, while Paul says, 'What then becomes of boasting?' these approaches actually leave us with something to boast about. The Reformers would most definitely say 'No' to that. If I boast, may I boast in the cross of my Lord Jesus Christ, because what he has done is free and sufficient to save me.

Bibliography

Biel, G., 'The Circumcision of the Lord', trans. P. L. Nyhus, in H. A. Oberman, *Forerunners of the Reformation: The Shape of Late Medieval Thought Illustrated by Key Documents*, 165–174, London: Lutterworth, 1967.

Bradwardine, T., 'The Cause of God against the Pelagians', trans. P. L. Nyhus, in H. A. Oberman (ed.), *Forerunners of the Reformation: The Shape of Late Medieval Thought Illustrated by Key Documents*, 151–162, London: Lutterworth, 1967.

Calvin, John, *Institutes of the Christian Religion*, trans. Ford Lewis Battles, ed. John T. McNeill, Philadelphia: Westminster, 1960.

Chemnitz, M., *Examination of the Council of Trent: Part 1*, trans. F. Kramer, St Louis: Concordia, 1971.

Cranmer, T., 'A Sermon of the Salvation of Mankind by Only Christ Our Saviour from Sin and Death Everlasting', in *Certain Sermons or Homilies Appointed to Be Read in Churches in the Time of Queen Elizabeth of Famous Memory*, 20–32. London: SPCK, 1864.

Hooker, R., 'A Learned Discourse of Justification', in *Of the Laws of Ecclesiastical Polity*, Books 1 to 4, London: Dent & Sons, 1907.

Irenaeus of Lyon, *The Demonstration of the Apostolic Preaching*, 31, Christian Classics Ethereal Library, <https://www.ccel.org/ccel/irenaeus/demonstr.iv.html>.

Pelikan, Jaroslav and Helmut T. Lehmann (eds.), *Luther's Works*, 55 vols., St Louis: Concordia; Philadelphia: Fortress Press, 1955–86.

Reu, J. M. (ed.), *The Augsburg Confession: A Collection of Sources*, St Louis: Concordia, 1983.

Solzhenitsyn, A., *The Gulag Archipelago 1918–1958: An Experiment in Literary Investigation*, trans. T. P. Whitney, New York: Harper & Row, 1973.

Wright, N. T., *Surprised by Scripture: Engaging Contemporary Issues*, New York: HarperCollins, 2015.

11. SCRIPTURE ALONE

Mark D. Thompson

In a landmark work from 1845, *The Principle of Protestantism*, church historian Philip Schaff (1819–93) distinguished the formal and material principles of the Reformation. The formal principle, he argued, 'consists in this, that the word of God, as it has been handed down to us in the canonical books of the Old and New Testaments, is the pure and proper source as well as the only certain measure, of all saving truth'.[1] He had previously identified the material principle as 'the doctrine of the justification of the sinner before God by the merit of Christ alone through faith'.[2] This is a characteristically Lutheran way of filling out the distinction.[3] In the seventeenth century, Reformed theologians preferred

---

1. P. Schaff, *The Principle of Protestantism as Related to the Present State of the Church*, trans. J. W. Nevin (Chambersburg: General Reformed Church, 1845), pp. 70–71.
2. Ibid., p. 2.
3. Schaff may have been influenced by August Twesten (1789–1876), a Lutheran who embraced the ideas of Schleiermacher: *Vorlesungen über die Dogmatik der evangelisch-lutherischen Kirche* (Lectures on the dogma of the evangelical–Lutheran Church), 2 vols. (Hamburg: Friedrich Perthes, 1838), 1:259, 269. However, note T. George, *Theology of the Reformers* (Nashville: Broadman, 1988), pp. 82, 85, who cites J. A. (*sic*) Dorner, actually another Lutheran, Isaac A. Dorner (1809–84).

to speak of God himself as the material principle.[4] Regardless of the room for debate on this issue – need the article of the standing and falling church be the ultimate subject matter of all theology? – both of the great traditions flowing out of the Reformation were agreed on the significance of Scripture.

To a certain extent, so too was the Roman Catholic Church. Luther would have gained no traction with his appeal to the authority of Scripture if it was entirely out of step with the Roman tradition. Medieval theologians, as well as those of the patristic period, claimed to acknowledge the authority of Scripture. Richard of St Victor (1110–73), an influential exegete and theologian of the High Middle Ages, commenting on the account of the Transfiguration in Matthew 17, remarked,

> Any truth that the authority of the Scriptures does not confirm is suspect in my eyes; I do not receive Christ in his brightness, unless Moses and Elijah are standing by . . . I do not receive Christ without a witness. No apparent revelation is ratified without the testimony of Moses and Elijah, without the authority of the Scriptures.[5]

Luther's constant reference to Scripture, and his monumental stand at Worms on the basis of the authority of Scripture, made sense and was incredibly powerful because all sides recognized that the Bible is indeed the word of the living God. His teaching was a devastating critique of Roman theology precisely because of this purportedly common ground. In fact, the Church of Rome claimed to be the guardian of Scripture. Yet in the centuries prior to the Reformation the authority of the papacy, the canon law and the pronouncements of church councils were also recognized alongside the authority of Scripture and in such a way that they, rather than Scripture, appeared to have the final word. The most extreme statement in this direction came from Silvester Mazzolini (Prierias), who penned the first official Roman response to Luther's Ninety-Five Theses: 'Whoever does not hold fast to the teachings of the Roman Church

4. Richard Muller, *Post-Reformation Reformed Dogmatics: The Rise and Development of Reformed Orthodoxy, Ca. 1520 to Ca. 1725*, 2nd edn, 4 vols. (Grand Rapids: Baker Academic, 2003), p. 434.
5. Richard of St Victor, *The Book of the Twelve Patriarchs*, p. 81 (*Patrologiae, cursus completes, series Latina*, ed J. P. Migne, 221 vols. [Paris: Migne, 1844–64], 196:57D). English translation cited in H. Feiss, *On Love: A Selection of the Works of Hugh, Dam, Achard, Richard and Godfrey of St Victor* (New York: New City Press, 2012), pp. 48–49.

and of the Pope as the infallible rule of faith, from which even Holy Scripture draws its strength and authority, is a heretic.'[6]

Perhaps the most obvious lasting legacy of the Reformers was their fresh and determined critique of all Christian thought and practice on the basis of the teaching of Scripture. Luther, Zwingli, Calvin, Cranmer and others challenged the place the church had given to tradition, scholastic theology had given to human philosophy and reason, and the Anabaptists had given to experience. The final unchallengeable authority over these three real but secondary authorities is the written word of God. Their challenge needs to be heard afresh today, in the light of new but strangely familiar calls to give sustained attention to the Christian tradition, reason or experience alongside Scripture. It is not too difficult to discern in contemporary theology a foregrounding of the Christian tradition, or the consensus of our communities on what is true and just and nourishing of life, or accounts of individual or corporate Christian experience. Biblicism is sometimes decried even by those who affirm their allegiance to the creeds and confessions which themselves proclaimed the supreme authority of Scripture. On the other hand, a more modern individualism is sometimes confused with Reformation biblicism. Scripture alone becomes 'the right of private judgment' where idiosyncratic interpretations must be respected without regard for those who have read the texts before us or alongside us. The Bible, and not our opinions (or the opinions of others) about the Bible, is the supreme authority and yet the Bible is not our sole and private possession: we read and teach it in the context of the communion of saints. So there is much to be gained by turning back to the Reformers themselves to see, by carefully paying attention to their own words, just what *they* meant by *sola scriptura* and more widely what they had to say about the nature, authority and use of the Bible.

Luther's appeal to *sola scriptura*

Luther's attitude towards Scripture never really deviated from that which he articulated in his stand at the Diet of Worms in April 1521:

> Unless I am convinced by the testimony of the Scriptures or by evident reason –
> for I can believe neither pope nor councils alone, as it is clear that they have

---

6. Silvestro Prierias, *De potestate papae dialogus* (1518), cited in Latin and English in H. A. Oberman, *The Reformation: Roots and Ramifications*, trans. A. C. Gow (Edinburgh: T&T Clark, 1994), p. 124.

erred repeatedly and contradicted themselves – I consider myself conquered
by the Scriptures adduced by me and my conscience is captive to the Word
of God. I cannot nor will not recant anything, since to act against conscience
is neither safe nor sound. Here I stand, I cannot do otherwise. God help me.
Amen.[7]

He used the expressions 'the Scriptures' and 'the Word of God' interchange-
ably. He considered the words of Scripture and clear reasoning from Scripture
a ground on which to stand firm against the Pope, the empire and the devil. He
considered his conscience captive to the Word of God. Luther would always
insist that it was not his personal courage or integrity that empowered such a
stand. It was rather the sheer power and authority of the word which God had
given us.

Luther never doubted the nature of Scripture as the word of God.[8] In 1522
he wrote, 'We have no other word than Scripture. That is why all the wicked
should be reproved with it.'[9] Later in the same treatise he would be most explicit:

Furthermore, I ask whether or not St. Paul's word and order are derived from God's
word and order? I think that the pope himself, with all his devils, even though he
suppresses every word of God, cannot deny that St. Paul's word is God's word and
that his order is the order of the Holy Spirit.[10]

Ten years later, commenting on Psalm 45:6, he would insist,

The Word is so irreproachable that not a single iota can err in the Law or the divine
promises. For that reason we must yield to no sect, not even in one tittle of Scripture,

---

7. The final line does not appear in the official record but in the transcripts made
   of the speech by friends of Luther who were present. It appears there was quite
   some noise in the crowded hall once Luther uttered the critical words *revocare neque
   possum nec volo*, 'I neither can nor will recant'. 'Luther at the Diet of Worms' (1521),
   LW 32:112 = *WA* 7:838.4–8.

8. Mark D. Thompson, *A Sure Ground on Which to Stand: The Relation of Authority
   and Interpretive Method in Luther's Approach to Scripture* (Carlisle: Paternoster, 2004),
   pp. 68–90.

9. *Against the Spiritual Estate of the Pope and the Bishops Falsely So Called* (1522),
   LW 39:250 = *WA* 10/2:108.25–26.

10. *Against the Spiritual Estate, LW* 39:277 = *WA* 10/2:139.14–18.

no matter how much they clamour and accuse us of violating love when we hold so strictly to the Word.[11]

It becomes apparent when we look at what Luther himself actually said that the modern attempts to distinguish between Scripture and the word of God are only anachronistically applied to him. Of course he knew that Jesus was designated the Word in John's Gospel. He knew the expression could be used of Jesus, the words Jesus spoke, the words proclaimed by the apostles and the written words of Scripture. The distinction between Jesus and Scripture was not that one was the Word of God and one was not, but that only Jesus is God.[12] For that reason, 'Christ is Lord over Scripture and over all works'.[13] However, to treat the Bible as the Word of God is not to dethrone Jesus, nor to engage in bibliolatry, but rather to take seriously what Jesus himself said about the Old Testament Scriptures and what the apostles understood about their own preaching and writing under the impress of the Spirit. We are humble and tremble before these words (Isa. 66:2) because they are the words by which God addresses us.

The famous hard case for Luther was the epistle of James. He had two difficulties with James. In the first instance, it was the epistle to which his opponents regularly turned to challenge his doctrine of justification by faith alone. After all, the only place where the expression 'justified by faith alone' is actually used in the New Testament (not counting Luther's controversial addition of the word *allein* in his German translation of Rom. 3:28) is James 2:24, and it is only used there in order to deny it: 'You see that a person is justified by works and not by faith alone' (Jas 2:24, ESV). Luther struggled with reconciling Paul and James. 'I will give my doctor's hat to the one who can reconcile [James and Paul],' he told his students.[14] In the second instance, clearly related to the first, he did not see James as an epistle that clearly put forward Christ. Luther was convinced that this was a fundamental interpretive principle: the Scriptures testify of Christ. In his words, we must look for *was Christum treibt*, 'what drives home Christ'.[15] With its emphasis on Christian living without an exposition of Christ and the salvation he accomplished, James was less useful, in Luther's view, when it came to preaching the gospel. For these two reasons he struggled with James. But he

---

11. *Lecture on Psalm 45* (1533), *LW* 12:242 = *WA* 40/2:531.30–34.

12. *Table Talk* 5177 (1540), *LW* 54:395 = *WATr* 4:695.16 – 696.2.

13. *Galatians Commentary* (1535), *LW* 26:295 = *WA* 40/1:458.20–21.

14. *Table Talk* 3292a (1532), *WATr* 3:253.27–28.

15. 'Preface to the Epistles of James and Jude' (1522), *LW* 35:396 = *WADB* 7:384.25–27.

could never simply dispose of it. He reordered his New Testament and put James at the back with Hebrews and Revelation. He made clear that he could not 'include it among the chief books [*der rechten Hauptbücher*]'.[16] Nevertheless, he did not feel free to remove it altogether, despite some exaggerated statements over dinner.[17] It never stopped being the word of God, which is why he could never stop wrestling with it.[18]

Seeing Scripture as the written word of God, Luther would speak in the strongest terms of Scripture's truthfulness. We have already seen that Luther could emphasize that 'not a single iota can err [*vitiosum sit*] in the Law or the divine promises'. Even when faced with difficulty, he insisted, 'we must honour the Holy Spirit by believing his words and accepting them as divine truth.'[19] These testimonies to Luther's view could be multiplied. The boldest of them all, perhaps, is the comment he made in his Galatians commentary of 1535: 'it is impossible that Scripture should contradict itself. It only appears so to senseless and obstinate hypocrites.'[20] The reason was simple, as he had made clear a few years before: 'For the Holy Spirit neither lies nor errs nor doubts.'[21]

Luther was entirely convinced that God had communicated clearly in his Word. The clarity of Scripture was a particular emphasis in *The Bondage of the Will*, written in response to Erasmus in 1525. He boldly declared, 'Moreover, against you I say concerning the entire Scripture: I want to call no part of it obscure.'[22] Of course he recognized that some parts of Scripture are more difficult than others. However, Luther saw this as the reader's problem rather than a problem with the text.

---

16. 'Preface to the Epistles of James and Jude' (1522), *LW* 35:397 = *WADB* 7:386.17–18.

17. 'We should throw the Epistle of James out of this school, for it doesn't amount to much.' *Table Talk* 5443 (1542), *LW* 54:424 = *WATr* 5:157.17–18. Cf. *Table Talk* 5854, *WATr* 5:382.14–18; *Table Talk* 5974, *WATr* 5:1–8.

18. In a more formal setting in 1542, at the same time as complaining 'I almost feel like throwing Jimmy into the stove, as the priest in Kalenberg did', he could talk about dealing with it and interpreting it 'according to the sense of *the rest of the Scriptures*' (emphasis added). *The Licentiate Examination of Heinrich Schmedenstede* (1542), *LW* 34:317 = *WA* 39/2:20–22, 24–25.

19. *Sermons on the Gospel of St John* (1537–8), *LW* 22:10 = *WA* 46:545.18–20.

20. *Commentary on Galatians* (1535), *LW* 26:295 = *WA* 40/1:458.35–36.

21. *Confession Concerning Christ's Supper* (1528), *LW* 37:279 = *WA* 26:4518.19–20

22. *The Bondage of the Will* (1525), *LW* 33:94 = *WA* 18:656.15–16. For a discussion of Luther on the clarity of Scripture, see Thompson, *A Sure Ground*, pp. 193–247.

I admit, of course, that there are many texts in the Scriptures that are obscure and abstruse, not because of the majesty of their subject matter, but because of our ignorance of their vocabulary and grammar; but these texts in no way hinder a knowledge of all the subject matter of Scripture.[23]

The clarity of Scripture was critical if there was to be genuine faith on the part of God's human creatures.

Thus it is not possible that a man, of his own reason and strength, should by works ascend to heaven, anticipating God and moving him to be gracious. On the contrary, God must anticipate all works and thoughts, and make a promise clearly expressed in words, which man then takes and keeps in good, firm faith. Then there follows the Holy Spirit, who is given to man for the sake of this same faith.[24]

Scripture also needed to be clear in and of itself if it was to function effectively as the final authority over and above the words of the Fathers.

Or tell me, if you can, who finally decides when two statements of the fathers contradict themselves? Scripture ought to provide this judgment, which cannot be delivered unless we give to Scripture the chief place in everything, that which is acknowledged by the fathers: that is, that it is in and of itself the most certain, the most accessible, the most clear of all, interpreting itself, approving, judging and illuminating all things.[25]

A clear and truthful word from God was more than sufficient ground on which to make a stand. Luther used the language of sufficiency explicitly in 1530, in the first four of the theses prepared to ensure his point of view was heard at the Diet of Augsburg:

1. The church of God has no power to enact any article of faith; nor has it established any, nor will it ever establish any.
2. The church of God has no power to impose any command of good works; nor has it ever imposed any, nor will it ever impose any.

---

23. *Bondage, LW* 33:25 = *WA* 18:606.22–24.
24. *A Treatise on the New Testament, That Is, the Holy Mass* (1520), *LW* 35:82–83 = *WA* 6:356.13–19.
25. *Assertion of All the Articles of M. Luther Lately Condemned by the Bull of Leo X* (1520), *WA* 7:97.19–24.

3. All of the articles are sufficiently established in the Holy Scriptures, so that there is no need for them to be established otherwise.

4. All of the commandments of good works are sufficiently established in the Holy Scriptures so that there is no need for them to be established otherwise.[26]

Luther was confident that the Christian person with the Word of God was in a strong position in the face of the devil's lies. 'Hold to Scripture and the Word of God,' he wrote in 1521 in the light of his pending excommunication. 'There you will find truth and security – assurance and a faith that is complete, pure, sufficient, and abiding.'[27] A year later, in a sermon on Matthew 2, Luther wrote:

> [Christ] did this [allowed his birth to be searched for in Scripture] to teach us to cling to Scripture and not to follow our own presumptuous ideas or any human teaching. For it was not his desire to give us his Scripture in vain. It is in Scripture and nowhere else, that he permits himself to be found. He who despises Scripture and sets it aside, will never find him.[28]

Luther pioneered an appeal to Scripture that was more thoroughgoing and more consistent than that of the Roman church. One of his favourite biblical texts, judging by how often it was quoted by him, was 1 Thessalonians 5:21 – 'Test everything; hold fast what is good' (ESV). The measure by which everything was to be tested was undoubtedly the Bible. Luther understood the Bible to be the word of God, carrying his authority, effectively communicating his truth, without distortion or error or falsehood, and sufficient for the purpose for which it was given: that we might live by faith in Christ.

Zwingli's joy in the powerful and effective Word of God

Huldrych Zwingli, the pioneer of the Reformation in Zurich, laid the ground-work for changing the city with a new pattern of preaching. Upon taking up the post of parish priest (*Leutpriester*) in the Grossmünster on 1 January 1519,

---

26. *Articles against the Whole School of Satan and All the Gates of Hell* (1530), *WA* 30/2:420.5–16.

27. *Defence and Explanation of All the Articles* (1521), *LW* 32:98 = *WA* 7:455.22–24.

28. 'Gospel for the Festival of the Epiphany', *Church Sermons* (1522), *LW* 52:171 = *WA* 10/1/1:576.6–10.

he abandoned the lectionary and began to preach sequentially through Matthew's Gospel. That one decision moved the Bible to the centre of the service and the centre of the Reformation in Zurich. It 'became the primary place to encounter God'.[29] Zwingli's enthusiasm for direct and sustained engagement with Scripture arose from his own experience. He explained in 1522,

> When I was younger, I gave myself overmuch to human teaching, like others of my day, and when about seven or eight years ago I undertook to devote myself entirely to the Scriptures I was always prevented by philosophy and theology. But eventually I came to the point where led by the Word and Spirit of God I saw the need to set aside all these things and to learn the doctrine of God direct from his own Word. Then I began to ask God for light and the Scriptures became clearer to me – even though I read nothing else – than if I had studied many commentators and expositors. Note that that is always a sure sign of God's leading, for I could never have reached that point by my own feeble understanding. You may see then that my interpretation does not derive from the over-estimation of myself, but the subjection.[30]

The paradox of freedom and joy found in subjection to the Word of God was a characteristic feature of Zwingli's engagement with the Bible.[31] So too was his understanding of the creative and transforming power of God's Word:

> The Word of God is so sure and strong that if God wills all things are done the moment that he speaks his Word.[32]
> Thus we see that the whole course of nature must be altered rather than that the Word of God should not remain and be fulfilled . . . Nothing is too hard or distant for the Word of God to accomplish.[33]
> The Word of God is so alive and strong and powerful that all things have necessarily to obey it, and that as often and at the time that God himself appoints.[34]
> His Word can never be undone or destroyed or resisted. For if it could, if God could not always fulfil it, if some other were stronger than he and could resist it, it would not

---

29. Peter Opitz, 'The Authority of Scripture in the Early Zurich Reformation (1522–1540)', *Journal of Reformed Theology* 5 (2011), p. 298.
30. 'On the Clarity and Certainty of the Word of God' (1522), in G. W. Bromiley, *Zwingli and Bullinger* (Philadelphia: Westminster Press, 1953), pp. 90–91 = *Z* 1:379.21–30.
31. Ibid., p. 68 = *Z* 1:352.33 – 353.3. Opitz, 'Authority of Scripture', pp. 296, 300.
32. 'Clarity and Certainty' (1522), in Bromiley, *Zwingli and Bullinger*, p. 68 = *Z* 1:352.8–9.
33. Ibid., p. 70 = *Z* 1:355.5–6, 29–30.
34. Ibid., p. 71 = *Z* 1:356.28–30.

be almighty. But it must always be fulfilled. If it is not fulfilled at the time when you desire, that is not due to any deficiency of power but to the freedom of his will.[35]

The power and efficacy of Scripture arises from the very fact that it is the word *of God*. Zwingli would point this out in the starkest of terms, anticipating a later enigmatic statement by William Tyndale: 'Note, you cavillers, who have no trust in the Scriptures, that it is the word of God, which is God himself, that lighteth every man.'[36] This conviction explains his approach to reform in the churches of Zurich. The central place he gave to Scripture was a way of ensuring that God himself directed the reform. In his exposition of Christian freedom in the light of the controversial breaking of the Lenten fast in 1522, and again in the great disputations held in Zurich in 1523, Zwingli insisted that only Scripture be used in debate.[37] As he insisted, his great desire for himself and his people was that they be '*theodidacti*, that is, taught of God'.[38]

Once again it would be too easy for modern commentators, influenced by the theology of the twentieth century, to distinguish between this powerful word of God and the written words of Scripture. However, throughout the sermon 'On the Clarity and Certainty of the Word of God', from which these quotes come, Zwingli moves regularly and unselfconsciously from the expression 'word of God' to the word 'Scripture'. In the conclusion to his explanation of the Sixty-Seven Theses, he was more explicit:

> Should I have erred regarding the meaning of scripture, and should this be demonstrated here and there on the basis of scripture, I offer to be corrected – not by human teaching and statutes, of course, but through scripture which is *theopneustos*, i.e. inspired by God. Further, the meaning of scripture must be verified,

35. Ibid., p. 72 = *Z* 1:357.15–23.
36. Ibid., p. 79 = *Z* 1:365.30–32. The quote from Tyndale is 'God is nothing but his law and his promises; that is to say, that which he biddeth thee to do, and that which he biddeth thee believe and hope. God is but his word, as Christ saith, John viii. "I am that I say unto you"; that is to say, That which I preach am I; my words are spirit and life. God is that only which he testifieth of himself; and to imagine any other thing of God than that is damnable idolatry.' W. Tyndale, 'The Obedience of the Christian Man', in H. Walter (ed.), *Doctrinal Treatises* (Cambridge: The Parker Society, 1848), p. 160. See P. F. Jensen, 'God and the Bible', in D. A. Carson (ed.), *The Enduring Authority of the Christian Scriptures* (Grand Rapids: Eerdmans; London: Apollos, 2016). pp. 477–478.
37. *Regarding the Choice and Freedom of Foods* (1522), *Z* 1:91.14–15.
38. 'Clarity and Certainty' (1522), in Bromiley, *Zwingli and Bullinger*, p. 89 = *Z* 1:377.19–20.

not from the writings of the Fathers, but from scripture itself. I, in turn, offer to clarify the dark passages of scripture, not from the top of my head and through useless prattle; the meaning I elicit from scripture, I shall also support from scripture. Scripture must be my judge as well as the judge of everyone else; but no person must ever be judge of the word of God.[39]

As he would say in a marginal comment of a manuscript from 1523: 'Scripture alone is the leader and teacher of the godly.'[40]

Zwingli's commitment to the role of the Spirit, not so much as an interpreter of Scripture but as the one who brings Scripture to the human heart and moves the believer to faith and obedience, was not a move away from an earlier confidence in the biblical text itself.[41] Rather, the address of God using these words is entirely in the hands of God as a sovereign work of the Spirit. He insisted that Paul's declaration that 'faith comes from hearing and hearing through the word of Christ' (Rom. 10:17 ESV) 'does not mean very much can be accomplished by the preaching of the external word apart from the internal address and compulsion of the Spirit'.[42] Just as critical for his understanding of Scripture, though, is the next line: 'Therefore it is necessary not merely to instil faith into the young by the pure words which proceed from the mouth of God, but to pray that he who alone can give faith will illuminate by his Spirit those whom we instruct in his Word.'[43] The efficacy of the word of God is not something that can be separated from the illumining and convicting work of the Spirit. The record of the first Zurich Disputation (January 1523) has Zwingli exclaiming, 'I will accept no one as judge and witness except the Scriptures, the Spirit of God speaking from the Scriptures.'[44]

---

39. 'Exposition and Basis of the Conclusions or Articles Published by Huldrych Zwingli, Zurich, 29 January, 1523', in E. J. Furcha and H. W. Pipkin, *Huldrych Zwingli Writings*, trans. H. W. Pipkin (Allison Park: Pickwick Publications, 1984), p. 373 = *Z* 2:457.7–17.

40. 'A Defence of Ultimate Principles' (1522), *Z* 1:306.

41. Contra G. R. Chatfield, *Balthasar Hubmaier and the Clarity of Scripture: A Critical Reformation Issue* (Cambridge: James Clarke, 2013), p. 65.

42. 'Of the Education of Youth' (1523), in Bromiley, *Zwingli and Bullinger*, p. 104 = *Z* 2:538.20–21.

43. Ibid., p. 104 = *Z* 2:538.21–23.

44. 'The Acts of the First Zurich Disputation, January 1523', in Samuel Macauley Jackson (ed.), *Ulrich Zwingli 1484–1531: Selected Works* (Philadelphia: University of Pennsylvania Press, 1972), p. 103 = *Z* 1:558.2–5.

The correlate of this was, of course, the effectiveness of God's communication to his people in Scripture, encapsulated in the doctrine of the clarity of
Scripture. 'When the Word of God shines on the human understanding,' he
wrote in his famous tract on the subject, 'it enlightens it in such a way that it
understands and confesses the Word and knows the certainty of it.'[45] Zwingli
surveyed seven passages from the Old Testament leading to his conclusion that

> God's Word can be understood by a man without any human direction: not that this
> is due to man's own understanding, but to the light and Spirit of God, illuminating
> and inspiring the words in such a way that the light of the divine content is seen
> in his own light.[46]

Zwingli then quotes Psalm 36:9: 'in your light do we see light' (ESV). His survey
of New Testament passages touching upon the same theme concludes similarly:

> the simplicity of the disciples was instructed only by God, which is an example
> to us, that we might seek the form of divine doctrine from God alone. The doctrine
> of God is never formed more clearly than when it is done by God himself and in the
> words of God.[47]

Zwingli's exposition of the clarity of Scripture is one of the boldest from
the Reformation period.

> our view of the matter is this: that we should hold the Word of God in the highest
> possible esteem – meaning by the Word of God only that which comes from the
> Spirit of God – and we should give to it a trust which we cannot give to any other
> word. For the Word of God is certain and can never fail. It is clear, and will never
> leave us in darkness. It reaches its own truth. It arises and irradiates the soul of man
> with full salvation and grace. It gives the soul sure comfort in God. It humbles it,
> so that it loses and indeed condemns itself and lays hold of God.[48]

Once again the link between word and Spirit, which is characteristically
Zwinglian, is to the fore when he speaks about the clarity of Scripture. The
clarity of Scripture remains the clarity *of Scripture*, but Scripture does not exist

---

45. 'Clarity and Certainty' (1522), in Bromiley, *Zwingli and Bullinger*, p. 75 = *Z* 1:361.31–32.
46. Ibid., p. 78 = *Z* 1:365.15–19.
47. Ibid., pp. 89–90 = *Z* 1:378.14–18.
48. Ibid., p. 93 = *Z* 1:382.21–28.

in isolation from the one who inspired it nor from his sovereign illumining and convicting work. So Zwingli can insist, 'The comprehension and understanding of divine doctrine comes then from above and not from interpreters', and more boldly, 'Even if you hear the gospel of Jesus Christ from an apostle, you cannot act upon it unless the heavenly Father teach and draw you by the Spirit.'[49]

It is this sure confidence in the authority, clarity and sufficiency of Scripture which explains not only Zwingli's approach to preaching in the Grossmünster in Zurich but also the founding of the *Prophezei* in 1525.[50] This gathering of scholars and teachers to study the Old Testament in Hebrew, Greek and Latin, and then to hear a sermon preached on the passage they had just examined, epitomized a new seriousness about the text of Scripture as God's agent of change. This was the means by which he would reform a church or a city just as it was the means by which he would reform the heart of the individual sinner. Zwingli's confidence was expressed in the prayer he used to start the gatherings of the *Prophezei*:

> Almighty, eternal and merciful God, whose Word is a lamp unto our feet and a light unto our path, open and illuminate our minds, that we may purely and perfectly understand thy Word and that our lives may be conformed to what we have rightly understood, that in nothing we may be displeasing unto thy majesty, through Jesus Christ our Lord. Amen.[51]

Calvin and the self-authenticating Word of God

The first edition of John Calvin's *Institutes of the Christian Religion,* published in Basel in 1536, did not include a discrete chapter on the doctrine of Scripture. In 1539 Calvin reworked the book, and the expanded first paragraph on the knowledge of God included Calvin's first exposition of the authority of Scripture:

> For Scripture provides no less evidence of its truth than white or black objects do of their colour, or sweet or bitter things of their taste. If we truly want to help men's consciences so that they are not gripped by perpetual doubt, we must derive the

---

49. Ibid., p. 79 = *Z* 1:366.1–3, 30–33.
50. B. Gordon, *The Swiss Reformation* (Manchester: Manchester University Press, 2002), pp. 232–239.
51. Gottfried W. Locher, *Zwingli's Thought: New Perspectives* (Leiden: Brill, 1981), p. 28.

authority of Scripture from a higher source than human reasoning, evidence or conjecture. We must, that is, base it on the inner witness of the Holy Spirit.

Although Scripture's own majesty is enough to command our reverence, it really begins to affect us only when it is sealed in our hearts by the Holy Spirit.[52]

This is worth comparing with similar statements spread over the five paragraphs of Book 1, chapter 7, in the definitive 1559 edition:

Hence the Scriptures obtain full authority among believers only when men regard them as having sprung from heaven, as if there the living words of God were heard ... Scripture exhibits fully as clear evidence of its own truth as white and black things do of their color, or sweet and bitter things do of their taste ... We ought to remember what I said a bit ago: credibility of doctrine is not established until we are persuaded beyond doubt that God is its Author. Thus, the highest proof of Scripture derives in general from the fact that God in person speaks in it ... The same Spirit, therefore, who has spoken through the mouths of the prophets must penetrate into our hearts to persuade us that they faithfully proclaimed what has been divinely commanded ... Let this point therefore stand: that those who the Holy Spirit has inwardly taught truly rest upon Scripture, and that Scripture indeed is self-authenticated; hence, it is not right to subject it to proof and reasoning. And the certainty it deserves with us, it attains by the testimony of the Spirit. For even if it wins reverence for itself by its own majesty, it seriously affects us only when it is sealed upon our hearts through the Spirit.[53]

Calvin's final treatment of the subject had first examined other avenues to the knowledge of God: an innate human consciousness of the divine (chs. 3–4) – this 'seed of religion' in sinful men and women tends only towards idolatry; and the creation's testimony to God (ch. 5), which remains inchoate and unfocused without the word of God (ch. 6). Scripture is the word of the living God, and the living God is active in and through it to draw and inflame his

---

52. J. Calvin, *Institutes of the Christian Religion: Translated from the First French Edition of 1541*, trans. R. White (Edinburgh: Banner of Truth, 2014), p. 20. The French edition of 1541 (recently translated into English) was Calvin's own translation of the Latin edition of 1539 = *CR* 29:294, 295.

53. John Calvin, *Institutes of the Christian Religion*, trans. Ford Lewis Battles, ed. John T. McNeill (Philadelphia: Westminster, 1960), I.vii.1, 2, 4, 4, 5 = *CR* 30:56, 57, 58, 59, 60.

people 'knowingly and willingly, to obey him'.[54] Calvin spelt this out in more
detail than did Zwingli, or even Bullinger, Zwingli's successor in Zurich. He
grounded the Christian's confidence in Scripture as the word of God in God's
address of the human heart with these words by his Spirit. This is how Scripture
is self-authenticated (*autopiston*). However, once this is granted, there remains
room – and a legitimate role – for secondary, confirmatory evidences. Calvin
considered the majesty of Scripture, its antiquity, the miracles, fulfilled prophecy,
the preservation and transmission of Scripture, the testimony of the church
and the witness of the martyrs. These are useful aids, 'not strong enough before
to engraft and fix the certainty of Scripture in our minds', but now wonderful
confirmations of what we know as a result of the Spirit's work.[55] Calvin's heirs
would continue to ponder this connection between self-authentication and
genuine confirmatory evidence, over time placing (theo-)logical weight at
different points.[56]

Around the time that Calvin was embarking on his first expansion of
the *Institutes*, he also penned a response on behalf of the city of Geneva to the
overtures made by Cardinal Sadoleto. As he countered the cardinal's call to
return to the Catholic church, Calvin stressed the inseparability of the bond of
Spirit and word in the most emphatic terms: 'It is no less unreasonable to boast
of the Spirit without the Word than it would be absurd to bring forward the
Word itself without the Spirit.'[57]

Calvin, like Luther and Zwingli, affirmed the clarity of Scripture as well as
its ultimate divine origin and authority. However, he was willing to recognize
that this did not mean that Scripture was always easily understood and that some
clarity was what we might label 'hard-won'. When, in 1552, he lectured on Acts
8 and the account of the Ethiopian eunuch, he remarked,

> So, if we are conscious of our ignorance and do not disdain to submit ourselves
> to learning, the Lord will also present Himself as a teacher to us children. And just
> as the seed lies hidden for a time under the ground where it has been cast, so the
> Lord, by the illumination of His Spirit will cause a reading, that is sterile, unfruitful

---

54. Ibid., I.vii.5 = *CR* 30:60.
55. Ibid., I.viii.1 = *CR* 30:61.
56. See Henk van den Belt, *The Authority of Scripture in Reformed Theology* (Leiden: Brill,
    2008); Andrew M. Leslie, *The Light of Grace: John Owen on the Authority of Scripture
    and Christian Faith* (Göttingen: Vandenhoeck & Ruprecht, 2015).
57. John Calvin, 'Calvin's Reply to Sadoleto', in John Olin (ed.), *A Reformation Debate*
    (Grand Rapids: Baker, 1966), p. 61 = *CR* 33:393–394.

and producing nothing but boredom, to take on the clear light of understanding. Indeed the Lord never keeps the eyes of His own so closed that the way of salvation in Scripture does not lie open to them right from the first moment, and that they do not profit immediately from their reading. But he often allows them to be stuck, and their way to be blocked, as though by a barrier placed there, sometimes to test the endurance of their faith; sometimes to train them in humility after reminding them of their ignorance; now to make them shake off their torpor and to be more attentive; now to kindle the flames of prayer; again, by the very longing for it, to urge them on to a greater love of the truth, and, yet again, the better to commend the superiority of His heavenly wisdom, which is sometimes not valued as it should be. But even if the faithful may not reach the goal of complete knowledge at once, yet they will always realize that their labour is not wasted, provided that they do not close the road for themselves by haughty contempt.[58]

It is a wonderfully pastoral exploration of how to deal with difficulties in understanding, with the example of the eunuch – whose difficulty was not so much with the meaning of the text but its referent, since he did not have the whole Scripture in front of him – providing the opportunity to encourage perseverance. A year earlier Calvin had dealt with the other New Testament passage which raises questions about the extent of Scripture's clarity. Commenting on 2 Peter 3:16 – 'wherein are some things difficult to understand' – he wrote,

It may be asked whence this obscurity is, for Scripture shines for us like a lamp, and guides our steps with certainty. My answer is that it is not to be wondered at that Peter attributes obscurity to the mysteries of the kingdom of Christ, especially when we think how hidden they are from our carnal perception. The method of teaching which God adopts, however, is so arranged that those who do not refuse to follow the Holy Spirit as the guide of their way have in Scripture a clear light. There are many who are blind and stumble even at noonday, and others who are proud and wander through byways. They hasten over the rough places and fall headlong.[59]

Calvin's confidence in the communicative effectiveness of Scripture through the ministry of the Spirit allowed him to see difficulties much as the Church Fathers had done, as divine incentives to humility and attentiveness. God's

---

58. *Calvin's New Testament Commentaries: The Acts of the Apostles*, Vol. 1, trans. W. J. G. McDonald (Grand Rapids: Eerdmans, 1965), p. 251 = *CR* 76:195.

59. *Calvin's New Testament Commentaries: Hebrews and I and II Peter*, trans. W. B. Johnston (Grand Rapids: Eerdmans, 1963), pp. 367–368 = *CR* 83:478.

communicative purpose does not fail, but God has determined the means as well as the end.

With closer resonances with Luther, perhaps, than with Zwingli, Calvin's high view of Scripture did not lead him to disdain the teaching of the Church Fathers and those faithful theologians who had gone before him. The *Institutes*, for instance, is replete with quotations from Augustine, Jerome, Hilary and others. Yet Calvin always respected a distinction between the written word of God and the words of men, between the role of the human authors of Scripture and that of later theologians. In the final Latin edition of the *Institutes*, he wrote:

> Yet this, as I have said, is the difference between the apostles and their successors: the former were sure and genuine scribes of the Holy Spirit, and their writings are therefore to be considered oracles of God; but the sole office of others is to teach what is provided and sealed in the Holy Scriptures. We therefore teach that faithful ministers are now not permitted to coin any new doctrine, but that they are simply to cleave to that doctrine to which God has subjected all men without exception.[60]

In many ways Calvin's theology was clarified and developed with successive editions of the *Institutes* and as he continued to lecture and preach through the Old and New Testaments. However, his stance towards Scripture was set very early on, when he first expounded the doctrine of Scripture as part of that initial revision of the *Institutes* he completed while in exile in Strasbourg in 1539:

> But while no daily revelations are given from heaven anymore, the Scriptures alone remain, wherein it pleased the Lord to consecrate his truth to everlasting remembrance; it must also be noticed how they will justly receive authority among believers and be heard as the living voices of God himself.[61]

Cranmer and the profitable reading of the Word of God

While Calvin was exercising an international ministry in Geneva, Thomas Cranmer was trying to negotiate the delicate political situation of Tudor England. Two of the Thirty-Nine Articles which he helped to draft (originally

---

60. Calvin, *Institutes (1559)*, IV.viii.9 = *CR* 30:851–852.
61. Calvin, *Institutes* (1539), I.21 = *CR* 29:293 (English translation modified from van den Belt, p. 18).

Forty-Two Articles under the reign of Edward VI) touch upon the authority of Scripture.

> VI. Holy Scripture contains all things necessary to salvation: so that whatsoever is not read therein, nor may be proved thereby, is not to be required of any man, that it should be believed as an article of the faith, or be thought requisite [as] necessary to salvation . . .
>
> XX. The Church has power to decree Rites or Ceremonies, and authority in controversies of faith: And yet it is not lawful for the Church to ordain any thing that is contrary to God's word written, neither may it so expound one place of scripture, that it be repugnant to another. Wherefore, although the Church be a witness and a keeper of holy writ: yet, as it ought not to decree any thing against the same, so besides the same, ought it not to enforce any thing to be believed for necessity of salvation.[62]

What is particularly interesting in Article VI is the statement that nothing that is not read in Scripture or proved by Scripture is to be set up as a binding article of faith. Here in effect is Cranmer's confession of *sola scriptura*. Proposed articles of faith are to be tested by the plain reading of Scripture – 'read therein' and 'proved thereby'. Neither the church nor the king may bind the conscience of believers beyond what can be read or proved on the basis of Holy Scripture. Yet, importantly, the article was not *narrowly* biblicist: it spoke very specifically about 'all things necessary to salvation' and 'articles of faith'. This was what must be read in or proved on the basis of Holy Scripture.

This becomes clearer in Article XX with its acknowledgment that 'the Church has power to decree rites and ceremonies and has authority in controversies of faith'. Cranmer could hardly have written otherwise, given the relationship of church and state in England. Yet a statement like this was not unusual in other Reformation confessions. The ordering of common life was the prerogative of the church so long as what was instituted did not contravene the Word of God. The settling of religious controversy was a collective activity of believers rather of a single solitary believer, no matter what his title. Therefore this, too, rightly falls within the responsibility of the church. Nevertheless, 'it is not lawful for the church to ordain anything that is contrary to God's word written'.

---

62. P. Schaff, *The Creeds of Christendom*, Vol. 3: *The Evangelical Protestant Creeds*, 1876 repr. edn (Grand Rapids: Baker, 2007), pp. 489, 500. [I have modernized the spelling.]

The identification of Scripture as 'God's word written' is significant even if, as we have seen, it is rather unexceptional. The authority carried by Scripture is directly related to this identification. Since this is God's word, not simply a human response of one kind or other to God's word, it carries God's own authority. Just as importantly, since it is all God's word written, an assumption of consistency and coherence – a fundamental unity of the Scriptures in their unfolding witness to Christ – directs the way it is to be read and applied. The Continental Reformers had spoken of Scripture as its own interpreter. The Articles spell out what this means for the church: the church may not so expound one part of Scripture that it conflicts with or contradicts another. Here is Cranmer's fundamental hermeneutical principle.

What is taught in summary in the Articles is unpacked in the homily 'A Fruitful Exhortation to the Reading and Knowledge of Holy Scripture'. However, here in particular we see Cranmer's characteristic emphasis on the transforming power of the Scripture, something that explains the central place of an extensive and unadorned reading of Scripture in the liturgies he prepared.

> The words of holy scripture be called words of everlasting life: for they be God's instrument, ordained for the same purpose. They have power to convert through God's promise, and they be effectual through God's assistance; and, being received in a faithful heart, they have ever an heavenly spiritual working in them ... there is nothing that so much establishes our faith and trust in God, that so much conserves innocence and pureness of the heart, and also of outward godly life and conversation, as continual reading and meditation of God's Word.[63]

The second part of this homily treats two objections which Cranmer antici-pates might keep people from this 'continual reading and meditation of God's Word'. He insists they are 'vaine and fained excuses' and yet he sets out to answer them. The first is that through ignorance the reader might fall into error:

> And if you be afraid to fall into error by reading of Holy Scripture, I shall show you how you may read it without danger of error. Read it humbly, with a meek and a lowly heart, to the intent you may glorify God, and not yourself, with the knowledge of it; and read it not without daily praying to God, that he would direct your reading

---

63. R. B. Bond, *Certain Sermons or Homilies (1547) and a Homily against Disobedience and Wilful Rebellion (1570): A Critical Edition* (Toronto: University of Toronto Press, 1987), pp. 62, 63.

to good effect; and take upon you to expound it no further than you can plainly
understand it . . . Presumption and arrogance is the mother of all error: and humility
needs to fear no error. For humility will only search to know the truth; it will search
and will confer one place with another: and where it cannot find the sense, it will
pray, it will inquire of other that know, and will not presumptuously and rashly define
anything which it knows not. Therefore, the humble man may search any truth boldly
in the Scripture without any danger of error.[64]

The second concern was that Scripture was just too hard to understand:

If we read once, twice or thrice, and understand not, let us not cease so, but still
continue reading, praying, asking of other and so by still knocking, at the last the
door shall be opened, as Saint Augustine says. Although many things in the Scripture
be spoken in obscure mysteries, yet there is nothing spoken under dark mysteries in
one place, but the self-same thing in other places is spoken more familiarly and plainly
to the capacity both of learned and unlearned. And those things in the Scripture that
be plain to understand and necessary for salvation, every man's duty is to learn them,
to print them in memory, and effectually to exercise them; and as for the obscure
mysteries, to be contented to be ignorant in them until such time as it shall please
God to open those things unto him.[65]

Cranmer sought to expose the men and women of England to as much of
Scripture as possible, trusting that this would transform lives and so reform the
nation. He understood that this was a process and would take time. Not
everything could be understood at once. Nevertheless, underlying this commitment were convictions he held in common with his Continental counterparts:
the unique and final authority of Scripture, its accessibility to all with faith and
dependence upon the Spirit, and its sufficiency for life for disciples of Christ.
As he wrote in his notebook:

If the church and the Christian faith did not rely upon the certain word of God as
a firm foundation, no one could know whether he had faith, whether he were in the
church of Christ or the synagogue of Satan.[66]

---

64. Ibid., p. 65.
65. Ibid., p. 66.
66. 'Cranmer's Great Commonplaces', British Library Royal MS 7.B.XI, fol. 22v. I am
    very thankful to my friend Dr Ashley Null for drawing my attention to Cranmer's
    comments about Scripture in the 'Great Commonplaces'.

Conclusion

At the heart of the legacy of the Reformation is this new orientation towards the teaching of Scripture. Wherever the Reformation took hold, reading and being taught from the Scriptures became a more prominent part of corporate and individual Christian life. What we have seen to be common to these four major Reformers, with all their differences of expression and emphasis, was also characteristic of many other influential voices and the churches they served. Precisely because God has spoken, his word must take precedence over all other words. Everything (doctrine and behaviour) must be tested by this measure: whether it arises from, and is consistent with, the teaching of Scripture.

That this fresh turning to the Scriptures was a cause for rejoicing was due to the generous character of the God who has spoken. His Word brings faith and life and hope. Luther could speak of his conscience being bound but also of having the gates of paradise opened to him through his reading of the Scriptures. Zwingli could speak of the joy that comes from the fear of God produced by the Word and the Spirit.[67] Calvin spoke of the sweetness of taste and the clarity of vision associated with Scripture, and Cranmer could write of its comfort and encouragement. The formal principle of the Reformation was a wonderfully liberating discovery: that God's Word nourishes life and shines light into our darkness.

Bibliography

Baum, W. et al., *Corpus Reformatorum*, 101 vols., Berlin/Leipzig/Zurich: Theologischer Verlag, 1834–).

Belt, Henk van den, *The Authority of Scripture in Reformed Theology*, Leiden: Brill, 2008.

Bond, R. B., *Certain Sermons or Homilies (1547) and a Homily against Disobedience and Wilful Rebellion (1570): A Critical Edition*, Toronto: University of Toronto Press, 1987.

Bromiley, G. W., *Zwingli and Bullinger*, Philadelphia: Westminster Press, 1953.

Calvin, J., 'Calvin's Reply to Sadoleto', in John Olin, *A Reformation Debate*, 49–94, Grand Rapids: Baker, 1966.

———, *Institutes of the Christian Religion: Translated from the First French Edition of 1541*, trans. R. White, Edinburgh: Banner of Truth, 2014.

———, *Institutes of the Christian Religion*, trans. Ford Lewis Battles, ed. John T. McNeill, Philadelphia: Westminster, 1960.

---

67. 'Clarity and Certainty' (1522), in Bromiley, *Zwingli and Bullinger*, p. 95 = *Z* 1:384.17–19.

Calvin's New Testament Commentaries: The Acts of the Apostles, Vol. 1, trans. W. J. G.
McDonald, Grand Rapids: Eerdmans, 1965.

Calvin's New Testament Commentaries: Hebrews and I and II Peter, trans. W. B. Johnston,
Grand Rapids: Eerdmans, 1963.

Chatfield, G. R., *Balthasar Hubmaier and the Clarity of Scripture: A Critical Reformation Issue*,
Cambridge: James Clarke, 2013.

Correspondence of Erasmus, Vol. 5: *Letters 594 to 841*, trans. R. A. B. Mynors and D. F. S.
Thomson, Toronto: University of Toronto Press, 1979.

Feiss, H., *On Love: A Selection of the Works of Hugh, Dam, Achard, Richard and Godfrey
of St Victor*, New York: New City Press, 2012.

Furcha, E. J. and H. W. Pipkin, *Huldrych Zwingli Writings*, trans. H. W. Pipkin, Allison
Park: Pickwick Publications, 1984.

George, T., *Theology of the Reformers*, Nashville: Broadman, 1988.

Gordon, B., *The Swiss Reformation*, Manchester: Manchester University Press, 2002.

Jackson, Samuel Macauley (ed.), *Ulrich Zwingli 1484–1531: Selected Works*, Philadelphia:
University of Pennsylvania Press, 1972.

Jensen, P. F., 'God and the Bible', in D. A. Carson (ed.), *The Enduring Authority
of the Christian Scriptures*, Grand Rapids: Eerdmans; London: Apollos, 2016.

Knaake, J. K. F., G. Kawerau et al. (eds.), *D. Martin Luthers Werke, Kritische
Gesamtausgabe: Die Deutsche Bibel*, 12 vols., Weimar: Hermann Böhlaus Nachfolger,
1906–61.

———, *D. Martin Luthers Werke, Kritische Gesamtausgabe: Schriften*, 66 vols., Weimar:
Hermann Böhlaus Nachfolger, 1883– .

———, *D. Martin Luthers Werke, Kritische Gesamtausgabe: Tischreden*, 6 vols. (Weimar:
Hermann Böhlaus Nachfolger, 1912–21.

Leslie, Andrew M., *The Light of Grace: John Owen on the Authority of Scripture and Christian
Faith*, Göttingen: Vandenhoeck & Ruprecht, 2015.

Locher, Gottfried W., *Zwingli's Thought: New Perspectives*, Leiden: Brill, 1981.

Muller, Richard, *Post-Reformation Reformed Dogmatics: The Rise and Development of Reformed
Orthodoxy, Ca. 1520 to Ca. 1725*, 2nd edn, 4 vols., Grand Rapids: Baker Academic, 2003.

Oberman, H. A., *The Reformation: Roots and Ramifications*, trans. A. C. Gow, Edinburgh:
T&T Clark, 1994.

Opitz, Peter, 'The Authority of Scripture in the Early Zurich Reformation (1522–1540)',
Journal of Reformed Theology 5 (2011), pp. 296–309.

Pelikan, Jaroslav and Helmut T. Lehmann (eds.), *Luther's Works*, 55 vols., St Louis:
Concordia; Philadelphia: Fortress Press, 1955–86.

Schaff, P., *The Creeds of Christendom*, Vol. 3: *The Evangelical Protestant Creeds*, 1876 repr. edn,
Grand Rapids: Baker, 2007.

———, *The Principle of Protestantism as Related to the Present State of the Church*, trans.
J. W. Nevin, Chambersburg: General Reformed Church, 1845.

Thompson, Mark D., *A Sure Ground on Which to Stand: The Relation of Authority and Interpretive Method in Luther's Approach to Scripture*, Carlisle: Paternoster, 2004.

Tyndale, W., 'The Obedience of the Christian Man', in H. Walter (ed.), *Doctrinal Treatises*, Cambridge: The Parker Society, 1848.

Huldreich Zwinglis sämtliche Werke, Berlin: Schwetschke; Leipzig: Hensius; Zurich: Berichthaus/Theologischer Verlag, 1905–1991.

12. THE PRIESTHOOD OF ALL BELIEVERS: NO MEDIATOR BUT CHRIST; A 'NEW' SHAPE TO MINISTRY

Chase R. Kuhn

'The priesthood of all believers' is often considered one of the significant doctrines of the Reformation that was retrieved by Martin Luther. In recent years, though, this narrative has been challenged.[1] In this chapter we will examine this doctrine again, briefly looking at its historical background before concentrating on Martin Luther. We will conclude with a consideration of the contemporary significance of the doctrine.

Historical developments (or disturbances)

In the first and second centuries, the universal priesthood was a common theological belief and practice. There were some early challenges to the doctrine, such as Ignatius's ecclesiological emphasis on the centrality of the bishop in the church.[2] However, it wasn't until the third century that the language of 'laity',

---

1. See Bernhard Lohse, *Martin Luther's Theology: Its Historical and Systematic Development*, trans. Roy A. Harrisville (Minneapolis: Fortress Press, 1999), pp. 286–289.
2. Ignatius, 'Epistle to the Smyrneans', in Alexander Roberts and James Donaldson (eds.), *Ante-Nicene Fathers*, Vol. 1 (Peabody: Hendrickson, 1994), chs. VIII and IX, pp. 89–90.

'clerics' and 'sacrifice' appeared and began to threaten severely the universality of the priesthood. We will here look briefly at a few major ways that the doctrine changed between the time of the early church and the Reformation.

Tertullian was the first who used the language of the offices of the priests and the laics. He wrote,

> Vain shall we be if we think that what is not lawful for priests is lawful for laics. Are not even we laics priests? It is written: 'A kingdom also, of priests to His God and Father, hath he made us.' It is the authority of the Church, and the honour which has acquired sanctity through the joint session of the Order, which has established the difference between the Order and the laity. Accordingly, where there is no joint session of the ecclesiastical order, you offer, and báptize, and are priest, alone for yourself. But where three are, a church is, albeit they be laics. For each individual lives by his own faith, nor is there exception of persons with God; since it is not hearers of the Law who are justified by the Lord, but doers, according to what the apostle withal says. Therefore, if you have the *right* of a priest in your own person, in cases of necessity, it behoves you to have likewise the *discipline* of a priest whenever it may be necessary to have the right of a priest.[3]

Tertullian's point was that the church does not rise and fall with a formal priesthood (clerical order); instead the Lord has made all of his new-covenant people priests. Indeed, the church exists wherever a few are gathered, even if only 'laics'. Tertullian reserved a place for the ordained ministry, as the last line in the above quote demonstrates, but in the absence of such ordained persons the ministries that would otherwise be conducted by them might be carried forward by the laity; all are priests. Tertullian used this as an opportunity to exhort laypeople to holiness as would be expected within the ranks of the ordained. In other words, he does the reverse of what might be expected: rather than lifting the clergy above the lay in status or holiness, he raises the laity to match the clergy in standards. Thus, the priesthood of all believers does not permit a more 'spiritual' order; rather it demands that all live equally unto the Lord as his holy people.

It was Cyprian who formalized the most apparent divide in ranks, and his epistles are replete with sacerdotal language. He refers to his colleagues in the episcopate as priests, and sets this college of clergy over against the people.

---

3. Tertullian, 'On Exhortation to Chastity', in Alexander Roberts and James Donaldson (eds.), *Ante-Nicene Fathers*, Vol. 5 (Peabody: Hendrickson, 1994), ch. VII, p. 54.

Cyprian's concern in the epistle is to caution against some who have followed after heretics. He wrote,

> [Novatian] himself had excluded himself and could not by any of us be received into communion, as he had attempted to erect a profane altar, and to set up an adulterous throne, and to offer sacrilegious sacrifices opposed to the true priest; while the bishop Cornelius was ordained in the Catholic Church by the judgment of God, and by the suffrages of the clergy and the people.[4]

As well as distinguishing between clergy and people, Cyprian provides insight into the democratic process by which leadership was identified in the church. Here he also identifies the true priesthood over against a false priesthood; this distinction was less about the universal versus particular priesthood, but instead about the true versus false church. It is clear that Cyprian identified a class of priest designated for the ministry. Incorporated in this ministry was a notion of sacrifice. Cyprian wrote, '[I]t is long since bidden by the voice of Heaven and prescribed by the law of God, who and what sort of persons ought to serve the altar and to celebrate the divine sacrifices.'[5] Thus the ordained clergy were those (and only those?) who served at the altar of the Lord in a sacrificial work.

Augustine was among the first to nominate ordination as a sacrament. As such, ordination was rendered an irrevocable grace. In the context of the Donatist controversy, Augustine wrote,

> For as those who return to the Church, if they had been baptized before their secession, are not rebaptized, so those who return, having been ordained before their secession, are certainly not ordained again; but either they again exercise their former ministry, if the interests of the church require it, or if they do not exercise it, at any rate they retain the sacrament of their ordination; and hence it is, that when hands are laid on them, to mark their reconciliation, they are not ranked with the laity.[6]

It may be fair to assume that Augustine was practically rather than theologically motivated. Those who had lapsed under the threat of severe persecution ought

---

4. Cyprian, 'Epistles of Cyprian', in Alexander Roberts and James Donaldson (eds.), *Ante-Nicene Fathers*, Vol. 5 (Peabody: Hendrickson, 1994), Epistle LXVI, p. 366.

5. Ibid., Epistle LXVII, p. 370. Cyprian moves on to quote Exod. 19:22; 28:43; and Lev. 21:17.

6. Augustine, 'On Baptism, Against the Donatists', in P. Schaff (ed.), *Nicene and Post-Nicene Fathers: First Series*, Vol. 4 (Peabody: Hendrickson, 1994), 1.2, p. 412.

not to feel as though the time before their struggle was insignificant or ineffect-ive. Rather, on their repentance they were to be welcomed back to the Lord and his church. What remains clear is that there was a special demarcation of ordained clergy over the laity, and with Augustine this was an indelible grace given to them. Thus, though practically motivated, sacramental theology was attached to ordination.

In the eleventh century the Gregorian reforms presented further challenges to the priesthood.[7] In the papal bull *In Nomine Domini* (1059), Pope Nicholaus II declared that the leadership of the church, namely the Pope, should be chosen by the leaders of the church and from among them. Furthermore, Pope Gregory VII's *Dictatus Papae* (1075) stated that the Pope was the supreme and universal ruler of the church. With this, the Pope was now declared to be above all emperors with the power to depose these rulers. Claiming infallibility and exemption from judgment, the Pope was now exalted to a place of power as never before. The consequence of the Gregorian reforms was a greater chasm between the clergy and the laity, even between ecclesial authority and secular authority, with the leadership of the church being protected and nominated only by those holding power in the church. Thus, what was centuries earlier a democratic process (recall Cyprian's comments on the suffrages of the people) now belonged exclusively to the clergy.

By the end of the thirteenth and beginning of the fourteenth century, the fight for power had only got worse. In the papal bull *In Clericis Laicos* (1296), Boniface reminded the secular powers that they had no power over the church, but instead the church had power over them.[8] The Pope assured the secular authorities that threatening this position would amount to facing the wrath of almighty God. In 1302, Boniface authored the papal bull *Unam Sanctum*, further offending the secular rulers, especially those of France.[9] In the bull he articulated how the church has two swords in her power (Luke 22:38), one being spiritual, the other being temporal. He explained that the temporal sword was under the power of the church, belonging to the kings and captains, and it was to be used *for* the church by permission of the priests. The spiritual sword was wielded by the priests, and was to be used *by* the church. 'The one sword, then, should be under the other, and temporal authority subject to the spiritual.' Ultimately, all humanity was to be subject to the Roman pontiff.

---

7. See Henry Bettenson, *Documents of the Christian Church*, 2nd edn (Oxford: Oxford University Press, 1965), pp. 101–110.
8. Ibid., pp. 113–115.
9. Ibid., pp. 115–116.

It was not long after this bull that Boniface was taken prisoner and died in his cell.

A succinct and helpful exposition of the development of sacerdotal theology and practice, is provided by Bishop J. B. Lightfoot.[10] When first considering how the sacerdotal understanding of the priesthood developed, it is most natural to assume that it was a direct imposition of levitical practice upon the Christian ministry. Priestly intercession, especially in order to make atonement for the people, belonged to the priestly class. But against this understanding Lightfoot identified the development of the Christian priestly class with Gentile, rather than Jewish, influence. He believed that the Jewish threats to the gospel and the ministry in early Christianity latched onto false doctrine regarding feast days, circumcision and law-keeping. But it was in the distinctively pagan regions where the church was planted that sacerdotal seeds took root and grew. This he attributed to the much more vibrant participation in sacerdotal activities of the Gentiles. These practices would have been foreign to the Jews in the diaspora who were unable to keep sacerdotal rites.[11] So Lightfoot's theory is that cultural influence determined the practice.

Uche Anizor and Hank Voss argue, following Eastwood, that the development of the sacerdotal ministry – especially with relationship to episcopal authority – was strongly tied to the need for unity in the church in the Roman empire.[12] The bishop was a focus of unity in the church and thereby served the interests of the unity of the empire. For example, Constantine insisted that the bishops come to an agreement at Nicaea, which served his political purposes. 'Entrance and continuance in the church were dependent on the bishop, thus enabling him to wield unprecedented power in the life of the church.'[13] This control of power, in time, led to the spiritually elite status of the priestly class, as well as the tainting of doctrine as it served the will of that powerful class.

Overall, we can detect a fairly uniform pattern of movement towards an institutional hierarchy, with the bishop as a key figure, especially the bishop of Rome. This trend progressed from the early church until the eve of the Reformation. It was in this context that Martin Luther fought for reform. The church

---

10. See J. B. Lightfoot, *The Christian Ministry* (Wilton: Morehouse-Barlow, 1983), pp. 93–115.

11. See ibid., pp. 106–111.

12. Uche Anizor and Hank Voss, *Representing Christ: A Vision for the Priesthood of All Believers* (Downers Grove: IVP Academic, 2016), pp. 61–62.

13. Ibid., p. 62.

had come to be spiritually divided into two classes or estates, as we saw in *Unam Sanctum*. The priests were given a spiritual position, an indelible grace, with the special privilege of access to divine rites. This was physically represented in the medieval churches by the screen that divided the clergy from the laity; the priests engaged with God on one side separated from the people who received ministrations on the other side. The celebration of the Eucharist had become a sacrificial mass, offering again and again the sacrifice of Christ. How could people believe rightly and receive any comfort in the gospel if the gospel was not being proclaimed by the priests and the practices of the priests undermined its message?

Reforming the ministry

> Where does this new interpretation come from? I will tell you. They have sought by this means to set up a seed bed of implacable discord, by which clergy and laymen should be separated from each other farther than heaven from earth, to the incredible injury of the grace of baptism and to the confusion of our fellowship in the gospel. Here, indeed, are the roots of that detestable tyranny of the clergy over the laity. Trusting in the external anointing by which their hands are consecrated, in the tonsure and in vestments, they not only exalt themselves above the rest of the lay Christians, who are only anointed with the Holy Spirit, but regard them almost as dogs and unworthy to be included with themselves in the church. Hence they are bold to demand, to exact, to threaten, to urge, to oppress, as much as they please. In short, the sacrament of ordination has been and still is an admirable device for the establishing of all the horrible things that have been done hitherto in the church, and are yet to be done. Here Christian brotherhood has perished, here shepherds have been turned into wolves, servants into tyrants, churchmen into worse than worldlings.[14]

So Luther identified corrupt and distorted patterns of leadership as the root of many of the problems in the church of his day. The clergy had usurped authority from the Word of God and in doing so oppressed the people in their care. Luther believed that the guise of a spiritual estate masked a dreadful injustice in which the people of God were being preyed upon.

For Luther, all Christians were spiritual people and all were made priests at their baptism.

---

14. Martin Luther, *The Babylonian Captivity of the Church*, *LW* 36:112.

Therefore, we are all priests, as many of us as are Christians. But the priests, as we call them, are ministers chosen from among us. All that they do is done in our name; the priesthood is nothing but a ministry. This we learn from 1 Corinthians 4 [v. 1].[15]

There might well be a distinction in office, but not in estate.

A new challenge

Theological reflections like these are the reason why the doctrine of the priest-hood of all believers – or the universal priesthood – has long been ascribed to Martin Luther.[16] In recent years, however, the identification of Luther with this notion has been challenged. Was he really the one who retrieved this doctrine? Indeed, does the 'priesthood of all believers' feature at all in Luther's works?

Among those who deny Luther's affiliation with the doctrine is Timothy Wengert. In response to recent (and not so recent) trends in Lutheranism, Wengert distances Luther from the priesthood of all believers in the concern that misappropriations of that doctrine have been justified by wrongly associ-ating the doctrine with the great Reformer.[17] He is adamant that Luther was not extending the priesthood – pastoral ministry – to all believers. Instead, Luther was concerned not to divide Christians into two estates, or *Stände*. The pastoral office remained, and was to remain distinct – for those who were agreed upon (ordained) by the congregation. But for Wengert, this understanding of the priesthood is not congruent with what followed Luther. Instead, he believes more is owed to Philip Jacob Spener than to Luther.

Wengert's concerns about pinning the universal priesthood on to Luther are tied to contemporary problems he wishes to avoid. Whether or not the doctrine causes problems today is not the primary issue of concern. Instead, the focus should be on whether or not the doctrine came from Luther. Wengert's unease about the 'pious myth' of the priesthood of all believers is based almost entirely on a word study on Luther's works. He concludes that Luther never used the phrase 'priesthood of all believers'. However, even if Luther did not coin the phrase precisely, it is worth asking whether the *concept* is present in his writings, in either seed form or full flower. We will examine the question by identifying four of Luther's key concerns.

---

15. Ibid., p. 113.

16. See Lohse, *Martin Luther's Theology*, pp. 289–291.

17. Timothy J. Wengert, *Priesthood, Pastors, Bishops: Public Ministry for the Reformation and Today* (Minneapolis: Fortress, 2008), pp. 1–16.

Reclaiming the universal priesthood: one estate

Luther's primary concern as he challenged the Roman doctrine of ministry was the claim that there were two estates (*Stände*) in the church: a 'spiritual estate' for the clergy and a 'temporal estate' for the laity.[18] Luther was adamant that there was only a single spiritual estate shared by all who were baptized and had faith in Christ. Jerome Emser was Luther's principal opponent at this point. Against Emser, Luther wrote, 'The priesthood of which Emser has dreams and the church of which the papists write agree with Scripture as life agrees with death.'[19] In order to embrace the two estates of Christians put forward by the Roman church, Christians would need to deny the Scriptures and its teaching about the gospel and Christian identity.

Though Luther identified a single estate for Christians, he maintained a distinction of roles. This was not a contradiction in Luther's view, for he understood estate and roles to be two different things. He wrote,

> There is no true, basic difference between laymen and priests, princes and bishops, between religious and secular, except for the sake of office and work, but not for the sake of status. They are all of the spiritual estate, all are truly priests, bishops, and popes. But they do not all have the same work to do.[20]

Luther's distinction within the one body of the church was of office over against ontology, function against status or being. In contrast, the Roman church believed that ordination conferred a change of estate that was irreversible and irrevocable. Luther wrote,

> I cannot understand why one who has been made a priest cannot again become a layman; for the sole difference between him and a layman is his ministry . . . unless I am greatly mistaken, if this sacrament and this fiction ever fall to the ground, the papacy itself with its 'characters' will scarcely survive. Then our joyous liberty will be restored to us; we shall realize that we are all equal by every right. Having cast off the yoke of tyranny, we shall know that he who is a Christian has

---

18. Martin Luther, 'To the Christian Nobility of the German Nation Concerning the Reform of the Christian Estate', *LW* 44:117–217, here p. 127. Cf. Wengert's discussion of the matter in *Priesthood*, p. 5.

19. Martin Luther, *Answer to the Hyperchristian, Hyperspiritual, and Hyperlearned Book of Goat Emser in Leipzig – Including Some Thoughts Regarding His Companion, the Fool Murner* (1521), *LW* 39:153–154.

20. Luther, *To the Christian Nobility*, p. 129.

Christ; and that he who has Christ has all things that are Christ's, and can do all things [Phil. 4:13].[21]

There is only one Christian estate because all Christians are similarly, and on the same ground, in Christ, by the Spirit, through faith. Luther believed that until the falsity of the Roman church's ministry was exposed, Christ would not be truly appreciated, nor would Christians comprehend their true spiritual status.

Preserving the dignity and place of the pastor (priest)

We have seen that although Luther insisted on no distinction between Christians as to their status and manner of life before God – all are spiritual – he upheld a clear distinction of office. This distinction was a functional one. Luther believed, as Paul had taught (1 Cor. 12:14–31), that believers were to use their individual office and gifts for mutual service. Those ordained were faithfully to carry on the ministry of the Word and sacrament for the benefit of those who were not so ordained.

> Every one must benefit and serve every other by means of his own work or office
> so that in this way many kinds of work may be done for the bodily and spiritual
> welfare of the community, just as all the members of the body serve one another
> [1 Cor. 12:14–26].[22]

In Luther's eyes, the priesthood was something that belonged to all, but the office of priest belonged to those who had been set apart to serve others in this way. Luther cautioned against a reckless abuse of privileged status since all were priests:

> [W]hoever comes out of the water of baptism can boast that he is already
> consecrated priest, bishop, and pope, although of course it is not seemly just
> anybody should exercise this office. Because we are all priests of equal standing,
> no one must push himself forward and take it upon himself, without our consent
> and election, to do that for which we all have equal authority. For no one dare take
> upon himself what is common to all without the authority and consent of the
> community.[23]

---

21. Luther, *Babylonian Captivity*, p. 117.
22. Luther, *To the Christian Nobility*, p. 130.
23. Ibid., p. 129.

So Luther's commitment to a single common estate in which all Christians participated did not mean the office of the ministry was common. That responsibility was entrusted to those tested, called and authorized. Luther would later write against 'Infiltrating and Clandestine Preachers'.[24]

The true ministry of the priesthood: priority of the Word

Luther guarded the ordained office because he believed that office guarded the ministry of the Word. In fact, the primary difference that Luther's followers identified between their own ministries and those of the priests of the Church of Rome was that they attended to the ministry of the Word.[25] For Luther, ordination was only ever about the choosing of preachers.[26]

> The duty of a priest is to preach, and if he does not preach he is as much a priest as
> a picture of a man is a man ... It is the ministry of the Word that makes the priest
> and the bishop.[27]

Luther believed that the perversion of the Roman church's ministry lay in its exchange of Word ministry for a sacerdotal one. Their priests, he declared, were idolatrous and 'really such priests as Jeroboam ordained, in Beth-aven, taken from the lowest dregs of the people, and not of Levi's tribe [1 Kgs 12:31]'.[28] Luther's followers expanded upon his critique of the falseness of the Roman ministry, berating the Roman notion of a sacrificial mass offered for the forgiveness of the sins of the people. In contrast, the Lutherans boldly declared confidence in the work of Christ and the proclamation of the Word for the communication of the gospel.

> We teach that the sacrificial death of Christ on the cross was sufficient for the sins
> of the entire world and that there is no need for additional sacrifices, as though
> Christ's sacrifice was not sufficient for our sins. Therefore, human beings are justified
> not on account of any other sacrifice except the one sacrifice of Christ when they
> believe that they have been redeemed by that sacrifice. Thus, priests are not called

---

24. Martin Luther, *Infiltrating and Clandestine Preachers* (1532), *LW* 40:379–394.
25. 'Apology of the Augsburg Confession, Article XXIV: The Mass', in Robert Kolb and Timothy J. Wengert (eds.), *The Book of Concord: Confessions of the Evangelical Lutheran Church* (Minneapolis: Fortress, 2000), p. 267.
26. Luther, *Babylonian Captivity*, p. 113.
27. Ibid., p. 115.
28. Ibid., p. 113.

to offer sacrifices for the people as in the Old Testament law so that through them they might merit the forgiveness of sins for the people; instead they are called to preach the gospel and to administer the sacraments to the people.[29]

Luther's reform of ministry practice was motivated and shaped by his deeply theological convictions. He was convinced the ministry must agree with the message. By offering the mass as a sacrifice, the Roman church had undermined the true gospel that declared that Christ was sacrificed once for all.

Mediation?

While Luther upheld a priestly office within the church, this did not mean that *all* ministry was reserved for the ordained.[30] He continued to teach that each Christian has a responsibility, and an opportunity, to both pray for others and teach others divine truth.[31] Luther explained that as priests, all Christians have access to the Father through the Son. In Christ, Christians are counted worthy to appear before the Father and make petitions to him. 'Praying for one another, we do all things that pertain to the duties and visible works of priests.' That is, in prayer we offer mediation for others in the form of intercession. This mediation, however, is only ever because of the high-priestly work of Christ in whom all believers are granted priestly status. Our prayers and intercessions are a participation in his prayers and intercessions. Luther explained,

> Nor does [Christ] only pray and intercede for us but he teaches us inwardly through the living instruction of his Spirit, thus performing the two real functions of a priest, of which the prayers and preaching of human priests are visible types.[32]

So, as all Christians perform their priestly service, they entrust themselves and those they serve to the work of Christ in his priestly perfection.

After Luther, Spener

Before moving on to consider the practical implications of the priesthood of all believers today, it is worth looking briefly at the work of Philip Jacob Spener.

---

29. 'Apology of the Augsburg Confession, Article XIII: The Number and Use of the Sacraments', in Robert Kolb and Timothy J. Wengert (eds.), *The Book of Concord: Confessions of the Evangelical Lutheran Church* (Minneapolis: Fortress, 2000), p. 220.
30. Martin Luther, *Concerning the Ministry* (1523), *LW* 40:21–22.
31. Martin Luther, *The Freedom of a Christian* (1520), *LW* 39:354–355.
32. Ibid., p. 354.

Spener belonged to the German Pietistic tradition and wrote more than a hundred years after Luther. He sought to continue the work that was begun by Luther at the Reformation. Likening the Reformation to the Jews returning from Babylonian exile (an image very prominent in Luther), he believed there was work that remained lest they face the threat of being returned to exile. Spener wrote, '[W]e . . . ought not to be satisfied with the knowledge that we have gone out of Babel but we ought to take pains to correct the defects which still remain.'[33] He knew that, in order for this to be done, there would be more work required than the ordained clergy could handle. The matter was not merely practical, but anchored in a theology of the ministry that gave expression to the universal priesthood.

Concerning the universal priesthood, Spener believed that all Christians had a duty to fulfil their priestly service to others, especially those within their homes.[34] He sought to correct a common misconception of his day, that the ordained officeholder was the only one who did the work of ministry. Any sloth or complacency in the work of ministry amongst the laity was due to a misconception about the pastoral office. He charged every Christian to fulfil his or her priestly duty.

> No damage will be done to the ministry by a proper use of this priesthood. In fact, one of the principal reasons why the ministry cannot accomplish all that it ought is that it is too weak without the help of the universal priesthood. One man is incapable of doing all that is necessary for the edification of the many persons who are generally entrusted to his pastoral care. However, if the priests do their duty, the minister, as director and oldest brother, has splendid assistance in the performance of his duties and his public and private acts, and thus the burden will not be too heavy.[35]

This exhortation reflects Paul's teaching on how Christ's church is built when every member does his or her part (Eph. 4:7–16). Thus, Spener believed that, in order for the church to continue to be properly Reformed, the priesthood of all believers must be rightly understood and practised. Only then would the Word do the work of bringing maturity by the Spirit.

Luther's theological and pastoral concern can be found in Spener. Between them, of course, stood others who found creative ways to affirm ministerial responsibility and the priesthood of all believers. Calvin and the Reformed

---

33. Philip Jacob Spener, *Pia Desideria*, trans. Theodore G. Tappert (Philadelphia: Fortress, 1964), p. 73.

34. Ibid., p. 94.

35. Ibid., pp. 94–95.

tradition addressed these same questions in a different but robust manner. Some of the Anabaptists rejected the notion of office, which Luther retained, in an effort to give greater voice to the laity. However, it is now worth us concluding with reflections on some contemporary implications of this doctrine.

Ministry today

Lay and clergy? Who does the work of ministry?

Timothy Wengert has cautioned that a wrong understanding or misapplication of the doctrine of the universal priesthood could have devastating consequences in the church. He writes,

> The Protestant and pietistic misappropriation of these terms turns everything on its head and replaces service with power grabbing and the unity of Christ's body with the disunity of individualistic spirituality. As Paul Rorem of Princeton Theological Seminary once said, the democratic, American misconstrual of the priesthood of all believers means, in actuality, the priesthood of no believers.[36]

Is this really just an American problem, allowing democratic ideals to override theology? Wengert's concern is more theological: if the lines between lay and clergy are dissolved, no priesthood remains. In order for there to be an appreciation and appropriation of the priestly ministry, there must be a distinction of roles even though there is only one estate.

What are the theological boundaries that must not be crossed if there is to be a faithful distinction of ecclesial roles? Luther drew the first by demonstrating that, while all Christians are equal in standing, each has a different role in service of the church. T. F. Torrance takes this further:

> The real priesthood is that of the whole Body, but within that Body there takes place a membering of the corporate priesthood, for the edification of the whole Body, to serve the whole Body, in order that the whole Body as Christ's own Body may fulfil His ministry of reconciliation by proclaiming the Gospel among the nations. Within the corporate priesthood of the whole Body, then, there is a particular priesthood set apart to minister to the edification of the Body until the Body reaches the fullness of Christ (Eph. 4:13).[37]

---

36. Wengert, *Priesthood*, p. 8.

37. T. F. Torrance, *Royal Priesthood: A Theology of Ordained Ministry*, 2nd edn (Edinburgh: T&T Clark, 1993), p. 81.

So each reconciled person plays a necessary part. Rather than a democratization of the pastorate, as Wengert feared, this participation arises from an appreciation of the place of each person in the body of Christ. It is a rich picture of how Christ brings maturity to those in his church.

Equality, gender and ministry

It is not difficult to imagine how the doctrine of the priesthood of all believers could be used to advocate the ordination of women to the priesthood (e.g. the role of presbyter/elder). If all people who belong to Christ are priests, why should women not have equal opportunity to be ordained and fulfil this role? Obviously, this has been a severely contentious issue, especially throughout the last hundred years since the rise of women's suffrage and feminism. It is true that in society and in the church women have been undervalued and mistreated. As part of God's design for humanity he created men and women in his image, as equal (Gen. 1:27). On this basis, the dignity and fair treatment of women in every sector of society is something for which Christians should continue to fight, not least in ecclesial contexts.

Equality, though a term in which the New Testament is singularly uninterested, does not rise and fall with function. Biological diversity makes this clear. Men and women are made for different but complementary roles in God's wonderful design for humanity.[38] Diversity in ministry does not simply boil down to a difference in biological parts. Instead, such profound value and variety is reflective of the fact that God, even in our biological design, made us equal but distinct,[39] in order that man and woman might complement each other. This complementarity extends to God's design for the home and for the church (Eph. 5:21–33; 1 Tim. 2:11 – 3:7).

Within the ministry of the church, the priesthood of all believers teaches us the beauty of complementarity. There is *no priestly class*; all are equal in Christ. Never can it be attributed to officeholders that they are more spiritual or of greater standing before God (or other people, for that matter). The cross levels the playing field for all Christians, men and women alike. When we think of humanity in the church, we think of Christ who purchased men and women to be a people – a bride, even – for himself. But, as Luther was careful to identify, *there are offices that remain.* These offices are for the good of the church in God's

---

38. Claire Smith, *God's Good Design: What the Bible Really Says about Men and Women* (Kingsford, NSW: Matthias Media, 2012).

39. I am indebted to my colleague Jane Tooher for the phrase 'equal but distinct' as a more helpful way of expressing the point than the common 'equal but different'.

purposes for seeing all to maturity in Christ. As Scripture teaches, these offices are not open to all (e.g. 1 Tim. 3:1–7; Titus 1:5–9) but only to those who are called, equipped and authorized. The distinction in the New Testament is that, while men and women of good faith and practice may serve as deacons, eldership (presbyterate, priesthood) is reserved for men of good faith and practice. However, it has been a careful proviso throughout history that the church does not exist only where the leadership is (contra Cyprian). The church is where Christ is, and when two or more gather in his name there is a church. In special circumstances, for instance where there is an absence of ordained clergy, others may fulfil the function of the ordained minister in Word and sacrament.[40] Such a provision ensures that the Word of God is not dependent on the ministrations of a priestly class.

An important caveat is that, while a particular office may be reserved for men in the church, this does not mean that *all* Word ministry is reserved for men only. As the Word of God is proclaimed to the congregation, both men and women are equipped for further service in the church, especially for speaking the truth in love to one another (Eph. 4:7–16). As men and women do this good service, Christ builds his church. It is wonderful that God uses all of his people – both men and women – in this work. So, though certain roles are reserved for particular people, the work is shared in other contexts, with each member of the same body playing its part; each member equally valuable and part of the same whole, even if having a different function (1 Cor. 12:14–31).

Mediation: 'representing Christ'[41]
What does the ministry of every Christian entail? The priesthood of all believers is a ministry of mediation: all are Christ's witnesses in light of our reconciliation

---

40. We have focused little on what 'work' the ordained clergy are to do. Most have reserved Word and sacrament for this office, especially sacrament. We would advocate lay administration and lay preaching, but would view Word and sacrament as preaching activities, and therefore appropriate only for men to practise in a mixed congregation. With regards to the office, the ordained priesthood (elder, presbyter) has responsibility and authority for guarding the truth in the church. This means that while unordained men may preach or administer the sacrament, these ministries of the Word are conducted under the care of the ordained officeholder(s) (the one(s) chosen by the church to serve in this capacity). For more on administration of the sacrament, see Peter Bolt, Mark Thompson and Robert Tong (eds.), *The Lord's Supper in Human Hands: Who Should Administer?* (Camperdown, NSW: Australian Church Record, 2008).
41. I'm indebted to Anizor and Voss for the phrase 'Representing Christ'.

and commission (Matt. 28:18–20). Yet we should be cautious and exercise this ministry in its appropriate context. The mediation of the Christian, especially intercession, is a work that is carried forward only ever because of the perfect and full mediation of Christ our great high priest.[42]

> Since then we have a great high priest who has passed through the heavens, Jesus the Son of God, let us hold fast our confession . . . Let us then with confidence draw near to the throne of grace, that we may receive mercy and find grace to help in time of need. (Heb. 4:14, 16)[43]

Our mediation consists of intercession, not atonement. The Christian priest makes no sacrifice for sin; that sacrifice has been given once and for all.

> And every priest stands daily at his service, offering repeatedly the same sacrifices, which can never take away sins. But when Christ had offered for all time a single sacrifice for sins, he sat down at the right hand of God . . . For by a single offering he has perfected for all time those who are being sanctified. (Heb. 10:11–12, 14)

There is one priest, Christ; one altar, the cross; one sacrifice, his own body and blood.

In addition to mediating prayers on behalf of other believers, Christians represent Christ to one another. This representation is conducted in word and in deed. Christians consider how they might 'stir up one another to love and good works' (Heb. 10:24). The Reformation retrieved a ministry of the Word of God. Those holding ministerial office are first and foremost preachers of the Word. Most importantly, this proclamation, or speaking of the Word, is not restricted to the pulpit. In fact, the way that Christians best mediate Christ to others is by 'speaking the truth in love' (Eph. 4:15). It is through this speaking that the body of Christ is built up (Eph. 4:15–16). Without reflection in the life of the believer our words would sound like hypocrisy. Christians let the word of Christ dwell in them richly (Col. 3:16) as they demonstrate lives clothed in love (Col. 3:14).

As Christians participate in this work of mediation, glory will be given to Christ. Prayers will be offered in confidence in the work of Jesus our great high priest. Words will be spoken in boldness because it is Christ, the Word of God,

---

42. Zacharias Ursinus, *Commentary on the Heidelberg Catechism*, trans. G. W. Williard (Grand Rapids: Eerdmans, 1956), p. 96.

43. All Scripture quotations in this chapter are from the ESV.

who has ascended to his heavenly throne. Lives will be lived in love, knowing what wonderful love the Father has shown in giving his Son for sinners. All glory will indeed be given to Christ as Christ's body works together in the ministry of the Word according to the promises of the Word.

Conclusion

Luther's monumental contribution extends to this area of the theology of ministry. It is appropriate to give thanks to God for that contribution. Today, as in the sixteenth century, the church and its practices are reformed by clear and courageous proclamation of God's Word. With the retrieval of right theology came the retrieval of right practice. If it is to last, it must come in that order. The nexus between theology and practice is vital. If the churches today are to remain faithful to the gospel, the ministry must match the message. What we have learnt from Luther is that this does not mean the removal of all ecclesial offices in the interest of the priesthood of all believers. In fact, it means protecting these offices, by keeping them to their primary task: proclaiming the Word, while calling on all Christians to play their part in gospel ministry. As Spener wisely indicated, the ordained clergy cannot do it all! Christ builds his church as every member takes his or her place of service in the body.

Bibliography

Anizor, Uche and Hank Voss, *Representing Christ: A Vision for the Priesthood of All Believers*, Downers Grove: IVP Academic, 2016.

'Apology of the Augsburg Confession', in Robert Kolb and Timothy J. Wengert (eds.), *The Book of Concord: Confessions of the Evangelical Lutheran Church*, Minneapolis: Fortress, 2000.

Augustine, 'On Baptism, Against the Donatists', in P. Schaff (ed.), *Nicene and Post-Nicene Fathers: First Series*, Vol. 4, Peabody: Hendrickson, 1994.

Bettenson, Henry, *Documents of the Christian Church*, 2nd edn, Oxford: Oxford University Press, 1965.

Bolt, Peter, Mark Thompson and Robert Tong (eds.), *The Lord's Supper in Human Hands: Who Should Administer?*, Camperdown, NSW: Australian Church Record, 2008.

Cyprian, 'Epistles of Cyprian', in Alexander Roberts and James Donaldson (eds.), *Ante-Nicene Fathers*, Vol. 5, Peabody: Hendrickson, 1994.

Ignatius, 'Epistle to the Smyrneans', in Alexander Roberts and James Donaldson (eds.), *Ante-Nicene Fathers*, Vol. 1, Peabody: Hendrickson, 1994.

Lightfoot, J. B., *The Christian Ministry*, Wilton: Morehouse-Barlow, 1983.

Lohse, Bernhard, *Martin Luther's Theology: Its Historical and Systematic Development*, trans. Roy A. Harrisville, Minneapolis: Fortress Press, 1999.

Pelikan, Jaroslav and Helmut T. Lehmann (eds.), *Luther's Works*, 55 vols., St Louis: Concordia; Philadelphia: Fortress Press, 1955–86.

Smith, Claire, *God's Good Design: What the Bible Really Says about Men and Women*, Kingsford, NSW: Matthias Media, 2012.

Spener, Philip Jacob, *Pia Desideria*, trans. Theodore G. Tappert, Philadelphia: Fortress, 1964.

Tertullian, 'On Exhortation to Chastity', in Alexander Roberts and James Donaldson (eds.), *Ante-Nicene Fathers*, Vol. 5, Peabody: Hendrickson, 1994.

Torrance, T. F., *Royal Priesthood: A Theology of Ordained Ministry*, 2nd edn, Edinburgh: T&T Clark, 1993.

Ursinus, Zacharias, *Commentary on the Heidelberg Catechism*, trans. G. W. Williard, Grand Rapids: Eerdmans, 1956.

Wengert, Timothy J., *Priesthood, Pastors, Bishops: Public Ministry for the Reformation and Today*, Minneapolis: Fortress, 2008.

13. DISCIPLESHIP IN ALL OF LIFE: RETURNING TO BIBLICAL MODELS OF CHRISTIAN ETHICS

Andrew Bain

As he writes the opening of the initial edition of the first Protestant systematic theology in early 1521, in the months between Luther's condemnation by the Pope and his confrontation with the emperor at the Diet of Worms, Philipp Melanchthon makes two things abundantly clear to his readers. The first is that he pens Christian doctrine in a manner which is thoroughly practical: not only is his *Loci Communes* written in a readily accessible way, but in virtually every section he seeks to indicate the relevance of what is taught to the salvation and life of his readers. In this way, Melanchthon establishes a pattern followed by the best of the Protestant authors who follow in his footsteps in the years and centuries afterwards, in which Christian ethics and practical teaching is based at every step upon Christian theology, and in which the latter always, inevitably and appropriately, issues forth in the former.

That said, Melanchthon is not interested merely in *any* relationship, however close, between doctrine and ethics. He begins by concentrating on certain biblical doctrines which he considers to be particularly important as foundations for both systematic theology and ethics, which brings us to the second thing that Melanchthon makes clear to his readers. His starting point is the freedom of the human will, which may seem an unusual topic with which to begin a work of systematic theology, until we notice his purpose in doing so.[1] Melanchthon

---

1. Philip Melanchthon, *Theological Commonplaces*, trans. Christian Preus (St Louis: Concordia, 2014), pp. 18ff.

argues against the common supposition that humans can will freely, primarily to point out the depths of human sin and the fact that the human will is not free, as the will is directed by the affections and often in an uncontrollable manner, with the affections themselves being thoroughly enslaved to sin. When considering our actions from an external point of view we might fool ourselves that we are the masters of our own conduct and can will – and will the good – freely. However, a right consideration of the matter indicates that our wills are the slaves of our affections, and the Bible informs us that these affections are controlled by the sinful nature, making it impossible for us to will the good consistently, let alone to respond to the will of God at all. Therefore, Melanchthon goes on to explain, we are completely and utterly dependent upon the grace of God in both our salvation and the conduct of our daily lives.

This insight of Melanchthon's is shared by virtually all of the key magisterial Reformers, and lies at the foundation of their contribution to Christian ethics and the theology of the Christian life. For above all, the Reformers remind us that ethics is a response to the gospel, not part of our way of salvation, and this provides the life of discipleship with its fundamental shape. Cutting this nexus also leads to some surprising and deeply transforming consequences for particular areas of ethics, as we shall see below.

Most follow the example of the scholastics, to whom Melanchthon opposes his construction of a biblical view, in understanding human activity from the starting point of the freedom of the will. Melanchthon believes that practical theology prior to the Reformation, and indeed theology as a whole, had at its root this false fundamental assumption, which leads to Christian discipleship being completely misunderstood. Once we grasp that we are not free, but slaves to sin, and that it is only the gospel of grace received through faith which can grant us the kind of freedom which God intends for humanity, only then can we understand not only the basis of our salvation but also the Christian life and all that pertains to ethics.

The Reformers and the place of the good life

Ethics is commonly understood as the science of either right willing, right acting or right (or virtuous) existence, or some combination of these three. The most fundamental contribution of the Reformers to Christian ethics is not in the area of applied theology *per se*, but in relation to soteriology. For it is their restatement of a biblical soteriology which facilitated the rediscovery of a biblical understanding of the human will, human actions and human character. The strong claim of the Reformers that humans inevitably act sinfully, because our wills along with the affections that direct us are so corrupted by sin that we cannot turn God-wards, and indeed that our nature or very character is thus sinful, stands with Augustine (and Scripture itself) against the mainstream of Western philosophical thought from at least Plato and Aristotle onwards. It has the famous and celebrated effect of declaring that any supposed contribution to salvation from the human side is completely ineffective, but also of separating the Christian life and the practice of Christian discipleship from contributing to the mechanism of God-given salvation.[2] Late medieval theology, in its various forms, had seen the Christian life and what we would today call theological ethics as being tied up, in semi-Pelagian fashion, with the process of justification, as members of the church willed to cooperate in their thoughts, words and deeds with the divine grace granted to them in baptism and supported through the other parts of the sacramental apparatus of the church. This cooperative work, though in most medieval schema (and in the formal theology of the modern Roman Catholic Church) at least initiated by divine sacramental grace, contributes towards the attainment of eternal life for the Christian. It tends to shape the life of discipleship in an uncertain and anxiety-raising direction.

The Reformers' teaching on justification completely severed the medieval connection between the life of discipleship of Christians as lived in the present, and salvation: 'we do not become righteous by doing righteous deeds, but, having been made righteous, we do righteous deeds.'[3] In so doing, it established a new foundation for Christian ethics, and the Christian life, today. The contrast to the medieval alternative is further strengthened when the Reformers' approach to justification is taken together with the Reformers' fresh emphasis on the fact that all of the other elements of the scheme of salvation, such as sanctification, are God-given and all of grace. The work of Christ applied to the believer both changes our identity and places the Holy Spirit in us, and enables us to do works that are truly good, since these are no longer grubby, ineffectual attempts at self-justification, but good works which are directed towards the true God and shaped by his faithful love and promises towards his people. We do good works as a grateful, right and naturally appropriate response to the great work of salvation which has been accomplished in Christ and applied to us by the Holy Spirit, the same Spirit who enables us to live in a God-ward pattern, the form of which was most commonly summed up by the Reformers as becoming more

---

2. E.g. John Calvin, *Institutes of the Christian Religion*, trans. Ford Lewis Battles, ed. John T. McNeill (Philadelphia: Westminster, 1960), 3.11.1–2, 21–23.

3. M. Luther, *Disputation against Scholastic Theology*, *LW* 31:11.

Christlike, and loving our neighbour.[4] As Luther famously puts it in his *Freedom of a Christian*, we become slaves of all in response to our having been freed by Christ: for the Christian, discipleship and ethics are above all a response to our having been freed from sin, death and the devil by the gospel of grace.[5] The Reformers recognize that where the redeemed life is consistently characterized, not by the works of the Spirit, but by the works of the flesh, this can and should raise doubts about the final salvation of the person in question, while emphasizing that causation runs in one direction only, from salvation to godly living – never the reverse. According to the Reformers, much has been misunderstood in relation to the Christian life by confusing and conflating its good works in particular with the means of our salvation, and in their view disentangling the two, and clearly placing them in their right relationship is the fundamental first step to establishing a biblical view of Christian living.

Once this is done, ethics, understood as right existence, right willing and right action, can be understood in a Christian manner, transformed by the gospel. The Reformers assist us to see that virtuous existence is not habituated as in Aristotelian and Thomist schema, but granted by the grace of God in Christ. Right willing is not a matter of expressing personal autonomy to improve ourselves or even cooperate with God's work, but begins with an acceptance of God's will to save us from sin through the gospel. Right action is a response to this and nothing more, shaped by the gracious action of God in Christ to and for us. In this light, the good life becomes not a search for self-transformation or identity-creation, but is about service of others. This was a strange and yet liberating word in the world of the sixteenth century, and is all the more so in our contemporary context for people within as well as outside the church.

A common life

Within the Reformers' understanding of the gospel, there is a consistent recognition that all apart from Christ are in the same place with respect to sin, and that in Christ all of God's people occupy the same familial and priestly relationship to God. That all Christians are saved by exactly the same means, and have the same positional and ontological status before God, has the important implication that the Christian life has the same essential character and shape

---

4. E.g. Calvin, *Institutes* (1559), III.vi.2–3.

5. M. Luther, *Freedom of a Christian, LW* 31:343, 360.

for all of God's people. Our life in Christ in the present age has the same common features, being characterized for all by a lifelong struggle for godliness and against sin, as we continually seek to trust in the promises of God in every situation, rejoicing in his salvation.[6] Different circumstances, life stages and personalities might mean that we experience the details of the Christian life in somewhat different ways from others, but our underlying position before God and our experience is the same. For the Reformers, this had the well-known implication of reducing the distinction between clerical and lay vocations to a purely functional level, in which the clergy are simply those with recognized qualifications and gifts to serve in certain vital biblical roles, alongside lay-people who serve in a variety of other, complementary, roles.[7] While the ministry of Word and sacrament undertaken by the clergy was seen as being of central importance to the life of the church and its members, these and other actions taken by the clergy were at bottom regarded as a form of loving one's neighbour alongside other forms of Christian service.[8] The Reformers regarded the ministry of the clergy as a great and grave responsibility and in a functional sense the ministry of Word and sacrament in particular as having a special role at the heart of church life, but which did nothing to change the experience or status of the Christian life as lived by the individual clergy in person.

Likewise, the prayers and services performed by monks and nuns in the 'religious' life were seen by the Reformers as having no special status or role compared with prayers offered up by others or acts performed out of godliness by any Christian person. Again, monks and nuns were understood as having exactly the same positional status before God as other Christian people, and their experience of the Christian life was understood as being subject to hopes and challenges in the same way as others'. As a result, the medieval idea that the saints together with some monks and nuns could perform works of supererogation was swept away, in the light of the fact that all Christians had taken on the same status, as had all of their good works, which were simply the fruits of

---

6. Some of the Anglican materials of Edward VI's reign express this particularly well; for example, the private prayers to be said at the start and end of the day which are provided within the *Primer or Book of Private Prayer* of 1553, in J. Ketley, *The Two Liturgies, AD 1549 and AD 1552: With Other Documents Set Forth by Authority in the Reign of King Edward VI* (Cambridge: Cambridge University Press, 1844), pp. 378–381.

7. E.g. Calvin, *Institutes* (1559), VI.i.6.

8. E.g. Luther, *Freedom of a Christian*, p. 336.

the Spirit in the life of those redeemed by grace.[9] The monastic life in and of itself conferred no special spiritual advantages or benefits, and the Reformers recognized that, for some, monasticism could lead to temptations all of its own. Luther, for example, comments that often people will appear to choose the monastic life out of sinful motives.[10]

Not only are the lives of all Christians placed on the same level by the Reformation, but there is also a certain levelling of the various actions and activities that Christians perform in the course of their lives in Christ. Because the Christian life has been reconfigured for all as a life lived in response to the gospel of grace, all conceivable parts of that life take on a spiritual importance. All Christians are called to be godly and to love their neighbours in all that they do, which is the content of the 'holy' life understood biblically. Therefore, how a Christian performs any action or responds to any circumstance provides as much opportunity to please God as the routines of the monastic life or the prayers of the clergy. The key is godliness, or more specifically a Christlike response to the God of the gospel, shaped by Scripture, in the light of one's present circumstances. For example, when Luther makes his often-quoted remarks affirming the value of simple and menial household tasks, such as fathers washing diapers for their children, he observes that God 'is smiling – not because that father is washing diapers, *but because he is doing so in Christian faith*'.[11] The life of discipleship thus becomes a life filled with opportunities to love and serve our neighbour, in response to the fact of our salvation by grace. It is a life of struggle against sin as we rejoice at being freed from the dominion of sin by living in the power of the Spirit according to God's law.[12]

For the Reformers, what we have in common, and who we are in common, is stressed above the things that distinguish us from each other. What we share with each other is what is of the greatest importance ethically, whereas what is unique or distinctive is usually of more marginal ethical significance. On this point, the Reformers' perspective pushes in a different direction from the present tendency to emphasize tribal or sub-group identity both in the church and in broader society, through contemporary phenomena such as Bibles aimed at specific self-conscious identity groups or an over-use of the homogeneous

---

9. E.g. Calvin, *Institutes* (1559), III.xx.19–20, 26. Cf. B. Wannenwetsch, 'Luther's Moral Theology', in D. K. McKim (ed.), *The Cambridge Companion to Martin Luther* (Cambridge: Cambridge University Press, 2003), p. 122.

10. M. Luther, *The Estate of Marriage, LW* 45:39.

11. Ibid., p. 40. Italics mine.

12. E.g. Calvin, *Institutes* (1559), III.vii.1.

unit principle beyond virtually necessary circumstances such as linguistic differences between Christian groups.

Christians, churches and government

In freeing God's people to live in response to the grace of God, the Reformers sought to dispel the confusion which had arisen, first, by placing the Christian life in its right relation with salvation, and, second, by clarifying the fundamental equality of status and experience that exists between all of God's people in the present age. They also believed that the Christian life had become misconceived due to the development during the medieval period of unbiblical assumptions as to the roles of the key institutions of church and state in relation to law, life and ethics. As a result, various of the Reformers sought to establish a right understanding of the relationship between the church and the secular governments of their day, particularly with a view to enabling them to perform their God-given functions in supporting godly living, without unhelpful interference in one another's domains.

The magisterial Reformers were virtually unanimous in opposing the role which the medieval church had taken on in relation to matters which they regarded as belonging, biblically speaking, to the state.[13] Not only were ministers of the gospel exceeding their mandate when they took on the role of worldly princes, as the Pope and many other bishops had done, but they were to avoid meddling in political matters and in the making and unmaking of laws for states. For the Reformers, the role of the clergy was to teach and proclaim the Word and to care for the spiritual needs of God's people, and by no means to act as governors or law-makers.[14] To do otherwise was to neglect the vital work of the gospel, and also to trespass on the God-given domains of others. For both Luther and Calvin, and many of their associates, the various worldly governments have been put in place by God as his agents for restraining human evil in response to the fall, and for maintaining some degree of right order within God's creation.[15] As such, they are to be obeyed by private citizens and by the church except where they command the church and its members to act contrary to the Word of God, by commanding Christians to desist from gospel

13. E.g. M. Luther, *On Marriage Matters*, *LW* 46:317–318; and Calvin, *Institutes* (1559), IV.xx.1.
14. E.g. Calvin, *Institutes* (1559), IV.v.1–4.
15. Ibid., IV.xx.3–5.

proclamation or to engage in sinful conduct.[16] Even when governments are tyrannical or enforcing seriously deficient or unjust laws, Christians are to live quiet lives, patiently bearing the yoke, and the church itself is not to engage in rebellious conduct against the authorities. Calvin and many of his followers differ from Luther in explicitly allowing intermediate magistrates (government officials, judges, and members of parliaments and governmental assemblies), but not private citizens, to act to remove tyrannical rulers under some circumstances: however, this point of difference is a secondary one, in the context of the magisterial Reformers' general posture of encouraging Christian submission to the authorities under all circumstances.[17] Even poor governments ordinarily have some elements of just law-making and law-enforcement and God's good order for human social life about them, and therefore are to be accepted as examples of God's common grace, and as providing the opportunity for the Holy Spirit to put down our pride and teach us humility.

Conversely, the secular authorities are not to take on the role of the church.[18] Princes and magistrates are to remember that it is the church through its preaching which makes God known in the world, and that while the state might make and enforce laws against ungodliness, it is only the ministry of Christ through his church which can make the ungodly to be godly. Christian princes might provide funds to support the preaching of the gospel, and may make laws protecting Christian preaching and even against counterfeit Christian preaching, but they cannot themselves *as princes* preach the gospel or sit in judgment over the church and its doctrine, nor make determinations as to how the church will fulfil its spiritual responsibilities. In so far as churches are operating within the framework of general social laws, the Reformers typically regarded the church as subject to the decisions of the state – for example, in matters of property, or where the clergy (like any other citizens) fall foul of the criminal law of the state.[19] On this point the Reformers distinguished themselves from the practices of the contemporary Roman Catholic Church, to clear away abuses such as exemptions for clergy from the civil courts system that had arisen

---

16. Ibid., IV.xi.30.

17. E.g. in Calvin's case, his advice to the intermediate magistrates in *Institutes* IV.xx.31 follows shortly after a lengthy series of warnings to Christians against disobedience and rebellion towards even unjust rulers in IV.xx.22–29.

18. On the points that follow in this paragraph, see Calvin, *Institutes* (1559), IV.xi.3–5 and IV.xx.1–3.

19. On ecclesiastical property, see, for example, Luther's *On the Ordinance of a Common Chest, LW* 45:170–171.

through the church taking to itself worldly privileges which rightly belonged to the state. Such privileges tended to support the unbiblical distinction discussed above between the clergy and the remainder of Christian society. However, when it came to the spiritual 'core business' of the church, the Reformers were clear that the church retains its right to settle its own affairs without civil interference and to resist any attempt on the part of the other authorities to regulate its internal life or doctrine. The Reformers' primary contribution to ethical thinking in this area was to disentangle church and state from each other so that each was free to pursue its own distinctive responsibilities, while promoting the possibility of a constructive partnership between them.

This is not to say that the Reformers had no interest in the operations of government. Luther himself advised many German princes on a range of matters, Calvin authored a constitution for the city of Geneva and was consulted by the city council on a good number of occasions, and Cranmer was for many years a member of the royal council, and a particularly influential one under Edward VI. As a result, the advice of various of the magisterial Reformers played a significant role in shaping governmental structures and policies in some European contexts where Protestantism came to be predominant. However, it is this very category of *advice* which the Reformers saw as the appropriate one for any role which the church might have in relation to the state. Christian leaders may seek to urge princes and magistrates in the direction of just governance, but they must remember that they have no special role with respect to the state and, therefore, their advice may be ignored, and rightly ignored in a theological sense, by those whom the Lord has placed in the seat of civil authority.[20]

However, in the explicitly Christian contexts of the sixteenth century, when rulers were normally Christian or at least claiming to be such, it was a not unreasonable expectation that those such as the leading Reformers would be asked for advice and would provide it. This certainly did occur, and most commonly this advice consisted of urgings to rule justly and in accordance with the general principles (though not normally the specifics) given in the 'juridical' law of the Old Testament, and above all to care for the poor and needy under their rule.[21] For the Reformers, behind and alongside these concerns stood the intention of giving the same broad advice as they might give to all other classes

20. E.g. Calvin, *Institutes* (1559), IV.x.1 and IV.xi.8.

21. C.f. W. R. Stevenson, 'Calvin and Political Issues', in D. K. McKim (ed.), *The Cambridge Companion to John Calvin* (Cambridge: Cambridge University Press, 2004), pp. 179–180.

of people: to be godly and to love their neighbours – which in the case of princes was typically understood as not allowing their high position to lead them to be proud, but rather to be humble, moderate, generous towards the needy, and just rather than showing favouritism. However, it is notable how reluctant the Reformers could sometimes be to play this part, reflecting their caution about setting a pattern of church interference in state affairs. For example, Luther, even in writing on a critical social issue such as marriage, indicates that he is only doing so having been pestered for some advice by many people over a long period of time, and he pointedly indicates that his comments should not be seen as binding upon rulers, while carefully circum-scribing the scope and extent of the advice that he gives.[22] Calvin is a little more forward – for example, in the Preface to his *Institutes*, where he gives guidance to Francis I (and any other princes who might be reading along) that is somewhat more pointed.[23] However, even in this example, it is to be noted that Calvin is chiefly concerned, not with instructing Francis on how to rule in a general sense, so much as reminding him that a 'true' king recognizes that the Lord is the source of his authority and that he is merely the Lord's steward, and as such he ought to protect rather than persecute the true church of the Protestants.

The advice of the Reformers on the Christian life as it is lived in relation-ship with all of the various civil authorities is to remember what is the proper and biblically determined character of the church, of the state and other civil institutions, and of the individual Christian in relation to these. The role of the government is not to build the kingdom of God, but rather to restrain sin, uphold justice and the social order, and create a space in which the church can perform its role: but Christians and their churches are to respect this work of the state as God-given and for their good. The state, not being created as part of the economy of salvation, cannot itself participate in the work of bringing the Lord's salvation to the world, even when it comprises Christians, but must leave this to the church. Individual Christians should recognize the state and the various civil institutions that surround it as part of God's provision for human life and for the life of the church, and live under it in contented obedience, serving as active and dutiful citizens and loving their neighbours within the framework made available by their own society's institutions where these do not conflict with the Word of God. At the same time, they should actively serve within the church, remembering

22. Luther, *On Marriage Matters*, pp. 266–267.
23. Calvin, *Institutes* (1559), Preface, p. 8.

that it is the work of the church and not the state to bring the gospel of grace to all.

It is in this area that the Reformers' ethical vision most clearly departs from contemporary evangelical practices. The Reformers are distinguished by their robust ethical framework for the roles of church and state that has a clear role for each, and yet allows for the possibility of a constructive partnership. Their understanding of this ethical domain is thoroughly theological, and it is expressed in their willingness to actively speak the principles of the gospel's implications into political life, while leaving political leadership to craft the concrete policies. In comparison, contemporary evangelicalism can on occasions present as confused and atheological in its approach to these matters, sometimes pushing aggressively for specific regulations or solutions within the sphere of the civil magistrate, and at others offering pointed advice which is not clearly grounded in biblical teaching on sin, grace and the gospel. This would be firmly rejected by the Reformers who did not envision Scripture as functioning to enshrine a new religious leadership caste over society to the detriment of the proper roles of church and state. However, they would also probably reject the counter-tendency appearing today to mute Christian witness to the moral order as the unviability of the previous efforts at hegemony become clear. There remains a constructive role for the church in its relationship to the state.

The law and the Christian life

Given the Reformers' emphasis on the grace of God, and the opposition between law and grace which is sometimes set in place by Luther and some of the other Reformers, it might be considered an unexpected development that the law in general and the Decalogue in particular is given greater attention by the Reformers – Luther included – than by most of their medieval predecessors.[24] However, when the way in which the Reformers use the law is considered, the reasons for this development become obvious. A common approach is to begin by recognizing that the first table of the law contains more than simply a list of commands, but functions as a summary of the Christian's relationship to God and of the Christian life as a whole. The Christian life in its entirety is one of worship, of single-minded devotion to the one true God, and above all it is this that the first table of the law teaches, summarizing the Old Testament's teaching on faithful discipleship for Israel and for individual

---

24. Wannenwetsch, 'Luther's Moral Theology', p. 121.

Israelites.[25] It can only be known by special revelation. The second table of the law, on the other hand, can be known at least partially by members of the community more widely, and finds expression (albeit quite imperfectly, and in some cases very imperfectly) in the law codes of civil societies. This is because it relates to the right ordering of society, and human beings even when un-regenerate tend to have some care corporately for the operations of their social and political context.[26] In a sense, therefore, both the church and civil society are concerned with the horizontal laws summarized in the second table of the Mosaic law. However, it is important to bear in mind that they do so for very different reasons, and therefore any scope for meaningful cooperation is limited. As governments uphold good laws, laws which mirror God's law to a degree, they are doing something quite different from the church: the church teaches the law in order to bring about awareness of sin and for some Reformers also to inform of God's character and the Christian life, whereas governments enforce more than teach the law, for the purpose of restraining lawlessness and upholding the general social order.

The second table of the law, and indeed all of the other commandments concerning relationships between human beings in Scripture, find real meaning only when they are understood in the light of the first table, and ultimately the gospel which makes possible the right worship of which it speaks. Commentators often remark upon the differences between Luther and Calvin particularly regarding the emphasis which Calvin and other Reformed theo-logians place on the 'third' use of the law[27] – and this was not an unimportant matter in the sixteenth century; however, significant as this question is, it must not be allowed to obscure that what the magisterial Reformers taught in common regarding the law was both more extensive and more significant. Their emphasis on the law's initial spiritual function in making humans aware of their sin and consequent need for the gospel of grace contrasted and still contrasts sharply with the semi-Pelagian tendency to regard the law as a pathway to righteousness. Their common recognition that the second table of the law acts to restrain wickedness and thereby create a space for the ministry of the church in society furnished Protestant Christians with a

---

25. E.g. Calvin, *Institutes* (1559), II.iii.3, 9; and Luther, *The Large Catechism*, in T. G. Tappert, ed., *The Book of Concord: The Confessions of the Evangelical Lutheran Church* (Philadelphia: Muhlenburg Press, 1959), pp. 369–371.

26. E.g. Calvin, *Institutes* (1559), II.ii.13.

27. E.g. J. P. Wogaman, *Christian Ethics: A Historical Introduction*, 2nd edn (Louisville: Westminster John Knox, 2011), pp. 124–125.

theologically defensible and workable means of relating biblical law and structures to the laws of their local contexts. Most importantly, though, the Reformers' presentation of the law as rightly and most appropriately understood in the wider context of God's redemptive relationship with his people to which the first table gestures, enabled the law to be grounded in their theology of the gospel of grace.

It can often seem odd to modern eyes that one of the effects of the Reformers' appropriation of the gospel of grace is a renewed emphasis on the law in the Christian life, and it is sometimes considered as a surprisingly legalistic misstep on their part. This is to misunderstand them completely. Their focus on the law was intended to promote the interests of true Christian freedom. Coming out of the medieval period, and faced with the Anabaptist movements of their day, the Reformers could see that human beings will always gravitate to a moral order to guard against chaos in their lives. However, left to their own devices, human beings will constantly invent more and more moral mandates – for themselves, and for each other – whose fulfilment is required for self-justification. With the focus on the biblical law a multitude of obligations, which often vary depending on one's social identity and whose ambiguity leaves people unclear as to when they have discharged them, are cleared away by a small set of basic words that are clear and which deal with the everyday life that we have in common. Understood against the gospel of grace, the law thus serves to promote genuine freedom for believers, the freedom to truly serve God and one's neighbour, which is the good life.

The Christian life and the vocations

As well as those matters to which the Reformers give surprisingly substantial attention, such as the Decalogue, there are other areas which receive less emphasis than we might expect. Given the Reformers' stress on the importance of Christian discipleship in the *whole* of life, it seems natural to assume that they would have written very substantially on the matter of vocations and the workplace. The Reformers do make clear that all legitimate work which does not necessarily involve its practitioners in ungodliness is potentially as pleasing to God and provides as much opportunity for godliness and love of neighbour as the work of the clergy. Indeed, the magisterial Reformers are keen to assert positively the appropriateness of Christians serving in certain 'worldly' and yet legitimate occupations, such as Luther's reassurance that Christian soldiers may continue in their line of work and need not be troubled by their consciences or the objections of some radical Protestant teachers.[28] However, the question of vocations comes up relatively infrequently in their writings, and receives less extended attention than many other topics: Calvin, in his *Institutes*, for example, devotes one short section within a single chapter (III.10.6) to offering more than a passing commentary on the topic. More importantly, though, is what exactly concerns the Reformers when they write about human vocations. Their predominant interest is in urging Christians to function in a godly manner as they perform their daily work, shaped by the gospel of grace: for example, as Lindberg observes, 'the centre of Luther's ethic of vocation is not self-sanctification, but the neighbour's needs', daily employment like all other kinds of 'good work' having been shifted out of the realm of self-transformation, where medieval theology had placed it, and into the sphere of service of others in response to the gospel.[29] Although they will at points trace out how godliness might look in concrete terms in a particular type of work, they show little interest in producing developed theologies of the various specific vocations. Thus, in Calvin's brief section in the *Institutes* on the vocations, he clearly does assume a creational order within which vocations exist within society and are occupied variously by individuals, but he does not seek to argue for this order, let alone outline a theology of the vocations. Instead, he argues briefly and simply for godliness in the Christian's work, particularly biblical patience, humility and contentment.[30] In so doing Calvin builds directly upon his discussion in the previous five sections of the chapter, where the patient and humble taking up of one's cross as the heart of the life of discipleship is critical. Christians are to glorify and worship God in their conduct of their work, but for the Reformers this is ordinarily expressed in undertaking this work in a godly manner, loving their neighbour at every opportunity. Christian literature produced by the magisterial Reformation for popular use underlines this same point. For example, in the collects attached to the Catechism of Edward VI, we may find prayers for, among others, landlords, merchants, lawyers, labourers, as well as mothers, fathers and children, and the wealthy and the poor. In every case, these prayers begin by noting the theological context of the specific persons prayed for, but when they turn to make their petition, they pray largely and sometimes exclusively for the godliness of the subjects in

---

28. M. Luther, *On Whether Soldiers, Too, Can Be Saved*, LW 46:94.

29. Carter Lindberg, 'Luther's Struggle with Social–Ethical Issues', in D. K. McKim (ed.), *The Cambridge Companion to Martin Luther* (Cambridge: Cambridge University Press, 2003), p. 170.

30. Calvin, *Institutes* (1559), III.10.6.

relation to the temptations and opportunities for service which they face in their daily lives.[31]

One contemporary statement seeks to speak into this space in the following way:

> Christians glorify God not only through the ministry of the Word, but also through their vocations of agriculture, art, business, government, scholarship – all for God's glory and the furtherance of the public good . . . The gospel is seen as a means of finding individual peace and not as the foundation of a worldview – a comprehensive interpretation of reality affecting all that we do. But we have a vision for a church that equips its people to think out the implications of the gospel on how we do carpentry, plumbing, data-entry, nursing, art, business, government, journalism, entertainment, and scholarship. Such a church will not only support Christians' engagement with culture, but will also help them work with distinctiveness, excellence, and accountability in their trades and professions.[32]

The Reformers would find much to strongly affirm here, while urging us to apply such statements in those ways which they believed to be most central to the biblical message. To the suggestion that the church should promote a vision for the church that equips its people to think out the implications of the gospel for the various trades and professions, their answer would be, 'Be godly and love your neighbour as your particular work provides the opportunity to do so.' To the recommendation to regard the gospel as 'a comprehensive interpretation of reality affecting all that we do', the Reformers would cheer loudly, and would urge us never to forget that at the heart of that comprehensive interpretation of reality is the fact of complete human slavery to sin, answered by the gospel of unadulterated grace. Christians would be expected to be distinctive in the workplace, but by dint of their godliness; to excel, as those who work as though working for the Lord who has bought them from slavery to sin and death; to be accountable, as those who know they must give account to their master in heaven.

It is in this light that we are to understand the Reformers' approach to the matter of changing work roles or vocations. They certainly did live in an economic context which was considerably more static than that found in many

---

31. In Ketley, *Two Liturgies*, pp. 457–466.

32. The Gospel Coalition, 'Foundation Documents: Vision', V. 4. Available at The Gospel Coalition, <https://www.thegospelcoalition.org/about/foundation-documents/vision>.

countries today, and in settings where social mobility was very low by modern standards, and for this reason the question of 'changing careers' was far less pressing than is the case today: although we must be careful not to overstate this consideration, remembering that for a pre-industrial society some parts of Europe did have considerable social and vocational mobility, and parents in a rather modern fashion would seek to use educational opportunities to send their children on new vocational trajectories (bearing in mind the example of Luther himself, who entered a different profession from that of his father, who in turn engaged in different work from that of Luther's grand-father). However, there is more to the Reformers' perspective than their having written for another time and place, and this becomes apparent when the content of their comments on the matter is considered. When writing about the possibility that someone may change his or her work, the Reformers caution against this. The reason given is godliness: they echo the biblical advice to be content and patient, and to live in the condition in which one has been called (1 Cor. 7:17–24).

In summary, the Reformers' teaching on vocations embodies their thinking on the central matters we have discussed above. What we share together as Christians on the common way of discipleship is much more important than the vocations and other features that differentiate us. Our contemporary hunger for a fully-developed theology of each trade and profession contrasts with the Reformers' stress that the good life is primarily about service built on our primary identity as sinners graciously joined to Christ. The former risks a drift back towards seeing the good life as composed partly of self-transformation, identity-creation and the prioritizing of difference by giving it more theological weight than is appropriate. If done crudely, it also blurs the line between the church and civil institutions, and potentially multiplies obligations upon us, making them specific to different identity groups.

Conclusion: the centrality of the gospel of grace for Christian ethics

Writing on Psalm 45, Luther summed up theology in relation to human activity in the following terms, urging that we not

> think of man as the master of his property, the way the lawyer does; or of his health, the way the physician does. But let him think of man as sinner. The proper subject of theology is man guilty of sin and condemned, and God the Justifier and Savior of man the sinner . . . Therefore this theological knowledge is necessary: A man should know himself, should know, feel, and experience that he is guilty

of sin and subject to death; but he should also know the opposite, that God is the Justifier and Redeemer of a man who knows himself this way. The care of other men, who do not know their sins, let us leave to lawyers, physicians, and parents, who discuss man differently from the way a theologian does.[33]

This statement reminds us of the basic reality which lay at the heart of the magisterial Reformers' teaching on Christian ethics and discipleship. The Christian life, biblically speaking, can only be truly lived when at its centre stands an awareness of ourselves as sinners rescued from death by the grace of God in Christ. With this gospel-centred awareness in place, a right understanding of the good life becomes possible. We recognize the proper place of our own works as completely separate from our justification, and we recognize the proper place of the law in relation to life both with and without Christ. We are also able to grasp the proper place of both the church and the civil institutions of society in relation to the purposes of God in showing grace within his created order. We will also come to appreciate that we have much more in common as fellow believers – as sinners justified and saved by God – and that the consequent struggle for godliness and towards service of neighbour that we all share is more important than the details of vocational theology or any other secondary questions.

Bibliography

Calvin, John, *Institutes of the Christian Religion*, trans. Ford Lewis Battles, ed. John T. McNeill, Philadelphia: Westminster, 1960.

Ketley, J., *The Two Liturgies, AD 1549 and AD 1552: With Other Documents Set Forth by Authority in the Reign of King Edward VI*, Cambridge: Cambridge University Press, 1844.

Lindberg, Carter, 'Luther's Struggle with Social–Ethical Issues', in D. K. McKim (ed.), *The Cambridge Companion to Martin Luther*, 165–178, Cambridge: Cambridge University Press, 2003.

Melanchthon, Philip, *Theological Commonplaces*, trans. Christian Preus, St Louis: Concordia, 2014.

Pelikan, Jaroslav and Helmut T. Lehmann (eds.), *Luther's Works*, 55 vols., St Louis: Concordia; Philadelphia: Fortress Press, 1955–86.

Stevenson, W. R., 'Calvin and Political Issues', in D. K. McKim (ed.), *The Cambridge Companion to John Calvin*, Cambridge: Cambridge University Press, 2004.

---

33. M. Luther, *Selected Psalms I, LW* 12:311–312.

Tappert, T. G. (ed.), *The Book of Concord: The Confessions of the Evangelical Lutheran Church*, Philadelphia: Muhlenburg Press, 1959.

Wannenwetsch, B., 'Luther's Moral Theology', in D. K. McKim (ed.), *The Cambridge Companion to Martin Luther*, Cambridge: Cambridge University Press, 2003.

Wogaman, J. P., *Christian Ethics: A Historical Introduction*, 2nd edn, Louisville: Westminster John Knox, 2011.

PART 3

THE REFORMATION IN RETROSPECT

Andrew Leslie

Introduction

It would be no small feat to cover all the issues relevant to assessing the significance of the Reformation in the seventeenth century. Given its close proximity to the tumultuous political, social, intellectual and not least spiritual events of the 1520s and 1530s, intuition alone suggests these effects would continue to reverberate profoundly in the century to come: a century which presented its own fair share of social and intellectual upheaval. Such an intuition is, of course, correct. Yet the impact of the Reformation in the seventeenth century can be traced along so many different axes – politically, socially, intellectually, spiritually – and the scope of literature, whether primary or secondary, is so vast that our discussion of this impact will necessarily be brief and incomplete. The question posed by the title of this chapter gives us a helpful cue. It directs us to consider the Reformation either as some social ideal or as an intellectual and spiritual set of convictions – or perhaps even an interrelated combination of the two – that is somehow capable of being 'lost'. And the very act of posing this question suggests it is one needing our attention; that there is a perception, at least, that within a century or so some achievement of the Reformation was undone or misplaced. It is not an easy question to answer, not least because it can be tackled on numerous fronts, but also because it is a question with a vexed and controversial history of its own. Not surprisingly, theologians and historians of theology have typically addressed it by concentrating on the fate of distinctively Reformed principles or convictions. And that is a sensible way for us to proceed too.

Judged from a purely theological perspective, an apparent declension from some Reformed ideal could be a good or a bad thing, depending on where your sympathies lie. Either way, to make such an assessment the theologian needs to be confident that he or she has fairly assessed the facts on their own terms to decide there is such a declension in the first place. Anything short of this and the theologian's pretended historical evaluation may not amount to much more than a search for one's own reflection: a kind of 'whig history', as it is often pejoratively put. Over the past thirty years or so, historians of Early Modern (that is, sixteenth to eighteenth century) Protestantism have championed an approach to its ideas or intellectual content that puts one's own theological convictions to one side with the aim of accurately discerning not just the content of those ideas, but also their origin, variety and evolution, within their own context. An attention to context entails an evaluation of people, their writings (in original languages, of course), the sources and influences for their ideas, their contemporaries, their sympathizers, their opponents, and so on. It is a laborious task, requiring the sensitivity of a theologian coupled with the analytical skill and precision of an historian. But it is a necessary task, not least because there is a principle of charity at stake. Love for one's neighbour must surely embrace a fair representation of that neighbour's views; even, perhaps especially, if the neighbour happened to have lived several centuries ago.

The recent revival in this intentionally historical approach to Early Modern Protestantism has partly emerged from a feeling that, for the previous century or so, post-Reformation theology has too often been the victim of overly hasty and inaccurate assessment from theologians and historians who have had their own particular axes to grind. As Carl Trueman points out,[1] sometimes this problem has emerged from would-be sympathizers who might go looking for an authoritative precedent for a particular set of doctrines – encapsulated, perhaps, in the acronym 'TULIP' – presenting a picture of seventeenth-century Reformed thought that is far more monolithic, doctrinaire or reductionist than it actually was. But more often than not – in older scholarly literature at least – the tendency has emanated from theological critics of post-Reformation Protestantism. The Protestant thought of seventeenth-century Europe has often been sharply opposed to that of the two isolated heroes of the Reformation, Martin Luther and John Calvin. Whereas, say, Calvin's output represents the perfect

---

1. Carl R. Trueman, 'Calvin and Calvinism', in Donald K. McKim (ed.), *The Cambridge Companion to John Calvin* (Cambridge: Cambridge University Press, 2004), p. 226.

marriage of a 'humanist' ideal – attention to sources – with a Reformational commitment to Scripture and the person of Christ, later Reformed theologians were overtly predestinarian and relentlessly 'scholastic' in their approach. By 'scholastic', what is typically meant is a doctrinal content and method which privileges systems, reason, logic and metaphysical speculation over careful biblical exegesis.[2] Amongst other things, the era has been characterized as embracing a woodenly propositional, dictation theory of revelation, speculative doctrines like 'limited atonement' which are grounded in logic rather than Scripture, and a rigid 'covenant theology' which elevates human response to the detriment of God's grace, the work of Christ and personal assurance of salvation.

All these assessments, and many more like them, have been so thoroughly overturned by intellectual historians in the last thirty years that they can no longer be held with any credibility. It is beyond us to summarize this discussion here, but fortunately there are now numerous introductions to this debate, as well as more extended treatments of various contentious issues available to the reader.[3] Suffice to say, a very different picture of post-Reformation Protestantism

---

2. A classic example of this is the taxonomy in Brian G. Armstrong, *Calvinism and the Amyraut Heresy: Protestant Scholasticism and Humanism in Seventeenth-Century France* (Madison: University of Wisconsin Press, 1969), p. 32.

3. The best general introduction to the historiography and recent reappraisal is Willem van Asselt (ed.), *Introduction to Reformed Scholasticism* (Grand Rapids: Reformation Heritage Books, 2011). See too the essays Willem van Asselt and Eef Dekker, 'Introduction', in Willem van Asselt and Eef Dekker (eds.), *Reformation and Scholasticism: An Ecumenical Enterprise* (Grand Rapids: Baker Academic, 2001); Richard Muller, 'The Problem of Protestant Scholasticism: A Review and Definition', in Willem van Asselt and E. Dekker (eds.), *Reformation and Scholasticism: An Ecumenical Enterprise* (Grand Rapids: Baker, 2001); Trueman, 'Calvin and Calvinism'; Richard Muller, 'John Calvin and Later Calvinism', in David Bagchi and David C. Steinmetz (eds.), *The Cambridge Companion to Reformation Theology*, ed. (Cambridge: Cambridge University Press, 2004); Willem van Asselt, 'Reformed Orthodoxy: A Short History of Research', in Herman J. Selderhuis (ed.), *A Companion to Reformed Orthodoxy* (Leiden: Brill, 2013). The following paragraph draws from and summarizes some of the material in these overviews. More detailed discussions of the general historiographical issues can be found in Richard Muller, *After Calvin: Studies in the Development of a Theological Tradition*, Oxford Studies in Historical Theology (New York: Oxford University Press, 2003), pp. 1–46, 63–102; Richard Muller, *Calvin and the Reformed Tradition: On the Work of Christ and the Order of Salvation* (Grand Rapids: Baker Academic, 2012), pp. 13–69.

has emerged. Within the Reformed context, for instance, it is simply a mistake to identify Calvin as the founder of a particular tradition, since Early Modern Reformed identity never coalesced around one particular person, however much he was revered.[4] It was shaped instead by the various national confessional documents of the sixteenth and seventeenth centuries into which numerous theologians had input, and concerning which individuals – including Calvin – often had to compromise on issues of secondary importance to achieve consensus. Indeed, Reformed 'orthodoxy', as defined by these great confessions, was sufficiently 'catholic' to allow for considerable variety on all kinds of doctrines, including the extent of the atonement and the covenants.[5] Yet amidst this variety, there is a remarkable degree of confessional consensus concerning the key Reformational convictions: the authority of Scripture, the person and work of Christ, the character of faith and justification, and so on. Moreover, while there is no doubt that many post-Reformation theologians adopted what may rightly be called a 'scholastic' method in their writings, historians such as Paul Kristeller and others have demonstrated that Renaissance scholasticism was sufficiently eclectic that it cannot be pitted against humanism, nor can it be defined as privileging particular theological content.[6] Rather, in its broadest sense it best describes a particular method of disputation emanating from the Mediaeval schools and carrying over into the Renaissance university and academy. As orthodox Protestant reflection passed into its second and third generations, there was an increasing need to accommodate it within the academy and defend it from both external and internal opposition. The existing scholastic method was thus an entirely appropriate and, indeed, necessary vehicle for such discussion. Yet, however much this form of disputation was widely adopted by theologians into the seventeenth century, it was by no means the exclusive mode of theological discourse, and it certainly did

---

4. On the specific question of Calvin's later influence, see Richard Muller, 'Reception and Response: Referencing and Understanding Calvin in Seventeenth-Century Calvinism', in Irena Backus and Philip Benedict (eds.), *Calvin and His Influence, 1509–2009* (Oxford: Oxford University Press, 2009).

5. A good introduction to some of this diversity in the British scene, for instance, can be found in the following collection: Michael A. G. Haykin and Mark Jones (eds.), *Drawn into Controversie: Reformed Theological Diversity and Debates within Seventeenth-Century British Puritanism* (Göttingen: Vandenhoeck & Ruprecht, 2011).

6. See, e.g., Paul Oskar Kristeller, *Renaissance Thought and Its Sources* (New York: Columbia University Press, 1979).

not supplant the more foundational Reformation tradition of biblical commentary and exegesis.

Without wanting to draw the lines too sharply, a pioneer in the recent
scholarly resurgence, Richard Muller, charts the development of post-
Reformation orthodoxy of the specifically Reformed variety in three stages.[7]
The period from about 1560 (following the deaths of second-generation
Reformers like Calvin, Vermigli and Musculus) till the aftermath of the Synod
of Dort (1618–19) represents an era of significant confessional codification,
together with a remarkably productive extension and development of the
Reformational exegetical and dogmatic tradition. It was also a time when central
Reformed convictions, such as the authority and clarity of Scripture, began to
face robust and formidable critique in the wake of the Counter-Reformation
from immensely learned Catholic apologists such as Robert Bellarmine and
Fransico Suárez. Controversial even within its own Catholic context, Jesuit
teaching on the divine will and human contingency also exercised considerable
influence on the Dutch Protestant Jacobus Arminius and his Remonstrant
supporters. All these developments, and others like them (such as the rise of
a Protestant anti-trinitarianism), required Reformed thinkers to formulate
considered theological responses, which continued to grow in refinement
and sophistication throughout the following period, what Muller calls 'High
Orthodoxy', from about 1640 till 1700. From the 1650s onwards, the rise of
anti-dogmatic rationalism and Cartesian philosophy represented a new front
on which Reformed thought needed to contend. Indeed, as the century drew
to a close, it is possible to witness the beginnings of an eventual collapse in
confessionalism which befell Reformed thought in the eighteenth century, or
Muller's final period of 'Late Orthodoxy'. The radical philosophical developments of the late seventeenth century forced self-identified Reformed
theologians to decide on the extent to which they should be embraced or
rejected. An increasing inability to find consensus is surely a key factor in the
eventual fragmentation of confessionalism within the Protestant academy. It
is not that Reformed confessionalism was completely eclipsed in the eighteenth

---

7. See, e.g., Muller, *After Calvin*, pp. 4–7. A useful discussion of each era can be found
   in van Asselt, *Introduction*, pp. 103–193. Our discussion will focus on the Reformed
   context, but for developments in Early Modern Lutheran orthodoxy, the classic
   scholarly study is R. D. Preus, *The Theology of Post-Reformation Lutheranism*, Vol. 1:
   A Study of Theological Prolegomena (St Louis: Concordia, 1970); R. D. Preus, *The
   Theology of Post-Reformation Lutheranism*, Vol. 2: *God and His Creation* (St Louis:
   Concordia, 1972).

century, but, as Muller points out, it tended to live on in a new context, having lost connection to much of the new philosophy and anti-dogmatic exegetical approaches of the academy.[8]

Trueman rightly cautions against assessing the development of post-Reformation theology in terms of a simplistic continuity–discontinuity paradigm.[9] Differences in formulation and even doctrine clearly did emerge over subsequent generations, as one would naturally expect in a changing intellectual and political environment, notwithstanding any underlying confessional consistency. Rather than repeating the general summaries of these developments which readers can readily access elsewhere, in the body of this chapter we have chosen to focus on a particular Reformational conviction, what we might call the 'Protestant Scripture principle', or the supreme and infallible authority of Scripture, which began to face sustained pressure throughout the second half of the seventeenth century, and certainly featured in the general decline of Reformed orthodoxy into the eighteenth century. Obviously we will not be able to address every complexity associated with these developments, and there is always a risk that by pointing to general 'trends' and 'tensions' a rather simplistic and two-dimensional picture will emerge.[10] Instead, we will simply illustrate the way in which the Reformational commitment to Scripture's authority was compromised by some, but, as we shall see, not by all self-identifying Protestants in the late seventeenth century.

The Protestant Scripture principle restated: Petrus van Mastricht (1630–1706)

To begin with, it is worth outlining a classic 'High Orthodox' statement of the Protestant Scripture principle from one of the ablest theologians of the era, Petrus van Mastricht (1630–1706), a German-born Dutch pastor and theologian who was professor of Hebrew and theology first in Duisburg, then later at Utrecht. Compared with some of his contemporaries, such as Francis Turretin

---

8. See Richard Muller, *Post-Reformation Reformed Dogmatics: The Rise and Development of Reformed Orthodoxy, Ca. 1520 to Ca. 1725*, 2nd edn, 4 vols. (Grand Rapids: Baker Academic, 2003), I.82–84. Hereafter cited as *PRRD*.
9. Carl R. Trueman, 'The Reception of Calvin: Historical Considerations', *Church History and Religious Culture* 91, no. 1 (2011).
10. For a fuller picture, readers may consult Muller's magisterial discussion of the issues in the second volume of his *PRRD*.

or John Owen, van Mastricht is still relatively unknown to English-speaking audiences, not least because his output is still untranslated. Even still, van Mastricht was a formidable exegete, dogmatician and defender of Reformed orthodoxy, so much so that the renowned American theologian Jonathan Edwards famously remarked that, 'for divinity . . . doctrine, practice and controversy', van Mastricht's *magnum opus, Theoretico-Practica Theologia* (first published in 1682 and revised in 1698), 'is much better than Turretin or any other book in the world, excepting the Bible'![11]

As was typically the pattern in High Orthodox theological compendiums, the *Theoretico-Practica Theologia* is arranged according to various theological topics or 'loci', and in this case the author tends to address each topic under different sections: a dogmatic summary, followed by a much fuller elenctic discussion where controversies over the doctrine are addressed, and concluding with a section spelling out the practical implications of the doctrine. As Muller points out, High Orthodox compendiums would not only state the confessional consensus on a particular doctrine, but would also often summarize the standard Reformed responses to various objections to the doctrine over the preceding hundred years.[12] And in an elenctic section of the locus *De Sacra Scriptura* ('On Holy Scripture'), van Mastricht restates the Reformational Scripture principle by distinguishing it from the opinions of three kinds of 'pseudo-Christians'.

The first he mentions are the 'Enthusiasts', the spiritual descendants of the so-called Radical Reformation.[13] This group may retain some notion of an authoritative divine 'Scripture' or infallible 'word of God', he says, but they insist that it can only be interpreted through continuing 'inspirations of the Spirit' which function like an 'internal word'. To this group, the written text is but a 'dead letter' without the Spirit's 'private interpretation', alluding to the apostle Paul in 2 Corinthians 3:6, as they frequently did. Summarizing the standard Reformed response to the Enthusiasts, van Mastricht readily acknowledges that the biblical patriarchs and apostles were directly inspired by the Spirit, but denies that believers experience this today since the Spirit's internal work is now limited to conversion and sanctification. The Enthusiasts make two basic errors, he claims. First, they undermine the perfection and sufficiency of Scripture as the supreme 'rule of faith and life'. Second, they assert that an

---

11. Quoted in Adriaan C. Neele, *Petrus van Mastricht (1630–1706): Reformed Orthodoxy: Method and Piety* (Leiden: Brill, 2009), p. 11.

12. Muller, *PRRD*, I.74.

13. Here I am summarizing and, at points, translating Petrus van Mastricht, *Theoretico-Practica Theologia* (Utrecht: W. van de Water, 1724), I.ii.33 (30b–31a).

infallible internal spiritual revelation, different from that contained in Scripture itself, remains necessary for the interpretation of Scripture. Not only is this necessity never taught in the 'sacred text', Scripture explicitly rejects it on the grounds of its inherent sufficiency and perfection, whilst warning against the dangers of Satanic delusion (e.g. 2 Cor. 11:4; 2 Thess. 2:2; 1 John 4:1–2).

The second kind of 'pseudo-Christians' are what he generically calls the 'Socinians'.[14] This group distinguishes itself by arguing that human reason is the 'infallible norm' for expounding Scripture on the pretext that reason is the ultimate authority in religious matters. In outlining the Reformed position, van Mastricht acknowledges that reason can function either as an 'instrument', an 'argument' or as a 'norm' or 'foundation'. While he points to an anti-rational biblicism among some Protestants, the Reformed readily maintain that reason is a 'necessary' instrument for unfolding and inquiring into the truth contained in Scripture. It can also be 'useful' as an argument to support or confirm the truths which have their ultimate foundation in Scripture. But for a number of reasons they deny it can act as a norm or foundation of the realities Christians believe. Not only is fallen reason prone to error and deception (cf. 1 Cor. 2:14, 15; John 1:5; Rom. 1:21), but the spiritual truths of Christian faith transcend its natural grasp (cf. 1 Tim. 3:16; Matt. 13:11; 1 Cor. 2:7, 14). For the apostles and even Christ himself, inspired Scripture always retains a unique authority to prescribe the principles of faith and determine the limits of rational argument or interpretation. Therefore, to allow reason a place at the foundation of Christian faith robs Scripture of its proper office and dignity.

Finally, there are the Roman Catholics, or the 'Pontificii', who argue that the divine authority of Scripture depends on the infallible testimony of the church.[15] As van Mastricht indicates, the Catholics do not so much deny the unique divine authority of inspired Scripture 'in itself'. Rather, their claim is that its authority cannot be properly recognized by us without the testimony of the church. Against this, the Reformed insist that it is impossible to separate the authority of Scripture (and our perception of it) from Scripture itself. Scripture is itself a testimony whose authority depends solely on the veracity of its divine author. In other words, its authority is necessarily 'self-authenticating' (*autopistos*) and 'trustworthy' (*axiopistos*) in itself. As van Mastricht puts it, 'in every respect, the authority of Scripture depends on Scripture itself and the divine splendour which is evident within it'. And therefore, the authority of the church must ultimately give way to the authoritative testimony of Scripture. Van Mastricht

---

14. Drawing from ibid., I.ii.34 (31a–b).

15. Drawing from ibid., I.ii.37 (32b).

then goes on at great length to outline the standard Reformed responses to the extensive charges Catholics have levelled against the Protestant Scripture principle over the preceding century or so.[16]

Of these challenges to the classic Reformational affirmation of scriptural authority, van Mastricht clearly considers the second to pose the most immediate threat within his own context. By the mid- to late seventeenth century, Roman Catholicism continued to present a formidable alternative to the Protestant faith, but the religious wars that tore Europe apart earlier in the century had ceased, and the intellectual polemics were now formalized without the fresh intensity they possessed a century earlier.[17] Moreover, the memories of recent bitter conflicts undoubtedly contributed to a new intellectual climate which, amongst other things, harboured a widespread suspicion of religious 'enthusiasm' with its uncomfortably radical and sectarian appeals to the supernatural work of the Spirit. Alongside this wariness towards fanaticism emerged a new-found confidence in human reason as the proper arbiter of religious truth.[18]

Van Mastricht himself specifically points to the impact of Socinianism. As he mentions, the label 'Socinian' was originally attached to the teachings of an anti-trinitarian sect which broke away from the Polish Reformed church in the late sixteenth century. Faustus Socinus (1539–1604), whose name gave rise to the label, came to fame with his *Racovian Catechism* in which he excluded doctrines such as the Trinity and Christ's divinity. Aside from their unitarianism, the Socinians were particularly infamous for the place they ascribed to reason in biblical interpretation. Although they acknowledged the infallible authority of Scripture, the only acceptable interpretations of its teachings were those which conformed to reason, and it was on this basis that they rejected trinitarian orthodoxy. Socinian writings were circulated widely throughout Europe in the seventeenth century and eventually the label 'Socinian' became a term of derision used to describe any significant deviation from Protestant orthodoxy, especially where it was seen to entail the inflation of human reason over biblical authority.[19]

---

16. Ibid., I.ii.38–60 (32b–39b).

17. See Muller, *PRRD*, I.75.

18. On the phenomenon labelled 'enthusiasm' and the reaction to it in the seventeenth century, see Michael Heyd, 'The Reaction to Enthusiasm in the Seventeenth Century: Towards an Integrative Approach', *The Journal of Modern History* 53, no. 2 (1981), pp. 258–280; Michael Heyd, *'Be Sober and Reasonable': The Critique of Enthusiasm in the Seventeenth and Early Eighteenth Centuries* (Leiden: Brill, 1995).

19. Important studies on Socinianism include H. John McLachlan, *Socinianism in Seventeenth-Century England* (Oxford: Oxford University Press, 1951); Martin Muslow

Consequently, aside from the Socinians themselves, under the broad label of 'Socinianism' van Mastricht will also refer to those he describes as 'Rationalist Theologians'. These have 'lately arisen before us', he says, and they insist that the divine authority of Scripture cannot be proven except by reason, and maintain that if there is any 'tension' between Scripture and reason, the latter is 'to be more strongly heard than Scripture'.[20] As Goudriaan observes, van Mastricht seems to be at least partly alluding to a controversy that erupted at Franeker in 1687 over a university disputation by G. W. Duker.[21] Amongst other things, Duker had argued that the 'divinity of Scripture is not able to be established other than from reason'.[22] Van Mastricht himself probably stayed out of this particular debate, but his remark alone highlights for us two major points of tension for the Protestant Scripture principle stemming from a rapidly dissolving classical hegemony of faith over reason in the late seventeenth century. The first concerns the means by which Scripture's authority may be discerned or established. The second relates to the interpretation of Scripture. Let us examine and illustrate these in turn.

Discerning the authority of Scripture

As van Mastricht notes above, an important corollary of the Protestant commitment to the supremacy of Scripture over unaided rational inquiry or church dogma was a conviction that its infallible divine authority is ultimately 'self-authenticating' (*autopistia*) in the process of drawing a person to faith. Inevitably this involved an appeal to the work of the Holy Spirit. Calvin captured this appeal with famous clarity when he insisted that 'those whom the Holy Spirit

---

(note 19 *cont.*) and Jan Rohls (eds.), *Socinianism and Arminianism: Antitrinitarians, Calvinists and Cultural Exchange in Seventeenth-Century Europe* (Leiden: Brill, 2005); Sarah Mortimer, *Reason and Religion in the English Revolution: The Challenge of Socinianism* (Cambridge: Cambridge University Press, 2010); Paul C. H. Lim, *Mystery Unveiled: The Crisis of the Trinity in Early Modern England* (New York: Oxford University Press, 2012).

20. Mastricht, *Theologia*, I.ii.34 (31a).
21. Aza Goudriaan, *Reformed Orthodoxy and Philosophy, 1625–1750* (Leiden: Brill, 2006), p. 64. On the controversy, see Aza Goudriaan, 'Ulrik Huber (1636–1694) and John Calvin: The Franeker Debate on Human Reason and the Bible (1686–1687)', *Church History and Religious Culture* 91 (2011), pp. 165–178.
22. Latin quoted in Goudriaan, 'Franeker Debate', p. 169; translation mine.

has inwardly taught truly rest upon Scripture, and that Scripture indeed is self-authenticated; hence, it is not right to subject it to proof and reasoning'. Any 'certainty' a believer might experience in relation to Scripture is 'attained by the testimony of the Spirit'.[23] Orthodox Reformed theologians throughout the seventeenth century consistently maintained this commitment to the ultimate self-authenticating spiritual authority of Scripture. Van Mastricht describes the efficacy of Scripture as an instrument of the Spirit or 'arm of God' which 'pierces the heart', 'exposes' what is hidden in it, 'penetrates' and 'wondrously affects' the soul, 'illumines' the mind, 'regenerates' the heart, 'kindles' faith, 'sanctifies' the whole man, 'strengthens', 'comforts' and eternally 'saves'.[24]

It is true that soon after the Reformation the role of rational argumentation or 'proofs' which lend support to the divine authority of Scripture became increasingly prominent in Reformed apologetics. Someone like Calvin readily appreciated the value in this well-established tradition of identifying various evidences which might rationally support its divine authority. To his mind, these proofs are sufficiently compelling that anyone with 'pure eyes and upright senses' will immediately recognize the 'majesty of God' in Scripture. 'Yet', as he goes on to say, 'they who strive to build up firm faith in Scripture through disputation are doing things backwards'.[25] These arguments may be useful in quelling irrational opposition to Scripture. They may even serve to strengthen the faith of those who *already* believe. But for Calvin, they cannot play any role in the foundation of faith: a role which must be reserved for the testimony of the Spirit alone. Yet within a generation, it was virtually commonplace for Reformed thinkers to maintain that the Spirit may somehow incorporate these objective evidences into his own internal testimony. For instance, someone like the important Elizabethan divine William Whitaker readily agrees that these evidences are incapable of inducing faith on their own. Yet, when the Spirit's testimony is 'added' to them, he says, 'it fills our minds with a wonderful plenitude of assurance, confirms them, and causes us most gladly to embrace the Scriptures, giving force to the preceding arguments'.[26]

---

23. John Calvin, *Institutes of the Christian Religion*, trans. Ford Lewis Battles, ed. John T. McNeill (Philadelphia: Westminster, 1960), I.vii.5. Cf. I.vii passim.

24. Mastricht, *Theologia*, I.ii.21 (23a).

25. Calvin, *Institutes* (1559), I.vii.4. Calvin outlines numerous arguments and defends their usefulness throughout, ibid., I.viii.

26. William Whitaker, *A Disputation on Holy Scripture: Against the Papists, Especially Bellarmine and Stapleton*, trans. William Fitzgerald (Cambridge: Cambridge University Press, 1849), p. 295.

Referring to a similar shift in the writings of Theodore Beza, Jeffrey Mallinson suggests this move may have partly been a response to sceptical attacks from humanist and Catholic quarters that were wary of Protestant appeals to the Spirit's subjective work.[27] Certainly, for Catholic polemicists like Thomas Stapleton, a mere reliance on some 'private' spiritual testimony provided no safeguard against the possibility of Satanic delusion – a hint at the dangers of 'spiritualism', or the 'enthusiasm' so derided by Catholics and mainstream Protestants alike.[28] Sensitive to this kind of concern, van Mastricht denies that the Spirit's internal testimony amounts to 'an enthusiasm of sorts'.[29] Rather, consistent with the pattern set by Whitaker and others, he responds by tying the Spirit's testimony to the objective evidences in the text itself. He refers to the 'marks of divinity' impressed on Scripture by God, such as the sublime character of its content, its inherent harmony and the unadorned majesty of its written style. These essentially amount to what are often described as evidences 'internal' to Scripture itself which were typically considered superior to 'external' evidences (such as those derived from miracles, the preservation of the text or the testimony of martyrs), and van Mastricht points the reader to his more extensive discussion of them elsewhere in the chapter.[30] The Spirit's effectual 'internal persuasion' does not whisper some message about Scripture directly into the mind, he insists. Rather it elevates the 'power of understanding' so that it is able to grasp the 'marks of divinity' which God has impressed into Scripture. This, he suggests, is how the Holy Spirit effectively functions as a 'co-witness' with our own spirit (Rom. 8:16).

While this move to ground the Spirit's testimony in objectively discernible proofs or arguments is understandable when it has been tarred with the brush of enthusiasm, it has been seized upon as evidence of a general declension into 'rationalism' by second-generation Reformed theologians, effectively betraying the Protestant hegemony of faith over reason and its associated Scripture

---

27. Jeffrey Mallinson, *Faith, Reason and Revelation in Theodore Beza, 1519–1605*, Oxford Theological Monographs (Oxford: Oxford University Press, 2003), p. 98.

28. Thomas Stapleton, *Principiorum Fidei Doctrinalium* (Paris, 1579), p. 336. On the degree to which reliance on the Spirit's authority to undergird religious certainty was already a contentious issue in the mid-sixteenth century, see Susan E. Schreiner, *Are You Alone Wise? The Search for Certainty in the Early Modern Era* (Oxford: Oxford University Press, 2011).

29. For this, see Mastricht, *Theologia*, I.ii.62 (40a–b).

30. On the standard set of 'internal' and 'external' evidences, see, e.g., Muller, *PRRD*, II.267–281.

principle.[31] Is the Holy Spirit's illuminative work limited merely to a restoration of natural reason, so that Christian faith in the Word of God ends up piggybacking on some rational argument that could, in theory, convince anyone in his or her right mind, with or without the Spirit? As scholars like Helm and van den Belt are right to point out, for Calvin it is vital that Christian faith rests directly on the divine testimony of Scripture itself, effectually communicated and authenticated by the same Spirit who inspired its very words. In other words, the grounds for believing Scripture to be God's word must be the very same grounds as for faith itself: not a rational demonstration, but the authoritative testimony of the Holy Spirit in the word itself, effectually communicated to the heart.[32]

The detection of a rationalizing trajectory among later Reformed writers is tempting, but in reality the situation is far more nuanced. For High Orthodox theologians like van Mastricht and Francis Turretin, there is no sense that faith in Scripture's infallible authority ultimately rests on a natural or rational argument. Van Mastricht speaks of the need for the mind to be 'elevated', not just healed from its fallen prejudices, suggesting that the 'marks of divinity' impressed by God in Scripture are such that their full force cannot be detected by the mind in its natural state. Reason needs to be spiritually raised above its natural powers. In any event, he anticipates this very objection. Responding to the claim that 'the characters of divinity from which the divinity of Scripture is demonstrated are of reason', he answers, 'those characters are in Scripture [itself], so that Scripture is recognized as divine from itself and not from rational demonstration, just as the sun is recognized by its own light and not another'.[33] Similarly, Turretin argues that the full 'theological certainty' believers enjoy about Scripture only arises when their minds and senses are so renewed by the Spirit that they are able to discern the supernatural light and truth spiritually impressed on Scripture 'by its own light'.[34]

---

31. See, e.g., Jack B. Rogers and Donald K. McKim, *The Authority and Interpretation of the Bible: An Historical Approach* (San Francisco: Harper & Row, 1979), pp. 176–177, 207; and in a much more measured fashion, Henk van den Belt, *The Authority of Scripture in Reformed Theology* (Leiden: Brill, 2008), pp. 155–158, 176–177.

32. See, e.g., Paul Helm, *John Calvin's Ideas* (Oxford: Oxford University Press, 2004), pp. 278–281. Cf. van den Belt, *Scripture*, pp. 49–70.

33. Mastricht, *Theologia*, I.ii.34 (31b).

34. Francis Turretin, *Institutes of Elenctic Theology*, trans. George Musgrave Giger, ed. James T. Dennison Jr., 3 vols. (Phillipsburg: P&R, 1992), II.vi.11. For a slightly fuller defence of Turretin's position, see Andrew M. Leslie, *The Light of Grace: John Owen on the Authority of Scripture and Christian Faith* (Göttingen: Vandenhoeck & Ruprecht, 2015), pp. 29–30.

Writing after the English Restoration in 1660, John Owen certainly does register various hesitancies about the way some Reformed writers had incorporated the standard, rationally discernible proofs, such as the inherent excellency of Scripture's doctrine, into the Spirit's internal testimony. He would rather adopt an approach similar to Calvin's, insisting that the Spirit's internal testimony works directly through his own unique supernatural testimony inspired in Scripture itself. Even so, given that the standard Reformed position still insists upon 'the necessity of an internal, effectual work of the Holy Spirit, in the illumination of our minds, so enabling us to believe with faith divine and supernatural', he does not detect any substantial theological departure.[35] Nonetheless, he does anticipate a much bigger threat. In his mature treatise *Reason of Faith* (1674), he locks horns with a recent propensity he detects in Protestant apologetics to defend the authority of Scripture on purely rational grounds.[36] Apparently it had become increasingly commonplace to exclude the testimony of the Holy Spirit altogether from a Christian's belief in the authority of Scripture. Instead, through deployment of the standard internal and external arguments alone, it was felt a person could attain a sufficiently high degree of rational certainty regarding the divine authority of Scripture, enabling him or her to believe in its content. The Spirit may be necessary to heal the moral prejudices of fallen reason; he may also enable someone to believe doctrines contained within Scripture which transcend the grasp of natural reason, such as the Trinity; but when it comes to a belief in the authority of Scripture itself, the foundation of that conviction must emphatically be tied to the deductions of 'right reason' from the rationally discernible proofs. And because human reason, even when healed of its fallen prejudices, is still potentially prone to error, the highest degree of certainty a believer may possess is 'moral' but not 'infallible'. In other words, the evidences are sufficiently strong to prove its authority 'beyond reasonable doubt', but not to exclude all possibility of error or deception, which is simply beyond our rational grasp.

Owen does not name his opponents, but it is not hard to find this sort of approach being championed in England throughout the seventeenth century.[37] One of its earliest advocates was the Laudian confrère William Chillingworth, responding to the Catholic polemicist Edward Knott in his 1637 treatise *The*

---

35. John Owen, *The Works*, ed. William H. Goold (Edinburgh: Johnstone & Hunter, 1850–1855), IV.53. Cf. Leslie, *Light*, pp. 58–64.

36. For the following, see Leslie, *Light*, pp. 42–49, 56–64. Cf. Owen, *Works*, IV.5–6, 45–69, 100–108.

37. For the following, see Leslie, *Light*, pp. 42–49, 59–60.

Religion of Protestants, A Safe Way to Salvation.[38] After the Restoration, learned establishment figures, such as the Archbishop of Canterbury John Tillotson or the one-time Dean of St Paul's Cathedral Edward Stillingfleet, as well as numerous others, argued similarly.[39] On the Continent, a similar trend is evident, initially among Arminian theologians such as Jean Le Clerc, but it eventually took hold within the Reformed context as well. We have already noted the controversy at Franeker in 1687 over G. W. Duker's disputation, to which van Mastricht alludes. By the turn of the century in the Genevan Academy, Francis Turretin's son, Jean-Alphonse Turretin, had virtually excluded the Spirit's internal testimony from the grounds of faith, leaning heavily on the standard apologetic arguments instead.[40] Likewise, a few decades later in Franeker once again, Hermann Venema resolutely maintained that the truthfulness and authority of Scripture can be established only on rational grounds.[41]

This more radical apologetic strategy was undoubtedly driven, as ever, by an attempt to stave off accusations of irrational and potentially seditious enthusiasm at one end, and, at the other, to defend Scripture against the rising tide of scepticism emerging from freethinking voices outside the church structures. Scholars have drawn attention to a growing anti-clerical quest to emancipate religion and philosophical inquiry from its traditional confessional context, spurred on by the radical and often sceptical writings of laymen such as Lord Herbert of Cherbury,

---

38. See William Chillingworth, *The Works* (Philadelphia: R. Davis, 1844), pp. 17–522.

39. See, e.g., John Tillotson, *The Works*, ed. Thomas Birch (London: Richard Priestley, 1820), IX.173–346; Edward Stillingfleet, *A Rational Account of the Grounds of Protestant Religion* (Oxford: Oxford University Press, 1844), I.321–373. For further examples, see the discussion in Barbara J. Shapiro, *Probability and Certainty in Seventeenth-Century England: A Study of the Relationships between Natural Science, Religion, History, Law and Literature* (Princeton: Princeton University Press, 1983), pp. 74–118; Gerard Reedy, *The Bible and Reason: Anglicans and Scripture in Late Seventeenth-Century England* (Philadelphia: University of Pennsylvania Press, 1985), pp. 20–62; John Spurr, '"Rational Religion" in Restoration England', *Journal of the History of Ideas* 49, no. 4 (1988), pp. 563–585; Martin I. J. Griffin Jr., *Latitudinarianism in the Seventeenth-Century Church of England* (Leiden: Brill, 1992), pp. 72–104. Cf. Henry G. van Leeuwen, *The Problem of Certainty in English Thought, 1630–1690* (The Hague: Nijhoff, 1963).

40. See Martin I. Klauber, *Between Reformed Scholasticism and Pan-Protestantism: Jean-Alphonse Turretin (1671–1737) and Enlightened Orthodoxy at the Academy of Geneva* (Selinsgrove: Susquehanna University Press, 1994), pp. 107–112.

41. Hermann Venema, *Institutes of Theology*, trans. Alex W. Brown (Edinburgh: T&T Clark, 1850), pp. 71, 96–97.

René Descartes, Thomas Hobbes, Baruch Spinoza and John Toland.[42] Take, for instance, the Royalist philosopher Hobbes, who wrote his famous political treatise *Leviathan* (1651) whilst exiled in Paris during the Interregnum. Aside from its provocative espousal of Epicurean materialism and a host of other idiosyncratic theological ideas, *Leviathan* proposes an extreme Erastianism which strictly grounds the binding canonical authority of scriptural laws in the Commonwealth and its sovereign.[43] Moreover, when it comes to matters of faith, Hobbes is dismissive of attempts to prove Scripture's divine authority through rational argument, appeals to the church or the Spirit's inward testimony, claiming it is impossible to 'know' that the Bible truly is the word of God. A Christian can only 'believe' in its divinity, and such belief normally arises through the instruction of 'teachers', such as our parents, and, of course, pastors who receive their licence to preach from the sovereign.[44] If Hobbes essentially domesticates the authority of Scripture to the state, the Jewish philosopher Baruch Spinoza is more radical still. Spinoza entirely dispensed with the notion of a divinely inspired text, treating its human authors as just that, releasing the Bible from its dogmatic stronghold and translating it into a mere species of natural religious history.[45] To make matters worse, a number of Catholic apologists were advancing the sceptical cause by adopting an ancient 'Pyrrhonic' rhetorical strategy to undermine Scripture as the supreme 'rule of faith' in favour of the church's infallible authority, which, they argued, could be established on purely rational grounds.[46]

---

42. See, e.g., Gerald R. Cragg, *From Puritanism to the Age of Reason: A Study of Changes in Religious Thought within the Church of England, 1660 to 1700* (Cambridge: Cambridge University Press, 1950); Spurr, 'Rational'; J. A. I. Champion, *The Pillars of Priestcraft Shaken: The Church of England and Its Enemies, 1660–1730* (Cambridge: Cambridge University Press, 1992).

43. See, e.g., Thomas Hobbes, *Leviathan* (Cambridge: Cambridge University Press, 1996), XXXII (255–259); XXXIII.199 (260); 205–256 (267–259).

44. Ibid., XL.323–324 (405–327). Cf. XXXIII.205–326 (267–329).

45. On this, see, e.g., J. S. Preus, *Spinoza and the Irrelevance of Biblical Authority* (Cambridge: Cambridge University Press, 2001), pp. 154–202. Cf. Richard Popkin, *The History of Scepticism: From Savonarola to Bayle* (Oxford: Oxford University Press, 2003), pp. 239–253. For a more measured account of Spinoza's aims with this approach vis-à-vis Scripture, see Nancy K. Levene, *Spinoza's Revelation: Religion, Democracy, and Reason* (Cambridge: Cambridge University Press, 2004).

46. See, e.g., the relentless approach of John Sergeant, *Faith Vindicated from Possibility of Falsehood . . .* (London, 1667), pp. 67–70, passim. On this generally, see further, Popkin, *Scepticism*, pp. 67–77; Griffin Jr., *Latitudinarianism*, pp. 54–57.

Someone like Owen feels the strain of these developments as acutely as anyone. In this respect he applauds the apologetic efforts of his contemporaries to shore up orthodox, biblical Christian faith against the onslaught of what many were now labelling 'atheism'.[47] Yet by insisting that the grounds of Christian faith – the Scriptures – may be established purely through rational argument, without recourse to the Spirit's infallible and irresistible testimony, Owen believes they have conceded far too much ground, hastening the eventual collapse of Protestant orthodoxy. The same may be said for van Mastricht, or Ulrik Huber, who forcefully opposed Duker in Franeker by referring directly to Calvin's argument, no less, for the critical importance of the Spirit's internal testimony at the foundation of Christian faith.[48] In other words, by the end of the seventeenth century, there remains a readily identifiable group of High Orthodox theologians who are resolutely committed to the classic, confessional Protestant affirmation of Scripture's self-authenticating, spiritual authority as the exclusive ground of Christian faith. Undoubtedly we can trace some development in the way this was expressed, with an increased emphasis on objectively discernible 'evidences', most likely in response to polemical charges of enthusiasm from the middle of the sixteenth century onwards. Yet these theologians continued to recognize the critical and distinctive place of the Spirit's effectual testimony alongside the written word, ensuring that the confessional Protestant hegemony of Scripture over reason remained intact.

Such an emphasis on the Spirit's work would become increasingly difficult to maintain, however, in the face of more radical attacks on the traditional dogmatic priority of Scripture over reason. And throughout the late seventeenth century, numerous Protestant apologists simply found it no longer desirable, or necessary, to prioritize the Spirit's work in drawing a person to trust in Scripture as the word of God. This critical shift, as writers like Owen and van Mastricht feared, represented a key move in the eventual demise of confessional orthodoxy within the Protestant establishment by the early eighteenth century.

The place of reason and the interpretation of Scripture

From the mid-seventeenth century onwards, a similar tension between Scripture and reason would also begin to manifest itself in the context of biblical interpretation. As we noted above, in the late sixteenth century the Socinians had

---

47. Owen, *Works*, IV.5–6, 20–21, 47. Cf. XVI.334, 337.
48. See Goudriaan, 'Franeker Debate'.

already distinguished themselves with their ruthlessly rational approach to
biblical interpretation which dismissed all dogma that did not conform to a
strictly literalistic reading of the text. By the middle of the seventeenth century,
a more explicitly rationalistic method would find support within the mainstream
Protestant academy among certain devotees of Cartesian philosophy. A particularly controversial publication was Ludwig Meyer's *Philosophia Sacrae Scripturae
Interpres* ('Philosophy: the interpreter of sacred Scripture'), which appeared in
1666.[49] Meyer was a freethinking Dutch physician and philosopher who felt that
the seemingly intractable impasse between rival interpretations of Scripture
could be broken through the guidance of philosophical reasoning, as the title
of his treatise suggests.[50] Meyer was certainly committed to the authority and
truthfulness of Scripture, but was sufficiently sceptical about its inherent clarity
or unity that he dismissed the possibility of discerning its truth through a simple
application of the classic Protestant principle that 'Scripture is its own interpreter'. Instead, proceeding from the Cartesian assumption that God has
furnished the mind with infallibly 'clear and distinct' ideas, he proposes that
right reason is naturally capable of discerning the intended divine meaning
expressed through the inspired authors of Scripture. Though Meyer's approach
can almost give the impression that scriptural revelation adds nothing to what
God has already revealed to natural reason, more theologically astute contemporaries like Ludwig Wolzogen and Lambert van Velthuysen were willing
to grant that God does reveal new truths in Scripture, while applying a similarly
naturalistic philosophical method to the discernment of such truth.[51]

Unsurprisingly, numerous Reformed thinkers directly resisted this kind of
hermeneutical approach in the following decades, especially among the followers
of Descartes' great nemesis in Utrecht, Gisbertus Voetius. Without denying the
necessary instrumental role of reason in biblical interpretation, theologians like
Voetius himself or his successor at Utrecht, van Mastricht, continued to stress
that its natural limitations and depravity mean that it cannot assume a foundational role.[52] Rather, to discern God's truth in Scripture aright, Christians are

---

49. Ludwig Meyer, *Philosophia S. Scripturae Interpres* (Eleuthropoli [Amsterdam]: [n.p.],
    1666).

50. In this paragraph, I am drawing on the analysis of Preus, *Spinoza*, pp. 34–67.

51. See discussion in ibid., pp. 107–153. Cf. Ernst Bizer, 'Reformed Orthodoxy and
    Cartesianism', *Journal for Theology and the Church* 2 (1965), pp. 45–52.

52. See, e.g., Goudriaan, *Orthodoxy*, pp. 29–65. Cf. Aza Goudriaan, 'Theology and
    Philosophy', in Herman J. Selderhuis (ed.), *A Companion to Reformed Orthodoxy*,
    ed. (Leiden: Brill, 2013), pp. 55–56.

chiefly dependent on its inherent perspicuity alongside the Spirit's internal illumination. This ensures that the Holy Spirit is properly recognized as the final and authoritative interpreter and teacher of the truth he has inspired within the biblical text. As Voetius insists, in opposition to this new rationalistic hermeneutic,

> the highest, absolute, infallible judge and interpreter of Scripture is the Holy Spirit speaking to us in Scripture, and through what is written; and internally impressing and communicating to us the sense and truth of Scripture, enabling us to understand, assent and believe, so that as we are enabled, we may understand, believe, and live accordingly.[53]

Not only was the authority of reason increasingly leveraged to break the impasse between rival dogmatic and sectarian interpretations of Scripture, it also assumed a more foundational interpretive role in the wake of substantial scientific developments throughout the seventeenth century, particularly within geology and astronomy. Shortly after his appointment to the newly formed theological faculty at Duisburg in 1653, the German-born Christoph Wittich caused a stir with the publication of his *Dissertationes Duae* ('Two Dissertations'), in the first of which he sets out to examine both the 'misuse' of Scripture in philosophical matters, and the planetary motion of the earth according to the theory espoused by the 'most noble Descartes'.[54] Wittich's most controversial claim is probably his contention that the 'light of reason' gives natural philosophy an authority autonomous from Scripture since such light grants us sufficient perception of its divinely instilled foundational principles that we ought to be able to avoid 'falling into errors'.[55] The Bible does not overturn the 'light of reason', he claims, and more significantly, Scripture's own infallible and inerrant authority can safely be limited to matters of faith and salvation, quoting 2 Timothy 3:17. In issues outside these core doctrines of salvation, Wittich believes that the Holy Spirit often allowed the human authors of Scripture to speak according to their ancient common perceptions, which may have been erroneous or imprecise when evaluated according to the principles of natural reason or philosophy.

---

53. Gisbertus Voetius, *Selectarum Disputationum Theologicarum*, 5 vols. (Utrecht: J. à Waesberge, 1648–67), V.421.
54. Christoph Wittich, *Dissertationes Duae* (Amsterdam: Ludovicum Elzevirium, 1653).
55. Ibid., 1–2. Wittich sets out his basic hermeneutical convictions in chapter 1 of the first dissertation: ibid., pp. 1–5.

There has been much written about the principle of biblical 'accommodation' in the writings of early Reformed theologians like Calvin.[56] That God accommodates truth about himself, ourselves or the world, to reveal it in Scripture through human language and idioms, is by no means controversial within confessional Protestant orthodoxy, let alone the wider Catholic tradition. Far more contentious is Wittich's claim that divine accommodation may embrace human error, and that autonomous reason can make such a determination in the process of biblical exegesis.[57]

Throughout the two dissertations, Wittich provides plenty of cases where he believes that Scripture contains an error about a natural phenomenon, or even, in some instances, about a moral or practical matter. For example, in referring to Genesis 1:16 and its description of 'two great lights', the sun and the moon, he believes that this is a purely phenomenological description based on a 'common' perception (*opinionem vulgi*) which contains factual error. In reality, the moon is neither 'great', he argues, nor is it strictly a 'light', since unlike the sun, it merely reflects rather than emits light.[58] Likewise, the growing consensus concerning a Copernican or heliocentric astronomical model rather than a geocentric one compels Wittich to detect an error in Joshua 10:13, where the narrator remarks that the 'sun stood still, and the moon stopped' (ESV), according to Joshua's command. Once again, the narrator's observation merely reflects the 'common' perception of what happened and which is factually incorrect, Wittich maintains, since only the moon literally 'stopped', not the sun.[59]

---

56. The literature includes D. Wright, 'Calvin's Pentateuchal Criticism: Equity, Hardness of Heart, and Divine Accommodation in the Mosaic Harmony Commentary', *CTJ* 21 (1986), pp. 33–50; D. Wright, 'Calvin's Accommodating God', in *Calvinus Sincerioris Religionis Vindex: Calvin as Protector of the Purer Religion*, Sixteenth Century Essays & Studies (Kirksville: Sixteenth Century Journal Publishers, 1997); Jon Balserak, *Divinity Compromised: A Study of Divine Accommodation in the Thought of John Calvin* (Dordrecht: Springer, 2006); Arnold Huijgen, *Divine Accommodation in John Calvin's Theology: Analysis and Assessment* (Göttingen: Vandenhoeck & Ruprecht, 2011). For a recent historical overview of the principle, see Glenn S. Sunshine, 'Accommodation Historically Considered', in D. A. Carson (ed.), *The Enduring Authority of the Christian Scriptures* (Grand Rapids: Eerdmans, 2016).

57. On Wittich's hermeneutical approach, see, e.g., discussion in Bizer, 'Orthodoxy', pp. 52–68; or briefly in Huijgen, *Accommodation*, pp. 30, 32, 33.

58. Wittich, *Dissertationes Duae*, pp. 52–58.

59. Ibid., pp. 251–259.

Modern readers of Scripture may have their own approaches to the challenge of reconciling biblical remarks about natural phenomena with the scientific consensus, but for someone like the young van Mastricht, Wittich's general hermeneutical approach was the thin end of a wedge. In 1655, at the age of twenty-five, van Mastricht published his first major treatise, which was a response to Wittich's *Dissertationes Duae*, namely, *Vindiciae Veritatis et Authoritatis Sacrae Scripturae in rebus Philosophicis* ('Defences of the Truthfulness and Authority of Holy Scripture in Philosophical matters').[60] Van Mastricht begins by re-framing the relationship between Scripture and philosophy in a manner consistent with the Protestant Scripture principle.[61] For him, all human sciences must ultimately be subordinate to theology, which is derived from biblical revelation. Even if philosophy has its own unique principles as a discipline, the veracity of those principles must ultimately be regulated by Scripture. It is not that van Mastricht denies the instrumental role of reason in theology or biblical interpretation, or its critical place within various human disciplines, but it cannot be the final arbiter of human knowledge after the fall, even within natural sciences like philosophy. After the fall, he remarks, the light of reason is only perfectly expressed in Scripture, and thus 'there is no principle more certain or solid upon which a science can be built than holy Scripture. Con-sequently, whatever agrees with it is to be received as truth; whatever contends in opposition with it is to be rejected as a falsehood.'[62] Not surprisingly, then, van Mastricht goes on to reject Wittich's revision of biblical accommodation which embraces the likelihood of human error within the text, even where it is limited to matters outside the scope of faith and salvation.[63] For him, the prospect that the Spirit of truth may bear false testimony in Scripture is both absurd and destructive of Christian faith: a prospect Wittich's position inevitably entails.[64]

We might expect that, when put into practice, van Mastricht's hermeneutical convictions will result in more literalistic exegesis compared with Wittich's

---

60. Petrus van Mastricht, *Vindiciae Veritatis et Authoritatis Sacrae Scripturae in rebus Philosophicis* . . . (Utrecht: Johannis à Waesberg, 1655). In 1677, van Mastricht would publish a more extensive refutation of the Cartesian incursion into Reformed theology: Petrus van Mastricht, *Novitatum Cartesianarum Gangraena* (Amsterdam: Jansson, 1677).

61. On this, see Mastricht, *Vindiciae*, pp. 1–6.

62. Ibid., p. 5.

63. For his extended set of arguments, see ibid., pp. 6–13.

64. See, especially, ibid., pp. 13–20.

approach. The situation is actually more nuanced.[65] Sometimes van Mastricht effectively castigates Wittich for overly literalistic exegesis, or for reading physical descriptions into the text where they plainly do not belong. In Genesis 1:16, for instance, van Mastricht denies that describing the sun and moon as 'great lights' implies an erroneous claim that they are somehow physically bigger than other stars.[66] It simply ought to be read as a straightforward reference to their effects – greater luminosity, radiance, and so on – relative to those of other stars.[67] Likewise, even if Wittich's astronomical observations about the moon are correct (and van Mastricht disputed this), he refused to concede that the moon's reflected radiance is only 'light' in a purely 'equivocal' sense, as if there is no analogical proportion between the rays of the sun and the reflection from the moon. In other places, such as Deuteronomy 30:4; 2 Samuel 22:8; Job 26:11; Psalms 18:8–9; 48:10; 103:12; 139:8–10; and Isaiah 13:5, van Mastricht similarly denies the presence of literal scientific error in these lofty phenomenological descriptions since they are plainly 'metonyms', 'synecdoches' or 'hyperbolic' figures of speech.[68]

Even still, given the fallibility of human reason, van Mastricht generally prefers the Bible's straightforward claims about natural phenomena to the conjectures of science, especially where they seem to contradict. Sometimes, then, he will clearly insist upon a more literal reading of certain texts than Wittich will allow. For instance, where the sun is said to 'stop' (Josh. 10:13), he is convinced this necessarily implied its regular motion.[69] Once again, he did not woodenly reject any accommodation to human perception. Isaiah's report of the 'declining sun' is clearly stated from the perspective of a person located on the earth (see Isa. 38:8, ESV). Yet, to his mind, both Joshua 10:13 and Isaiah 38:8, as well as other texts such as Psalms 19:5–7 and 93:1, contain a literal truth about the movement of the sun relative to the earth, notwithstanding some accommodation to human perception or the embellishment of metaphor.[70]

We might wonder if van Mastricht has conceded the point to Wittich by granting that the Bible's description of phenomena is sometimes accommodated to human perception, which may not precisely square up with scientific or

---

65. On the response of orthodox writers like Voetius and van Mastricht to the new exegetical approaches to various biblical descriptions of natural phenomena, see Goudriaan, *Orthodoxy*, pp. 85–141.

66. For his comments on this verse, see Mastricht, *Vindiciae*, pp. 98–112.

67. Ibid., p. 100.

68. Ibid., pp. 93–97.

69. For his discussion of the issues surrounding Josh. 10:12–13, see ibid., pp. 121–134.

70. See his discussion of these verses, ibid., pp. 135–188.

physical description. After all, as Wittich and his sympathizer Jacob Lansberg are quick to point out, Calvin himself could admit that where the psalmist speaks of God building a 'tent for the sun' in Psalm 19 (ESV), the Holy Spirit did not waste time attempting 'to teach the secrets of astronomy to the rude and unlearned' but was content to speak 'in a homely style'.[71] Yet while van Mastricht can readily agree that Scripture freely embraces metaphor and phenomenological descriptions without always adopting technical precision, he will not grant the possibility of any real error in such analogous or accommodated descriptions; nor does he believe Calvin would either.[72] The difference is that, a century later, the scientific advances are such that van Mastricht is forced to confront the hermeneutical challenges of upholding inerrancy in a way Calvin never had to. A modern reader may well disagree with some of his judgments concerning the degree to which specific texts speak to literal scientific or physical truths. Yet, however we may choose to approach these texts, van Mastricht is adamant that capitulating to a theory of accommodation which embraces the possibility of errors in the text would not only betray the Reformational commitment to the supremacy of Scripture over human reason, but would also entail a very real blasphemy against the Holy Spirit.

For van Mastricht, the central issue is Wittich's unmitigated confidence in the power of human reason, which grants science not only an authority autonomous from Scripture, but even one capable of detecting error within the text: even if, for now, that error is limited to matters outside the core doctrines of faith. If Meyer effectively collapses Christian faith into philosophy, Wittich begins to prize them apart, much in the way Jean-Alphonse Turretin would a few decades later in Geneva.[73] Either way, by the second half of the seventeenth century, the critical Reformational hegemony of Scripture over reason was beginning to collapse. No longer assuming an instrumental role in human knowledge, the new hermeneutic endows reason with foundational authority in certain matters, quite deliberately distinct from, and even superior to, the domain of Scripture. Notwithstanding substantial orthodox resistance to this

---

71. John Calvin, *Commentary on the Book of Psalms* (Grand Rapids: Eerdmans, 1949), I.315. Cf. Wittich, *Dissertationes Duae*, pp. 266–267.

72. Mastricht, *Vindiciae*, p. 174. As he points out in chapter 1, such metaphors are true, albeit analogous descriptions of the scientific facts; ibid., pp. 10–11, 12.

73. The junior Turretin's notion of biblical accommodation bears strong similarities to Wittich's. On Turretin, see Martin I. Klauber and Glenn S. Sunshine, 'Jean-Alphonse Turrettini on Biblical Accommodation: Calvinist or Socinian?', *Calvin Theological Journal* 25, no. 1 (1990), pp. 7–27.

trajectory throughout the latter half of the century, Samuel Preus is undoubtedly correct to argue that with the publication of Spinoza's *Tractatus* the rift between these domains was soon cast in a way that would exercise profound influence over biblical exegesis from the seventeenth century up to our own day.[74] Spinoza's theory of accommodation is so radical that it entirely dispenses with all dogmatic assumptions about Scripture and its content. Scripture merely represents a human history of religion, and therefore it is no longer necessary nor appropriate to wed its claims with those of the philosopher. And so, with Spinoza's thoroughly 'naturalized' Bible, a new approach to exegesis – the method of historical criticism – is unleashed.

Conclusion

These illustrations of a gradual accommodation of biblical authority to human reason among otherwise largely orthodox late seventeenth-century Protestant thinkers should not be interpreted either as an outright attack on the faith or a declension from genuine piety. Someone like Wittich is very keen to assert his Reformed credentials, and he too will engage in a forceful critique of Spinoza's far more radical attack on the authority of Scripture. Instead, what ought to be clear is that revolutionary developments within the intellectual climate of the late seventeenth century would put an increasing strain on Protestant theologians and exegetes in their attempts to uphold the doctrinal convictions not just of the Reformation, but of a Christian worldview stretching back at least as far as Augustine – strains which an earlier generation of Reformers largely had the luxury of being able to avoid. As we have seen, theologians like Voetius, Owen and van Mastricht are scrupulous in attempting to maintain their Reformational convictions, even while being forced to engage polemically and constructively with these emerging developments. Some, like Wittich and the junior Turretin, will broker something of a compromise, bringing with it an inevitable declension from the orthodoxy of the Reformational confessions. Others still, like Jean-Alphonse Turretin's more orthodox older cousin, Benedict Pictet, will adopt an almost anti-scholastic stance, pointing to the way in which Reformational orthodoxy would tend to live on outside the establishment in more pietistic circles throughout the eighteenth century.[75]

---

74. On Spinoza's hermeneutical method, see Preus, *Spinoza*, especially chapter 5.
75. Van Asselt, *Introduction*, pp. 184–189. Cf. Muller, *PRRD*, I.82–84; Muller, *After Calvin*, p. 7.

The effects of this gradual collapse in the Christian worldview, with its hegemony of faith and Scripture over autonomous human reason, is, of course, something we continue to feel today. That is what makes this period of church history so fascinating and important. It affords us a vital opportunity to learn from the way our early Protestant ancestors attempted to discern precisely what biblical and doctrinal principles were at stake as they engaged with the worldview of their neighbours; navigating these challenges, no doubt, with greater success in some cases than in others.

Bibliography

Armstrong, Brian G., *Calvinism and the Amyraut Heresy: Protestant Scholasticism and Humanism in Seventeenth-Century France*, Madison: University of Wisconsin Press, 1969.

van Asselt, Willem van (ed.), *Introduction to Reformed Scholasticism*, Grand Rapids: Reformation Heritage Books, 2011.

——, 'Reformed Orthodoxy: A Short History of Research', in Herman J. Selderhuis (ed.), *A Companion to Reformed Orthodoxy*, 11–26, Leiden: Brill, 2013.

Asselt, Willem van and Eef Dekker, 'Introduction', in Willelm van Asselt and Eef Dekker (eds.), *Reformation and Scholasticism: An Ecumenical Enterprise*, 11–43, Grand Rapids: Baker Academic, 2001.

Balserak, Jon, *Divinity Compromised: A Study of Divine Accommodation in the Thought of John Calvin*, Dordrecht: Springer, 2006.

Belt, Henk van den, *The Authority of Scripture in Reformed Theology*, Leiden: Brill, 2008.

Bizer, Ernst, 'Reformed Orthodoxy and Cartesianism', *Journal for Theology and the Church* 2 (1965), pp. 20–82.

Calvin, John, *Commentary on the Book of Psalms*, Grand Rapids: Eerdmans, 1949.

——, *Institutes of the Christian Religion*, trans. Ford Lewis Battles, ed. John T. McNeill, Philadelphia: Westminster, 1960.

Champion, J. A. I., *The Pillars of Priestcraft Shaken: The Church of England and Its Enemies, 1660–1730*, Cambridge: Cambridge University Press, 1992.

Chillingworth, William, *The Works*, Philadelphia: R. Davis, 1844.

Cragg, Gerald R., *From Puritanism to the Age of Reason: A Study of Changes in Religious Thought within the Church of England, 1660 to 1700*, Cambridge: Cambridge University Press, 1950.

Goudriaan, Aza, *Reformed Orthodoxy and Philosophy, 1625–1750*, Leiden: Brill, 2006.

——, 'Theology and Philosophy', in Herman J. Selderhuis (ed.), *A Companion to Reformed Orthodoxy*, 27–63, Leiden: Brill, 2013.

——, 'Ulrik Huber (1636–1694) and John Calvin: The Franeker Debate on Human Reason and the Bible (1686–1687)', *Church History and Religious Culture* 91 (2011), pp. 165–178.

Griffin Jr., Martin I. J., *Latitudinarianism in the Seventeenth-Century Church of England*, Leiden: Brill, 1992.

Haykin, Michael A. G. and Mark Jones (eds.), *Drawn into Controversie: Reformed Theological Diversity and Debates within Seventeenth-Century British Puritanism*, Göttingen: Vandenhoeck & Ruprecht, 2011.

Helm, Paul, *John Calvin's Ideas*, Oxford: Oxford University Press, 2004.

Heyd, Michael, *'Be Sober and Reasonable': The Critique of Enthusiasm in the Seventeenth and Early Eighteenth Centuries*, Leiden: Brill, 1995.

———, 'The Reaction to Enthusiasm in the Seventeenth Century: Towards an Integrative Approach', *The Journal of Modern History* 53, no. 2 (1981), pp. 258–280.

Hobbes, Thomas, *Leviathan*, Cambridge: Cambridge University Press, 1996.

Huijgen, Arnold, *Divine Accommodation in John Calvin's Theology: Analysis and Assessment*, Göttingen: Vandenhoeck & Ruprecht, 2011.

Klauber, Martin I., *Between Reformed Scholasticism and Pan-Protestantism: Jean-Alphonse Turretin (1671–1737) and Enlightened Orthodoxy at the Academy of Geneva*, Selinsgrove: Susquehanna University Press, 1994.

Klauber, Martin I. and Glenn S. Sunshine, 'Jean-Alphonse Turrettini on Biblical Accommodation: Calvinist or Socinian?', *Calvin Theological Journal* 25, no. 1 (1990), pp. 7–27.

Kristeller, Paul Oskar, *Renaissance Thought and Its Sources*, New York: Columbia University Press, 1979.

Leeuwen, Henry G. van, *The Problem of Certainty in English Thought, 1630–1690*, The Hague: Nijhoff, 1963.

Leslie, Andrew M., *The Light of Grace: John Owen on the Authority of Scripture and Christian Faith*, Göttingen: Vandenhoeck & Ruprecht, 2015.

Levene, Nancy K., *Spinoza's Revelation: Religion, Democracy, and Reason*, Cambridge: Cambridge University Press, 2004.

Lim, Paul C. H., *Mystery Unveiled: The Crisis of the Trinity in Early Modern England*, New York: Oxford University Press, 2012.

McLachlan, H. John, *Socinianism in Seventeenth-Century England*, Oxford: Oxford University Press, 1951.

Mallinson, Jeffrey, *Faith, Reason and Revelation in Theodore Beza, 1519–1605*, Oxford Theological Monographs, Oxford: Oxford University Press, 2003.

Mastricht, Petrus van, *Novitatum Cartesianarum Gangraena*, Amsterdam: Jansson, 1677.

———, *Theoretico-Practica Theologia*, Utrecht: W. van de Water, 1724.

———, *Vindiciae Veritatis et Authoritatis Sacrae Scripturae in rebus Philosophicis . . .* Utrecht: Johannis à Waesberg, 1655.

Meyer, Ludwig, *Philosophia S. Scripturae Interpres*, Eleuthropoli [Amsterdam]: [n.p.], 1666.

Mortimer, Sarah, *Reason and Religion in the English Revolution: The Challenge of Socinianism*, Cambridge: Cambridge University Press, 2010.

Muller, Richard, *After Calvin: Studies in the Development of a Theological Tradition*, Oxford
    Studies in Historical Theology, New York: Oxford University Press, 2003.
————, *Calvin and the Reformed Tradition: On the Work of Christ and the Order of Salvation*,
    Grand Rapids: Baker Academic, 2012.
————, 'John Calvin and Later Calvinism', in David Bagchi and David C. Steinmetz
    (eds.), *The Cambridge Companion to Reformation Theology*, 130–149, Cambridge:
    Cambridge University Press, 2004.
————, *Post-Reformation Reformed Dogmatics: The Rise and Development of Reformed Orthodoxy,
    Ca. 1520 to Ca. 1725*, 2nd edn, 4 vols., Grand Rapids: Baker Academic, 2003.
————, 'The Problem of Protestant Scholasticism: A Review and Definition', in Willem
    van Asselt and E. Dekker (eds.), *Reformation and Scholasticism: An Ecumenical Enterprise*,
    45–64, Grand Rapids: Baker Academic, 2001.
————, 'Reception and Response: Referencing and Understanding Calvin in
    Seventeenth-Century Calvinism', in Irena Backus and Philip Benedict (eds.), *Calvin
    and His Influence, 1509–2009*, 182–201, Oxford: Oxford University Press, 2009.
Muslow, Martin and Jan Rohls (eds.), *Socinianism and Arminianism: Antitrinitarians,
    Calvinists and Cultural Exchange in Seventeenth-Century Europe*, Leiden: Brill, 2005.
Neele, Adriaan C., *Petrus van Mastricht (1630–1706): Reformed Orthodoxy: Method and Piety*,
    Leiden: Brill, 2009.
Owen, John, *The Works*, ed. William H. Goold, Edinburgh: Johnstone & Hunter, 1850–1855.
Popkin, Richard, *The History of Scepticism: From Savonarola to Bayle*, Oxford: Oxford
    University Press, 2003.
Preus, J. S., *Spinoza and the Irrelevance of Biblical Authority*, Cambridge: Cambridge University
    Press, 2001.
Preus, R. D., *The Theology of Post-Reformation Lutheranism*, Vol. 1: *A Study of Theological
    Prolegomena*, St Louis: Concordia, 1970.
————, *The Theology of Post-Reformation Lutheranism*, Vol. 2: *God and His Creation*, St Louis:
    Concordia, 1972.
Reedy, Gerard, *The Bible and Reason: Anglicans and Scripture in Late Seventeenth-Century
    England*, Philadelphia: University of Pennsylvania Press, 1985.
Rogers, Jack B. and Donald K. McKim, *The Authority and Interpretation of the Bible:
    An Historical Approach*, San Francisco: Harper & Row, 1979.
Schreiner, Susan E., *Are You Alone Wise? The Search for Certainty in the Early Modern Era*,
    Oxford: Oxford University Press, 2011.
Sergeant, John, *Faith Vindicated from Possibility of Falsehood . . .*, London, 1667.
Shapiro, Barbara J., *Probability and Certainty in Seventeenth-Century England: A Study of the
    Relationships between Natural Science, Religion, History, Law and Literature*, Princeton:
    Princeton University Press, 1983.
Spurr, John, '"Rational Religion" in Restoration England', *Journal of the History of Ideas* 49,
    no. 4 (1988), pp. 563–585.

Stapleton, Thomas, *Principiorum Fidei Doctrinalium*, Paris, 1579.

Stillingfleet, Edward, *A Rational Account of the Grounds of Protestant Religion*, Oxford: Oxford University Press, 1844.

Sunshine, Glenn S., 'Accommodation Historically Considered', in D. A. Carson (ed.), *The Enduring Authority of the Christian Scriptures*, 238–265, Grand Rapids: Eerdmans, 2016.

Tillotson, John, *The Works*, ed. Thomas Birch, London: Richard Priestley, 1820.

Trueman, Carl R., 'Calvin and Calvinism', in Donald K. McKim (ed.), *The Cambridge Companion to John Calvin*, 225–244, Cambridge: Cambridge University Press, 2004.

———, 'The Reception of Calvin: Historical Considerations', *Church History and Religious Culture* 91, no. 1 (2011), 19–27.

Turretin, Francis, *Institutes of Elenctic Theology*, trans. George Musgrave Giger, ed. James T. Dennison Jr., 3 vols., Phillipsburg: P&R, 1992.

Venema, Hermann, *Institutes of Theology*, trans. Alex W. Brown, Edinburgh: T&T Clark, 1850.

Voetius, Gisbertus, *Selectarum Disputationum Theologicarum*, 5 vols., Utrecht: J. à Waesberge, 1648–67.

Whitaker, William, *A Disputation on Holy Scripture: Against the Papists, Especially Bellarmine and Stapleton*, trans. William Fitzgerald, Cambridge: Cambridge University Press, 1849.

Wittich, Christoph, *Dissertationes Duae*, Amsterdam: Ludovicum Elzevirium, 1653.

Wright, D., 'Calvin's Accommodating God', in *Calvinus Sincerioris Religionis Vindex: Calvin as Protector of the Purer Religion*, Sixteenth Century Essays and Studies, 3–19, Kirksville: Sixteenth Century Journal Publishers, 1997.

———, 'Calvin's Pentateuchal Criticism: Equity, Hardness of Heart, and Divine Accommodation in the Mosaic Harmony Commentary', *Calvin Theological Journal* 21 (1986), pp. 33–50.

15. *SEMPER REFORMANDA*:
THE REVIVALISTS AND THE REFORMERS

Rhys Bezzant

One would be entitled to imagine a close relationship between conservative Protestants in the eighteenth century and their theological forebears in the sixteenth, though we have to proceed cautiously. There are signs that the path was not always straight. George Whitefield, for example, protested that he had never read Calvin, and John Wesley published extracts from Jonathan Edwards' writings but only after he had expurgated some of their Reformed ideas. Famously, John and Charles both fell out with Whitefield over the matter of election in the free grace episode of 1741. What is perhaps more surprising is that Jonathan Edwards dramatically distanced himself from Calvin in his preface to *Freedom of the Will*:

> the term 'Calvinist' is in these days, amongst most, a term of greater reproach
> than the term 'Arminian'; yet I should not take it at all amiss, to be called
> a Calvinist, for distinction's sake: though I utterly disdain a dependence on
> Calvin, or believing the doctrines which I hold, because he believed and taught
> them; and cannot justly be charged with believing in everything just as he
> taught.[1]

---

1. Jonathan Edwards, *Freedom of the Will*, in Paul Ramsey, ed., *The Works of Jonathan Edwards*, Vol. 1 (New Haven: Yale University Press, 1957), p. 131.

Further, there was a more radical tendency in the revivalists to reappropriate ancient or medieval priorities. Whitefield was greatly influenced by the fifteenth-century devotional guide *Imitation of Christ* by Thomas à Kempis, Wesley tried to recreate the primitive church in Georgia,[2] and Edwards built his theological system around the notion of beauty, attempted only once before by the medieval monk Bonaventure. We have to acknowledge that these men were not merely unthinking mimics of Luther, Calvin or Cranmer. What is more, the classic and Reformation way of securing Christian experience, namely 'territorial parishes, resident clergymen and parish churches', was not without qualification amongst those espousing vital piety in the eighteenth century.[3] The revived Protestantism of the eighteenth century was never merely wistfully nostalgic or backward-looking, but was deliberately engaged with the world as the revivalists found it, as the case of Methodism makes clear:

> [it] thrived in symbiosis with other changes in the English-speaking world
> in the late eighteenth and nineteenth centuries . . . It was a world-affirming
> movement, relatively free from the millenarian fantasies of other populist
> religious strains.[4]

How might we then best explain any relationship of dependence between the revivalists and the Reformers, a relationship recast in the first half of the eighteenth century?[5]

The goal of this chapter, then, is to draw a line from the eighteenth to the sixteenth century, and to highlight the sometimes obvious, sometimes subtle, theological appropriations of Reformation ideas and practice in England and its American colonies by John Wesley (1703–91), Jonathan Edwards (1703–58) and George Whitefield (1714–70). The revivalists were largely in agreement that the doctrinally Protestant churches of Europe had grown cold and to some degree nominal, and therefore needed a new birth of vital piety. The eighteenth century witnessed such a rebirth under modern conditions, along with new ways of justifying the progress of providence, and a deepening of lay involvement

---

2. See Geordan Hammond, *John Wesley in America: Restoring Primitive Christianity* (Oxford: Oxford University Press, 2014).

3. David Hempton, *The Church in the Long Eighteenth Century* (London: I. B. Tauris, 2011), p. 5.

4. Ibid., pp. 23, 31.

5. Rosemary O'Day, *The Debate on the English Reformation* (Manchester: Manchester University Press, 2014), p. 53.

in church life. Whether on the perimeter of empire or in the metropolitan heartland, revived Protestants drew upon the Reformation to tell their story and shape their faith in a new age. Though there were many different kinds of revivalist, reflecting on many different kinds of Reformer, we will discover nonetheless a common vision undergirding their ministries by examining some of their direct statements and unpacking their deeper assumptions concerning the place of the Reformation in God's plans.

John Wesley as confessional Protestant

It is of course a commonplace to recount the conversion of John Wesley on 24 May 1738 as he listened to a reading of Luther's Preface to the epistle to the Romans in a meeting of the Moravians on Aldersgate Street in London. Having just returned from a confusing stint of missionary service in the colony of Georgia, he was seeking a more personally satisfying theological foundation for his ministry aspirations. The example of the peacefully assured Moravians, whom he had met during his dangerous travels at sea, provoked him to attend such a meeting. With exuberance he declaimed that his heart had been strangely warmed (though of course affection and heart religion was not invented in the eighteenth century).[6] He may not have agreed with all of Luther's doctrinal convictions – for example, his view of sanctification or perfection[7] – but the essentially Protestant foundations of Wesley's Christian experience were now anchored.

But the Wesleys, both John and Charles, were not just generically Protestant. They were also saturatedly Anglican. As sons of the manse and Oxford graduates, they were literally and figuratively formed in the home of the Church of England. John even financed his career through a stipendiary fellowship at Lincoln College, Oxford. Symbolically, their connection with the founders of the Protestant Anglican Church is seen in their service to inmates in Oxford's Boccardo prison where, due to their Protestant convictions, Ridley and Latimer had been held before their execution just a few steps away on Broad Street. Charles even composed a hymn, outlining the eschatological framework of his beloved church:

---

6. See, for example, Abram C. van Engen, *Sympathetic Puritans: Calvinist Fellow Feeling in Early New England* (Oxford: Oxford University Press, 2015).

7. Leo G. Cox, 'John Wesley's View of Martin Luther', *Journal of the Evangelical Theological Society* 7, no. 3 (1964), pp. 83–90, especially p. 88.

Head of Thy church, attend
Our long-continued prayer,
And our Jerusalem defend,
And in Thy bosom bear
The sheep of England's fold,
Mark'd with their Shepherd's sign,
Bought with a price, redeem'd of old,
And wash'd in blood Divine.

Call'd out of Babylon
At Thy command they came;
Our ancestors their lives laid down,
And triumph'd in the flame:
The Church's seed arose
Out of the martyrs' blood,
And saw their anti-Christian foes
Before Thy cross subdued.[8]

John Wesley also exerted much energy to explain how his teaching was consistent with the formularies of the Church of England and to persuade his Methodist followers to remain committed to the church's life and polity. However, he also aspired to reform the established church from the ground up, for Methodism was essentially a small-group accountability network, set in parallel with traditional structures of the church's ministry of Word and sacraments, giving attention to transformation of the mind through preaching and transformation of the nation through the pursuit of holiness. He may have been *accused* of departing from traditional teaching on original sin, but he replied in 1738 with an abridgement of some of the sixteenth-century Homilies, entitled *The Doctrine of Salvation, Faith and Good Works*, highlighting the common ground between him and Cranmer on the nature of salvation,[9] and later in 1757 built a case against John Taylor's inadequate anthropology and his 'naively optimistic view of human nature' which espoused a rationalist Arminianism.[10]

---

8. John R. Tyson, *Assist Me to Proclaim: The Life and Hymns of Charles Wesley* (Grand Rapids: Eerdmans, 2007 [1781]), p. 286.

9. John Wesley, 'The Doctrine of Salvation, Faith, and Good Works', in R. L. Maddox (ed.), *The Works of John Wesley*, vol. 12 (Nashville: Abingdon Press, 2012).

10. John Wesley, 'The Doctrine of Original Sin: According to Scripture, Reason, and Experience', in ibid., p. 117.

Wesley *does not espouse* but *resists* the Arminianism of much of the church's leadership in his own day, which reflected the doctrinal commitments of Archbishop Laud's seventeenth-century anti-Puritan, political and quasi-Pelagian Arminianism.[11]

The question, then, is rightly asked, why does Wesley so boldly appropriate the term 'Arminian' by naming his periodical *The Arminian Magazine*? Perhaps it was because of the influence of his mother, or to defend preaching to a mass audience, or due to fears of antinominianism. His own views, however, are well described by Maddox as an 'alternative evangelical Arminianism'.[12] It is important to recognize that this loaded word could be set to many uses in the eighteenth century, and frequently functioned as a catch-all term to describe thinkers influenced by the Enlightenment more than by the Scriptures, who were deistic or semi-Pelagian in their views. Minkema points out that originally Arminianism was

> narrowly understood as a repudiation of John Calvin's supralapsarianism, but
> by the early eighteenth century the term came to encompass a broad spectrum
> of theologians, including the majority of the Anglican clergy, who emphasized good
> works over right doctrine and maintained the free will of humankind to accept or
> reject the grace of God.[13]

Burrows holds that Wesley's views actually represent instead 'a return from the world of synergism and self-determination to that of monergism and sovereign grace'.[14] Packer describes Wesley as 'an inconsistent Calvinist'.[15] Gatiss maintains the same line:

> Wesley was at heart an Arminian but, happily, an inconsistent one. Tensions and
> incoherencies are inevitable when a man who 'abhors' predestination also wants
> (rightly) to assert the Reformation doctrine of justification by grace alone through

---

11. Roland Burrows, *John Wesley in the Reformation Tradition: The Protestant and Puritan Nature of Methodism Rediscovered* (Stoke-on-Trent: Tentmaker Publications, 2009), p. 37.

12. Wesley, 'Doctrine of Original Sin', p. 117.

13. Kenneth P. Minkema, 'Preface to the Period', in K. P. Minkema (ed.), *Works of Jonathan Edwards*, Vol. 14 (New Haven: Yale University Press, 1997), p. 17.

14. Burrows, *John Wesley in the Reformation Tradition*, p. 47.

15. J. I. Packer, *Among God's Giants: Aspects of Puritan Christianity* (Eastbourne: Kingsway, 1991), p. 56.

faith alone . . . and enabled a degree of cooperation in mission, on occasion, between the Wesleys and Whitefield.[16]

Though John fell out with George Whitefield over the nature of free grace, this should not be understood to mean that Wesley preached works righteousness. Wesley's own position was more traditionally Augustinian, for it was the character of grace, not its centrality, which was in dispute in these eighteenth-century debates.[17]

Wesley is to be understood as situated within the bigger arc of the Reformation and its consequences. However, much historiography of the evangelical revivals has placed Wesley over and against the laxity of the church of his day, and therefore as someone who opposed the order of the Church of England, ushering in a new synthesis of Enlightened ideas, Catholic spirituality and democratic polity. This older 'secularization thesis' locates Wesley as someone captive to his world, shaped passively by the forces of 'industrialization, urbanization, and modernization' and occasionally advancing that very agenda.[18] In this telling of the story, he may have been a great leader, but a leader nonetheless who was increasingly distanced from the priorities and dynamics of the world of the Reformation. In this account, as Schmidt explains, 'Wesley construed the Reformation as a transient renewal rather than a dramatic resurgence of vital Christianity.'[19]

More recent writing has pushed back against this thesis. It may be true that Wesley ordained clergy for the American colonies even though he was not a bishop, which was of course a grievous breach of Anglican polity, but this should not be understood as opposition to Reformation formularies or convictions. An alternative to the secularization thesis is the 'Anglican stabilization

---

16. Lee Gatiss, *The True Profession of the Gospel: Augustus Toplady and Reclaiming our Reformed Foundations* (London: The Latimer Trust, 2010), p. 50.

17. G. Rupp, 'Son of Samuel: John Wesley, Church of England Man', in K. E. Rowe (ed.), *The Place of Wesley in the Christian Tradition: Essays Delivered at Drew University in Celebration of the Commencement of the Publication of the Oxford Edition of the Works of John Wesley* (Metuchen: The Scarecrow Press, 1976), p. 55.

18. David Hempton, *Methodism: Empire of the Spirit* (New Haven: Yale University Press, 2005), p. 189.

19. Darren Schmidt, 'The Pattern of Revival: John Wesley's Vision of "Iniquity" and "Godliness" in Church History', in K. Cooper and J. Gregory (eds.), *Revival and Resurgence in Christian History: Papers Read at the 2006 Summer Meeting and the 2007 Winter Meeting of the Ecclesiastical History Society, Studies in Church History* (Woodbridge: Boydell Press, 2008), p. 144.

thesis', which argues instead that Wesley was a defender of the role of the church in the life of the nation, for he opposed both the Roman Catholic pretender to the throne and Jacobist uprisings, and wanted to stabilize society by serving the marginalized and shoring up 'a confessional state in the eighteenth century [which] revolved around the development and deployment of a political theology that combined commitment to the Trinity and reception of the sacraments with a policy of toleration'.[20] The Halévy thesis, with its Marxist supporters, which suggested that the Methodists were politically quietist, is inadequate, for Wesley encouraged his Methodists not to be disengaged but to be 'busy developing and deploying a political strategy for the reconstruction and maintenance of England as a confessional state'.[21] On this account, Wesley is less a pawn of modern economic reality and more of a player in calling the church of his own day back to its Protestant roots.

It has been my intention in this section to outline Wesley's espoused views concerning the Protestant Reformation, and to suggest that, despite his innovations and context, his theological assumptions were neither primitivist nor speculative, but confessional. He may have been, according to his own words, a 'man of one book', but this book (the Bible) was the launching pad from which to defend and promote traditional Protestant teachings and appreciation of the established Church of England. Reg Ward makes the case with just a touch of sarcasm:

> though one might never guess it from modern historical writing, there was still a Protestant world in the eighteenth century to which the Church of England belonged, to which it was acknowledged to belong and to which it regarded itself as belonging.[22]

Jonathan Edwards as eschatological Protestant

While it may be true that Jonathan Edwards, the sage of Northampton, hesitated to name himself a Calvinist, his own understanding of providential history nonetheless highlighted the ministry of the Protestant Reformers and their place in God's purposes for the church and the world. Edwards listed Luther

---

20. Jason E. Vickers, *Wesley: A Guide for the Perplexed* (London: T&T Clark, 2009), p. 57.

21. Ibid., p. 45.

22. W. R. Ward, 'The Eighteenth-Century Church: A European View', in J. Walsh, C. Haydon and S. Taylor (eds.), *The Church of England c.1689–1833: From Toleration to Tractarianism* (Cambridge: Cambridge University Press, 1993), p. 285.

in his own reading in his 'Catalogue of Books', and lent a copy of Luther's sermons to his mentee, Samuel Hopkins, for his own edification. Edwards quoted most from Calvin's *Institutes* in his *Religious Affections*, revealing, if not dependence, then certainly dialogical delight. While the seventeenth-century divines are quoted more often, Edwards situates the Reformation, after the early church, as a high point in the story of the church's pilgrimage:

> So again, before the glorious times of the church commence, the church's wine runs
> very low, and is almost out; what they alouted [*sic*] with is water – human learning,
> sapless speculations and dispensations, and dead morality. Formerly the Christian
> church had wine, as in the times of the primitive church, and in the times of the
> Reformation, but now their wine is just gone. But after the beginning of those
> glorious times, their water shall be turned into wine, and much better wine than
> ever they had before.[23]

What is more, Edwards sees himself as part of that Reformation 'moment', for in his eschatological mind the achievement of the Reformation was in essence the defeat of the papal Antichrist, though the final victory would emerge only later in stages driven by episodes of revival. The Puritans represented a stage in the Antichrist's downfall when they migrated to America in the seventeenth century to complete the Reformation.[24] The Puritan 'errand into the wilderness' was the context of Edwards' ministry, which thereby accessed deep Reformation roots:

> And 'tis worthy to be noted that America was discovered about the time of the
> Reformation, or but little before: which Reformation was the first thing that God
> did towards the glorious renovation of the world, after it had sunk into the depths
> of darkness and ruin under the great antichristian apostasy. So that as soon as this
> new world is (as it were) created, and stands forth in view, God presently goes about
> doing some great thing to make way for the introduction of the church's latter-day
> glory, that is to have its first seat in, and is to take its rise from that new world.[25]

---

23. Jonathan Edwards, *Notes on Scripture*, in S. J. Stein (ed.), *The Works of Jonathan
    Edwards*, Vol. 15 (New Haven: Yale University Press, 1998), p. 359.
24. Perry Miller, *Errand into the Wilderness* (Cambridge, MA: Harvard University Press,
    1956), p. 11.
25. Jonathan Edwards, 'Some Thoughts Concerning the Revival', in C. C. Goen (ed.),
    The Works of Jonathan Edwards, Vol. 4 (New Haven: Yale University Press, 1972),
    pp. 355–356.

Edwards in his own day witnessed victories over the forces of the Antichrist – for example, the English defeat of the French at Louisbourg in 1745, or more spiritual victories during times of refreshment and revival in 1734–35 or 1740–41. His international perspective on the work of God in history empowered him to see his own work related to the trajectory of the Reformation, which itself was a unitary concept:

> And if I may be allowed humbly to offer what appears to me to be the truth
> with relation to the rise and fall of Antichrist; it is this. As the power of Antichrist,
> and the corruption of the apostate church, rose not at once, but by several notable
> steps and degrees; so it will in the like manner fall: and that divers steps and seasons
> of destruction to the spiritual Babylon, and revival and advancement of the true
> church, are prophesied of under one. Though it be true, that there is some particular
> event, that prevails above all others in the intention of the prophecy, some one
> remarkable season of the destruction of the Church of Rome and papal power
> and corruption, and advancement of true religion, that the prophecies have a
> principal respect to.[26]

Edwards gives further justification for his position through his historicist reading of the book of Revelation. He assumes here that the two witnesses spoken of in chapter 11 refer to movements of reform before the sixteenth century, either within the scriptural storyline or after the closing of the canon:

> 33. CHAPTER 11:3. 'And I will give power to my two witnesses.' By it may partly be
> intended those two nations, that were all along witnesses to Christianity, viz. the
> Waldenses and Albigenses.

> 45. CHAPTER 11:3 Hereby it is with me undoubted, that respect is had to Moses and
> Elias. For these witnesses are two prophets . . . But yet, I believe respect is also had
> to Zerubbabel and Joshua . . . who were God's instruments for the rebuilding and
> re-establishing of the church after the Babylonish captivity.[27]

---

26. Jonathan Edwards, *An Humble Attempt to Promote Explicit Agreement and Visible Union of God's People in Extraordinary Prayer for the Revival of Religion and the Advancement of Christ's Kingdom on Earth, Pursuant to Scripture-Promises and Prophecies Concerning the Last Time*, in S. J. Stein (ed.), *The Works of Jonathan Edwards*, Vol. 5 (New Haven: Yale University Press, 1977), pp. 407–408.

27. Edwards, 'Notes on the Apocalypse', in ibid. pp. 137, 144.

So the fifth vial (in modern parlance 'bowl') poured out, as described in Revelation 16, refers to the ministry of Luther and Calvin (amongst others), making the revivals of the eighteenth century the next step towards the outpouring of the sixth vial. Edwards' ministry was located between these fifth and sixth vials, making it a continuation of Reformation activity:

> If these things that have been spoken of, are intended in the prophecy of the sixth vial, it affords, as I conceive, great reason to hope that the beginning of that glorious work of God's Spirit, which in the progress and issue of it, will overthrow Antichrist, and introduce the glory of latter days, is not very far off. Mr. Lowman has, I think, put it beyond all reasonable doubt, that the 5th vial was poured out in the time of the Reformation. It also appears satisfyingly, by his late exposition, that take one vial with another, it has not been 200 years from the beginning of one vial to the beginning of another, but about 180 years. But it is now about 220 years since the 5th vial began to be poured; and it is a long time since the main effects of it have been finished. And therefore if the 6th vial han't already begun to be poured, it may well be speedily expected.[28]

Indeed, though Edwards surveys the history of the work of redemption and divides it into three periods (from creation to Christ, Christ's earthly ministry, then from Christ's exaltation to his return), this last and third period he further subdivides to explain the church's progress in history. The Reformation is significant, and receives due attention, but is not a turning point without relationship to the more important progress of the defeat of the Antichrist:

> This was begun about 220 years ago, first in Saxony in Germany by the preaching of Martin Luther, who being stirred in his spirit to see the horrid practices of the popish clergy, and having set himself diligently to inquire after truth by the study of the holy Scriptures and the writings of the ancient fathers of the church, very openly and boldly decried the corruptions and usurpations of the Romish church in his preachings and writings . . . it went on by the labors of Luther and Melanchthon in Germany, and Zwingli in Switzerland . . . and particularly Calvin who appeared something after the beginning of the Reformation . . . Thus God began gloriously to revive his church again and advance the kingdom of his Son after such a dismal night of darkness as had been before from the rise of Antichrist to that time.[29]

---

28. Edwards, 'Humble Attempt', in ibid., p. 421.
29. Jonathan Edwards, *A History of the Work of Redemption*, in John F. Wilson (ed.), *The Works of Jonathan Edwards*, Vol. 9 (New Haven: Yale University Press, 1989), pp. 421–422.

Edwards provides an eschatologically loaded reading of the place of the Reformation in God's purposes. God's victory is not outside history, but within it, though this is presented in gradualist terms. Doctrinal recalibration was certainly a gift of the sixteenth-century Reformers to the church, though Edwards believed that such refreshment was critical to any pilgrim army's need of sustenance in its forward march to defeat the powers that oppose God. As Zakai explains:

> Edwards's philosophy of history shows that he was a true heir of sixteenth- and seventeenth-century Protestant and Puritan historiography, which was founded upon an apocalyptic interpretation of history, although he radically transformed some of its basic assumptions. Edwards inherited the quest to establish the closest possible link between prophecy and history ... Yet, in contrast to the Protestant assumption that the historical process is based ultimately on social, political, and ecclesiastical changes, such as the struggle against the Church of Rome, Edwards held that the principal source governing the historical process is God's redemptive plan.[30]

Edwards' commitment to Reformation teaching is beyond dispute, but he also made seventeenth-century Continental dogmaticians leading conversation partners. We note that his Reformed teaching is not constituted by exposition of the five sixteenth-century *sola*s alone:

> Jonathan Edwards is most certainly a Reformed theologian of the first rank, and the most influential theologian yet to appear on the American continent. Nevertheless ... Edwards was not concerned merely to transmit a tradition, or to reiterate certain confessional standards ... He was a constructive theologian whose appeal was to Scripture rather than tradition ... His theological formation was in the Puritan and continental post-Reformation traditions ... He was a kind of intellectual magpie, gathering up useful material wherever he found it.[31]

The Reformation of the sixteenth century was for Edwards a powerful example of faith persevering under trial, a phase of the work of the Spirit promoting divine providential plans and a conversation partner in resourcing

---

30. Avihu Zakai, *Jonathan Edwards's Philosophy of History: The Reenchantment of the World in the Age of Enlightenment* (Princeton: Princeton University Press, 2003), pp. 161–162.

31. Oliver D. Crisp, *Jonathan Edwards among the Theologians* (Grand Rapids: Eerdmans, 2015), pp. 3–4.

evangelism in a spiritually dozing world. It was his Protestant conviction that laid the groundwork for his Puritan theologizing and his evangelical priorities.

George Whitefield as populist Protestant

Amongst the leaders introduced in this chapter, it is George Whitefield who perhaps more than the others can be unambiguously identified as a defender of the teachings of the sixteenth-century Reformers. His theological convictions are on the whole unexceptional, and his references to the views and practices of the Reformers are overwhelmingly positive; for example:

> Had you been with me, I know you would have joined me in praising and gratefully adoring the LORD of all lords, for the great wonder of the reformation, and also for that glorious deliverance wrought out for us a few years past, in defeating the unnatural rebellion. O what a mighty spirit and power from on high must Luther, Calvin, Melancthon [*sic*], Zuinglius, and those glorious reformers, have been unnecessarily endued with, who dared first openly to oppose and stem such a torrent of superstition and spiritual tyranny! And what gratitude we owe to those, who, under God, were instrumental in saving us from the return of such spiritual slavery, and such blind obedience to a papal power! To have had a papist for our kind; a papist, if not born, yet from his infancy nursed up at Rome a papist, one of whose sons is advanced to the ecclesiastical dignity of a cardinal, and both under the strongest obligations to support the interest of that church, whose superstitions, as well as political state principles, they have sucked in and imbibed even from their infancy. But, blessed be God, the snare is broken, and we are delivered. O for Protestant practices to be added to Protestant principles![32]

Others also spoke exuberantly of his Protestant convictions: 'Many thousands at his chapel and Tabernacle, and in other places, were witnesses that he faithfully endeavored to restore the interesting doctrines of the reformation, and the purity of the church to its primitive glory.' Amongst those 'interesting doctrines', in his sermon 'The Lord our Righteousness' Whitefield like Luther held 'Christ's imputed righteousness' as the 'article upon which the church stands or falls'.[33]

---

32. John Gillies, *Memoirs of Rev. George Whitefield: Revised and Corrected, with Large Additions and Improvements, to Which Is Appended an Extensive Collection of his Sermons and Other Writings* (New Haven: Whitmore & Buckingham and H. Mansfield, 1834), p. 154.

33. Ibid., pp. 224, 301.

He fully recognized as well that these foundational truths were no longer commonplace in the church of his day:

> Blessed be God, there are some left among us who dare maintain the doctrines
> of the reformation … the generality of the clergy are fallen from our articles,
> and do not speak agreeably to them, or to the form of sound words delivered
> in the scriptures. Woe be unto such blind leaders of the blind![34]

Indeed, as his career progressed and his sojourns in America had more and more of an impact on him, Whitefield's anti-Catholicism came increasingly to the surface.[35] Anti-papalism was of course a staple amongst the revivalists, but Whitefield embodied a new personal justification for this stance. His travels across the seas had been impeded by the outbreak of the Seven Years War (1756–63) fought between Protestant Britain and Catholic France for global hegemony; his freedom to preach out of doors, increasingly against Jacobite rebellion at home, was therefore dependent on British military ascendancy. Some of his most popular printed sermons from the 1750s were on imperial themes: for example, 'Britain's Mercies' and 'A Short Address to Persons of All Denominations'.[36] Furthermore, the theological opposition he faced, both in the colonies and in Britain, was to some degree moderated when he could show through his patriotic preaching that he was on the same side as many of his critics. Attempts to silence him by the Bishop of London (responsible for Anglican order outside England) could themselves appear treacherous under such political conditions. He was afforded a warm welcome by non-Anglicans in America, which further functioned to sharpen his sympathy with the colonial cause and to highlight the synergy of Protestant theology with defence of religious liberty and freedom of conscience.

Anti-Catholicism had in the eighteenth century become a chief organizing principle of states and peoples, and was therefore a contributor to the centralizing spirit of the metropolitan leaders and to the waxing of national spirit amongst the American colonists, amongst whom Whitefield was a vanguard voice.[37] His Protestant credentials were also enhanced in a Roman Catholic territory through his determination to sponsor a vernacular Bible in Irish Gaelic,

---

34. Ibid., p. 428, in the sermon 'The Indwelling of the Spirit'.
35. Hempton, *Methodism: Empire of the Spirit*, pp. 166–167, 203.
36. Thomas S. Kidd, *George Whitefield: America's Spiritual Founding Father* (New Haven: Yale University Press, 2014), p. 227.
37. Hempton, *The Church in the Long Eighteenth Century*, p. 196.

and to encourage vernacular preaching of the same.[38] His anti-papalism served an imperial agenda and the Protestant interest, which in turn secured his status and prospered his preaching:

> The gospel of the new birth remained Whitefield's central concern, but he also realized that without the political and religious liberty afforded under British Protestant rule, the preaching of that gospel could be at risk. Wartime anti-Catholicism proved a potent source of British unity.[39]

In Whitefield's example, we see how Reformation priorities were appropriated and refreshed. The so-called eighteenth-century twist in conservative Protestantism gave birth to modern evangelicalism, in which human agency and authority were prized (exemplified by the possibilities of individual mobility), protest against Catholic imperial hegemony was emboldened, and vital piety was defended and promoted in contrast with the stale orthodoxy of state churches. As Pelikan argues, the eighteenth century witnessed an 'affective turn' in matters theological.[40] Where once theologically ordered church buildings gave shape to ministerial authority and social decorum, now through field preaching ecclesiastical order was threatened. Out of doors, rich and poor, black and white, men and women mingled, shouted out or were distracted, creating disorder and danger. The charismatic personality of the preacher, not the height of the pulpit nor the robes of the officiant, bound the listeners together. The revivals engendered an international frame of reference, transcending local contingencies and relationships of deference, and replaced them with a 'dynamic, expansive, potentially global religious orientation', in which Christians could experience 'permeable boundaries and long-distance, affective ties'.[41] This is a great awakening, or the Great Awakening.

Whitefield upheld Reformation doctrine, but under these conditions he functioned as the bellwether for a movement coalescing around the preaching of regeneration and the potency of the laity. He even described the sermonic event

---

38. Kidd, *George Whitefield*, p. 58.

39. Ibid., p. 222.

40. Jaroslav Pelikan, *Christian Doctrine and Modern Culture (since 1700)*, The Christian Tradition: A History of the Development of Doctrine (Chicago: University of Chicago Press, 1989), p. 128.

41. Timothy D. Hall, *Contested Boundaries: Itinerancy and the Reshaping of the Colonial American Religious World* (Durham, NC: Duke University Press, 1994), pp. 82, 103.

in which he participated using the language of the tabernacle, where he was effectively the locus of the holy! This would have been unconscionable amongst sixteenth-century preachers, who were trying to persuade their own hearers of the transcendence of God in worship, not his capture in the material. The Reformers of the sixteenth century re-eschatologized the church, but were highly unlikely to place themselves at its centre. In the eighteenth century, however, with the declericalization of ministry, sacred place and sacred time were being reinvented. Whitefield, for example, referring to the opposition he had personally faced, says:

> the tabernacle of the Lord is already driven into the wilderness: the ark of the Lord is fallen into the unhallowed hands of uncircumcised Philistines ... Men in power have been breathing out threatenings: we may easily guess what will follow, imprisonment and slaughter. The storm has been gathering some time; it must break shortly. Perhaps it may fall on me first.[42]

Whitefield had a distinct role amongst the revivalists. Wearing a wig to preach, Edwards was an establishment figure, despite the momentary affliction when he was ejected from his pulpit. Wesley in some minds was identified with the cause of the establishment due to his authoritarian leadership style. Whitefield, however, was an outsider, not just occasionally but in most of the contexts in which he worked: his successful but unusual itinerancy on two continents, his episcopal warrant which licensed him to the orphanage of Bethesda and not to a traditional parish or academic ministry, theological alienation from the majority of English Methodists, suspicion of him from Scottish Presbyterians and English Dissenters, and his increasingly loose ties to his home in the British Isles themselves meant that the current of his populism flowed into his identity as an outlier. In terms of the audience reached, the style of communication adopted and his ambiguous ecclesiastical status, his ministry bore the least resemblance of any here discussed to sixteenth-century Reformation norms. Yet his doctrinal conservatism did find a place within his ministry innovations and created a potent new rallying-point for the Protestant cause. It was to be Whitefield's booming voice during his expansive travels that provided some kind of unity amongst his listeners, and loosened their loyalty to institutional or formal authority.

---

42. George Whitefield, 'Persecution: Every Christian's Lot', in E. Bence (ed.), *Sermons of George Whitefield* (Peabody: Hendrickson, 2009), p. 310.

Revivals and reformations as pedagogical Protestantism

It has been my intention to demonstrate that on the surface and in historiographic depth the revivalists of the eighteenth century saw themselves as participating in a larger project, namely defending and prospering the *theological* priorities of sixteenth-century reform, though their individual *ministry* priorities may have encouraged new structures, generated from the bottom up. We note the contrast with the Reformation in England (as elsewhere), which was of course built around a top-down reform agenda, which destabilized the body politic and became a concern for contemporaries and later commentators alike. No wonder, then, that structured preparation for conversion and penitential disciplines were prominent in England, where fears of instability as a result of the Wars of the Roses, growing poverty and homelessness, or the potential for ecclesiastical or royal dynastic impotency coloured theological debates and developments.[43] This gives us pause to reconsider whether the relationship between the sixteenth- and eighteenth-century stages in renewal was as coherent as I have suggested. It does appear at first blush that movements for renewal in the eighteenth century were of a very different shape and dynamic.

However, more recent scholarship about the Reformation has reminded us of the *purpose* of reforming efforts, which provides even more substantiation of the claims in this chapter that the two historical 'moments' under consideration were profoundly connected. Though Luther renewed debate on the doctrine of justification and reconceptualized the shape of Sunday worship, though Calvin rejected the traditional threefold order of the church's polity and wrested some responsibility for discipline from the town council, they both had the goal of *re-evangelizing and training the laity*.[44] Indeed, the slogan associated with Luther, 'the priesthood of all believers', though often misunderstood to suggest the redundancy of clergy, nevertheless gets close to one of the overarching themes of sixteenth-century reform.[45] This missiological goal in

---

43. Theodore Dwight Bozeman, *The Precisianist Strain: Disciplinary Religion and Antinomian Backlash in Puritanism to 1638*, Omohundro Institute of Early American History and Culture (Chapel Hill: University of North Carolina Press, 2004), pp. 13, 21.

44. Hempton, *Methodism: Empire of the Spirit*, p. 30.

45. Carl R. Trueman, 'Reformers, Puritans and Evangelicals: The Lay Connection', in D. W. Lovegrove (ed.), *The Rise of the Laity in Evangelical Protestantism* (London: Routledge, 2002), pp. 19–20.

the sixteenth century was exemplified by production of the Scriptures in the vernacular, which in turn encouraged preaching and liturgy in the same, whether by Tyndale, Luther or Cranmer. Even Calvin's French had wide impact in ennobling the common tongue to transmit transcendent ideas. Singing hymns or psalms allowed the laity to participate more fully in Sunday services, and the Book of Common Prayer was 'common' because the priest and people used the same one! Communion was offered to the laity in two kinds, not one.[46] As Scott Hendrix has argued, in all their various forms, the different reformations of the sixteenth century were intent on the same outcome: the re-Christianization of western Europe.[47] The revivalists would have cheered.

It has been evident from our survey that empowerment of the laity grew and developed from the sixteenth to the eighteenth century, by which time there were of course already translations of the Scriptures in the vernacular, and preaching and liturgy in the heart language of the hearers was expected as the norm. At this juncture in history, however, through innovations like lay exhorting, Concerts of Prayer organized by non-clergy, greater attention to the movement of the Spirit, theological rationale for flexible ecclesiologies, the propriety of itinerating, small groups for accountability and the doctrine of regeneration as the driving validation for a new view of human agency, Reformation priorities were rediscovered and applied anew. Stephen Neill is so bold as to say, 'Here was a calling of the layman into responsible activity in the Church on a scale that had hardly ever been before',[48] and Mark Noll echoes this sentiment: 'It is axiomatic that the personal religion of evangelicalism pushed in the direction of heightened lay involvement.'[49]

Increasingly, authority for ministry was derived not from the education of the clergy nor from institutional imprimatur, but from the gifting or experience

46. For further examples of the role of the laity in the sixteenth century, see G. Rupp, 'The Age of the Reformation, 1500–1648', in S. C. Neill and H.-R. Weber (eds.), *The Layman in Christian History: A Project of the Department on the Laity of the World Council of Churches* (London: SCM, 1963), pp. 141–146.

47. Scott H. Hendrix, *Recultivating the Vineyard: The Reformation Agendas of Christianization* (Louisville: Westminster John Knox, 2004), pp. xvii, 35, 43.

48. Stephen Neill, 'Britain, 1600–1780', in S. C. Neill and H.-R. Weber (eds.), *The Layman in Christian History: A Project of the Department on the Laity of the World Council of Churches* (London: SCM, 1963), p. 207.

49. Mark A. Noll, 'National Churches, Gathered Churches, and Varieties of Lay Evangelicalism, 1735–1859', in D. W. Lovegrove (ed.), *The Rise of the Laity in Evangelical Protestantism* (London: Routledge, 2002), p. 140.

of individual leaders. This was not an unalloyed success, but it reflected none-theless a gospel trajectory which the sixteenth-century Reformers had unleashed. Lay autonomy was sometimes treated with suspicion, with Edwards rebuking untethered exhortation and Wesley maintaining tight control of the movement, but their hesitations could not deny the hopes they had for a new birth of piety which would reach deep into the souls of the faithful, and which would also, blown along by the Spirit, have significant impact on the world. The planting of Protestant faith in Australia is therefore just one of the results of this great Reformation project, mediated by those touched by the eighteenth-century revivals. Gregory reminds us of the importance of patience in working for reform:

> Even if the political Reformation had been won by the seventeenth century, there was still much to do in bringing the Protestant faith to the hearts and minds of the English people, and this was a process which took centuries rather than years or decades.[50]

Sometimes we define evangelicalism in relation to common doctrines upheld by Reformers and revivalists alike, but sometimes it repays our effort to see not just common beliefs but common aspirations or motivations emerging out of those beliefs. We inherit the task of reforming and renewing the church when we too set ourselves the goal of reevangelizing the church, redoubling our commitment to a ministry of Word and sacrament, and making plain the promises and purposes of God to a world in need of new life, even when we do this using instruments which would have been foreign to sixteenth-century leaders. We too may well need to combine the insights and innovations of different ages of the church to create a rationale for ministry which is fully orbed, recognizing, for example, the ways in which the doctrines of justification and regeneration have worked together for the flourishing of the church, and the importance of the laity in this vision. Even Luther recognized that his attempts at reform were just the beginning. On his deathbed, he confessed that lives around him were not Christian enough. The revivalists took up the challenge and decided to make good the deficit.

---

50. Jeremy Gregory, 'The Making of a Protestant Nation: "Success" and "Failure" in England's Long Reformation', in N. Tyacke (ed.), *England's Long Reformation 1500–1800* (London: UCL Press, 1998), p. 314.

Bibliography

Bozeman, Theodore Dwight, *The Precisianist Strain: Disciplinary Religion and Antinomian Backlash in Puritanism to 1638*, Omohundro Institute of Early American History and Culture, Chapel Hill: University of North Carolina Press, 2004.

Burrows, Roland, *John Wesley in the Reformation Tradition: The Protestant and Puritan Nature of Methodism Rediscovered*, Stoke-on-Trent: Tentmaker Publications, 2009.

Cox, Leo G., 'John Wesley's View of Martin Luther', *Journal of the Evangelical Theological Society* 7, no. 3 (1964), pp. 83–90.

Crisp, Oliver D., *Jonathan Edwards among the Theologians*, Grand Rapids: Eerdmans, 2015.

Engen, Abram C. van, *Sympathetic Puritans: Calvinist Fellow Feeling in Early New England*, Oxford: Oxford University Press, 2015.

Gatiss, Lee, *The True Profession of the Gospel: Augustus Toplady and Reclaiming Our Reformed Foundations*, London: The Latimer Trust, 2010.

Gillies, John, *Memoirs of Rev. George Whitefield: Revised and Corrected, with Large Additions and Improvements, to Which Is Appended an Extensive Collection of His Sermons and Other Writings*, New Haven: Whitmore & Buckingham and H. Mansfield, 1834.

Goen, C. C. (ed.), *The Works of Jonathan Edwards*, Vol. 4, New Haven: Yale University Press, 1972.

Gregory, Jeremy, 'The Making of a Protestant Nation: "Success" and "Failure" in England's Long Reformation', in N. Tyacke (ed.), *England's Long Reformation 1500–1800*, London: UCL Press, 1998.

Hall, Timothy D., *Contested Boundaries: Itinerancy and the Reshaping of the Colonial American Religious World*, Durham, NC: Duke University Press, 1994.

Hammond, Geordan, *John Wesley in America: Restoring Primitive Christianity*, Oxford: Oxford University Press, 2014.

Hempton, David, *The Church in the Long Eighteenth Century*, London: I. B. Tauris, 2011.

———, *Methodism: Empire of the Spirit*, New Haven: Yale University Press, 2005.

Hendrix, Scott H., *Recultivating the Vineyard: The Reformation Agendas of Christianization*, Louisville: Westminster John Knox, 2004.

Kidd, Thomas S., *George Whitefield: America's Spiritual Founding Father*, New Haven: Yale University Press, 2014.

Maddox, R. L. (ed.), *The Works of John Wesley*, Vol. 12, Nashville: Abingdon Press, 2012.

Miller, Perry, *Errand into the Wilderness*, Cambridge, MA: Harvard University Press, 1956.

Minkema, Kenneth P., 'Preface to the Period', in K. P. Minkema (ed.), *Works of Jonathan Edwards*, Vol. 14, New Haven: Yale University Press, 1997.

Neill, Stephen, 'Britain, 1600–1780', in S. C. Neill and H.-R. Weber (ed.), *The Layman in Christian History: A Project of the Department on the Laity of the World Council of Churches*, London: SCM, 1963.

Noll, Mark A., 'National Churches, Gathered Churches, and Varieties of Lay Evangelicalism, 1735–1859', in D. W. Lovegrove (ed.), *The Rise of the Laity in Evangelical Protestantism*, London: Routledge, 2002.

O'Day, Rosemary, *The Debate on the English Reformation*, Manchester: Manchester University Press, 2014.

Packer, J. I., *Among God's Giants: Aspects of Puritan Christianity*, Eastbourne: Kingsway, 1991.

Pelikan, Jaroslav, *Christian Doctrine and Modern Culture (since 1700)*, The Christian Tradition: A History of the Development of Doctrine, Chicago: University of Chicago Press, 1989.

Ramsey, Paul (ed.), *The Works of Jonathan Edwards*, Vol. 1, New Haven: Yale University Press, 1957.

Rupp, G., 'The Age of the Reformation, 1500–1648', in S. C. Neill and H.-R. Weber (eds.), *The Layman in Christian History: A Project of the Department on the Laity of the World Council of Churches*, London: SCM, 1963.

———, 'Son of Samuel: John Wesley, Church of England Man', in K. E. Rowe, *The Place of Wesley in the Christian Tradition: Essays Delivered at Drew University in Celebration of the Commencement of the Publication of the Oxford Edition of the Works of John Wesley*, Metuchen: Scarecrow Press, 1976.

Schmidt, Darren, 'The Pattern of Revival: John Wesley's Vision of "Iniquity" and "Godliness" in Church History', in K. Cooper and J. Gregory (eds.), *Revival and Resurgence in Christian History: Papers Read at the 2006 Summer Meeting and the 2007 Winter Meeting of the Ecclesiastical History Society*, Studies in Church History, Woodbridge: Boydell Press, 2008.

Stein, S. J. (ed.), *The Works of Jonathan Edwards*, Vol. 5, New Haven: Yale University Press, 1977.

———, *The Works of Jonathan Edwards*, Vol. 15, New Haven: Yale University Press, 1998.

Trueman, Carl R., 'Reformers, Puritans and Evangelicals: The Lay Connection', in D. W. Lovegrove (ed.), *The Rise of the Laity in Evangelical Protestantism*, London: Routledge, 2002.

Tyson, John R., *Assist Me to Proclaim: The Life and Hymns of Charles Wesley*, Grand Rapids: Eerdmans, 2007.

Vickers, Jason E., *Wesley: A Guide for the Perplexed*, London: T&T Clark, 2009.

Ward, W. R., 'The Eighteenth-Century Church: A European View', in J. Walsh, C. Haydon and S. Taylor (eds.), *The Church of England c.1689–1833: From Toleration to Tractarianism*, Cambridge: Cambridge University Press, 1993.

Whitefield, George, 'Persecution: Every Christian's Lot', in E. Bence (ed.), *Sermons of George Whitefield*, Peabody: Hendrickson, 2009.

Wilson, John F. (ed.), *The Works of Jonathan Edwards*, Vol. 9, New Haven: Yale University Press, 1989.

Zakai, Avihu, *Jonathan Edwards's Philosophy of History: The Reenchantment of the World in the Age of Enlightenment*, Princeton: Princeton University Press, 2003.

16. THE REFORMATION:
A VICTORIAN VIEW

Edward Loane

I was recently given an 1844 edition of the Parker Society's *Writings and Translations of Myles Coverdale*.[1] This delightful work is not only a testimony to the theological prerogatives of an early English Reformer, but also an important primary source for understanding how the Reformation was perceived and contended for in Victorian Britain. The volume opens with Coverdale's 'The Old Faith' (1547) which is an appropriate tract to take primary place considering the nineteenth-century polemic the Parker Society was seeking to counter. Indeed, the Victorian era was a time of major controversy relating to the Reformation and this itself has proved to be a fertile area of scholarship. In 2014 the *Bulletin of the John Rylands Library* dedicated an entire 382-page edition to essays by leading academics on the theme 'Reinventing the Reformation in the Nineteenth Century: A Cultural History'. As Richard Rex states, 'When Queen Victoria came to the throne, the Reformation was under threat.'[2] This chapter will explore the way the Reformation was perceived in the early nineteenth century and how various ecclesiastical forces in Victoria's reign repudiated its

---

1. Myles Coverdale, *Writings and Translations of Myles Coverdale, Bishop of Exeter*, ed. George Pearson, The Parker Society (Cambridge: Cambridge University Press, 1844).
2. Richard Rex, 'Introduction: The Morning Star or the Sunset of the Reformation?', *Bulletin of the John Rylands Library* 90, no. 1 (Spring 2014), p. 7.

principles and legacy. Other forces, however, took up their cudgels in defence of the Reformation. They celebrated and commemorated significant moments and, more importantly, they preached and defended Reformed theology. The Victorian view of the Reformation became increasingly polarized, with different sides using it as a weapon to wield in contemporary polemics. What had for centuries been a distinguishing feature of the national church and, in turn, of the nation itself, underwent a transmogrification from a unifying identity marker into the contested battlefield of an increasingly partisan church.

Early nineteenth-century milieu

Obviously no religious controversy takes place in a vacuum and there were certainly numerous antecedent factors that shaped the events that transpired in the Victorian church. These included social and political factors, as well as religious movements. It is worth briefly surveying some of these influences as a prelude to evaluating the Victorian view of the Reformation. Important issues include the political landscape, particularly in relation to the volatile situation in Ireland, the social consequences of the Industrial Revolution and the influence of the eighteenth-century evangelical revival. Before proceeding, however, it is worth noting that in many ways, the neat distinction between political, social and religious factors is somewhat artificial when considering early nineteenth-century history. For example, to which of these categories does the work of William Wilberforce belong? Surely all three. These categories interpenetrate one another and cannot be considered mutually exclusive. Nevertheless, we can distinguish important events that took place in the government, among the population and within the church which provide an important background for our present study.

Political and social factors

When Victoria acceded to the throne in 1837, the question of how the British were to govern Ireland effectively had been a hot potato for decades. Ireland had joined the United Kingdom in 1801 and, with the vast majority of its population identifying as Roman Catholic, there were always going to be challenges with incorporating them into a nation that staunchly defined itself as 'Protestant'. One pressing issue was the question of representation and enfranchisement, because a requirement of becoming a Member of Parliament was to identify as an Anglican. This nexus was broken by allowing Nonconformists to enter Parliament in 1828, and then, the following year, the Emancipation of Catholics Act extended this privilege to Roman Catholics. From the perspective of the twenty-first century such measures hardly seem controversial, but in the 1820s tensions ran high. The chief issues were the place of the established church and the national identity as a Protestant kingdom. Victoria's uncle had argued in the House of Lords against the Emancipation of Catholics, staking the issue on whether the country was to be a Protestant country with a Protestant government. When his elder brother, George IV, was required to sign the bill, the king sobbed, fearing that he was violating his coronation oath.[3] The evangelical bishop J. B. Sumner – later Archbishop of Canterbury – justified supporting the change on the grounds that 'the papal cause is a declining cause, and will become so more and more', and the Prime Minister argued that the bill would strengthen the Protestant and Anglican establishment.[4] Nevertheless, for many this bill was a state-sanctioned undermining of the United Kingdom's Reformation heritage.

It would be a dubious conclusion, however, to argue that the opposition in the general population arose primarily from theological convictions. The burgeoning Industrial Revolution in England was transforming the social landscape. One result was unprecedented Irish immigration to Britain, generally in the form of low-paid labouring classes. The discontent felt among British lower classes easily translated into sectarian hostility and anti-Catholic prejudice. On the other hand, in Ireland there was widespread resentment against being forced to pay tithe revenue to an established church to which most of the population was opposed. The government in London sought to relieve this tension in 1833 by passing the Irish Church Temporalities Act, which almost halved the number of bishoprics in Ireland and dramatically reduced the revenue the Anglican Church could extract from the population. In turn, this was perceived to be a further state-sanctioned assault on the Protestant established church and was the catalyst for the beginning of the Oxford Movement, which, as we shall see, was one of the most significant influences through the entire Victorian period. Peter Nockles helpfully points out that 'the political origins of the rise of the Oxford Movement are too often overlooked'.[5]

Religious factors
Since the time the Reformation began in England, there had been calls that the reforms had not gone far enough. There is a plausible argument that a number

---

3. Owen Chadwick, *The Victorian Church*, 3rd edn, 2 vols., Vol. 1 (London: Adam & Charles Black, 1971), pp. 7–8.

4. Ibid., p. 10.

5. Peter Nockles, *The Oxford Movement in Context: Anglican High Churchmanship, 1760–1857* (Cambridge: Cambridge University Press, 1994), p. 67.

of the clerical corruptions often cited as sources of discontent in pre-Reformation England were never suitably dealt with. Issues like plurality and non-residence were rife in the early nineteenth century. A decade before Victoria became queen, nineteen bishops held between them a total of sixty-one pieces of preferment, and of the 10,533 livings, only 4,413 incumbents were resident.[6] The Convocations (Provincial Synods) had been supressed in 1717 and the church had little opportunity for self-government. Even if it did, the level of vested interest in the *status quo* would have mitigated movement towards reform. There were advocates of reform, such as Thomas Arnold, author of *Principles of Church Reform*, but his Broad Church perspective was received with antagonism by ecclesiastical authorities. It was, however, throughout the Victorian period that reformation on issues like plurality and non-residence finally took place. It was in this period that the Convocations were revived and synodical government became paradigmatic in the burgeoning Anglican Communion, including the establishment of the Lambeth Conference in 1867. Nevertheless, prior to 1833 the Reformation was not a particularly contentious issue among English churchmen.[7] Conceding this, in the early nineteenth century there was one ecclesiastical group that particularly identified themselves as heirs of the Reformation and sought to rejuvenate the Church of England by propagating Protestant theology: the evangelicals.

The most remarkable ecclesiastical movement of the eighteenth century was the evangelical revival. This movement was instigated by John Wesley and George Whitefield a century before Victoria's reign began. Both Wesley and Whitefield declared their loyalty to the Reformation formularies of the Church of England. After Wesley's death most of his followers formally left the church and became Methodist dissenters. There was, however, a small group of evangelical clergy and laity in the national church who worked to

---

6. Chadwick, *Victorian Church*, p. 34.

7. This is not to say that there were no attacks on the received understanding of the Reformation. Perhaps the most damaging was William Cobbett's *History of the Reformation* (1824–6), which sold over 700,000 copies. Cobbett's thesis is that the English Reformation was 'engendered in beastly lust, brought forth in hypocrisy and perfidy, and cherished and fed by plunder, devastation, and by rivers of innocent English and Irish blood'. Cf. D. G. Paz, 'The Chartists and the English Reformation', *Bulletin of the John Rylands Library* 90, no. 1 (Spring 2014), p. 28; Peter Nockles, 'The Reformation Revised? The Contested Reception of the English Reformation in Nineteenth-Century Protestantism', *Bulletin of the John Rylands Library* 90, no. 1 (Spring 2014), p. 236.

multiply their number and influence. One of the most significant leaders in the expansion of evangelicalism across the country was Charles Simeon, the long-serving rector of Holy Trinity, Cambridge (1783–1836). Simeon's influence on the wider church was substantially a result of his strategic position in the university, of which more than half the graduates became clergymen.[8] As such, the number of evangelical clergy continued to rise in the first half of the nineteenth century. Peter Toon's research estimated that, in the first decade, about one-twentieth of clergy were evangelical; by 1820, one-tenth were; by 1839, a fifth were; and, by one calculation, in 1853 they numbered over a quarter of clergy in England and Wales.[9]

The perceived threat from Roman Catholicism in the early nineteenth century, along with the increasing popularity of their movement, mobilized evangelicals to defend and promote the Protestant cause with increased vigour. Through the 1820s new evangelical publications were begun, including the *Christian Examiner* and *The Record*.[10] They added to the existing publications, such as the *Christian Observer* and the *Christian Guardian*, in serving as mouthpieces for the Protestant cause and were often filled with sharp polemic. Coupled with these publications, new societies were formed. One example is the Protestant Reformation Society, which was founded in 1827 to promote 'the Religious Principles of the Reformation'. John Wolffe points out two underlying assumptions of this goal. First, the nature of such principles of the Reformation was taken for granted and apparently required no further definition. Second, the Reformation was not settled in the sixteenth century, but was perceived to be a continuing

---

8. Peter Searby states, 'During the 120 years considered in this volume [1750–1870] Cambridge was an Anglican seminary.' This was a declining percentage over this period, however, as between 1752 and 1769 more than three-quarters (76%) of Cambridge graduates became clergymen, but by 1870–86 that percentage had reduced to 38%. Nevertheless, it was still the most popular graduate profession. Peter Searby, *A History of the University of Cambridge*, Vol. 3: *1750–1870* (Cambridge: Cambridge University Press, 1997), p. 76.

9. Peter Toon, *Evangelical Theology 1833–1856: A Response to Tractarianism* (London: Marshall, Morgan & Scott, 1979), p. 2.

10. *The Record* was founded in 1828 and within fifteen years claimed to have a circulation greater than that of *The Globe* and virtually the same as that of *The Standard*. This was quite an achievement for a periodical setting forth an explicit Calvinistic evangelicalism. Throughout the Victorian era some evangelicals were known simply as 'Recordites'. Ibid., p. 7.

process.[11] The English and Irish Bible Societies were also very active, claiming that there was need of a new reformation in Ireland.[12] The evangelicals believed they were the heirs of the Reformation and conceived their growth as an important bulwark in protecting national Protestant identity. In 1826–7 there was a feeling among evangelicals that a full-scale Irish reformation was taking place; however, a number of setbacks, including the government's concessions to Roman Catholics, shattered these hopes and Protestantism's advance took a gloomy turn.[13]

Repudiating the Reformation

The Oxford Movement

As already mentioned, the government's decision radically to curtail the work of the Protestant established church in Ireland in 1833 instigated one of the most significant religious movements of the nineteenth century. It was launched by a small group of Oxford scholars who were increasingly concerned with government interference in ecclesiastical affairs. On 14 July 1833 John Keble preached on the 'National Apostasy' that had taken place.[14] He was invited to do so by his friend and the vicar of the University Church of St Mary the Virgin, John Henry Newman. Newman, Keble, Edward Pusey and others began publishing a series of *Tracts for the Times* which promoted their particular brand of High Church theology. Ninety tracts were published between 1833 and 1841. An often-overlooked fact is that in the early days many evangelicals – such as the Bishop of Winchester, C. R. Sumner – were very sympathetic to the Oxford Movement.[15] It became clear, however, that the objectives of the Tractarians were fundamentally at odds with what evangelicals held dear and what was considered to be the Protestant and Reformed faith of the Church of England.

---

11. John Wolffe, 'The Commemoration of the Reformation and Mid-Nineteenth-Century Evangelical Identity', *Bulletin of the John Rylands Library* 90, no. 1 (Spring 2014), p. 49.

12. Chadwick, *Victorian Church*, p. 49.

13. Wolffe, 'Commemoration of the Reformation', p. 51.

14. Interestingly, the evangelical *Record* responded to the act in a very similar fashion. Ibid., p. 53.

15. Toon, *Evangelical Theology*, p. 21; Alister E. McGrath, *Iustitia Dei: A History of the Christian Doctrine*, 2 vols., Vol. 2 (Cambridge: Cambridge University Press, 1986), pp. 121–122.

The radical change in this scenario was that the threat to the nation's Protestant heritage was not from the outside, but came 'from within the heart of the establishment, from within the Church of England itself and indeed its leading university'.[16]

Newman was the leader of the Oxford Movement. He had been converted to Calvinistic evangelicalism under the influence of a schoolmaster at the age of fifteen.[17] When he went up to Oxford he maintained his convictions and threw himself into evangelical organizations such as the local branch of the CMS, being elected secretary as late as 1829.[18] During the 1820s, however, Newman's theology shifted substantially on issues such as baptismal regeneration, the authority of the church and apostolic succession.[19] Through the 1830s Newman's opposition to Reformation theology became more vehement. His hand was involved in thirty of the ninety tracts published and he authored several that deliberately attempted to undermine the concept that the Church of England was Protestant. The climax of this attack was *Tract 90*, in which Newman argued that churchmen ought to understand the Anglican formularies in 'the most Catholic sense they will admit' because there is no duty to understand them in accordance with their framers' intentions. He maintained that the Thirty-Nine Articles are, 'through GOD's good providence, to say the least, not uncatholic, and may be subscribed by those who aim at being Catholic in heart and doctrine'.[20] The outcry over this tract was not because Newman was seeking to read the Articles broadly (there was precedent for that amongst Laudians and Latitudinarians), but it was that 'he understood them in a Roman Catholic direction'.[21] The *Morning Chronicle* stated that, 'According to the authors of the Tracts, we are all good papists without even knowing it'.[22]

In 1837, just as the Victorian era was dawning, Newman delivered a series of lectures on the doctrine of justification which were published the following year and are arguably the most significant theological work arising from the

---

16. Rex, 'Introduction', p. 11.

17. John Henry Newman, *Apologia Pro Vita Sua* (London: Collins, 1864), pp. 97–98.

18. Chadwick, *Victorian Church*, p. 69.

19. S. Gilley, 'Life and Writings', in Ian Ker and Terrence Merrigan (eds.), *The Cambridge Companion to John Henry Newman* (Cambridge: Cambridge University Press, 2009), p. 3.

20. John Henry Newman, *Tract 90: Remarks on Certain Passages in the Thirty-Nine Articles* (1841).

21. Owen Chadwick, *The Spirit of the Oxford Movement: Tractarian Essays* (Cambridge: Cambridge University Press, 1992), pp. 15–16.

22. Cited in Chadwick, *Victorian Church*, p. 185.

Oxford Movement.[23] The *Lectures on the Doctrine of Justification* argued for a *via media* between Protestant and Roman Catholic conceptions of the doctrine. Newman stated, 'Justification by faith only, thus treated, is an erroneous, and justification by obedience is a defective, view of Christian doctrine. The former is beside, the latter short of the truth.'[24] In contrast to understanding these doctrines in isolation, he argued that together they truly reflected the biblical teaching that humanity is justified by faith *and* obedience. The lectures proved to be influential in undermining a central Reformation doctrine and shifting the Church of England closer to the Roman Catholic position.

At the same time that Newman was working on redefining justification he edited a collection of writings by his recently deceased close friend Hurrell Froude. The first volume of Froude's *Remains* was published in 1838 and caused quite a stir, not least because of Froude's comments, 'I hate the Reformation and the Reformers more and more' and 'the Reformation was a limb badly set: it must be broken again to be righted'.[25] Likewise, Newman did not keep his disdain of Continental Protestants a secret. He once wrote to the Bishop of Oxford, 'Lutheranism and Calvinism are heresies repugnant to Scripture.'[26] These comments were both inflammatory to those advocating the Protestant nature of the Church of England and motivational to those who repudiated that nature. Simon Skinner has shown that the Tractarians 'reinforced their manifest theological distaste for the Reformation by attributing to it the commercial spirit and an attendant maldistribution of property'.[27] By the 1840s two powerful factions were at work within the Church of England: those advocating Protestant theology and those who 'declared war on the principles of the Reformation'.[28]

---

23. For claims along these lines, see McGrath, *Iustitia Dei*, p. 122; Ian Ker (ed.), *Newman the Theologian: A Reader* (London: Collins, 1990), p. 29. Cf. John Perry, 'Newman's Treatment of Luther in the Lectures on Justification', *Journal of Ecumenical Studies* 36, no. 3–4 (Summer–Fall 1999), p. 303; Gilley, 'Life', p. 8.

24. John Henry Newman, *Lectures on the Doctrine of Justification* (London: Longmans, Green, 1908 [1874]), p. 2.

25. Hurrell Froude, *Remains of the Late Reverend Richard Hurrell Froude*, 2 vols., Vol. 1 (London: J. G. and F. Rivington, 1838), pp. 389, 433.

26. 'Protest', 11 Nov. 1841, in Newman, *Apologia*, p. 208.

27. Simon Skinner, '"A Triumph of the Rich": Tractarians and the Reformation', *Bulletin of the John Rylands Library* 90, no. 1 (Spring 2014), p. 77.

28. This phrase is used by Ward who, after the publication of his *Ideal of a Christian Church*, was divested of his Oxford degrees. Chadwick, *Victorian Church*, pp. 207, 210–211.

Newman's own affiliation with the established church terminated in 1845 when he was received as a Roman Catholic. It was a fitting outcome, and an acceptance of where his heart and theology actually lay. Sheridan Gilley concluded that Newman had 'given some of his best thought to the question of the identity of Anglicanism, and concluded that it was essentially Protestant'.[29] This fact is something of an indictment on the subsequent rise of Anglo-Catholicism which, over the next century, appeared to flow, at first as a trickle and later like a flood. Nockles has stated that 'Newman's *via media* theory had a long "shelf life", even if he himself soon abandoned it'.[30] On the other hand, this may be seen as just another in the series of paradoxes to have marked the Oxford Movement from its outset. It was a movement born out of the attack on the Protestant Church of Ireland by a government seeking to enfranchise Roman Catholicism. Its objective was to advocate for the catholicity of Anglicanism and the apostolic authority of its episcopacy. This, however, meant reinventing the church's past and interpreting its confessions in plain contradiction to their meaning. Moreover, when the bishops sought to exercise their 'apostolic authority' by checking Anglo-Catholic excesses, those who had championed their rights to do so deliberately subverted it for not aligning with Catholic principles. Newman's realization that the Church of England was fundamentally Protestant, although removing Anglo-Catholicism's ablest leader, did not hinder the movement in its attempt to 'unprotestantize' the national church. By the end of the nineteenth century, Anglo-Catholics were portraying their movement's success as the true English Reformation.[31]

The Ecclesiological Society

Some scholars have argued that the Oxford Movement was primarily theological, at least in its early years, and that leaders such as Pusey and Keble were opposed to ritualistic innovation as it would distract from the primary issues.[32] There is some truth to the fact that Pusey and Keble were conservative in relation to ritual; however, the relationship between the Oxford Movement and ritual has

---

29. Gilley, 'Life', p. 13.
30. Peter Nockles, 'Newman's Tractarian Receptions', in Frederick Aquino and Benjamin King (eds.), *Receptions of Newman* (Oxford: Oxford University Press, 2015), p. 138.
31. Nockles, 'Reformation Revised?', p. 243. This notion is still prevalent, e.g. Dominic Janes, *Victorian Reformation: The Fight over Idolatry in the Church of England, 1840–1860* (Oxford: Oxford University Press, 2009).
32. E.g. Chadwick, *Victorian Church*, p. 212.

been shown to be more complex than such a simple delineation indicates.[33] Nevertheless, for our purposes it is worth highlighting a movement deriving from the other university that did promote a return to pre-Reformation practice in the worship of the English church: the Ecclesiological Society. The rise of Romanticism had ushered in an increased interest in and sympathy for the Middle Ages. One result was the establishment of this society – originally named the Cambridge Camden Society – in 1839, and its influence was magnified from 1841 through the publication of its journal, *The Ecclesiologist*. The society began to advocate for medieval architecture and ritual, promoting the power of symbolism in church practice. The interiors of church buildings were significantly rearranged. For example, chancels in ordinary parishes – which had been used as storehouses or schools apart from the very infrequent celebration of Holy Communion – were adorned with stalls for surpliced choirs, and services introduced novelties such as sung responses. In the sanctuary, tables were replaced with stone altars. Gothic architecture was ubiquitously revered, such that even Baptist chapels began to be built in prominent places in Gothic style.[34] One contemporary observer declared, 'Romanism is taught *Analytically* at Oxford, it is taught *Artistically* at Cambridge . . . it is inculcated theoretically in tracts at the one university and is *sculptured*, *painted* and *graven* at the other.'[35]

Various practices that had specifically been repudiated at the Reformation were reintroduced. Over the course of the century, one area in which this was particularly evident was in the adoption of pre-Reformation vestments. In 1846 John Mason Neale, the founder of the Ecclesiological Society, wrote to a friend persuading him to introduce wearing the cope in services, with a greater purpose in mind. He wrote, 'The greatest use of the cope is, it strikes me, to accustom our people to coloured vestments; once do that . . . and the chasuble follows without difficulty.'[36] Four years later, in 1850, Neale took that further step, being one of the first Anglicans to wear a chasuble. Over the next sixty years there was a steady increase in ritualism throughout the Church of England which became intimately tied to Anglo-Catholicism, the successor of the Oxford Movement. Although this trend towards ritualism has been labelled the 'Victorian

33. Nigel Yates, *Anglican Ritualism in Victorian Britain, 1830–1910* (Oxford: Oxford University Press, 1999), pp. 48–63.
34. Chadwick, *Victorian Church*, pp. 213–214, 221, 417.
35. Toon, *Evangelical Theology*, p. 67.
36. Cited in Janet Mayo, *A History of Ecclesiastical Dress* (New York: Holmes & Meier, 1984), p. 104. This book also gives a helpful account of how clerical dress was transformed through the Reformation period, pp. 62–76.

Reformation', it was essentially a repudiation of Reformation ideals through innovation in ritual, music and architecture.[37]

'Papal Aggression'

We have seen how outrage over concessions to popular Roman Catholicism in Ireland ironically spurned internal Anglican repudiations of the Reformation through the Oxford Movement. In something of a recursive loop, we now focus on how the development of such repudiations, along with high-profile defections like that of Newman, provided fertile ground for the establishment of Roman Catholic hierarchy in England. In 1850, a major controversy had played out between the High Church Bishop of Exeter, Henry Phillpotts, and an evangelical clergyman, George Gorham. The bishop insisted that Gorham subscribe to a strict view of baptismal regeneration, but Gorham refused. The case was taken all the way to the Privy Council, which sided with Gorham. The situation deteriorated to the point where Phillpotts threatened to excommunicate the evangelical Archbishop of Canterbury, John Bird Sumner. Furthermore, the judicial finding was considered a major blow to Anglo-Catholic assumptions about Anglican catholicity, and a number of prominent people joined the Church of Rome as a result. Seizing on the opportunity, in September the Pope established thirteen dioceses in England, including an Archdiocese of Westminster. This action was widely referred to as the Papal Aggression.[38] In 1850 Nicholas Wiseman became England's first Cardinal Archbishop since Reginald Pole died in 1558. Chadwick argued that 'Calamitous timing, and unlucky choice of persons to introduce it, made it look like an assault upon the Archbishop of Canterbury or even upon Queen Victoria'.[39] Newman's *Lectures on Certain Difficulties Felt by Anglicans in Submitting to the Catholic Church* was an unsubtle appeal to members of the Oxford Movement to defect. He argued, not that the movement was uncatholic, but rather that, because it *was* Catholic, it did not belong in the Church of England. This argument included two implicit assumptions. First was the belief that, by nature, Anglicanism is Protestant. Second, despite the doctrinal affinities, according to the Pope Anglo-Catholicism was an illegitimate ecclesiastical position to hold. This stance was emphatically

---

37. For more information on the influence of the Ecclesiologists, see Dale Aldermann, *The Contribution of Cambridge Ecclesiologists to the Revival of Anglican Worship, 1839–62* (Sydney: Ashgate, 1997); James White, *The Cambridge Movement: The Ecclesiologists and the Gothic Revival* (Cambridge: Cambridge University Press, 1962).

38. Toon, *Evangelical Theology*, p. 97.

39. Chadwick, *Victorian Church*, p. 279.

affirmed towards the end of the century, in 1896, when Pope Leo XIII issued *Apostolicae curae*, which condemned Anglican orders as null and void, and in doing so scuppered Anglo-Catholic attempts for papal recognition. Mark Chapman has demonstrated that since the beginnings of the Oxford Movement, 'Despite some of their rhetoric, the likelihood of [ecumenical] success was negligible in an ecclesiastical situation marked by competition and historical conflict.'[40]

Liberalism

Perhaps the most significant repudiation of Reformation principles in the Victorian era was one that was much more subtle than those mentioned thus far. The rise of biblical criticism in the latter half of the eighteenth century undermined the foundation from which Reformed theology was based: the authority of Scripture. Although the Queen's Consort, Prince Albert, was descended from those who protected Luther, the German influence that he brought to bear on the academic scene in England was liberal scholarship. From the late 1850s, significant works undermined traditional confidence in the Bible from philosophical, scientific and historic perspectives. Some examples are Henry Mansel's *The Limits of Religious Thought* (1858) which applied Kant's metaphysical agnosticism to theology, Charles Darwin's *Origin of Species* (1859) which posited evolution as an alternative to divine creation, and *Essays and Reviews* (1860) which was a controversial exposition of liberal theology from a group of Oxford scholars. Such works publicly challenged and even altered received religious beliefs.[41] John Colenso, Bishop of Natal (1853–83), produced a series of treatises critically challenging the historicity of the Pentateuch and book of Joshua which had direct implications for the infallibility of the Bible.

Although these developments were initially vehemently opposed by Anglo-Catholic and evangelical alike, liberal conclusions filtered into both parties. The 1889 volume *Lux Mundi*, organized by Charles Gore, is an early example of what would become known as Liberal-Catholicism. It presented an Anglo-Catholic understanding of church tradition and sacraments while adopting a liberal stance on the historical reliability of the Old Testament. A strong case can be made that the advance of biblical criticism in the latter half of the nineteenth century was one of the greatest repudiations of the

---

40. Mark Chapman, *The Fantasy of Reunion: Anglicans, Catholics, and Ecumenism, 1833–1882* (Oxford: Oxford University Press, 2014), p. 27.

41. J. C. Livingston, *Religious Thought in the Victorian Age: Challenges and Reconceptions* (London: T&T Clark, 2006), p. 4.

Reformation the Victorian period produced. Considering the Oxford Movement and the rise of ritualism within the Church of England, as well as the advance of Roman Catholicism itself, to say that biblical criticism was an equally significant repudiation is no small claim. But it struck at the heart of Protestant theology's source of authority.

Revering the Reformation

The numerous forces at work in Victorian England undermining the achievements of the Reformation led other groups to a closer identification with, and polemical defence of, the Protestant character of their church and country. Primarily this defence is associated with evangelicals, but identification as 'Protestant' was by no means limited to this party.[42] Three important aspects marked this identification in the nineteenth century. First, effort was put into remembering the Reformation by memorializing sixteenth-century people and events, as well as publishing English Reformers' writings. Second, there was a concerted defence of Reformed theology and practice, often in response to ritualist advances. Third, those who revered the Reformation aimed not just to maintain it as a museum piece, but rather to proclaim the central truths of the Reformation in their contemporary context. Both at home and abroad they championed the authority of the Bible as God's revelation, and salvation that is by the grace of God through faith in Christ alone. In this way, the spirit of the Reformation was alive and well in the Victorian church.

Remembering the Reformation

One of the interesting recent avenues of nineteenth-century ecclesiastical research has been the study of memorials commemorating English Reformers. Andrew Atherstone has been at the forefront of this research. He states, 'between 1828 and 1910 tablets, crosses and obelisks were erected in public locations' right across the country to memorialize sixteenth-century Protestant martyrs.[43] One of the most prominent was the memorial to the Oxford Martyrs

---

42. For example, Charles Golightly did not identify as evangelical but was one of the chief defenders of Protestantism in Oxford responding to Tractarians. See Andrew Atherstone, *Oxford's Protestant Spy: The Controversial Career of Charles Golightly* (Milton Keynes: Paternoster, 2007).

43. Andrew Atherstone, 'Memorializing William Tyndale', *Bulletin of the John Rylands Library* 90, no. 1 (Spring 2014), p. 155.

which commemorates the burning of Nicholas Ridley, Hugh Latimer and
Thomas Cranmer in 1555–6.[44] Not only were these bishops chief architects of
the Protestant Church of England, they were put to death in the very town
where Newman, Keble and Pusey were undermining what they stood for.
Although there had been plans for a memorial before the 1830s, the developments of that decade were catalysts that got the project off the ground. As
such, Peter Toon is correct in his assessment that the memorial 'stands today
reminding those who study it not only of the martyred bishops but also of
the strong Protestant feeling in Oxford in the early years of the reign of Queen
Victoria'.[45]

It was not only through the building of monuments that the Reformation
was remembered. Numerous anniversaries were commemorated by large-scale
gatherings and nation-wide celebrations. Wolffe has detailed the efforts that
went into the tercentenary of William Tyndale's martyrdom in 1835 by both
Anglicans and Dissenters.[46] Tyndale served as a unifying figure, as all Protestants
enjoyed the benefits of the English Bible. Later in the century, other dates were
similarly observed, from the accession of Elizabeth I to the birth of Luther.
Interestingly, not every significant date was celebrated on a national scale and
some, like the anniversary of the introduction of the Prayer Book and the
martyrdoms of Ridley, Latimer and Cranmer, passed by with relatively little
fanfare.[47] Nevertheless, it should be noted that in contrast to commemorations
of the Reformation on the Continent, the internal battle for identity in the
Church of England meant that national celebrations generally proved to be less
than unifying.[48]

Another avenue that was pursued in commemorating the Reformation
in England was the republication of the writings of English Reformers.
The Parker Society was begun in late 1840, motivated in part by the Oxford
Movement's efforts at translating and publishing the early Church Fathers,
as well as by their general undermining of the Reformers. The stated aim of
the Parker Society was 'to re-publish the entire mass of the printed works
of the leading divines of our reformed church, who flourished in the age
when the Roman yoke, which pressed so grievously upon our forefathers, was

44. Andrew Atherstone, 'The Martyrs' Memorial at Oxford', *Journal of Ecclesiastical
    History* 54 (2003).
45. Toon, *Evangelical Theology*, p. 41.
46. Wolffe, 'Commemoration of the Reformation'.
47. Ibid., p. 61.
48. Nockles, 'Reformation Revised?', p. 246.

broken'.[49] This was a significant undertaking and much of this work had not been republished since the sixteenth century. The committee was dominated by Anglican evangelicals and they aimed at having 2,000 subscribers to support the publishing initiative. Within a few months, however, they had more than double that number, and by 1842 almost 7,000 subscribers had enlisted, each paying £1 per year.[50] This indicates the remarkable popularity of the endeavour. By 1855 the Society had published no fewer than fifty-four volumes, the last of which was a general index. Richard Rex has described this as a 'herculean publishing effort'; indeed, it was the largest venture of its kind in the nineteenth century.[51] In fourteen years the Society had finished the task it was set up for and, that being so, it was wound up. There is little doubt that the wholesale republication of the English Reformers' work ensured deeper and richer reflection, not just on the foundational theology of the Protestant Church of England, but also on the nation's Protestant identity.

Defending the Reformation

Those in the nineteenth century who revered the Reformation not only celebrated the events that had taken place three hundred years earlier, they also defended the practices and theology that were established at that time. Three important areas of scholarly contention were Reformation history, the authority of the Bible and justification by faith. But it was not only the cerebral defence offered in ink that was prevalent; the Victorian era also witnessed a great struggle against innovations in liturgical practice, which included the undignified practice of public legal battles. In general, there was a sense of indignation amongst evangelicals that such arguments should be necessary within the Church of England itself. For example, the *Christian Observer* said:

> If the battles of the Reformation are to be fought over again, not with avowed
> Romanists but with professed Anglicans, who account popery their 'dear sister' and
> consider Protestantism as a rational neologian schism, the friends of the pure Gospel
> of Christ, unsophisticated by human devices, have only to take up the spiritual arms

---

49. 'The Thirteenth and Final Report of the Council of the Parker Society', in Henry Gough, *General Index to the Publications of the Parker Society* (Cambridge: Cambridge University Press, 1854), p. i.

50. Wolffe, 'Commemoration of the Reformation', p. 61; Andrew Cinnamond, 'The Reformed Treasures of the Parker Society', *Churchman* 122 (2008), p. 221.

51. Rex, 'Introduction', p. 16.

of their godly forefathers, and with the Bible in their hands to contend for the faith
once delivered to the saints.[52]

Indeed, the defence of the Reformation resulted in hundreds of tracts,
pamphlets, printed sermons and books, as well as numerous newspapers and
journals that promoted the Protestant cause. The Reformation was certainly
strongly defended, but the effectiveness, or otherwise, of that defence continues
to be a matter of debate.

Nineteenth-century Reformation historiography is a fascinating area of study,
as the polarizing effect of ecclesiastical divisions ensured that 'conviction history'
of sixteenth-century events was rife. As Eamon Duffy has stated, 'Catholic and
Protestant alike chronicled or commemorated the religious upheavals of the
sixteenth century in order to confute opponents, underpin party positions, or
consolidate denominational allegiances.'[53] Each side searched for evidence to
maintain its stance and the increased prevalence of source material, such as that
provided by the Parker Society, ensured that historical scholarship improved.
The interpretation of the Reformation by Catholic and Tractarian leaders has
already been noted; it is also essential to observe the increase in interest in the
Protestant articulation of Reformation history. Nineteenth-century evangelicals identified with the Reformation far more vigorously than did their
eighteenth-century predecessors, who were primarily concerned with religious
indifference.[54] For example, the nineteenth century saw a large upswing in the
popularity of John Foxe's sixteenth-century polemical history.[55] Between 1856
and 1870 James Froude – younger brother of Hurrell who had declared that
'the Reformation was a limb badly set' – produced his monumental *History of
England from the Fall of Wolsey to the Defeat of the Spanish Armada*. This twelve-
volume work was heavily dependent on archival sources and argued for the
positive impact of the Reformation on the nation. It was a firm and scholarly
historical defence against the influential presentation that the Reformation had
been disastrous for England, which had been argued, for example, by John

---

52. *Christian Observer*, 1838, pp. 52 and 258; cited in Peter Toon, 'A Critical Review of
    John Henry Newman's Doctrine of Justification', *Churchman* 94, no. 4 (1980), p. 336.
53. Eamon Duffy, 'Afterword', *Bulletin of the John Rylands Library* 90, no. 1 (Spring 2014),
    p. 369.
54. Wolffe, 'Commemoration of the Reformation', p. 60.
55. See Nockles, 'Reformation Revised?', pp. 232–239; and Elizabeth Evenden, 'John
    Foxe, Samuel Potter and the Illustration of the *Book of Martyrs*', *Bulletin of the John
    Rylands Library* 90, no. 1 (Spring 2014), pp. 207–209.

Lingard, a Catholic scholar. At a popular level, evangelicals such as J. C. Ryle were extremely effective in propagating support for the Reformation. Ryle's address 'What Do We Owe to the Reformation?' was made into a pamphlet which sold 88,000 copies in one year.[56] In his final episcopal address in 1900, Ryle declared that England should 'Never forget that the principles of the Protestant Reformation made this country what she is, and let nothing ever tempt you to forsake them.'[57] Nevertheless, John Wolffe has argued that, despite the greater historical awareness of evangelicals, in the latter half of the Victorian era they continued 'to reinvent the Reformation in their own image, assuming rather than demonstrating continuity between the teachings and practice of the sixteenth century and that of the nineteenth'.[58]

The place and authority of the Bible was another central battleground in the Victorian contest for the legacy of the Reformation. This foundational aspect of Reformed theology was both subjugated by Tractarians, who championed the authority of tradition, and also condemned as an historically unreliable authority by certain biblical scholars. In the 1830s a series of publications undermined the Reformed concept of *sola scriptura*. These included Keble's *Primitive Tradition* (1836), Newman's *The Prophetical Office of the Church* (1837) and Henry Manning's *The Rule of Faith* (1838).[59] In response, significant evangelicals offered defences of the Reformed doctrine. Two important examples are Bishop Daniel Wilson's *The Sufficiency of Holy Scripture as the Rule of Faith* (1841) and William Goode's *The Divine Rule of Faith and Practice* (1842). The increase of biblical criticism in Victorian England also resulted in something of a scholarly *ad fontes* in defence of the Bible's historical reliability. Alfred Edersheim's *The Life and Times of Jesus the Messiah* (1883) was a very significant work produced by a Jewish convert to Christianity which demonstrated the consistent reliability of the Gospel accounts in relation to their first-century milieu. Perhaps of greatest significance was the 'Cambridge Triumvirate' of J. B. Lightfoot, B. F. Westcott and F. E. A. Hort. These three friends made great advances in biblical scholarship and, like Erasmus in the sixteenth century, Westcott and Hort produced an important critical edition of the Greek New Testament. While none of these three was evangelical, their biblical scholarship served the Protestant cause by defending the historical reliability of the New Testament. Evangelicals such as

---

56. Iain Murray, *J. C. Ryle: Prepared to Stand Alone* (Edinburgh: Banner of Truth, 2016), p. 117.

57. J. C. Ryle, *Charges and Addresses* (Edinburgh: Banner of Truth, 1978), p. 368.

58. Wolffe, 'Commemoration of the Reformation'.

59. Toon, *Evangelical Theology*, p. 113.

H. C. G. Moule, who was himself an accomplished biblical scholar in Cambridge, built upon the work of the Cambridge Triumvirate. Indeed, Moule succeeded Westcott (who had succeeded Lightfoot) as Bishop of Durham in 1901. Through their work, the place of the Bible was reaffirmed as of central importance for the doctrine of the church.

If *sola scriptura* was the foundation doctrine of the Reformation, the doctrine of *sola fide* was at its heart. As has been shown, John Henry Newman's *Lectures on the Doctrine of Justification* (1838) was a polemic against faith alone and instead argued that the biblical doctrine was that sinners are justified by faith and works. Protestants quickly condemned Newman's position. G. S. Faber's second edition of *The Primitive Doctrine of Justification Investigated* included two appendices dealing with Newman and his doctrine in which he concluded that Newman's *Lectures* exhibited 'a strange and mischievous attempt, to mix up together, wholesome food and rank poison, the sound doctrine of the Church of England and the pernicious dogmas of the Church of Rome; Scriptural Orthodoxy and Popish Heterodoxy'.[60] There were several evangelical articulations of the doctrine of justification by faith in the years following the publication of Newman's lectures.[61] In 1866, when James Buchanan's Cunningham Lectures were published under the title *The Doctrine of Justification*, he maintained that Newman's theory of justification 'was ably answered' at the time.[62] Toon's assessment over a hundred years later was more nuanced. He argued that much of the contemporary response viewed Newman's doctrine as a recapitulation of the medieval position, so therefore they rehashed the arguments of the Protestant Reformers. He said, 'It is difficult to avoid the conclusion that the evangelicals never really answered the doctrine of justification proposed by Newman.'[63] They expounded arguments from the sixteenth and seventeenth centuries, but they failed to deal with Newman's position for what it was, and, of course, there was the constant danger of reducing the doctrine itself to merely a party slogan.[64] This critique

---

60. Cited in ibid., p. 144.

61. Important works included Renn Dickson Hampden's *The Lord Our Righteousness* (1839), Philip Shuttleworth's *Justification through Faith* (1840), James Bennett *Justification as Revealed in Scripture in Opposition to the Council of Trent and Mr. Newman's Lectures* (1840), Charles McIlvaine's *Oxford Divinity* (1841), Charles Heurtley *Justification* (Bampton Lectures 1845).

62. James Buchanan, *The Doctrine of Justification: An Outline of Its History in the Church and of Its Exposition from Scripture* (London: Banner of Truth, 1961 [1867]), p. 13.

63. Toon, *Evangelical Theology*, p. 168.

64. Ibid., p. 169.

notwithstanding, significant effort was expended in defending the Reformed doctrine of justification against the theological attacks of the nineteenth century.

The defence of the Reformation in Victorian England was not limited to the cloistered environs of academic treatises, but was also pursued through appeal to the law of the land. In one sense, the Gorham case discussed above gave Protestants a feeling that their position against the tide of ritualism could be vindicated through legal avenues. Indeed, after the 1860s a powerful movement grew which aimed to actively prosecute those pioneering ritualistic advances. In 1865 the Church Association was formed to uphold the Protestant nature of the Church of England. Large amounts of money were raised and spent in seeking out and prosecuting clergy whose ceremonial practices defied canon law. While this action was not universally advocated by evangelical leaders, some significant people, such as J. C. Ryle, were heavily involved in the Church Association and championed its causes.[65] Manuals such as Henry Millar's 1889 *Guide to Ecclesiastical Law* were produced, which have been described as handbooks 'for Protestant zealots intent on prosecuting anyone who breached the Constitutional Settlement of Church and State'.[66] Anglo-Catholics claimed that they were acting within the limits of the law but the repeated success of the Church Association's prosecutions demonstrated this to be false. The impact of this litigious route proved counterproductive, however, as public sympathy soon favoured the convicted clerics, a number of whom had been imprisoned for their stand. They were perceived to be pious and well-intentioned 'martyrs', while those prosecuting them were portrayed as Pharisaical and heartless. This was a significant shift in thinking, given the longstanding identification of Foxe's martyrs as national heroes who suffered unjustly for the Protestant cause. The shoe, it appeared, was now on the other foot. In this way, the Victorian defence of the Reformation could prove to be both successful and unsuccessful at the same time: winning the battle in the courtroom could lead to losing the war of public opinion.

Proclaiming the Reformed faith

In nineteenth-century England the Reformation was both celebrated and defended by those who revered it, but more significantly still, in this era the

---

65. For more detail on different attitudes to prosecution, see M. Wellings, *Evangelicals Embattled: Responses of Evangelicals in the Church of England to Ritualism, Darwinism and Theological Liberalism, 1890–1930* (Carlisle: Paternoster, 2003), pp. 100–104.

66. J. S. Peart-Binns, *Herbert Hensley Henson: A Biography* (Cambridge: Lutterworth, 2013), p. 54.

Protestant biblical faith was proclaimed throughout England and across the world. Missionary and Bible societies flourished and their efforts to take the written and preached word of God to all nations made great advances. At home, famous preachers spoke to large crowds proclaiming salvation by faith in Christ. At the universities, new movements were established that would, under God, continue to be of global significance for the advancement of Protestant Christianity. Indeed, institutions were begun independent of the universities to propagate the Protestant faith by training evangelical clergy and missionaries. Efforts such as these meant that the Reformation was not merely a crusty museum piece of English history, but a vibrant aspect of national culture.

One society that epitomized the ethos of the Reformation was the British and Foreign Bible Society. This organization was founded in 1804 but had grown substantially by the time Victoria ascended the throne. William Tyndale's famous declaration to a priest that he would 'cause the boy that drives the plough to know more of the Scriptures than you!' has generally been considered a statement of his motive to translate the Bible into the vernacular of the people. Translation into vernacular languages and the distribution of the Scriptures was also the *raison d'être* for the Bible Society. Foreign missionary societies also boomed in Victoria's reign. As the empire expanded, so did the horizon for English Protestants in relation to the need to preach the gospel. Many were sent to far-flung and hostile locations around the world. There were numerous examples of the country's 'best and brightest', such as the Cambridge Seven, giving up promising futures in the upper echelons of English society to be missionaries.[67] The Bible and missionary societies of Victorian Britain were responsible for a global expansion of Protestant Christianity that was unprecedented and truly captured the spirit of the Reformation in proclaiming the salvation that is found in Christ alone.

In England, great preachers of the Reformed faith were Victorian celebrities, attracting large crowds to hear them preach and even larger followings reading what they had to say. Two of the most popular in Victorian England were J. C. Ryle and Charles Spurgeon. Ryle was at Oxford during the early days of the Tractarian movement, but became convinced that the theology of the movement was repugnant to Scripture. As an evangelical clergyman, he was widely admired as a platform speaker and writer. By 1888, he had published between 200 and 300 tracts, with over 12 million issued.[68] Ryle was consecrated as the first Bishop of Liverpool in 1880 and remained in that influential position until his death in

---

67. John Pollock, *The Cambridge Seven* (London: Inter-Varsity Press, 1955).
68. Murray, *Ryle*, p. 124.

1900, just months before the Victorian era came to an end. Charles Spurgeon, on the other hand, was a Particular Baptist who became known as the 'Prince of Preachers'. He was the pastor of the same church in London for thirty-eight years, until his death in 1892. Thousands came to hear him each week and on occasions he preached to crowds in the tens of thousands. The 'Downgrade Controversy' was the result of a stand he made in 1887 against the Baptist Union's liberal attitude to the authority of the Bible and the centrality of the atonement. As a result of this bold resolve to maintain these Reformation truths, his church disaffiliated from the Union. The examples of Ryle and Spurgeon demonstrate that the Reformation touchstones were proclaimed, with great popularity, in the Victorian period.

The universities of Oxford and Cambridge were transforming throughout the nineteenth century. At the beginning of the century they were relatively narrow institutions, where most graduates became clergymen. By the end of the century the academics included those not ordained and there were burgeoning subjects within science and humanities.[69] Religious tests were abolished such that students no longer had to sign the Thirty-Nine Articles to receive their degree. In the midst of this, evangelical Christian students began forming societies.[70] In 1862, a group of students at Cambridge began the Daily Prayer Meeting, which by 1875 had 10% of students supporting it. From this group the Cambridge Inter-Collegiate Christian Union (CICCU) was formed, which became a model for other Protestant student Christian groups throughout Britain and the world. Around the same time that CICCU was getting started, a group of evangelicals, realizing that Reformed theology was by no means a staple aspect of university education, began their own training colleges. Wycliffe Hall opened in Oxford in 1877 and Ridley Hall opened in Cambridge in 1881. Indeed, the names of these institutions were themselves indicative of the shape of the theological education the founders hoped would be taught there. So in the Victorian era the universities were the cradles for both the Tractarians and the Ecclesiologists, and the Inter-Collegiate Christian Unions and the evangelical Halls, which were founded to proclaim and propagate the principles of the Reformation.

---

69. A. J. Engel, *From Clergyman to Don: The Rise of the Academic Profession in Nineteenth-Century Oxford* (Oxford: Clarendon, 1983), pp. 280–282; cf. Daniel Inman, *The Making of Modern English Theology: God and the Academy at Oxford, 1833–1945* (Minneapolis: Fortress Press, 2014).

70. Indeed, there were almost fifty such societies by the end of Victoria's reign. Wellings, *Evangelicals*, p. 74.

Conclusions

The Victorian era was certainly a period of intense religious struggle for
supremacy within English Christianity, much like the sixteenth century itself.
As Jeremy Morris has stated, 'No other period of church history could serve
the religious conflicts of the nineteenth century as well as could the Reformation.'[71] While 'Protestant' identity had been taken for granted in the 150 years
before Victoria, the signs appeared ominous at her accession. Throughout her
reign, various forces repudiated the principles of the Reformation. Indeed, the
course was set early: within her first fifteen years the Tractarians were adjusting
well to their post-Newman development, the Ecclesiologists were growing in
popularity and the Pope had re-established Roman hierarchy across England.
These threats led Protestants, and particularly evangelicals, to a greater polemical
identification with the sixteenth century. They celebrated anniversaries of what
had taken place three hundred years earlier in an unprecedented way. They
republished works, held national celebrations and erected monuments, which
stand today as much as a testimony to nineteenth-century religious conflict as
to the sixteenth century they purport to memorialize. Protestants also defended
the Reformation. Historical study was advanced, Reformed theology was
reiterated and even litigation was pursued. It could be argued that they became
overly *defensive* in this regard as they became unwilling to change or innovate
where necessary. Furthermore, there were times when tribalism and slogans
were easily substituted for sincere engagement with the issues of the day.
Undoubtedly, however, the greatest achievements of Victorian Christianity were
the efforts that were made to proclaim Reformation truths. This resulted
in Bible distribution, overseas missionary efforts and the proclamation and
propagation of Christ in England. There is no doubt that the shape of global
Christianity today has been profoundly affected by the shape of Victorian Christianity, and one of the most contested aspects of Victorian Christianity was the
appropriate reception of the Reformation.

Bibliography

Aldermann, Dale, *The Contribution of Cambridge Ecclesiologists to the Revival of Anglican
    Worship, 1839–62*, Sydney: Ashgate, 1997.

---

71. Jeremy Morris, 'Afterword', *Bulletin of the John Rylands Library* 90, no. 1 (Spring 2014),
    p. 378.

Atherstone, Andrew, 'The Martyrs' Memorial at Oxford', *Journal of Ecclesiastical History* 54 (2003), pp. 278–301.

———, 'Memorializing William Tyndale', *Bulletin of the John Rylands Library* 90, no. 1 (Spring 2014), pp. 155–178.

———, *Oxford's Protestant Spy: The Controversial Career of Charles Golightly*, Milton Keynes: Paternoster, 2007.

Buchanan, James, *The Doctrine of Justification: An Outline of Its History in the Church and of Its Exposition from Scripture*, London: Banner of Truth, 1961 (1867).

Chadwick, Owen, *The Spirit of the Oxford Movement: Tractarian Essays*, Cambridge: Cambridge University Press, 1992.

———, *The Victorian Church*, 3rd edn, 2 vols., Vol. 1, London: Adam & Charles Black, 1971.

Chapman, Mark, *The Fantasy of Reunion: Anglicans, Catholics, and Ecumenism, 1833–1882*, Oxford: Oxford University Press, 2014.

Cinnamond, Andrew, 'The Reformed Treasures of the Parker Society', *Churchman* 122 (2008), pp. 221–242.

Coverdale, Myles, *Writings and Translations of Myles Coverdale, Bishop of Exeter*, ed. George Pearson, The Parker Society, Cambridge: Cambridge University Press, 1844.

Duffy, Eamon, 'Afterword', *Bulletin of the John Rylands Library* 90, no. 1 (Spring 2014), pp. 369–375.

Engel, A. J., *From Clergyman to Don: The Rise of the Academic Profession in Nineteenth-Century Oxford*, Oxford: Clarendon, 1983.

Evenden, Elizabeth, 'John Foxe, Samuel Potter and the Illustration of the *Book of Martyrs*', *Bulletin of the John Rylands Library* 90, no. 1 (Spring 2014), pp. 203–230.

Froude, Hurrell, *Remains of the Late Reverend Richard Hurrell Froude*, 2 vols., Vol. 1, London: J. G. and F. Rivington, 1838.

Gilley, S., 'Life and Writings', in Ian Ker and Terrence Merrigan (eds.), *The Cambridge Companion to John Henry Newman*, 1–28, Cambridge: Cambridge University Press, 2009.

Gough, Henry, *General Index to the Publications of the Parker Society*, Cambridge: Cambridge University Press, 1854.

Inman, Daniel, *The Making of Modern English Theology: God and the Academy at Oxford, 1833–1945*, Minneapolis: Fortress Press, 2014.

Janes, Dominic, *Victorian Reformation: The Fight over Idolatry in the Church of England, 1840–1860*, Oxford: Oxford University Press, 2009.

Ker, Ian (ed.), *Newman the Theologian: A Reader*, London: Collins, 1990.

Livingston, J. C., *Religious Thought in the Victorian Age: Challenges and Reconceptions*, London: T&T Clark, 2006.

McGrath, Alister E., *Iustitia Dei: A History of the Christian Doctrine*, 2 vols., Vol. 2, Cambridge: Cambridge University Press, 1986.

Mayo, Janet, *A History of Ecclesiastical Dress*, New York: Holmes & Meier, 1984.

Morris, Jeremy, 'Afterword', *Bulletin of the John Rylands Library* 90, no. 1 (Spring 2014), pp. 380–382.

Murray, Iain, *J. C. Ryle: Prepared to Stand Alone*, Edinburgh: Banner of Truth, 2016.

Newman, John Henry, *Apologia Pro Vita Sua*, London: Collins, 1864.

———, *Lectures on the Doctrine of Justification*, London: Longmans, Green, 1908 (1874).

———, *Tract 90: Remarks on Certain Passages in the Thirty-Nine Articles*, 1841.

Nockles, Peter, 'Newman's Tractarian Receptions', in Frederick Aquino and Benjamin King (eds.), *Receptions of Newman*, Oxford: Oxford University Press, 2015.

———, *The Oxford Movement in Context: Anglican High Churchmanship, 1760–1857*, Cambridge: Cambridge University Press, 1994.

———, 'The Reformation Revised? The Contested Reception of the English Reformation in Nineteenth-Century Protestantism', *Bulletin of the John Rylands Library* 90, no. 1 (Spring 2014), pp. 231–256.

Paz, D. G., 'The Chartists and the English Reformation', *Bulletin of the John Rylands Library* 90, no. 1 (Spring 2014), pp. 25–47.

Peart-Binns, J. S., *Herbert Hensley Henson: A Biography*, Cambridge: Lutterworth, 2013.

Perry, John, 'Newman's Treatment of Luther in the Lectures on Justification', *Journal of Ecumenical Studies* 36, no. 3–4 (Summer–Fall 1999), pp. 303–317.

Pollock, John, *The Cambridge Seven*, London: Inter-Varsity Press, 1955.

Rex, Richard, 'Introduction: The Morning Star or the Sunset of the Reformation?', *Bulletin of the John Rylands Library* 90, no. 1 (Spring 2014), pp. 7–23.

Ryle, J. C., *Charges and Addresses*, Edinburgh: Banner of Truth, 1978.

Searby, Peter, *A History of the University of Cambridge*, Vol. 3: *1750–1870*, Cambridge: Cambridge University Press, 1997.

Skinner, Simon, '"A Triumph of the Rich": Tractarians and the Reformation', *Bulletin of the John Rylands Library* 90, no. 1 (Spring 2014), pp. 69–91.

Toon, Peter, 'A Critical Review of John Henry Newman's Doctrine of Justification', *Churchman* 94, no. 4 (1980), pp. 335–344.

———, *Evangelical Theology 1833–1856: A Response to Tractarianism*, London: Marshall, Morgan & Scott, 1979.

Wellings, M., *Evangelicals Embattled: Responses of Evangelicals in the Church of England to Ritualism, Darwinism and Theological Liberalism, 1890–1930*, Carlisle: Paternoster, 2003.

White, James, *The Cambridge Movement: The Ecclesiologists and the Gothic Revival*, Cambridge: Cambridge University Press, 1962.

Wolffe, John, 'The Commemoration of the Reformation and Mid-Nineteenth-Century Evangelical Identity', *Bulletin of the John Rylands Library* 90, no. 1 (Spring 2014), pp. 49–68.

Yates, Nigel, *Anglican Ritualism in Victorian Britain, 1830–1910*, Oxford: Oxford University Press, 1999.

17. ALWAYS REFORMING?
REFORMATION AND REVOLUTION IN THE AGE
OF ROMANCE

David A. Höhne

It is not historically controversial to say that, in 1517, when Martin Luther nailed his Ninety-Five Theses to the door of the Wittenberg cathedral, a revolution broke out. Many have written on the causal links between the defiant acts of this lone Augustinian monk and their contribution to the Modern age.[1] In fact, for many observers of Modern history, revolution has been a key characteristic of Western (especially European) culture:

> Between the middle of the eighteenth and the middle of the nineteenth centuries, Europe changed so rapidly and radically that one can reasonably speak of a watershed in world history. Those who lived through it were constantly using the word revolution to express their awareness that they were living in exciting times as in 'the American revolution', 'the French revolution', or 'the Industrial revolution'. To these historians have added several others, notably 'the agrarian revolution', the commercial revolution', 'the communications revolution', and the 'consumer revolution'.[2]

---

1. See, for example, Steven Ozment, *Protestants: The Birth of a Revolution* (New York: Doubleday, 1992), p. 100. Ozment argues that the actions of Luther ought to be contextualized within a *milieu* of discontent and calls for change throughout Europe and Germany in particular.
2. Tim Blanning, *The Romantic Revolution* (New York: Modern Library Chronicles, 2010), p. ix.

Dramatic upheaval of existing spiritual, philosophical, political or cultural norms has become a defining characteristic of the Modern Romantic Age and from the perspective of the late twentieth and early twenty-first century we could add the sexual, technological and financial revolutions to the list above.[3] To live in an age characterized by revolution means, however, that not only must it be radical when it comes – it must come! In fact *permanent* revolution is basic to that stalwart of Modernist thought, Marxism.[4]

It is against this background, where the language of change has become almost a cliché, that this chapter will consider whether and how the later Reformation catch-cry of *semper reformanda* (always reforming)[5] should be viewed differently from Marx's mantra. On the one hand, how should evangelical Protestants of the twenty-first century who understand themselves as believing in the Reformation tradition seek to change, refine or renew their faith if, as some have argued, the Protestant Reformation of the sixteenth century was 'the beginning of something and not the end',[6] while, at the same time, being distinct (holy) amidst our Romantic contemporaries and resisting infatuation with change for change's sake?

Perhaps we should recognize that the Reformation finished with the compilation of the various denominational confessions? Both Luther and Calvin, founders of the epoch in their own way, were not averse to suggesting that some of their contemporaries had gone too far in their efforts to purify Christian

---

3. While the study of Romanticism as a movement has previously been confined to the study of certain forms of art (poetry, music, etc.), a growing body of literature has identified various characteristics of the Modern era that can be collated under the heading of Romanticism, starting with Isaiah Berlin, *The Roots of Romanticism* (London: Pimlico, 2000). See also Frederick C. Beiser, *The Romantic Imperative* (Cambridge, MA: Harvard University Press, 2003). For the relationship between Romanticism and science, see Richard Holmes, *The Age of Wonder: How the Romantic Generation Discovered the Beauty and Terror of Science* (New York: Vintage, 2008).

4. Marx and Engels, 'Address of the Central Committee to the Communist League', London, March 1850: 'Their battle-cry must be: Permanent Revolution.'

5. Andrew Atherstone, 'The Implications of *Semper Reformanda*', *Anvil* 26, no. 1 (2009), p. 31. Atherstone finds the phrase in the Dutch Reformed church of the late seventeenth century and in the works of Jodocus van Lodenstein, Jacobus Koelman and Johannes Hoornbeeck.

6. A. T. B. McGowan, 'Introduction', in A. T. B. McGowan, *Always Reforming* (Leicester: Apollos, 2006), p. 13.

faith from the evils of Rome.[7] In that case, though, how shall we avoid, after half a millennium, Reformed orthodoxy simply becoming another rigid magisterium with its custodians taking the place of the Roman teaching church for the sake of the contemporary believing church?[8] In the light of the Modern propensity for upheaval or rebellion and during this auspicious season of Reformation commemoration it seems important to distinguish as clearly as possible (and uphold) the practice of 'always reforming' from the Romantic obsession with revolution.

To maintain the focus of this chapter we shall need to do two things. First, we must establish some means by which we can consider a continuing practice of reforming to be compatible with the Reformation tradition. Protestantism has always had within it the potential for fragmentation. The plethora of denominations and churches arising out of the sixteenth and seventeenth centuries is living testimony to the desire of various groups and the individuals within them to establish a *true* Christian faith and practice. Lately, however, a number of evangelical theologians have been drawing our attention back to the Reformation *sola*s (grace alone, faith alone, etc.) as a means by which we might establish a benchmark against which continuing reformation could be measured. For example, Kevin Vanhoozer writes of the *sola*s as the means by which Protestants might retrieve the fruit of Reformation theology and hence 'look back creatively' for the purpose of 'moving forward faithfully'.[9] Alternatively, though complementarily, Goldsworthy describes the *sola*s as the basic ontological, epistemological and hermeneutical presuppositions that underline Christian faith in the gospel of salvation from the Father, through his Son and in the power of the Holy Spirit.[10] Therefore, since we are seeking to distinguish a continuing desire for reformation from the Romantic *Zeitgeist*, we shall look to the five *sola*s for guidance to ensure that it is a Christian past that we are creatively retrieving.

---

7. Alister E. McGrath, *Christianity's Dangerous Idea* (New York: Harper Collins e-books, 2007), Kindle edn, p. 3. The Peasants War in 1525 brought Luther to the realization that the 'priesthood of all believers' was an idea that was 'ultimately uncontrollable'.

8. Richard Muller comments, 'The historical analysis of Protestant orthodoxy must describe development and change, continuity and discontinuity: it ought not to postulate golden ages or optimum moments from which all else is decline.' Richard Muller, *Christ and the Decree* (Grand Rapids: Baker, 2008), p. 180.

9. Kevin Vanhoozer, *Biblical Authority after Babel: Retrieving the Solas in the Spirit of Mere Protestant Christianity* (Grand Rapids: Brazos, 2016), ebook, loc. 603.

10. Graeme Goldsworthy, *Gospel-Centred Hermeneutics* (Nottingham: Apollos, 2006), p. 39.

Reformation, retrieval and the doctrine of the Trinity

The second aspect of focus for the present essay will be a particular doctrine that underwent something of a revival or rediscovery, or possibly even a reformation, during the twentieth century, namely, the doctrine of the Trinity. The Reformers themselves, while on occasion making ambiguous statements about the doctrine, embraced the classic ecumenical tradition. Their main debates were with their more radical brethren who sought 'purely' biblical doctrines with complaints not unlike those of the Arians of the fourth century.[11] Reformers like Calvin did tend to be sceptical towards some of the traditional proof texts for the Trinity thanks to the Renaissance/Humanist-tradition reading strategies that they employed. However, Luther's works show a mellowing towards especially the Old Testament as he matured – reassessing proof texts that he originally rejected.[12]

By contrast, within the last hundred years a distinctly Modern narrative of East–West division over this most ecumenical of doctrines has fuelled both claims of the doctrine's neglect and the perceived need for its retrieval. At the time of writing, both this narrative and the 'revolutionary recovery' that followed have subsequently come under scrutiny. For example, Sarah Coakley identifies three waves in the trinitarian revival of the last century.[13] The first wave involves a reigniting of old flames by Eastern theologians like Vladimir Lossky, who sought to free the Christian tradition from Western scholasticism dating back to Augustine.[14] A parallel Protestant movement started with the work of Karl Barth, who fought for Christian theology purified from the Romanticism of Schleiermacher and his heirs.[15] A third player in this first phase was (somewhat ironically in this context) the Jesuit theologian Karl Rahner. Rahner famously bemoaned the 'mere monotheism' of many Christians and their theological

---

11. Richard Muller, 'The Doctrine of the Trinity from the Sixteenth to the Early Eighteenth Century', in Richard Muller, *The Triunity of God*, Post-Reformation Reformed Dogmatics (Grand Rapids: Baker, 2003), p. 60.

12. Ibid.

13. Sarah Coakley, 'Afterword: "Relational Ontology", Trinity and Science', in John Polkinghorne (ed.), *The Trinity and an Entangled World* (Grand Rapids: William B. Eerdmans, 2010).

14. See Lossky, *The Mystical Theology of the Eastern Church* (Crestwood: St Vladimir's Press, 1957).

15. Karl Barth, *Church Dogmatics*, Vol. 1: *The Doctrine of the Word of God*, Part 1, ed. G. W. Bromiley and T. F. Torrance, 2nd edn (Edinburgh: T&T Clark, 1975), pp. 1–47.

texts and argued instead for a Christian discipleship founded in the grace 'of the Word who is to become man'.[16]

The second wave of revolution in Coakley's portrait includes the work of theologians like John Zizioulas, who championed the reappropriation of the Trinity for the purpose of combating what he saw as Modernity's obsession with the subjective. Zizioulas, in particular, argued for an anti-Augustinian rereading of the Patristic Fathers in order to make 'relationality' more basic to personhood than the resultant individuation it provides. In favouring a particular interpretation of the Cappadocian term *hypostasis*, Zizioulas, and those who followed him,[17] declared God's being as identical 'with an act of communion'.[18] As with God, so with humanity and especially in the church, personhood *is* the relations that create distinct individuals. Again, a parallel and distinctly German Reformed alternative emerged in the work of Jürgen Moltmann, who brought similar attacks upon the Romantic idolization of the individual but, as we shall see, skirted more explicitly round the boundaries of tri-theism with his explicitly 'social' exposition of the Trinity.[19]

In keeping with Newton's third law, enough time has passed in the Trinity revival for an equal and opposite reaction to appear – this is Coakley's third wave. This reaction involves mainly re-rereadings of the Patristic and scholastic sources of the doctrine led in a somewhat Tridentine manner by Roman scholars like Lewis Ayres and Michel Barnes.[20] These authors variously dispute the

---

16. Karl Rahner, *The Trinity*, trans. Joseph Donceel, Milestones in Catholic Theology (New York: Crossroads, 1999), p. 13.

17. Coakley draws particular critical attention to the late Colin Gunton and his works, such as Colin E. Gunton, 'Augustine, the Trinity and the Theological Crisis of the West', in Colin E. Gunton, *The Promise of Trinitarian Theology* (Edinburgh: T&T Clark, 1997). See also Stanley J. Grenz, *Rediscovering the Triune God* (Minneapolis: Fortress, 2004).

18. John D. Zizioulas, *Being as Communion: Studies in Personhood and the Church*, Contemporary Greek Theologians, Vol. 4, ed. C. Yannaras et al. (Crestwood: St Vladimir's Seminary Press, 1997), p. 44.

19. Jürgen Moltmann, *The Trinity and the Kingdom of God*, trans. Margaret Kohl (London: SCM, 1981). Coakley also names his pupil Miroslav Volf, *After Our Likeness* (Grand Rapids: Eerdmans, 1998).

20. Lewis Ayres, *Nicaea and Its Legacy* (Oxford: Oxford University Press, 2004). See also Lewis Ayres, *Augustine and the Trinity* (Cambridge: Cambridge University Press, 2010); Michel R. Barnes, 'Rereading Augustine's Theology of the Trinity', in Stephen T. Davis and Gerald O'Collins (eds.), *The Trinity: An Interdisciplinary Symposium on the Trinity* (Oxford: Oxford University Press, 1999).

portrait of the Cappadocians offered by the likes of Lossky and Zizioulas and seek to redeem the contribution of Augustine to the Western tradition. In all, Ayres and those of the third wave seek to highlight the consensus between East and West on the basic issues of trinitarian conceptuality or person and relation, denouncing as Modernist prior calls for a reformation.[21] Later still, and again with some irony, Protestants in the Reformed tradition have distanced themselves from prior 'infatuations with the East' of the second wave, especially the attempts to combat Modernism by applying divine *perichoresis* to creaturely relationality, analogically or otherwise. Instead, scholars like Stephen Holmes have returned to the work of Aquinas to promote divine aseity and renounced the whole project of trinitarian revival.[22]

Whole books have been and are being written offering various alternatives to Coakley's portrait of the Trinity debates in the twentieth century,[23] which means that a comparable survey is beyond the scope of this chapter. Instead, we shall focus on a few of the more pertinent positions put forward by the chief of Protestants in the twentieth century, Karl Barth, along with the subsequent reactions from theologians in Coakley's second and third waves. Now that Protestantism has passed the half-millennium mark there is no better time to consider what could or should be meant by the phrase *semper reformanda*, particularly in an age of permanent revolution. By investigating key contributions to the doctrine of the Trinity through the lens of the five *sola*s we shall suggest some guidelines for Christians who, should the Lord tarry, anticipate a future faithful to the Reformation tradition while creatively engaging with their Protestant heritage. We begin with the first and most basic element of the gospel of salvation, *sola gratia* – by grace alone.[24]

21. Lewis Ayres, 'Into the Cloud of Witnesses: Catholic Trinitarian Theology beyond and before its Modern "Revivals"', in Giulio Maspero and Robert J. Wozniak (eds.), *Rethinking Trinitarian Theology* (London: Continuum, 2012).

22. Stephen Holmes, *The Holy Trinity* (Milton Keynes: Paternoster, 2012). See also Paul D. Molnar, *Divine Freedom and the Doctrine of the Trinity* (Edinburgh: T&T Clark, 2002). Since his recent untimely death, many have acknowledged the growing emphasis on divine aseity in the works of John Webster. See, for example, John Webster, *God without Measure: Working Papers in Christian Theology*, Vol. 1 (Edinburgh: T&T Clark, 2015).

23. For a concise summary, see Fred Sanders, 'The Trinity', in Kelly Kapic and Bruce L. McCormack (eds.), *Mapping Modern Theology* (Grand Rapids: Baker Academic, 2012).

24. Here we take Vanhoozer's point that the *sola*s were never codified in a specific order nor necessarily appeared all together in Reformation texts. See Vanhoozer, *Biblical Authority after Babel*, pp. 26ff.

Sola gratia – all from **God** alone for us

In the first instance the Reformation definition of grace alone is focused on the mechanics of salvation – one obtains the righteousness of God entirely as a divine gift. This was Luther's great discovery as he lectured on Psalms and Romans in the period 1513 to 1516.[25] Consequently the Reformers tended to concentrate on the Trinity in the work of salvation as distinct from the Trinity *in se*. The *loci communes* format for dogmatic theology allowed them to discuss the Trinity one topic at a time, especially as a consequence of exegesis.[26] This does not mean they gave no time to the immanent Trinity, but rather they kept their reflections as those from the pages of Scripture. Hence, in chapter 13 of book 1 of the *Institutes*, Calvin wrote:

> [I]t is not fitting to suppress the distinction that we observe to be expressed in Scripture. It is this: to the Father is attributed the beginning of activity, and the fountain and wellspring of all things; to the Son, wisdom, counsel, and the ordered disposition of all things; but to the Spirit is assigned the power and efficacy of that activity.[27]

In this quote we may observe the broader significance of grace for the Reformation tradition both historically and theologically. From an historical point of view Calvin's words above are a contemporary restatement of that which was handed down from the early church. Thus in the writings of St Basil of Caesarea we read: 'And remember foremost that in the creation, the Father is the original cause of all things that are made, the Son is the creative cause; the Spirit is the perfecting cause.'[28] The Reformers were seeking a *refinement* of Christian orthodoxy for the present in order to maintain *appropriate* links with the past for the sake of the gospel of salvation.

The result, from a theological point of view, was that the Reformers maintained that grace is the manner in which God relates, from first to last, to that which is not God. As we may infer from Calvin's statement, the existence of

---

25. Alister E. McGrath, *Luther's Theology of the Cross* (Grand Rapids: Baker, 1990), p. 93.

26. Muller, 'Doctrine of the Trinity', p. 64.

27. John Calvin, *Institutes of the Christian Religion*, trans. F. L. Battles, ed. J. T. McNeil (Philadelphia: Westminster Press, 1969), I.xiii.18.

28. Basil, *Sur le Saint-Esprit*, trans. Benoît Pruche, 2nd edn (Paris: Cerf, 1968), 16.38.15. Calvin does not cite Basil directly but does refer to him three chapters later in the *Institutes*, on Providence: Calvin, *Institutes*, I.xvi.8.

creation is due to the gracious initiation of the Father, given its coherence through the Son and enacted in the Spirit. Creation is, in all ways, totally contingent upon the gracious activity of God. It is within this ontological framework that the more urgent Reformation focus on salvation of sinners takes place. Salvation is from the wrath of God incurred by humanity's rejection of the triune God's gracious gift of life. The logic of this is encapsulated for us in Paul's letter to the Colossians, where the royal and eternal Son is both 'the firstborn over all creation' and the 'head of the body, the church' (Col. 1:15, 18).[29] Christ Jesus is these because 'all things have been created through him and for him', and 'through him [the Father] has reconciled all things to himself' (vv. 16, 20). We otherwise were 'alienated from God, hostile in our minds and evil deeds' (v. 21).

The rise of philosophical naturalism in the Modern period has, of course, called much if not all of this theology into question. However, it is an oversimplification to assert that all Modern naturalism is entirely atheistic. In fact, there is a deep and rich vein of pantheism running through the Romantic tradition, thanks to the likes of Spinoza.[30] The Romantics maintained a particularly organic view of the Universe, such that the 'living force of things' was a purposeful system of life 'undergoing development from the inchoate to the organised, from the indeterminate to the determinate, from the potential to the actual'.[31] The 'natural' outcome of all this is that the Universe becomes necessary to the being of God. The ancient doctrine of creation *ex nihilo* (out of nothing) had been abandoned in favour of something more palatable to Modern thought.[32]

In the twentieth century, during Coakley's 'first wave', trinitarian theologians like Barth retrieved and upheld the appropriate distinction between Creator and creation: 'God is before the world in the strictest sense that He is its absolute

---

29. All Scripture quotations are the author's translation.

30. See the chapter 'The Paradox of Romantic Metaphysics' in Beiser, *Romantic Imperative*, pp. 131–152. Even the most vociferous naturalist critics of Christianity in more contemporary times have admitted to a form of pantheism, e.g. Richard Dawkins, *The God Delusion* (London: Bantam, 2006), p. 15. Dawkins' remarks are in relation to comments made by Einstein on the grandeur of the Universe.

31. Beiser, *Romantic Imperative*, p. 142. 'Spinoza rationalises religion for the Romantics because by making God and nature the same things, science is divinised and religion becomes scientific – faith and reason no longer need be in conflict.' Ibid., p. 175.

32. See, for example, Irenaeus, 'Against Heresies,' in A. Roberts and J. Donaldson (eds.), *Ante-Nicene Fathers* (Edinburgh: T&T Clark, 1993), 2.10.14.

origin, its purpose, the power which rules it, its Lord. For He created it. Through Him it came into being and through Him it is.'[33] Yet while Barth was explicitly trinitarian when discussing God's grace towards humanity in salvation (as we shall see), his doctrine of creation lacked the presence of triune mediation that we have observed above in Calvin and the earlier tradition. Consequently, Barth's pupils (theologians of Coakley's 'second wave') were determined to reform the Christian doctrine of creation, but with mixed results.

Jürgen Moltmann's attempt to articulate the triune activity of God in creation focused on 'life-centredness' to achieve a more ecological theology of life in relation to the triune God in the light of his coming kingdom.[34] In thinking ecologically about God, Moltmann argues, 'the centre of this thinking is no longer the distinction between God and the world'.[35] Instead, the centre becomes the recognition that God is present in the world and the world is present in God. In trinitarian terms this means that the 'triune God also un-remittingly breathes the Spirit into his creation'.[36] The Father creates through the operation of the Holy Spirit, who in turn bridges the gap between the transcendent God and creation. Yet the operations of the Spirit go far beyond creating a link between different ontologies (divine and creaturely). He portrays the Spirit as the principle of evolution; it is the design of creativity on all levels. The Spirit is the design of the organic nature of creation that brings harmony and *perichoresis* within ecosystems at every level (including between God and creation).[37] In fact, Moltmann equates the Spirit of God with *the cosmic spirit*, something that the early Church Fathers were keen to avoid. As Torrance noted, 'Athanasius . . . would have nothing to do with any attempt to reach an understanding of the Spirit beginning from manifestations of the Spirit in creaturely existence, in man or in the world.'[38]

To be fair, this is only the smallest of insights into Moltmann's work, but even this leaves us with the distinct impression that in Moltmann's work the doctrine of the Trinity may well have been 'over-reformed' if not *Romantically* redefined. The use of technical language like *perichoresis* (traditionally restricted

---

33. Karl Barth, *Church Dogmatics*, Vol. 3: *The Doctrine of Creation*, Part 1, ed. G. W. Bromiley and T. F. Torrance (Edinburgh: T&T Clark, 1958), p. 7.

34. See Jürgen Moltmann, *The Source of Life* (Minneapolis: Fortress, 1997).

35. Jürgen Moltmann, *God in Creation*, trans. Margaret Kohl (London: SCM, 1985), p. 13.

36. Ibid., p. 9.

37. Ibid., p. 100.

38. T. F. Torrance, *The Trinitarian Faith* (Edinburgh: T&T Clark, 1995), p. 201.

to descriptions of the mutual constitution of the Father, Son and Spirit in the immanent life of God) in the context of the relationship between God and the world has come under criticism from theologians of Coakley's 'third wave'.[39] Most importantly in this context, as Webster has pointed out, any description of God's relationship to the world that diminishes the ontological distance between us and God likewise diminishes the absolute character of God's grace towards the world.[40] The grace of God both in creation and in redemption demands human recognition (at the very least), but the human being has no inherent ability to do this. Hence the importance of the Protestant efforts to reform the Christian concept of faith.

Sola fidei – the gift of life in the Spirit

From the perspective of the Reformation the notion of *sola fidei* – faith alone – involves both 'the ontological inability of the sinner and the epistemological priority of the Holy Spirit'.[41] Since we are 'dead in our sins' (Eph. 2:1) we are unable even to trust the promises of God without his gracious intervention. Calvin encapsulates the Reformation definition of faith thus:

> Now we shall possess a right definition of faith if we call it a firm and certain knowledge of God's benevolence toward us, founded upon the truth of the freely given promise in Christ, both revealed to our minds and sealed upon our hearts through the Holy Spirit.[42]

As a direct corollary of *sola gratia* and via the same dynamic of divine action, faith occurs exclusively as a result of the Father's initiative through his Son and by the power of his Holy Spirit. As Luther 'discovered' in Paul's letter to the church in Rome, 'in [the gospel] the righteousness of God is revealed *from faith for faith* just as it is written, "the righteous will live by faith"' (Rom. 1:17). In fact, Luther's *theologia crucis* (theology of the cross) was founded on the maxim that the truth of the gospel could only be perceived by faith in God's hidden grace

39. See Kevin Vanhoozer, *Remythologizing Theology*, Cambridge Studies in Christian Doctrine (Cambridge: Cambridge University Press, 2010), ch. 3.
40. John Webster, 'Trinity and Creation', *International Journal of Systematic Theology* 12, no. 1 (2010), pp. 4–19.
41. Goldsworthy, *Gospel-Centred Hermeneutics*, p. 50.
42. Calvin, *Institutes*, III.ii.7.

in the cross of Christ: 'He deserves to be called a theologian, however, who comprehends the visible and manifest things of God seen through suffering and the cross.'[43] The cross of Christ is the promise of the Father to us, apprehended in the Spirit's gift of faith.

In the Modern era reason took over from faith as the means by which truth could be learnt, and not only did the triune nature of God's activities *for* faith suffer, the very doctrine of the Trinity as an article of faith succumbed to rational scepticism. Kant famously wrote:

> The doctrine of the Trinity, taken literally, has no practical relevance at all, even
> if we think we understand it; and it is even more clearly irrelevant if we realize that
> it transcends all our concepts. Whether we are to worship three or ten persons in the
> Deity makes no difference.[44]

Even when a Romantic like Schleiermacher made the concession to include the Trinity in his system, it was belatedly, and was virtually dismissive: 'it is important to make the point that the main pivots of the ecclesiastical doctrine – the being of God in Christ and in the Christian Church – are independent of the doctrine of the Trinity.'[45] At the same time, and in keeping with the Romantic emphasis on self-determination and self-expression,[46] Schleiermacher incorporated the language of intuition, feeling and imagination in order to transform the Reformation understanding of faith, such that 'to feel oneself absolutely dependent and to be conscious of being in relation with God are one and the same thing'.[47]

Two things should be noted here. First, it was this complete marginalization of the doctrine of the Trinity within Christian faith that prompted those mentioned in Coakley's 'first wave' to set about the task of retrieving the doctrine. Second, and perhaps more contentiously as we shall see, it was the

---

43. Martin Luther, *Heidelberg Disputation*, in Harold J. Grimm (ed.), *Luther's Works*, Vol. 31 (Philadelphia: Muhlenberg Press, 1957), p. 40.

44. Immanuel Kant, *Religion and Rational Theology* (Cambridge: Cambridge University Press, 1996), p. 264.

45. Friedrich D. E. Schleiermacher, *The Christian Faith* (Edinburgh: T&T Clark, 1968), p. 741.

46. See Martin Seel, 'Letting Oneself Be Determined: A Revised Concept of Self-Determination', in Nikolas Kompridis (ed.), *Philosophical Romanticism* (London: Routledge, 2006).

47. Schleiermacher, *The Christian Faith*, §4.4.17.

apologetic challenge thrown down by Modern thinkers like Kant that prompted theologians in the 'second wave' to consider whether the way Christians articulate this most central of doctrines should be reformed.

In reaction to Schleiermacher on faith and the Trinity, Barth retrieved the true Reformation concepts of grace and faith by articulating the doctrine of the Trinity as the threefold movement of God towards humanity in the act of revelation. Thus, '*God* reveals Himself, He reveals Himself through *Himself*, He reveals *Himself*. . . God, the Revealer, is identical with His act in revelation and also identical with its effect'.[48] God makes himself known right down to the point at which a person is able to hear and believe his call, and this is the ordinary outworking of his triune actions towards the world. Barth considered his position of starting with the Trinity or elevating the Trinity to the head of all dogmas not simply a retrieval of Reformation theology but a reformation of the Reformers themselves: 'Even Melanchthon and Calvin, and after them Protestant orthodoxy in both confessions, followed this pattern (of dealing first with Holy Scripture or the general existence of God) in a way that was strongly uncritical.'[49] The result, according to Barth, was that the most important question, 'Who is God?', was left too late in the foundations of Christian dogma, considering that

> The doctrine of the Trinity is what basically distinguishes the Christian doctrine of God as Christian, and therefore what already distinguishes the Christian concept of revelation as Christian, in contrast to all other possible doctrines of God or concepts of Revelation.[50]

From the epistemic perspective Barth insisted on God's freedom to reveal and, in fact, his freedom in the revelation and his freedom from human attempts to comprehend that revelation: 'Godhead in the Bible means freedom, ontological and noetic autonomy.'[51] God does not become Trinity in revelation, but rather, 'revelation is the basis of the doctrine of the Trinity; the doctrine of the Trinity has no other basis apart from this'.[52] Furthermore, and in keeping with these maxims, the incarnation of the eternal Son as the royal Son, Jesus the Christ – 'the fact that God takes form' – according to Barth 'means that God

---

48. Barth, *Church Dogmatics* I/i. 296.

49. Ibid., p. 300.

50. Ibid., p. 301.

51. Ibid., p. 307.

52. Ibid., p. 312.

Himself controls not only man but also the form in which He encounters man'.[53] The holiness of God in human faith as an act of grace is revealed here similarly, because 'Holiness is the separation in which God is God and in which as God, He goes His own way even and precisely as He is "God with us".'[54]

It has been questioned by some of Coakley's 'second wave' theologians whether Barth's attempt to retrieve Reformation theology by so uniting Trinity and revelation resulted in God being 'more of a thrice-repeated I than one whose being is constituted by the communion of Father, Son and Spirit'.[55] Nevertheless, against the Romantic tide, what Barth did recover for Reformation faith was the fact that knowledge of the truth, the truth of who God is as Lord and Saviour, is a gracious act of God as he regenerates the spiritually dead for faith in the Son by the power of the Spirit. Before affection, imagination or any other sensation as cognitive activity there is faith, but, lest this be confused again, we must consider the object of our faith.

Solus Christus – but from the Father in the Spirit

The adage 'Christ alone' 'points us to the soteriological and hermeneutical priority'[56] of Jesus Christ in the gospel of salvation. It is the message proclaimed by Peter from the very beginning: 'There is salvation in no other, for there is no other name under heaven given to humanity by which we might be saved' (Acts 4:12). It is the testimony from the Lord himself to his disciples: 'I am the way, the truth and the life, no one comes to the Father except through me' (John 14:6). The Reformers sought to return the church's attention to the fact the

---

53. Ibid., p. 321.

54. Ibid., p. 322.

55. Colin E. Gunton, 'The Knowledge of God', in Colin E. Gunton, *Theology through Theologians* (Edinburgh: T&T Clark, 1996), p. 68. Gunton was critical of what he perceived to be a *lacuna* in Barth's pneumatology that either reduced the third member of the Trinity to the knowledge that Father and Son have of each other or occasionally dropped the Spirit out of the transaction. Gunton cited: 'In and for Himself He is I, the eternal, original and incomparable I . . . God is object in Himself and for Himself: in the indivisible unity of the knowledge of the Father by the Son and the Son by the Father, and therefore in his eternal and irrevocable subjectivity' (Karl Barth, *Church Dogmatics*, Vol. 2: *The Doctrine of God*, Part 1, ed. G. W. Bromiley and T. F. Torrance [Edinburgh: T&T Clark, 1957], p. 57).

56. Goldsworthy, *Gospel-Centred Hermeneutics*, p. 48.

Christ and Christ alone is the one who mediates God to humanity and humanity to God. In terms of what we have thus far discussed, Christ is to be the sole object of faith in the grace of God the Father.

In the twentieth century another of Barth's innovations to reform Christian theology in the light of Schleiermacher's Romanticism resulted in the former's concentration on the theological significance of Jesus Christ, especially in the doctrine of election: 'God's eternal will is the election of Jesus Christ.'[57] Barth was reacting against the traditional Reformed view of a double decree concerning salvation and reprobation. He reacted against this concept for a number of reasons, but chiefly because, for him, it treated the Christian God in the abstract, 'determined by the fact that both quantities [the God who chooses and the humanity he chooses] are treated as unknown'.[58] He further claimed that the concept of God choosing for creation became obscured when theologians spoke of 'the book of life' as having two columns – one for life and one for death.[59] The 'axioms of reason and/or the datum of experience'[60] led Reformed scholars to raise questions over the doctrine, with the result that 'Scripture [was] no longer able to say freely what it [willed] to say. It [could] only answer the questions put to it by man'.[61] Such questions 'put by man' included both election in view of 'God as omnipotent Will',[62] and election in view of

> what we observe to be the evident contrast between those who through the Church hear the Gospel . . . obediently and with profit, and so to salvation, and those who hear with open hostility or without any result at all and so finally to condemnation.[63]

In terms of God's relationship with creation, the former represents a rational history predetermined by absolute coherence in God, with the latter representing an empirical history governed by correspondence with creaturely reality. Barth credits Aquinas with the development of the first view of election,[64] and Augustine with the beginning of the propagation of the second view, which

---

57. Karl Barth, *Church Dogmatics*, Vol. 2: *The Doctrine of God*, Part 2, ed. G. W. Bromiley and T. F. Torrance (Edinburgh: T&T Clark, 1957), p. 146.

58. Ibid.

59. Ibid., II/ii.16.

60. Ibid., II/ii.3.

61. Ibid., II/ii.41.

62. Ibid., II/ii.44.

63. Ibid., II/ii.38.

64. Ibid., II/ii.45.

flows through Calvin and on into the Reformed tradition.[65] Against the latter tradition, and Calvin in particular as the architect, Barth argued that the 'facts' of election and/or divine decree could be concretely determined only in the gospel of the Lord Jesus Christ: 'Its direct and proper object is not individuals generally, but one individual – and only in Him the people called and united by Him, and only in that people individuals in general in their private relationship with God.'[66] Christ Jesus is *the* elect man, but, of course, he is also the God who elects:

> Who and what is the God who rules and feeds His people, creating and maintaining the whole world for its benefit, and guiding it according to His own good-pleasure? ... If in this way we ask further concerning the one point upon which, according to Scripture, our attention and thoughts should and must be concentrated, then from first to last the Bible directs us to the name of Jesus Christ.[67]

Thus the Lord Jesus is both the electing God and the Elected human. This is the clear and concrete teaching of Scripture on the subject, in Barth's view, and therefore the starting place for discerning both the will of God and the meaning of history. In the context of grace, God is in no way compelled, especially by humanity, to be God this way, and hence his decision for man is both free and loving. Nevertheless, 'in a free act of determination God has ordained concerning Himself ... God has put Himself under obligation to man.'[68]

Barth's Christocentrism has come under intense scrutiny from church historians and systematic theologians alike. From an historical perspective, Barth's version of *solus Christus*, based on his reading of predestination in the Reformed tradition, has been dismissed by the likes of Richard Muller:

> Nowhere in this older theology [of the sixteenth and seventeenth centuries] do we encounter the problem of the *Deus nudus absconditus* – certainly not as Barth defines it. Nor ... does Barth's collapsing of election in Christ, so that the electing and elected

---

65. Ibid., II/ii.39. To be fair, Barth acknowledges that Calvin did not base his doctrine of predestination on experience: 'But he [Calvin] did buttress his doctrine so emphatically by the appeal to it that we can hardly fail to recognise that much of the pathos and emotional power with which he defended it ... was determined by his experience' (ibid.).

66. Ibid., II/ii.43.

67. Ibid., II/ii.53.

68. Ibid., II/ii.101.

Mediator is also the only elect and only reprobate man, stand in any real relation to
the theological material on which he has commented and from which he takes the
clue to his solution to the doctrinal problem that he has posed.[69]

For Muller, Barth's contribution could not really be considered a reformation
because it solved a problem that did not actually exist – there was no 'hidden
God' or 'unknown God' in the tradition.

From a more systematic and specifically trinitarian perspective, 'second wave'
theologians like Colin Gunton contended with Barth's *solus Christus* because too
much attention was being given to the divine nature of Christ at the expense
of his humanity. Many others in the Reformed tradition had already expressed
concern about Barth's doctrine of election insofar as it is difficult not to read
the latter as claiming that all humanity is ultimately the church of Christ.[70] In
addition, and in terms of God's choice, Gunton was keen to remind us that in
keeping with triune grace, both initiation and *continuance* of faith are a gift from
God. In the more protologically focused discussions of God's choice Gunton
notes a movement away from 'grace mediated communally', that is, away from
church as communion towards an individual, inward experience of grace, on
the one hand, and, on the other, away from the eschatological enabling of
humans by the Spirit towards a 'conception of grace as a semisubstantial force
either assisting or determining human perseverance causally'.[71] What is lost here
is the sense in which 'the Lord who is the Spirit' personally mediates the will of
God in the economy of salvation (2 Cor. 3:17–18). In line with what we have
been exploring, Gunton suggests, against Barth, that we ought to understand
the Spirit as the electing God. For it is the Spirit who 'gathers the Church to the
Father through Christ and in order that his will be done on earth'.[72] In this way
we might distinguish the Spirit's creating work, which is universal, from the

---

69. Richard Muller, 'What I Haven't Learned from Karl Barth', *The Reformed Journal* 37,
    no. 3 (1987), p. 17. In a different context, and far more harshly, Muller remarks of
    Barth's *solus Christus*, 'it turns radically away from the concrete historical existence
    of Jesus Christ and finds its basis in an extrapolation, a dogmatic abstraction, off of
    a series of doctrinal concepts'. Richard Muller, 'The Place and Importance of Karl
    Barth in the Twentieth Century: A Review Essay', *WTJ* 50 (1988), p. 150.
70. Colin E. Gunton, *The Promise of Trinitarian Theology*, 2nd edn (Edinburgh:
    T&T Clark, 1997), p. 66. Gunton cites Barth, *Church Dogmatics*, II/ii.67.
71. Colin E. Gunton, 'Election and Ecclesiology in the Post-Constantinian Age',
    in Colin E. Gunton, *Intellect and Action* (Edinburgh: T&T Clark, 2000), p. 146.
72. Ibid., p. 129.

Spirit's perfecting work, which though it achieves a universal end in all things being summed up in Christ Jesus (Eph. 1:9–10), is achieved through the particulars of the election of Israel and the resurrection of Christ Jesus from the dead. Calvin draws out this distinction in his commentary on Romans 8:14:

> But it is right to observe, that the working of the Spirit is various: for there is that which is universal, by which all creatures are sustained and preserved; there is that also which is peculiar to men, and varying in its character: but what Paul means here is sanctification, with which the Lord favours none but his own elect, and by which he separates them for sons to himself.[73]

Barth's *solus Christus* was certainly an imaginative look to the past, but the possibilities for faithfully moving forward are hampered by his historical reconstruction and the insufficiently trinitarian shape of his position. Nevertheless, Barth's insistence on the biblical character of his innovation brings us to one of the critical issues in the cry for *semper reformanda*, the reading of Scripture.

Sola scriptura – reading for reform

Appealing to Scripture alone has invariably caused vexation when it comes to the doctrine of the Trinity.[74] When Luther or Calvin first invoked this principle of *sola scriptura* they were seeking to relativize the authority of the Church Fathers and councils in relation to the Bible. In fact, 'the reformers insisted that the authority of Popes, councils and theologians is subordinate to that of the Scripture'.[75] Whatever authority might be ascribed to certain theologians or councils was derived from the Bible. Calvin summed up the relationship like this:

> For, although we hold that the Word of God alone lies beyond the sphere of our judgment, and that Fathers and Councils are of authority only in so far as they accord

---

73. John Calvin, *Romans* (Albany: AGES Software, 1998), CD ROM, pp. 227f.

74. In the fourth century AD Arians infamously complained that trinitarian language was not in the Bible – they too wanted Scripture alone. See Justo L. González, *A History of Christian Thought*, rev edn, Vol. 1 (Nashville: Abingdon Press, 1987), pp. 261ff.

75. Alister E. McGrath, *Reformation Thought* (Oxford: Blackwell, 1993), p. 142.

with the rule of the Word, we still give to Councils and Fathers such rank and honor as it is meet for them to hold, under Christ.[76]

One consequence of this stance towards tradition, particularly in the earlier period of the Reformation, was that the Reformers were reluctant to use some of the trinitarian language for God that was not taken directly from Scripture. According to Muller, it was not until around 1540, when 'the rise of anti-trinitarian teachings demanded [a] response from the reformers [that] the usefulness of traditional dogmatic language became increasingly evident'.[77] We can get a sense of the tensions involved in the following quote from Calvin's 1536 *Institutes*:

> That *ousia, hypostasis, essence*, persons, are names invented by human decision, nowhere read or seen in the Scriptures. But since they cannot shake our conviction that three are spoken of who are one God, what sort of squeamishness is it to disapprove of words that explain nothing else than what is attested and sealed by Scripture . . . what prevents us from explaining in clearer words those matters in Scripture which perplex and hinder our understanding yet which faithfully serve the truth of Scripture itself, and are made use of sparingly and modestly and not at the wrong occasion.[78]

The traditional language, though an addition to Scripture, can and should be invoked (judiciously) since it arises from the Scriptures and enhances our understanding of the truth those same Scriptures teach.

From what we have already seen, it was Barth's determination to have the exegesis of Scripture govern theology that prompted his reformulations of Christian faith as trinitarian and christological. When it came to the traditional language used in discussing Father, Son and Spirit Barth seemed equally concerned, if not more so, to ensure that Modern notions of 'personality' were kept distinct from the traditional language of persons in the Godhead: '"Person" as used in the Church doctrine of the Trinity bears no direct relation to personality.'[79] Barth's agenda here is to address divine being in an appropriate manner in the context of Romantic pantheism: 'The concept of the "personality" of

---

76. John Calvin, 'Reply by John Calvin to Cardinal Sadolet's Letter', in Henry Beveridge and Jules Bonnet (eds.), *Selected Works of John Calvin: Tracts Part 1* (Albany: AGES Software, 1998), p. 127.
77. Muller, 'Doctrine of the Trinity', p. 60.
78. Calvin, *Institutes* (1536), II.8; cited in ibid., p. 66.
79. Barth, *Church Dogmatics*, I/i.351.

God . . . is a product of the battle against modern naturalism and pantheism.'[80] Barth understood himself to be more diligent than the Western scholastic tradition in insisting that God is a personal agent, 'He, not an It', in relation to the world.[81] Consequently, the classic Latin concept of *persona* used to describe Father, Son and Spirit ought to be kept quite distinct from anything that could likewise be used of a human person: '"Person" as used in the Church doctrine of the Trinity bears no direct relation to personality.'[82] Even so, the question down through the ages has been the same: what do we mean when we use this term *persona* to describe each of Father, Son and Spirit in the one essence that is God? Having reviewed the history of attempts to define *persona* (or the Greek *hypostasis*), Barth concluded with Augustine, 'A really suitable term for it just does not exist.'[83] Nevertheless he did not reject the ancient terminology so much as seek to accommodate the classic intention to his temporal context: 'we do not use the term "person" but rather "mode (or way) of being", our intention being to express by this term, not absolutely, but relatively better and more simply and clearly the same things as is meant by "person."'[84] Barth wanted the central focus to be on the fact that God is God in a particular way – as Father and as Son and as Holy Spirit. He wanted neither participation in the divine essence nor 'the rational nature' of each to be the defining characteristic of *persona*.

Of course, in the context of discussing *sola scriptura* and with the guidance given by Calvin, the key question to put to Barth is whether his reform made any positive difference to understanding the truth of the Bible. At least in §9.2 of *Church Dogmatics*, where Barth introduces the term, his only direct appeal to Scripture is to Hebrews 1:3 – 'the son is the exact representation of God's being/nature [*hypostasis*]' – and this for the purpose of showing that Calvin basically agrees.[85] However, Barth was never one for proof texts. His holistic approach to the canon of Scripture, with prophets anticipating and apostles

---

80. Ibid.

81. Ibid., I/i.350.

82. Ibid., I/i.351.

83. Ibid., I/i.355. Barth appeals to Augustine's *De Trinitate* V.9 & VII.4; see Augustine, *The Trinity*, The Works of Saint Augustine, Vol. 5 (New York: New City Press, 1991).

84. Barth, *Church Dogmatics*, I/i.358.

85. Strictly speaking, Barth notes, 'in the *Congregation* [*de la divinité de Christ*] quoted earlier he [Calvin] expressly declared that with the Greeks, and on account of the Biblical basis in Heb. 1:3, he would regard the word . . . *hypostasis* as [most fit] in this matter.' Ibid., I/i.360.

reflecting on the Christ, was grounded in the understanding that the triune God testifies to himself in the whole of it.[86] For Barth, the Bible narrative renders the agency of Jesus Christ the exclusive mediator of God the Father.[87] Nevertheless, despite the language of 'modes of being' appearing in various contexts throughout *Church Dogmatics*,[88] the reform added little of significance and caused many to suspect the ancient heresy of Modalism.[89] Barth's desire to remove the Modern baggage[90] of 'personality' from the equation retrieved the necessarily abstract character of the traditional language, but, at the same time, restricted the sense in which we might talk about the '*dramatis dei personae*', or Father, Son and Spirit as 'characters of the drama of God'[91] whom the narrative of the Scriptures 'attests and seals' as Calvin preferred. In the fourth century, and in the sixteenth, the issue of non-biblical language in the doctrine of the Trinity was solved, not by appeals to Scripture alone (*scriptura nudus*) but by the reading strategies for Scripture invoked by the likes of Athanasius and Calvin. Devices

---

86. Francis Watson, 'The Bible', in John Webster (ed.), *The Cambridge Companion to Karl Barth* (Cambridge: Cambridge University Press, 2000), p. 64.

87. David H. Kelsey, *The Uses of Scripture in Recent Theology* (Philadelphia: Fortress, 1975), pp. 39ff.

88. Distinguishing Father and Son Barth writes, 'it is not the one nature of God as such with whose operation we have to do here. It is the one nature of God in the mode of existence of the Son, which became Man.' Karl Barth, *Church Dogmatics*, Vol. 1: *The Doctrine of the Word of God*, Part 1, ed. G. W. Bromiley and T. F. Torrance (Edinburgh: T&T Clark, 1956), p. 33. See also especially against *Patripassionism*, 'It is not at all the case that God has no part in the suffering of Jesus Christ, even in His mode of being as the Father . . . The suffering is not His own but the alien suffering of the creature, of man.' Karl Barth, *Church Dogmatics*, Vol. 4: *The Doctrine of Reconciliation*, Part 2, ed. G. W. Bromiley and T. F. Torrance (Edinburgh: T&T Clark, 1958), p. 357.

89. Some of Barth's pupils were not so much suspicious as convinced of Barth's heresy. Moltmann was direct in his assessment of the change from 'person' to 'mode' as 'a late triumph for Sabellian modalism'. Moltmann, *Trinity and the Kingdom of God*, p. 139. For a more measured assessment, see Michael J. Ovey, 'A Private Love? Karl Barth and the Triune God', in David Gibson and Daniel Strange (eds.), *Engaging With Barth* (Nottingham: Apollos, 2008).

90. Oliver O'Donovan, *Resurrection and Moral Order: An Outline for Evangelical Ethics* (Leicester: Apollos, 1994), p. 238.

91. Robert W. Jenson, *Systematic Theology*, Vol. 1 (New York/Oxford: Oxford University Press, 1997), p. 75.

like the five *solas* can create a reading strategy to govern our desire for *semper reformanda* that retrieves the best of Scripture, tradition and reason. To expand on this proposal, we shall bring this chapter to a conclusion with the help of the fifth *sola* (in this list).

Soli Deo gloria – for the Father, through the Son and in the Spirit

Perhaps the least contentious and therefore least defined of the *solas* was this last one, 'for the glory of God alone'. Both Protestants and Roman Catholics considered themselves to be serving this purpose; the disagreements rested on what they thought of each other's efforts – whether the revolution could be considered doxological or heretical.[92] Most agree, therefore, that this last 'alone' is the sum of all that which might precede it, regardless of the order in which they are expounded. Of course, our goal throughout has been to develop an understanding of continual reformation that is distinct from the Romantic mantra of perpetual revolution. Romantics have always had a fraught relationship with history: 'How can we begin anew and "yet remain authentic to what we have been"?'[93] From a Romantic perspective, trinitarian theology is a prime example of Wittgenstein's game theory of language.[94] Creative retrieval for the sake of faithful progress depends on ensuring that our language bears a sufficient number of 'familial resemblances'[95] in order to satisfy the rules of orthodox engagement. The key terminology is extra-biblical and therefore historically arbitrary. Yet, in order to grasp the significance of biblical language like 'Jesus, full of joy through the Holy Spirit, [praying] said, "I praise you, Father, Lord of heaven and earth"' (Luke 10:21), Christians in the Reformation tradition have to engage with the terminology of 'person' or 'relation', or even *perichoresis*.[96] However, in order to claim legitimately that one is always reforming, and this for the glory of God alone, one must commit to a process governed

---

92. Vanhoozer, *Biblical Authority after Babel*, p. 182.

93. David Kolb, 'Authenticity with Teeth', in Nikolas Kompridis (ed.), *Philosophical Romanticism* (London: Routledge, 2006), p. 51.

94. Ludwig Wittgenstein, *Philosophical Investigations*, trans. P. M. S. Hacker and J. Schulte, 4th edn (Oxford: Wiley-Blackwell, 2009).

95. Ibid., p. 65.

96. John Colwell, 'Reflecting on the Trinitarian Grammar of Intimacy and Substance', in T. A. Noble and Jason S. Sexton (eds.), *The Holy Trinity Revisited* (Milton Keynes: Paternoster, 2015).

by grace, through faith in Christ, as portrayed in Holy Scripture. In terms of our Modern trinitarian theology case study, and particularly now with reference to Coakley's second and third waves, our exposition of the *sola*s, albeit brief, has provided us with a number of principles for distinguishing reform from revolution as we creatively engage with the past for the sake of faithfully facing the future.

So, then, we shall glorify God through devotion to his grace. This is the critical description of God's relating to that which is not God in the economy of salvation for his creation. The ontological divide between Creator and creation means that all language seeking to expand on an account of the incarnate Son speaking to the Father in the Spirit (as above) must be analogical. Nevertheless, the relationship between the immanent and the economic Trinity – how God relates within himself in eternity as Father, Son and Spirit compared with how the Father relates to the Son in the Spirit in the economy of salvation – has been a critical issue in calls for trinitarian reform as well as in the later 'counter-Reformation'.[97] When Karl Rahner famously asserted that '"economic" Trinity is the "immanent" Trinity and the "immanent" Trinity is the "economic" Trinity', it was to uphold the doctrine of grace by ensuring that the same God who saves in history is the God worshipped in eternity, and this God is worshipped in eternity because he graciously intervenes in history for salvation.[98] Hence, when the Scriptures portray moments of interaction between Father, Son and Spirit, we take these as gifts of grace that enable genuine insights into the life of the eternal God, even if they are not exhaustive.

Consequently, we glorify God by understanding our triune faith as a gift of his grace. The wonder of the gospel of salvation is that the Father mediates new life to sinners in the power of his Spirit *for faith* in and through the righteous sacrifice of his Son, Jesus the crucified and risen Messiah. Our faith in this saving act and the triune God who effects, forms and finalizes our reconciliation with him is all a gift of grace. Furthermore, in the church that the Father constitutes by his Spirit for faith in his Son, Jesus Christ, Christians are blessed with a relation of sonship in the Spirit, 'as we cry Abba, Father' (Rom. 8:14–16). Hence our language for God is, in Barth's words, an analogy of faith (*analogia fidei*).[99] Our language is shaped by the dynamics of God the Father initiating restoration of a familial relationship with him, through his Son and in the power of his Spirit (see John 1:12–13). The dynamics of this relationship are founded

---

97. See Sanders, 'The Trinity', passim.
98. Rahner, *The Trinity*, pp. 22–23.
99. Barth, *Church Dogmatics*, I/i.243–244.

on the *sui generis perichoresis* of Father, Son and Spirit in eternity, yet, as Calvin's remarks imply, divine relationality is genuinely and formatively experienced by creatures as the Spirit perfects the 'wisdom, counsel and ordered disposition' of the Son for the Father in creation.[100]

The key qualifier for this description of eternal relations being prescriptive for creaturely relationships through the lens of the economy of salvation is that the trinitarian fullness of divine life is mediated to creation through Christ *alone* in the Spirit. God is ultimately glorified by his creation when in Christ Jesus alone divine life and human life come together with the ontological distinction between them upheld in the power of the Holy Spirit. The immanent life of the eternal God is opened by the Spirit to include creation, but only and exclusively in the union between the eternal and royal Son, Messiah Jesus (Rom. 1:3–4). In the power of his Spirit, Christ unites us to himself in faith, and through him, our great High Priest (Heb. 7:26), we enjoy, in the Spirit, Christ's eternal life with the Father. One consequence of this position is, however, that our understanding of the personhood of the eternal Son is generated from the career of the royal Son.[101] This is more than the traditional approach of defining divine personhood through 'relations of origin' or that 'the Son is eternally begotten of the Father'.[102] Yet, as Colin Gunton argued,

> The Father who begets and the Son who is begotten are together one God in the
> [communion] of the Spirit. They are one because the Son and the Spirit are, in
> a sense, though God as subordinate in the eternal [order] as they are in the economy.
> But in another sense they are not subordinate, for without his Son and Spirit, God
> would not be God.[103]

---

100. See above combining Calvin, *Institutes*, I.xiii.18, and Calvin, *Romans*, pp. 227f.

101. Colin E. Gunton, *Act and Being* (London: SCM Press, 2002), p. 136.

102. Something proposed by 'second wave' theologians like Pannenberg (Wolfhart Pannenberg, *Systematic Theology*, Vol. 1 [Edinburgh: T&T Clark, 1988], pp. 308–313), although in his case with an at times unhelpfully significant role for history in the life of God.

103. Colin E. Gunton, 'And in One Lord Jesus Christ . . . Begotten Not Made', in Colin E. Gunton, *Father, Son and Holy Spirit* (London: Continuum, 2003), p. 73. Talk of subordination in a trinitarian context immediately raises the spectre of Arianism. Yet Gunton qualified the above with, 'His [the Son's] proper autonomy derives rather from the freedom, given by the Spirit, to be the kind of subordinate Son that he is.' Ibid., p. 72.

Finally, we speak of Jesus as the royal and eternal Son of the Father in the Sprit in an attempt to glorify the God whom the grand narrative of the Bible portrays. The apostolic testimony of the New Testament configures many threads of historic and prophetic anticipation in the identities of the Son of God, the servant of YHWH or the chosen leader/saviour of God's people. Each of these characters depicts YHWH mediating his will and power for salvation in the Spirit – whether it is Moses (Num. 11:25), David (1 Sam. 17) or the more mysterious Servant of YHWH (Isa. 11; 61). Yet all of these are brought together with the resurrection of Jesus of Nazareth. Hence, with the outpouring of the Holy Spirit at Pentecost, the apostles proclaimed that this man Jesus, 'whom you crucified, God has made Lord and Messiah' (Acts 2:36).[104] The Spirit revealed to the apostles the presence of the eternal Son, the Logos who tabernacled among us (John 1:14), in the words and deeds of the Spirit-endowed Messiah (Isa. 61; cf. Luke 4:14). Even the humble details of Jesus' birth, in the Spirit, fulfilled the ancient promise that 'God is with us' (Luke 1:35; Matt. 1:22–23; cf. Isa. 7:14) – the recognition of which became for the apostles their anticipation of the universal and everlasting glorification of God the Father, since 'at the name of Jesus, every knee shall bow . . . and every tongue confess that Jesus Christ is Lord to the glory of God the Father' (Phil. 2:10–11). If the Scriptures are to have their preeminent authority desired by the Reformers, the narrative dynamics that we have explored to describe the gracious activity of God in creation through his Son and in his Spirit must play a role in determining the *form* of trinitarian language, not just its *content*. That is, regardless of the possible historical reconstructions of Eastern/Western debate over the definition of person, relation or even *perichoresis*,[105] the Son's interactions with the Father in the Spirit as recorded in Scripture must be admissible as the divine

---

104. Stephen Holmes, as the current leader of the 'third wave', is highly critical of trinitarian theology that rests too heavily on the New Testament and Gospel accounts in particular at the expense of the Old Testament resources employed by the Church Fathers: Stephen Holmes, *The Quest for the Trinity* (Downer's Grove: IVP Academic, 2012). While it is easy to agree that trinitarian theology that fails to acknowledge the apostolic dependence on 'the Law, the Prophets and the Writings' (see Luke 24:44) for its exposition is not in keeping with the tradition, not all reading strategies are the same despite their ecclesial pedigree. The Fathers' allegorical expositions of poetry or wisdom literature, not to mention the extra-canonical material, must be considered of less value to trinitarian theology than attention to the more accessible narratives of God's actions in creation for salvation.
105. See above Coakley's summary of twentieth-century trinitarian theology.

accommodation for an *analogia relationis* between the economic and the immanent Trinity. Barth famously coined the term in discussing the 'image of God' as used for humanity, stating,

> If the humanity of Jesus is the image of God, this means that it is only indirectly and not directly identical with God. It belongs intrinsically to the creaturely world . . . it does not belong to the inner sphere of the essence . . . *It does not present God in Himself and in His relation to Himself, but in His relation to the reality distinct from Himself.*[106]

Insofar as Barth goes on to discuss 'the image' in relation to those descended from Adam, it is easy to agree with him. However, if we may repeat the passage from Luke 10:21 quoted above, when 'Jesus, full of joy through the Holy Spirit, [praying] said, "I praise you, Father, Lord of heaven and earth"', ought we not to consider ourselves privy to a moment of divine self-communication, that here we do indeed have God in himself and in relation to himself? If Jesus Christ 'is the image of the invisible God . . . in whom all the fullness of God dwells in bodily form', as Paul tells the church in Colosse (Col. 1:15, 19; 2:9), ought we not to consider moments of divine interpersonal communication like Luke 10, Matthew 23:36–46 or John 17 as exemplary of God's immanent life? That in the Spirit-empowered discourse of the royal Son with his heavenly Father we also hear creaturely accessible echoes of the eternal Son's spiritual fellowship with God the Father?[107] If so, we could infer that the dynamics of relating that occur between Father, Son and Spirit as characters in the Gospel accounts (for example) are another kind of accommodation by God to creatures similar to that which Calvin proposed.[108] Keeping in mind the principles

---

106. Karl Barth, *Church Dogmatics*, Vol. 3: *The Doctrine of Creation*, Part 2, ed. G. W. Bromiley and T. F. Torrance (Edinburgh: T&T Clark, 1960), p. 219. Emphasis added.

107. For a more extensive treatment of these issues from a similar perspective, see Michael J. Ovey, *Your Will Be Done: Exploring Eternal Subordination, Divine Monarchy and Divine Humility* (London: Latimer Trust, 2016).

108. See Calvin, *Institutes*, I.xiii.1. Significantly, perhaps, Calvin here discusses divine accommodation in relation to anthropomorphisms of God's nature in Scripture, but then immediately proceeds to discuss 'The Three "Persons" in God'. Calvin defends the traditional trinitarian language of person 'because some hatefully inveigh against the word . . . as if humanly devised' (ibid., I.xiii.2). The Reformer stops short of acknowledging the terminology of *hypostasis/persona* as a divine accommodation, even though the first term comes directly from Heb. 1:3.

established in our first three *sola*s, from this we could infer that divine person-hood is the product of mutually constitutive relations analogous to characters established by their interactions in the plot of a narrative: the scriptural narrative being *sui generis* for narrativity as opposed to a projection of human culture on to divine life.[109] In this way *sola scriptura* serves as a discipline applied to the extra-biblical language of the tradition, such that 'Persons are those particular beings – *hypostases* – whose attributes are manifested in particular kinds of action, such as love, relationality, freedom, creativity'.[110]

Conclusion

The Romantic struggle for authenticity in the present results in the need to revolt perpetually against the past and reinvent the future, as we have seen. By way of contrast, *semper reformanda*, when organized by the five *sola*s, consists of creatively retrieving the past in order faithfully to anticipate the future. In terms of our case-study doctrine, the last hundred years have, in Coakley's account, brought wave upon wave of deliberation and debate over the being and activity of the triune God – especially the perceived (or otherwise) 'problems to be solved, opportunities to be seized, resources to be appropriated [and] dangers to be avoided'.[111] Our far too brief engagement with Barth's contributions may well be judged to have weighed more in terms of problems and dangers than in resources and opportunities. Nevertheless, while ever the church meets the problems of theological language with the resources of Scripture appropriated through the gospel of grace, the dangers of reformation will be eclipsed by the promise of a faith initiated, formed and perfected by the Father, through the Son and in the Holy Spirit.

Bibliography

Atherstone, Andrew, 'The Implications of *Semper Reformanda*', *Anvil* 26, no. 1 (2009), pp. 31–42.
Augustine, *The Trinity*, The Works of St Augustine, Vol. 5, New York: New City Press, 1991.

---

109. John Webster, *Holy Scripture* (Cambridge: Cambridge University Press, 2003).
110. Gunton, *Act and Being*, pp. 146f.
111. John Frame, 'Foreword', in A. T. B. McGowan (ed.), *Always Reforming* (Leicester: Apollos, 2006).

Ayres, Lewis, *Augustine and the Trinity*, Cambridge: Cambridge University Press, 2010.

———, 'Into the Cloud of Witnesses: Catholic Trinitarian Theology beyond and before its Modern "Revivals"', in Giulio Maspero and Robert J. Wozniak (eds.), *Rethinking Trinitarian Theology*, London: Continuum, 2012.

———, *Nicaea and Its Legacy*, Oxford: Oxford University Press, 2004.

Barnes, Michel R., 'Rereading Augustine's Theology of the Trinity', in Stephen T. Davis and Gerald O'Collins (eds.), *The Trinity: An Interdisciplinary Symposium on the Trinity*, 145–176, Oxford: Oxford University Press, 1999.

Barth, Karl, *Church Dogmatics*, Vol. 1: *The Doctrine of the Word of God*, Part 1, ed. G. W. Bromiley and T. F. Torrance, Edinburgh: T&T Clark, 1956.

———, *Church Dogmatics*, Vol. 1: *The Doctrine of the Word of God*, Part 1, ed. G. W. Bromiley and T. F. Torrance, 2nd edn, Edinburgh: T&T Clark, 1975.

———, *Church Dogmatics*, Vol. 2: *The Doctrine of God*, Part 1, ed. G. W. Bromiley and T. F. Torrance, Edinburgh: T&T Clark, 1957.

———, *Church Dogmatics*, Vol. 2: *The Doctrine of God*, Part 2, ed. G. W. Bromiley and T. F. Torrance, Edinburgh: T&T Clark, 1957.

———, *Church Dogmatics*, Vol. 3: *The Doctrine of Creation*, Part 1, ed. G. W. Bromiley and T. F. Torrance, Edinburgh: T&T Clark, 1958.

———, *Church Dogmatics*, Vol. 3: *The Doctrine of Creation*, Part 2, ed. G. W. Bromiley and T. F. Torrance, Edinburgh: T&T Clark, 1960.

———, *Church Dogmatics*, Vol. 4: *The Doctrine of Reconciliation*, Part 2, ed. G. W. Bromiley and T. F. Torrance, Edinburgh: T&T Clark, 1958.

Basil, *Sur le Saint-Esprit*, trans. Benoît Pruche, 2nd edn, Paris: Cerf, 1968.

Beiser, Frederick C., *The Romantic Imperative*, Cambridge, MA: Harvard University Press, 2003.

Berlin, Isaiah, *The Roots of Romanticism*, London: Pimlico, 2000.

Blanning, Tim, *The Romantic Revolution*, New York: Modern Library Chronicles, 2010.

Calvin, John, *Institutes of the Christian Religion*, trans. F. L. Battles, ed. J. T. McNeil, Philadelphia: Westminster, 1969.

———, 'Reply by John Calvin to Cardinal Sadolet's Letter', in Henry Beveridge and Jules Bonnet (eds.), *Selected Works of John Calvin: Tracts Part 1*, 91–129, Albany: AGES Software, 1998.

———, *Romans*, Albany: AGES Software, 1998, CD ROM.

Coakley, Sarah, 'Afterword: "Relational Ontology", Trinity and Science', in John Polkinghorne (ed.), *The Trinity and an Entangled World*, Grand Rapids: Eerdmans, 2010.

Colwell, John, 'Reflecting on the Trinitarian Grammar of Intimacy and Substance', in T. A. Noble and Jason S. Sexton, *The Holy Trinity Revisited*, Milton Keynes: Paternoster, 2015.

Dawkins, Richard, *The God Delusion*, London: Bantam, 2006.

Frame, John, 'Foreword', in A. T. B. McGowan (ed.), *Always Reforming*, Leicester: Apollos, 2006.

Goldsworthy, Graeme, *Gospel-Centred Hermeneutics*, Nottingham: Apollos, 2006.

González, Justo L., *A History of Christian Thought*, rev. edn, Vol. 1, Nashville: Abingdon Press, 1987.

Grenz, Stanley J., *Rediscovering the Triune God*, Minneapolis: Fortress, 2004.

Gunton, Colin E., *Act and Being*, London: SCM Press, 2002.

———, 'And in One Lord Jesus Christ . . . Begotten Not Made', in Colin E. Gunton, *Father, Son and Holy Spirit*, 58–74, London: Continuum, 2003.

———, 'Augustine, the Trinity and the Theological Crisis of the West', in Colin E. Gunton, *The Promise of Trinitarian Theology*, 30–48, Edinburgh: T&T Clark, 1997.

———, 'Election and Ecclesiology in the Post-Constantinian Age', in Colin E. Gunton, *Intellect and Action*, 139–155, Edinburgh: T&T Clark, 2000.

———, 'The Knowledge of God', in Colin E. Gunton, *Theology through Theologians*, 50–69, Edinburgh: T&T Clark, 1996.

———, *The Promise of Trinitarian Theology*, 2nd edn, Edinburgh: T&T Clark, 1997.

Holmes, Richard, *The Age of Wonder: How the Romantic Generation Discovered the Beauty and Terror of Science*, New York: Vintage, 2008.

Holmes, Stephen, *The Holy Trinity*, Milton Keynes: Paternoster, 2012.

———, *The Quest for the Trinity*, Downer's Grove: IVP Academic, 2012.

Irenaeus, 'Against Heresies', in A. Roberts and J. Donaldson (eds.), *Ante-Nicene Fathers*, 309–568, Edinburgh: T&T Clark, 1993.

Jenson, Robert W., *Systematic Theology*, New York/Oxford: Oxford University Press, 1997.

Kant, Immanuel, *Religion and Rational Theology*, Cambridge: Cambridge University Press, 1996.

Kelsey, David H., *The Uses of Scripture in Recent Theology*, Philadelphia: Fortress, 1975.

Kolb, David, 'Authenticity with Teeth', in Nikolas Kompridis (ed.), *Philosophical Romanticism*, London: Routledge, 2006.

Lossky, *The Mystical Theology of the Eastern Church*, Crestwood: St Vladimir's Press, 1957.

Luther, Martin, *Heidelberg Disputation*, in Harold J. Grimm (ed.), *Luther's Works*, Vol. 31 Philadelphia: Muhlenberg Press, 1957.

McGowan, A. T. B., 'Introduction', in A. T. B. McGowan (ed.), *Always Reforming*, 13–18, Leicester: Apollos, 2006.

McGrath, Alister E., *Christianity's Dangerous Idea*, New York: Harper Collins e-books, 2007, Kindle edn.

———, *Luther's Theology of the Cross*, Grand Rapids: Baker, 1990.

———, *Reformation Thought*, Oxford: Blackwell, 1993.

Molnar, Paul D., *Divine Freedom and the Doctrine of the Trinity*, Edinburgh: T&T Clark, 2002.

Moltmann, Jürgen, *God in Creation*, trans. Margaret Kohl, London: SCM, 1985.

———, *The Source of Life*, Minneapolis: Fortress, 1997.

———, *The Trinity and the Kingdom of God*, trans. Margaret Kohl, London: SCM, 1981.

Muller, Richard, *Christ and the Decree*, Grand Rapids: Baker, 2008.

———, 'The Doctrine of the Trinity from the Sixteenth to the Early Eighteenth Century', in Richard Muller, *The Triunity of God*, Post-Reformation Reformed Dogmatics, 59–140, Grand Rapids: Baker, 2003.

———, 'The Place and Importance of Karl Barth in the Twentieth Century: A Review Essay', *WTJ* 50 (1988), pp. 127–156.

———, 'What I Haven't Learned from Karl Barth', *The Reformed Journal* 37, no. 3 (1987), pp. 16–18.

O'Donovan, Oliver, *Resurrection and Moral Order: An Outline for Evangelical Ethics*, Leicester: Apollos, 1994.

Ovey, Michael J., 'A Private Love? Karl Barth and the Triune God', in David Gibson and Daniel Strange (eds.), *Engaging with Barth*, 198–231, Nottingham: Apollos, 2008.

———, *Your Will Be Done: Exploring Eternal Subordination, Divine Monarchy and Divine Humility*, London: Latimer Trust, 2016.

Ozment, Steven, *Protestants: The Birth of a Revolution*, New York: Doubleday, 1992.

Pannenberg, Wolfhart, *Systematic Theology*, Vol. 1, Edinburgh: T&T Clark, 1988.

Rahner, Karl, *The Trinity*, trans. Joseph Donceel, Milestones in Catholic Theology, New York: Crossroads, 1999.

Sanders, Fred, 'The Trinity', in Kelly Kapic and Bruce L. McCormack (eds.), *Mapping Modern Theology*, Grand Rapids: Baker Academic, 2012.

Schleiermacher, Friedrich D. E., *The Christian Faith*, Edinburgh: T&T Clark, 1968.

Seel, Martin, 'Letting Oneself Be Determined: A Revised Concept of Self-Determination', in Nikolas Kompridis (ed.), *Philosophical Romanticism*, 59–74, London: Routledge, 2006.

Torrance, T. F., *The Trinitarian Faith*, Edinburgh: T&T Clark, 1995.

Vanhoozer, Kevin, *Biblical Authority after Babel: Retrieving the* Solas *in the Spirit of Mere Protestant Christianity*, Grand Rapids: Brazos, 2016, ebook.

———, *Remythologizing Theology*, Cambridge Studies in Christian Doctrine, Cambridge: Cambridge University Press, 2010.

Volf, Miroslav, *After Our Likeness*, Grand Rapids: Eerdmans, 1998.

Watson, Francis, 'The Bible', in John Webster (ed.), *The Cambridge Companion to Karl Barth*, 57–71, Cambridge: Cambridge University Press, 2000.

Webster, John, *God without Measure: Working Papers in Christian Theology*, Vol. 1, Edinburgh: T&T Clark, 2015.

———, *Holy Scripture*, Cambridge: Cambridge University Press, 2003.

———, 'Trinity and Creation', *International Journal of Systematic Theology* 12, no. 1 (2010), pp. 4–19.

Wittgenstein, Ludwig, *Philosophical Investigations*, trans. P. M. S Hacker and J. Schulte, 4th edn, Oxford: Wiley-Blackwell, 2009.

Zizioulas, John D., *Being as Communion: Studies in Personhood and the Church*, Contemporary Greek Theologians, Vol. 4, ed. C. Yannaras et al., Crestwood: St Vladimir's Seminary Press, 1997.

18. THE REFORMATION IN AUSTRALIA

Colin Bale

The sixteenth-century Reformation in Europe occurred over two hundred and fifty years before the British first settled Australia in 1788. The Reformation in Britain, and its development until the late eighteenth century, was thus the main channel for Protestantism in Australia as immigrants brought with them the various expressions of British Protestant churches. Therefore, any discussion of the implications of the Reformation for Australia must consider not only the key features of the Reformation but how these were developed, or changed, in that intervening period in Britain. Also, how did Protestantism in Australia hold to the key features of the Reformation as the Protestant churches established themselves in the Antipodes and over time separated from their mother churches in Britain?

Before considering the British influence, which is the major focus of this chapter, it is only right to examine the small but important part played by Lutherans, the spiritual heirs of Martin Luther, in Australian Christianity. By the early nineteenth century, Frederick William III, the King of Prussia, himself an adherent of the Reformed tradition, sought to unite Lutherans and Calvinists in his kingdom in one Protestant church. This new church was to be in place by 1817 'as a fitting memorial to Luther's Ninety-five Theses of 1517'.[1]

---

1. E. W. Gritsch, *A History of Lutheranism* (Minneapolis: Fortress, 2002), p. 180.

However, some Lutherans in Prussia, who became known as 'Old Lutherans', were unwilling to join such a church, claiming that it compromised traditional Lutheran doctrine. In particular, they believed that a union of Lutheranism and Reformed churches would threaten Luther's understanding of the 'real presence' in the Lord's Supper.[2] The 'Old Lutherans' were repressed by the Prussian government, which imprisoned some of them for their intransigence. The persecution motivated a number of Lutherans to emigrate and seek religious freedom outside Europe. One group, led by Pastor August Kavel, chose to migrate to the new colony in South Australia. They left this farewell message to explain their reasons for leaving Prussia:

> Convinced that the truth in Jesus can alone make eternally free, our only reason for emigrating is this – that we may continue a truly evangelical community, founding our liberty not upon the permission of man, but upon the authority of Scriptural truth; we adhere to that view of Scriptural truth which Luther upheld, because we believe it to be the true one.[3]

Many of these German migrants built settlements in the Barossa Valley where they pursued farming, including wine-growing, for which the Barossa became famous.

Another group of Lutherans, led by Pastor Fritsche, arrived in South Australia in 1841. In 1846 a dispute arose between Kavel and Fritsche that led to the establishment of two rival Lutheran churches in Australia: the United Evangelical Lutheran Church in Australia led by Kavel and the Evangelical Lutheran Church in Australia led by Fritsche. At its heart the disagreement arose from Kavel's convictions regarding church government. It seems that after the experience of the Old Lutherans in Prussia, Kavel wanted to have the Lutherans in Australia free from either state or denominational hierarchical control.[4] The split continued for generations and it was only in 1966, when the Lutheran Church of Australia was established as the denomination for all Australian Lutherans, that the long separation ended.

The Lutherans have never been a large group in Australian Protestantism. At the highest point, they accounted for about 2% of Australian Christians

---

2. Ibid.

3. I. Breward, *A History of the Australian Churches* (St Leonards, NSW: Allen & Unwin, 1993), p. 39.

4. E. Leske, *For Freedom and Faith: The Story of Lutherans and Lutheranism in Australia 1838–1996* (Adelaide: Openbook Publishers, 1996), p. 51.

in the 1901 Australian Census of Population and Housing.[5] Moreover, the German cultural identity of Lutheranism meant that the denomination never had much resonance in the majority Protestant culture of Australia because of a strong anti-German sentiment that developed in the later nineteenth century and continued for most of the twentieth century.

The Lutheran Church of Australia claims it is a confessional and evangelical church. By 'evangelical' the Lutherans mean that it is based on the gospel of Jesus Christ whereby

> we receive forgiveness of sin and become righteous before God by grace, for Christ's sake, through faith, when we believe that Christ suffered for us and that for his sake our sin is forgiven and righteousness and eternal life are given to us.[6]

Being a 'confessional' church 'means that its pastors and people accept, without reservation, the confessions of the evangelical Lutheran Church as contained in the Book of Concord of 1580 as a true exposition of the teaching of the *Bible*'.[7]

When considering the main impact of the Reformation in Australia through the British experience, it must be recognized that there were both positive and negative elements. Protestantism first came to Australia via the evangelical revival in Great Britain. Stuart Piggin makes the point that 'Evangelicalism has been the commonest expression of Protestantism in Australian history. It is a conservative Protestant movement that grew out of the Protestant Reformation of the sixteenth century.'[8] Positively, then, the foundational features of the Reformation were brought to Australia in this way and significantly influenced life on the Continent from 1788.

For the first thirty-two years, the Church of England dominated the settlement in Sydney and Van Dieman's Land. The two penal colonies were subject to military rules and discipline until 1820 and thus the only authorized formal ministry, with a couple of brief exceptions, was conducted by ordained clergy

---

5. The 1901 Census figure for the Lutherans seems to have been the 'high-water mark' for the denomination. The figure declined to about 1.5% by mid-century and hovered at this mark for the rest of the twentieth century.

6. Augsburg Confession, Article 4.

7. D. Zweck, 'Lutherans', in J. Jupp (ed.), *The Encyclopedia of Religion in Australia* (Cambridge: Cambridge University Press, 2009), p. 394.

8. S. Piggin, *Evangelical Christianity in Australia: Spirit, Word and World* (Melbourne: Oxford University Press, 1996), p. vii.

of the Church of England who were viewed as military officers by the colonial administration. In the chaplaincy period of the settlements the Anglican chaplains/clergy were evangelicals.

The first chaplain was the Rev. Richard Johnson. From his letters and the only published work he produced, *An Address to the Inhabitants of the Colonies Established in New South Wales and Norfolk Island*, it is evident that he was a Reformation man. With regard to 'Scripture alone' he wrote: 'This sacred book ... contains all that is needful to make us wise unto salvation.'[9] His understanding of the doctrine of 'Christ alone' is also evident throughout the *Address*:

> So heinous was sin, in the sight of God, that rather than permit it to pass unpunished, he would punish it in the person of his own, his only, his well-beloved Son, who was made sin, that is, treated as a sinner deserved to be treated, for us. He was delivered up into the hands of wicked men, and crucified, that by his suffering and death, he might make atonement for our sins, and procure an honourable and happy reconciliation, between a righteous God, and offending sinners.[10]

Likewise, there is clarity about the right response to Christ's atoning death for sinners: 'repentance and faith are the gifts of God, which none can obtain by any endeavours of their own'.[11]

The chaplaincy period ended in 1820 and other Christian denominations commenced formal ministry from this time onwards. Culturally, the colony at Sydney was a majority Protestant community with a minority adhering to papal Catholicism. As each new colony was established on the Australian continent this pattern of a Protestant majority with a Catholic minority sub-culture continued.

From its beginnings in 1788 until the present, the Church of England, later the Anglican Church of Australia, in Sydney remained committed to its Reformed, evangelical, Protestant heritage. The same was not true of the Church of England in other parts of the continent. While there was an evangelical beginning in the Diocese of Melbourne under Bishop Perry (1847–74), this dissipated over time so that 'by the end of the [nineteenth] century the diocese had become more representative of the broad strands of Anglican

---

9. R. Johnson, *An Address to the Inhabitants of the Colonies Established in New South Wales and Norfolk Island* (London: R. Johnson, 1792), p. 37.

10. Ibid., p. 28,

11. Ibid., p. 14.

theology and churchmanship, and its choice of bishops less partisan'.[12] There remained a continuing strong evangelical presence in Melbourne, but it was never the dominant party as was the case in the Diocese of Sydney. The evangelical presence in other dioceses was limited, with usually only two regional dioceses at any one time standing with the evangelical party. However, the identity of the particular two dioceses varied over time.[13]

The reason why other Anglican dioceses did not adhere to evangelicalism was due to the influence of Tractarianism from the late 1830s onwards. Tractarianism evolved into the Anglo-Catholicism that has characterized much of the Church of England in Australia during its history. In the main, the simple reason for the influence of Tractarianism was that episcopal appointments were made in Britain when new Australian dioceses were created. Quite often a Tractarian was appointed and thus established this churchmanship in the diocese from its beginning. At other times, evangelical bishops were replaced by Tractarians appointed from London and this led to a diocese moving from the evangelical fold to Anglo-Catholicism. Ian Breward notes that Tractarian worship usually involved 'moving away from Word alone to more Catholic worship', and this signalled 'for some a sign of Rome-ward creep, designed to wean congregations from the simple verities of the Reformation'.[14]

The Anglican Diocese of Sydney has been marked for much of its history – and continues to be so – by its conservative evangelicalism that adheres to the 'Scripture alone' principle of the Reformation: the Bible takes precedence over church tradition, human reason and Christian experience.[15] This makes Sydney particularly distinctive not only in the Australian church but also in Anglicanism worldwide. Sydney's adherence to Reformed Protestantism is evident at Moore Theological College, the diocese's ordination training institution, where Calvin and other Reformed notables are celebrated as much as English Reformers. The commitment of the Diocese of Sydney to the theological tenets of the Protestant Reformation was clearly expressed by Archbishop Peter Jensen in 2002 when he spoke of the connection between Sydney Anglicans and other 'Bible-based' churches who were not Anglican, 'churches which owe their

---

12. Breward, *History*, p. 95.

13. In 1870 the Dioceses of Bathurst and Goulburn were evangelical; in 1915 it was the Dioceses of Bendigo and Gippsland; in 1990 it was the Dioceses of Armidale and North-West Australia.

14. Breward, *History*, p. 44.

15. P. F. Jensen, '"Presidential Address": 46th Synod of the Diocese of Sydney, October 2002', *Year Book of the Diocese of Sydney* (2003), p. 362.

theological structure to the Reformation, and who see their fundamental authority in the great "scripture alone" of the Reformation'.[16]

Criticism of Sydney's Reformation position has readily come from those in Australian Anglicanism and elsewhere who argue that Sydney is not inclusive enough for the contemporary Christian scene. Chris McGillion argued that Sydney's Reformation stance effectively excluded from its understanding of biblical Christianity 'more liberal members of the Uniting, Baptist and Lutheran churches, and arguably Anglo-Catholics and liberal Anglicans who were seen to have insufficiently embraced the principles of the Reformation, or else to have deviated from them'.[17] Likewise, Muriel Porter, a Melbourne Anglican, criticized the Diocese of Sydney in 2011 because it was 'still fighting Reformation battles, though this time against apostate Anglicans more than the Church of Rome'.[18] By 'apostate' Anglicans, Porter made it clear she meant Anglicans who did not hold to the norms of the Protestant Reformation. She elaborated this by criticizing Sydney's firm focus on Word-based ministry and its eschewing of 'religious ceremonial, liturgical dress, religious images, or anything that appeals primarily to the senses' when these distract from the Word.[19]

Porter's critique, while endeavouring to argue that Sydney was out of step with much of Anglicanism worldwide, ironically underlined Sydney's foundational commitment to the theological substance of the Protestant Reformation. This commitment has led to the Diocese of Sydney being at the forefront in the creation of the Global Anglican Future Conference (GAFCON), which at its heart is a movement of 'authentic Anglicans standing together to retain and restore the Bible to the heart of the Anglican Communion'.[20] The GAFCON website makes it clear that the movement's focus on the Reformation foundation of *sola scriptura* is to redress the contemporary situation of global Anglicanism in which 'a substantial portion of the church [is] forsaking the clear teaching of the Bible and conforming to the prevailing culture'.[21]

Like early evangelical Anglicans in Australia, when the Presbyterians and Congregationalists began formal ministry in Australia in the nineteenth century,

---

16. Ibid.
17. C. McGillion, *The Chosen Ones: The Politics of Salvation in the Anglican Church* (Crows Nest, NSW: Allen & Unwin, 2005), p. 148.
18. M. Porter, *Sydney Anglicans and the Threat to World Anglicanism* (Farnham: Ashgate, 2011), p. 24.
19. Ibid.
20. 'About GAFCON', GAFCON, <www.gafcon.org/about>.
21. 'History', GAFCON, <www.gafcon.org/about/history>.

they adhered to the Reformed tradition. Official Presbyterian ministry commenced in Sydney in 1823 with the arrival of the Rev. John Dunmore Lang. He was a controversial figure over his long ministry in Sydney (1823–78) but he remained a staunch Calvinist all that time.[22] By the late nineteenth century the theological orthodoxy of the Presbyterians, like that of all the other Protestant denominations, was under threat from new scientific theories and different thinking about biblical interpretation. This modernist movement sought to reinterpret old formularies, such as the Westminster Confession in the case of the Presbyterians.[23] Rowland Ward, the primary historian of the Presbyterian church in Australia, noted that the following comments on the situation for Canadian Presbyterianism were equally valid for Australia:

> the later 19th century had witnessed a steady erosion of the Calvinistic orthodoxy
> with which Presbyterianism had traditionally been identified. In part, this was in the
> direction of a Methodist type of pietism which placed the primary emphasis on
> feeling and experience rather than on purity of doctrine. In part, it was in the direction
> of theological liberalism . . . In such an atmosphere the sombre creed of Calvinism
> seemed an alien intrusion, and many Presbyterians were induced, consciously or
> unconsciously, to dilute it or adapt it to altered circumstances.[24]

Those who held to the Reformation foundations of Presbyterianism fought liberalism in the denomination throughout the first seventy years of the twentieth century, but they lost ground. By the mid-1970s in New South Wales and Victoria it was estimated that the number of Presbyterian ministers who could be considered orthodox by the standards of the Westminster Confession had decreased to about 40% of the total number.[25] The establishment of the Uniting Church in 1977, which saw two-thirds of Presbyterians move into the new denomination, proved to be a chance to reassert the traditional orthodoxy of Presbyterianism in Australia. Of the one-third who remained, many key leaders 'were determined to create a church purified of liberalism and

---

22. D. W. A. Baker, *Preacher, Politician, Patriot: A Life of John Dunmore Lang* (Carlton South: Melbourne University Press, 1988), p. 2.

23. Breward, *History*, pp. 93–94.

24. N. G. Smith, A. C. Farris and N. K. Markell, *A Short History of the Presbyterian Church in Canada* (Toronto: Presbyterian Publishing, 1965), p. 70; cited in R. S. Ward, *The Bush Still Burns: The Presbyterian and Reformed Faith in Australia 1788–1988* (Wantirna, Vic: Rowland S. Ward, 1989), p. 329.

25. Ward, *Bush*, p. 466.

true to the Westminster Confession'.[26] This indeed began to occur, so that by 1989 Rowland Ward was estimating that the proportion of evangelicals in Presbyterian ministry was about 80% and that most of the new ministers since 1977 were Calvinists.[27]

The number of Congregationalists in Australia declined over the course of the twentieth century, from 1.95% of the population in 1901 to 0.39% in 1976.[28] The drop in Congregational numbers was due to three factors: an increasingly secular society, the impact of liberal theology and the reduction in the number of migrants arriving from Britain. With the creation of the Uniting Church of Australia in 1977 most Congregational churches decided to join the Union, with only a few churches choosing to stay out. Interestingly, the continuing Congregational churches look back on the creation of the Union as a positive watershed for the denomination: 'liberalism, modernism and growing materialism influenced many in the Congregational church . . . [who] turned from their heritage, away from the truth of Scripture, from the authority of God's word'.[29] The 'Basis of Union' document was viewed by remaining Congregationalists as weak regarding the basis of salvation in Protestant terms and brittle about *sola scriptura*.[30]

Australian Methodists also claimed to be 'true heirs of the Reformation', influenced by the eighteenth-century revivals such that they thought of themselves as 'a better kind of Anglican – Protestant but also Evangelical and missionary'.[31] The great strength of Methodism in the nineteenth century was its active laity who were encouraged to be involved in ministry. In this way, the Methodists actively sought to actualize the 'priesthood of all believers' in their ministry practice. Nowhere was this more evident than in the Victoria goldfields in the 1850s where population movement was very fluid. Geoffrey Serle noted that the Methodists 'were the only denomination to have a striking success on the goldfields . . . in many places they often conducted more services than all

---

26. Breward, *History*, p. 183.

27. Ward, *Bush*, p. 466.

28. H. Carey, *Believing in Australia* (St Leonards, Sydney: Allen & Unwin, 1996), pp. 197–205.

29. 'Our History', Fellowship of Congregational Churches (Australia), <http://fcc-cong.org/about-us/our-history/>.

30. P. Curthoys, 'Congregationalism', in J. Jupp (ed.), *The Encyclopedia of Religion in Australia* (Cambridge: Cambridge University Press, 2009), pp. 299–304.

31. G. O'Brien, 'Conclusion', in G. O'Brien and H. M. Carey (eds.), *Methodism in Australia: A History* (Farnham: Ashgate, 2015), p. 273.

the other churches combined'.[32] The style of the revival meetings run by Methodists, with a simple gospel message focused on repentance and saving faith in Christ, seemed to suit the situation. Serle argued that the 'essential factor' in the Methodist success 'was the initiative allowed to laity who were thoroughly trained and disciplined and expected to assume the responsibility of preaching and pastoral work in the absence of clergy'.[33] This gave the Methodists much more 'people power' for gospel ministry than was found in the other denominations.

At the beginning of the twentieth century Methodists accounted for almost 13.5% of the Australian population and its members were generally active in the denomination.[34] However, the church was moving from its traditional conversionist approach to ministry to something broader.[35] This reflected, in part, the pressures of modernism and new thinking about biblical interpretation on the denomination. 'Methodists were more open to such ideas' because the denomination 'emphasised personal religious experience . . . more than theological ideas'.[36] Likewise, O'Brien has noted that a feature of Australian Methodism in the twentieth century 'was an ability to embrace a diversity of theological views'.[37] This caused a tension in the denomination between liberals and conservatives. The former wanted to emphasize social justice, caricatured as the 'social gospel', as the key activity of the church, while the latter were more focused on evangelism and mission.[38] Attempts to hold both as valid and complementary expressions of Methodism were not altogether successful. An example of this can be seen in Alan Walker's 'Mission to the Nation' in the 1950s. Many Methodists in Sydney, who were generally more conservative than their counterparts in Adelaide and Melbourne, 'were disenchanted with the social justice content of Walker's mission'.[39] When the denomination joined

---

32. G. Serle, *The Golden Age: A History of the Colony of Victoria 1851–1861* (Melbourne: Melbourne University Press, 1968), p. 342.

33. Ibid.

34. 1901 Australian Census of Population and Housing.

35. J. Stebbins, 'Historical Models for Christianity in Australia', in D. Harris, D. Hinds and D. Millikan (eds.), *The Shape of Belief: Christianity in Australia Today* (Homebush West: Lancer, 1982), p. 55.

36. Breward, *History*, p. 93.

37. O'Brien, 'Conclusion', p. 276.

38. R. C. Thompson, *Religion in Australia: A History* (Melbourne: Oxford University Press, 1994), p. 116.

39. Ibid., p. 118.

Congregationalists and majority Presbyterians in forming the Uniting Church in 1977 the tensions between liberals and conservatives did not disappear. However, the social gospel approach gained the ascendancy and, as Breward notes, 'commitment to evangelism and overseas mission weakened'.[40] So the claim of the Methodists to be 'heirs of the Reformation', while true for much of the nineteenth century, was less so in the twentieth century, and was looking less the case for the Uniting Church of Australia, of which the Methodists were the largest founding group.

Overall, the basic theological tenets of the Protestant Reformation of the sixteenth century have been evident in the various Protestant denominations that have been part of Australian religious life since 1788.[41] Although all the Protestant churches have been subject to the inroads of modernism, theological liberalism and other pressures, and some have succumbed to these more than others, it is fair to say that Reformation truths have been faithfully proclaimed across the generations from the first settlement to the present. This has meant that men, women and children in Australia since 1788 have not only heard the essential biblical teaching recovered by the Reformation, but they have responded to it with repentance and faith.

While the impact of the Protestant Reformation has been largely positive for Australia because of the influence of the various strands of Protestantism that were imported to Australia from Britain, there is one particularly negative aspect upon which comment must be made. The Protestant Reformation of the sixteenth century left a great deal of bitterness between Catholics and Protestants. This was especially the case in the British Isles. In Scotland and England, but particularly in England, given the efforts of the papacy to restore Catholicism in the second half of the sixteenth century, patriotism was shaped by anti-Catholicism.[42] In the aftermath of the English Civil War and the Glorious Revolution, the Act of Toleration (1689) modified penal laws against Dissenters but specifically excluded Roman Catholics from its provisions.[43] This was the

40. I. Breward, 'Methodism', in J. Jupp (ed.), *The Encyclopedia of Religion in Australia* (Cambridge: Cambridge University Press, 2009), p. 415.

41. I have not covered other Protestant denominations, such as the Baptists and the Brethren, in this discussion because of limitations of space, but much of what could be said about the non-Anglican Protestants is true of these groups as well.

42. D. MacCulloch, *Reformation: Europe's House Divided, 1490–1700* (London: Penguin, 2003), p. 339.

43. D. Thomson, *England in the Nineteenth Century* (Harmondsworth: Penguin, 1950), p. 58.

situation at the time the First Fleet sailed in 1787 – British law still penalized Catholics and their religion.[44]

The attitude of the majority Protestant culture to Roman Catholics in Australia in the nineteenth century exhibited the same sectarianism that had been evident in Britain from the Elizabethan period. As the greater number of Catholics who came to Australia originated from Ireland, this only exacerbated the divide, given the strong antipathy between the English and the Irish. As the number of Irish clergy increased from the 1850s onwards, 'for many the defence and support of Ireland and of the Catholic faith became inseparable. Irishism became a basic element in the identity of Australian Catholicism.'[45] This raised suspicion among Protestants about the loyalty of Catholics to Crown and Empire. The sectarian divide was heightened in 1868 when there was an assassination attempt on Prince Alfred, the Duke of Edinburgh. The duke was not seriously wounded, but the 'anti-Irish fears of the Protestant population were aroused by the fact that it had been an Irish Catholic, Henry James O'Farrell, who had done the shooting'.[46]

Two prominent Irish figures in Australian Catholicism, Cardinal Moran, Archbishop of Sydney (1884–1911), and Archbishop Mannix, Archbishop of Melbourne (1917–63), accentuated the sectarian divide. Moran had a knack of irritating Protestants with his pronouncements about Catholic achievements from time to time, such as his claim in 1900 that the European settlement of Australia was 'Catholic at birth', citing the work of de Quiros, the Spanish explorer in this region of the world in 1606.[47] Another verbal storm was created in the same year by an address given by Archbishop Redwood from Wellington, New Zealand, at St Mary's Cathedral in Sydney. Copies of the sermon were circulated to the press beforehand and contained these inflammatory comments:

> Protestantism . . . covered Europe with blood and ruins in the sixteenth century, and has ever been the helper and instrument of the worst foes of Christianity. It desecrated the home, it polluted the nuptial bed, it lowered the dignity of womanhood, it devastated the school.[48]

---

44. P. O'Farrell, *The Catholic Church in Australia: A Short History 1788–1967* (Melbourne: Thomas Nelson, 1968), p. 1.

45. Stebbins, 'Historical Models', p. 51.

46. M. Hogan, *The Sectarian Strand* (Ringwood, Vic: Penguin, 1987), p. 91.

47. P. Ayres, *Prince of the Church: Patrick Francis Moran, 1830–1911* (Carlton, Vic: Miegunyah Press, 2007), pp. 231–232.

48. E. Campion, *Australian Catholics* (Ringwood, Vic: Penguin, 1988), p. 63.

The comments were left out of the spoken address but they caused a furore. As the host of Archbishop Redwood, Cardinal Moran not only refused to apologize for the written comments, but said that they were an accurate reflection of history. Large meetings were held in protest by Protestants.

The presenting issue that clearly demonstrated the antipathy of Catholics and Protestants was elementary education. From the 1850s the Catholic Church in Australia worked towards a Catholic philosophy of education for the colonies. As the demand in colonies for 'free, compulsory and secular' education increased, and as state aid for church schools was trimmed, it became critical for the Catholic church to define how as a sub-culture it should educate the children of the 'faithful'. According to Patrick O'Farrell, who has been the pre-eminent historian of the Catholic Church in Australia, the Catholic bishops believed 'the catholic religion was best preserved by keeping its adherents apart from Protestants, and thus away from contamination'.[49] In a pastoral letter in 1879 the bishops of New South Wales set out their opposition to secular education. They asserted that it would be dominated by Protestantism and its evils, and so it was necessary to maintain separate Catholic schools once colonial governments enacted legislation removing state aid to church schools and funded only public schools:

> The Archbishops and Bishops . . . condemn the principle of secularist education,
> and those schools which are founded on that principle. We condemn them, first,
> because they contravene the first principles of the Christian religion; and,
> secondly, because they are the seed plots of future immorality, infidelity, and
> lawlessness, being calculated to debase the standard of human excellence,
> and to corrupt the political, social and individual life of future citizens.[50]

Thus, the church promoted Catholic schools as essential to the maintenance of the sub-culture. The church leaned heavily on its adherents to send their children to these schools. Parents were instructed that it was their duty to Mother Church to ensure their children received the essentials of the faith that only Catholic schools could provide. The church was prepared to take punitive action against those who did not comply. In 1872 Bishop Goold of Melbourne threatened to excommunicate parents who sent their children to

---

49. P. O'Farrell, *The Catholic Church and Community in Australia* (West Melbourne: Nelson, 1977), p. 152.

50. *Pastoral Letter of the Archbishop and Bishops of New South Wales* (Sydney: F. Cunninghame, 1879), p. 11.

state schools.[51] In 1885 the Australian Council of Bishops laid down that 'parents who without cause or permission sent their children to a state school were denied absolution in the confessional'.[52]

Another area where the Catholic church sought to preserve Catholic identity in colonial society was the issue of 'mixed marriages'. In the early colony, before Catholic priests had been allowed to exercise sacramental ministry, many Catholics had preferred de facto relationships rather than go through the form of a marriage ceremony before a Church of England chaplain.[53] It was not uncommon for Catholics of either sex to enter de facto relationships with non-Catholics.[54] By the 1860s, the issue of de facto relationships among Catholics was diminishing, but that of mixed marriages was of concern to the bishops. Individual bishops sought to denounce mixed marriages in their dioceses. For example, Bishop Murray of Melbourne rejected mixed marriages, arguing that 'fatal indifference to religion, which is the curse of this country ... has crept in through mixed marriages which have been so long tolerated'.[55] The Plenary Councils of 1885 and 1895 barred mixed marriages and this became the policy of all dioceses of the Catholic Church in Australia.[56] The action by the bishops took time to have its effect but 'the culture of Catholic hostility towards mixed marriages gradually filtered down from the Irish clergy to the laity'.[57]

Increasingly, Catholic schools were a visible reminder in suburbs, towns and villages that Catholics were a people separated from their neighbours. Likewise, the stance on mixed marriage hammered home the message to the wider community that Catholics were a people apart. While the strength of Catholicism in Australia has been a clarity about its own identity, which was strongly fostered by its aggressive education policy and marriage policy, that separatist identity was built and maintained at the cost of estrangement from the wider community.

As the Catholic Church in Australia became more assertive in the second half of the nineteenth century for the reasons outlined above, the Protestant majority culture reacted, often aggressively. The Protestant churches generally

---

51. Breward, *History*, p. 72.

52. Campion, *Australian Catholics*, p. 62.

53. P. Grimshaw et al., *Creating a Nation 1788–1900* (Ringwood, Vic: Penguin, 1994), p. 57.

54. Hogan, *Sectarian*, p. 117.

55. Cited in O'Farrell, *Catholic Church in Australia*, p. 141.

56. Ibid., p. 141.

57. Hogan, *Sectarian*, p. 117.

were willing to support the creation of large public education systems in the colonies in the 1870s and 1880s, even though it meant the loss of state aid to Protestant church schools, because it disadvantaged the Catholics. Protestant leaders knew that Catholic schools, which would cater mainly for the children of the working classes, would struggle to provide decent facilities without government financial aid. Anything that hampered Catholic schooling, and hence the Catholic faith, was desirable. At the heart of this attitude in many Protestants was a deep disdain of both popery and the Irishness of Australian Catholicism. In 1876, when the issue of compulsory public schooling was being widely canvassed, Anglican Bishop Barker of Sydney stated that Catholic schools would produce 'a generation of aliens, enemies of the English crown, of English laws'.[58] His comments summed up the prevailing sentiment of many Protestants about Roman Catholicism.

The Catholic policy on mixed marriages also hardened Protestant attitudes to Catholics. In 1875 Anglican Bishop Barker opened the Protestant Hall in Sydney. He was cheered by the audience when he warned them against mixed marriages, stating that it was unacceptable for a Protestant to marry a Catholic.[59] In 1907 the Pope issued a decree, *Ne temere*, which stated that any mixed marriage not celebrated by a Catholic priest was not valid. Protestant anger about *Ne temere* was intense and long-lasting. In 1924, in response to sustained Protestant anger about the decree, the New South Wales government 'brought forward legislation to amend the Marriage Act so as to prohibit the promulgation of the church's *Ne temere* decree'.[60] The bill was passed by the Lower House, the Legislative Assembly, but was narrowly defeated in the Upper House. Another attempt was made the following year to enact the legislation but 'it was amended by the Upper House in such a way as to destroy its intention and power'.[61]

As stated earlier, the attempted assassination of the Duke of Edinburgh in 1868 roused much Protestant antagonism towards Catholics. In the aftermath of the incident, the Protestant Political Association was formed. The organization declared its purpose to be the defeat of 'that political conspiracy against the rights and liberties of man, commonly called the Church of Rome'.[62] Other Protestant groups were also established to combat what was perceived as a more militant Catholicism in the colonies. The most strident Protestant political

---

58. O'Farrell, *Catholic Church in Australia*, p. 114.

59. Hogan, *Sectarian*, p. 117.

60. O'Farrell, *Catholic Church in Australia*, p. 240.

61. Ibid.

62. Cited in ibid., p. 114.

response was seen in the establishment of the Protestant Defence Association in 1901. The object of the constitution of the Association was 'to preserve and defend the general interests of Protestantism from attack'.[63] Although only ever having about 5% of the Protestant population in the Association, it did have some political strength to lobby governments and have its voice heard in the public domain.[64] For example, in 1903 Dill Macky, the president of the Association, verbally attacked the Prime Minister, Sir Edmund Barton, for visiting the Pope at the Vatican.[65] Dill Macky organized a petition of over 30,000 signatures to the Federal Parliament condemning the Prime Minister's visit.

It used to be a common saying among Australian families that it was best to have no talk about religion or politics. The problem with the latter was that politics was necessarily disputative and could place people, even family members, in opposing camps. The problem with the former was that it was viewed as divisive because of sectarianism. For large numbers of families and communities this was a very real and often painful experience. In 1998, in the Australian Broadcast Corporation's *Boyer Lectures*, the noted author David Malouf mused upon Australian culture, and he recalled the negativity of the sectarian divide. He recalled how,

> growing up in Brisbane in the late 1930s and early 1940s, Catholic and Protestant Australians lived separate lives . . . the division between them, the separation, the hostility, was part of the very fabric of living; so essential to life here, so old and so deeply rooted.[66]

He recalled the separateness that existed socially and culturally in Australia because of the sectarian divide, and how fearful Protestants were about increasing Catholic influence. Yet, he added,

> young people today not only feel none of the old hostility. For the most part they have never heard of it . . . If Australia is basically, as I believe it is, a tolerant place, that tolerance was hammered out painfully and over nearly 150 years, in the long

---

63. Speech by Dr Dill Macky, reported in *Sydney Morning Herald*, 25 September 1901, p. 8.
64. Breward, *History*, p. 103.
65. Ayres, *Moran*, p. 238.
66. D. Malouf, 'Lecture 6: A Spirit of Play: The Making of Australian Consciousness', *Boyer Lectures* (Australian Broadcast Corporation, 20 December 1998).

process by which Catholics and Protestants . . . turned away from history and learned to live with one another.[67]

Protestant–Catholic antipathy was imported to Australia with the Anglo-Celtic cultures that mainly shaped Australian society from 1788 until the second half of the twentieth century. In Australia, it took on a life of its own and was the cause of much bitterness and alienation. The Protestant cause in Australia was harmed by the religious sectarianism that marked Australian society in that period because it was more than a theological conflict. As in Britain, it was also a religious, cultural and racial divide that had long-lasting consequences. That needs to be acknowledged. However, despite that negative legacy there is much to celebrate regarding the positive influence of the Protestant Reformation in Australia via, in the main, the British strands of Protestantism. The biblical truths recovered at the Reformation have been evident in the Word ministries of the Protestant churches since 1788. People have been, and continue to be, saved by that Word and live by its precepts. To that end, the Protestant Reformation has had incredible significance for Australia, even though it occurred so long before the first British settlement at Sydney Cove in 1788. The truths recovered at the Reformation by the Reformers are valid for all peoples in all times, and that has been the case in Australia also.

Bibliography

Ayres, P., *Prince of the Church: Patrick Francis Moran, 1830–1911*, Carlton, Vic: Miegunyah Press, 2007.

Baker, D. W. A., *Preacher, Politician, Patriot: A Life of John Dunmore Lang*, Carlton South: Melbourne University Press, 1988.

Breward, I., *A History of the Australian Churches*, St Leonards, NSW: Allen & Unwin, 1993.

———, 'Methodism', in J. Jupp (ed.), *The Encyclopedia of Religion in Australia*, Cambridge: Cambridge University Press, 2009.

Campion, E., *Australian Catholics*, Ringwood, Vic: Penguin, 1988.

Carey, H., *Believing in Australia*, St Leonards, Sydney: Allen & Unwin, 1996.

Curthoys, P., 'Congregationalism', in J. Jupp (ed.), *The Encyclopedia of Religion in Australia*, Cambridge: Cambridge University Press, 2009.

Grimshaw, P., M. Lake, A. McGrath and M. Quartly, *Creating a Nation 1788–1900*, Ringwood, Vic: Penguin, 1994.

---

67. Ibid.

Gritsch, E. W., *A History of Lutheranism*, Minneapolis: Fortress, 2002.

Hogan, M., *The Sectarian Strand*, Ringwood, Vic: Penguin, 1987.

Jensen, P. F., '"Presidential Address": 46th Synod of the Diocese of Sydney, October 2002', *Year Book of the Diocese of Sydney*, 2003.

Johnson, R., *An Address to the Inhabitants of the Colonies Established in New South Wales and Norfolk Island*, London: R. Johnson, 1792.

Leske, E., *For Freedom and Faith: The Story of Lutherans and Lutheranism in Australia 1838–1996*, Adelaide: Openbook Publishers, 1996.

MacCulloch, D., *Reformation: Europe's House Divided, 1490–1700*, London: Penguin, 2003.

McGillion, C., *The Chosen Ones: The Politics of Salvation in the Anglican Church*, Crows Nest, NSW: Allen & Unwin, 2005.

Malouf, D., 'Lecture 6: A Spirit of Play: The Making of Australian Consciousness', *Boyer Lectures*, Australian Broadcast Corporation, 20 December 1998.

O'Brien, G. and H. M. Carey (eds.), *Methodism in Australia: A History*, Farnham: Ashgate, 2015.

O'Farrell, P., *The Catholic Church in Australia: A Short History 1788–1967*, Melbourne: Thomas Nelson, 1968.

———, *The Catholic Church and Community in Australia*, West Melbourne: Nelson, 1977.

Piggin, S., *Evangelical Christianity in Australia: Spirit, Word and World*, Melbourne: Oxford University Press, 1996.

Porter, M., *Sydney Anglicans and the Threat to World Anglicanism*, Farnham: Ashgate, 2011.

Serle, G., *The Golden Age: A History of the Colony of Victoria 1851–1861*, Melbourne: Melbourne University Press, 1968.

Smith, N. G., A. C. Farris and N. K. Markell, *A Short History of the Presbyterian Church in Canada*, Toronto: Presbyterian Publishing, 1965.

Stebbins, J., 'Historical Models for Christianity in Australia', in D. Harris, D. Hinds and D. Millikan (eds.), *The Shape of Belief: Christianity in Australia Today*, Homebush West: Lancer, 1982.

Thompson, R. C., *Religion in Australia: A History*, Melbourne: Oxford University Press, 1994.

Thomson, D., *England in the Nineteenth Century*, Harmondsworth: Penguin, 1950.

Ward, R. S., *The Bush Still Burns: The Presbyterian and Reformed Faith in Australia 1788–1988*, Wantirna, Vic: Rowland S. Ward, 1989.

Zweck, D., 'Lutherans', in J. Jupp (ed.), *The Encyclopedia of Religion in Australia*, Cambridge: Cambridge University Press, 2009.

INDEX